Fishing For Dummies®
Published by
John Wiley & Sons, Ltd
The Atrium
Southern Gate
Chichester
West Sussex
PO19 8SQ
England
www.wiley.com

WILEY

Fishing FOR DUMMIES®

by Peter Kaminsky,
with new material by Greg Schwipps

Adapted by Dominic Garnett

 WILEY

A John Wiley and Sons, Ltd, Publication

About the Authors

Peter Kaminsky caught his first fish, a 30-pound grouper, on a party boat in the Florida Keys. It was the first time he went fishing, and that grouper won $45 for the big fish of the day. Kaminsky was hooked. He was Managing Editor of *National Lampoon* at the time. Soon after, he began to write for *Outdoor Life, Field & Stream,* and *Sports Afield.* In 1985, he began his regular contributions to *The New York Times* 'Outdoors' column. Kaminsky also wrote 'The Underground Gourmet' in *New York* magazine and is a frequent contributor on food and dining in *Food & Wine* magazine. He has written numerous books on cooking and fishing. His current book is *Culinary Intelligence.* As a television producer, Kaminsky is a creator and executive producer of The Mark Twain Prize for American Humor and The Gershwin Prize for Popular Song. Kaminsky is a graduate of Princeton University and lives in Brooklyn.

Greg Schwipps fished the farm ponds around his home in Milan, Indiana, as soon as he could walk to them. He later earned an MFA at Southern Illinois University at Carbondale, and he now teaches creative writing at DePauw University in Greencastle, Indiana. His work has appeared in outdoor magazines such as *Outdoor Indiana, Indiana Game & Fish,* and *In-Fisherman.* In 2010, his first novel, *What This River Keeps,* won the Eugene and Marilyn Glick Indiana Authors Award in the Emerging Writer category. He lives with his wife, Alissa, and their two dogs in Wilbur, Indiana, and fishes the White and Ohio rivers. www.gregschwipps.com

Dominic Garnett fell in love with fishing aged three, sitting on the banks of the Thames with a fibreglass roach pole. Thirty years later, he has a garage full of random tackle and a strange-smelling car that rattles with rods and reels. From early encounters with minnows, roach and perch, he graduated to match fishing on the local canal and casting further afield to outfox pike and carp. A move to Devon stirred further interest in tackling sea fish and exploring trout streams with a fly rod. Even the discovery of loud music, beer and the opposite sex did little to curb his great enthusiasm for spending time on the bank.

As an English graduate Dominic followed his passion for writing with a spell in film journalism, before switching to his first love of fishing. An *Angling Times* correspondent and contributor to many fishing titles in the UK and beyond, he has written over 100 articles on many subjects and was recently described as 'Britain's most promising young angling writer'. Backed by Britain's longest running tackle company, Hardy Greys, he is also an avid photographer and the author of *Flyfishing for Coarse Fish.* These days you might find Dominic lure fishing for pike, sitting it out for a big carp or just as happily casting a fly for trout. His website (www.dgfishing.co.uk) showcases his articles and pictures, along with the regular misadventures he records in his blog 'Crooked Lines'. He lives in Exeter, Devon.

Dedication

From Peter: For Lucian and Honeybunch.

From Greg: For my dad and grandfather, who made the time to take me fishing.

From Dominic: To Dad, for taking me fishing. Also to my mother, and Jo Bliss.

Author's Acknowledgments

From Peter: There are many people to thank, but first an anonymous thank you to all the anglers – men and women who have shared their knowledge, companionship, and often their tackle with me over the years. I would especially like to acknowledge the late Gene Calogiero (forgive me, Gene, I'm just guessing at the spelling, and you're not around to correct me anymore), who first taught me how to tie flies and fish the Esopus Creek; Nick Lyons for his generous counsel and support as I tried to learn how to write about this wonderful sport; John Culler for buying my first fishing piece in *Outdoor Life;* Duncan Barnes for years of putting up with my ageing-hippy-writer's ways; Susan Adams for making a home for me at *The New York Times* (and Joe Vecchione for getting me started there); Tom Akstens for being an exemplar of a passionate and joyful angler; a debt beyond measure to the unsung Everglades guide Jack Allen, the most complete angler I know, who, by his example, has taught me that one can make a life out of angling; not rich in money, but face it, for most of us, the money isn't going to happen anyway, so we might as well enjoy the fishing.

From Greg: I should thank first the fine folks at Wiley who welcomed me into the 2nd Edition of *Fishing For Dummies:* Lindsay Lefevere for presenting the opportunity, and Sarah Faulkner and Elizabeth Rea for expertly shepherding me through the writing process. Thanks to copy editor Susan Hobbs, and to technical reviewer Jeff Knapp for his great insights. The fine angler Mikey Hemkens helped out, as well. Any writer would be lucky to have such a team. Thanks, too, to Lucia Watson, the super-chef who graciously shared some recipes with us, and a tip of the fishing cap to Doug Stange; he's a great fisherman and friend at *In-Fisherman* from way back.

I fish most often with my brothers, Tim and Ron, and our cousin, Ben. There are many lighthearted references to their prowess throughout this book. They're not quite as inept as I make them seem, but as always, I had fun making jokes about them in print. We fish most often for catfish, a long-neglected and maligned fish – may they continue to find their rightful place in anglers' good graces everywhere. (Right, Dr. Pepper?) Finally, thanks to my fishing partner, Alissa, who is a fine angler and a pretty danged good wife.

From Dominic: The world of fishing is such a great community and I'd like to thank many of you, not just for your support but for your friendship and encouragement. A big shout firstly to the Westcountry massive: Rob Darby, Seb Nowosiad, Nick Maye and Ian Nadin in particular, also Paul Hamilton, Steve Lockett and everyone at Exeter Angling Centre. To Bob James, for taking me under your wing and sharing your fantastic knowledge and enthusiasm. I would also like to thank all the editors I've worked with, but especially Steve Partner at Angling Times for bringing out the best in my writing and daring to entertain some of my madder ideas. Thanks also to Tom Legge and the late *Pike & Predators* editor James Holgate for giving me those crucial first chances to shine. To all the Garnetts – Alex, Ben and especially my mother, for everything! Lucy Bowden and all at Hardy Greys. Last but not least, I would also like to give a big mention to those organisations which represent a brighter future for fishing: The Westcountry Rivers Trust, The Pike Angler's Club of Great Britain and most of all The Angling Trust – if you enjoy this book please give them your support.

Publisher's Acknowledgments

We're proud of this book; please send us your comments at http://dummies.custhelp.com. For other comments, please contact our Customer Care Department within the U.S. at 877-762-2974, outside the U.S. at 317-572-3993, or fax 317-572-4002.

Some of the people who helped bring this book to market include the following:

Acquisitions, Editorial, and Vertical Websites

Project Editor: Simon Bell
  (Previous Edition: Elizabeth Rea)

Commissioning Editor: Mike Baker

Assistant Editor: Ben Kemble

Copy Editor: Kate O'Leary

Technical Editor: Jeff Knapp

Recipe Tester: Emily Nolan

Nutritional Analyst: Patricia Santelli

Cover Photo: © iStock / Sasha Radosavljevic

Cartoons: Ed McLachlan

Composition Services

Senior Project Coordinator: Kristie Rees

Layout and Graphics: Claudia Bell, Melanee Habig, Amy Hassos, Joyce Haughey, Lavonne Roberts

Proofreader: John Greenough

Indexer: BIM Indexing & Proofreading Services

Special Art: Ron Hildebrand, www.allthingsillustrated.com

Publishing and Editorial for Consumer Dummies

  Kathleen Nebenhaus, Vice President and Executive Publisher

  Kristin Ferguson-Wagstaffe, Product Development Director

  Ensley Eikenburg, Associate Publisher, Travel

  Kelly Regan, Editorial Director, Travel

Publishing for Technology Dummies

  Andy Cummings, Vice President and Publisher

Composition Services

  Debbie Stailey, Director of Composition Services

Contents at a Glance

Table of Contents

Introduction

Wherever you live in the UK, there is exciting fishing nearby. Whether that means a wild river or the local canal, the village pond or the open coast, there is another world waiting to be discovered. It is this 'other world' that captivates those who fish all over Britain. This other place, far from school, work and daily chores, means many things to the angler. It can be a calm, meditative experience, but it can also be utterly thrilling. It can be a sedate way to spend a perfect, sunny afternoon, or an adventure spanning miles of countryside. Make no mistake, fishing is a million miles away from the cliché of the bored-looking bloke who sits there like a statue. It's a process of continual fascination in which you never stop learning. Whether you're after that heart-stopping bite from a monster fish or just a few hours of relaxing fun, fishing has it all.

With such a huge range of beautiful waters and different fish species to catch, you might easily call fishing the most varied and absorbing of all outdoor sports. The anglers themselves are just as diverse. It doesn't matter whether you're young or old, rich or poor. Whatever your level of income or physical ability, fishing is available to you. It's a very welcoming sport in this way. It's also highly affordable, and for little more than the price of a rod licence and some basic tackle, you can enjoy hours of fresh air and fun. In this way it provides countless pensioners with a happy retirement, but also saves just as many youngsters from weekends spent slouching in front of computer and TV screens. It's also a great way to spend time with family and friends.

Perhaps the only major conundrum is where to start. After all, fishing is such a vast sport it can be a confusing place. This is where *Fishing For Dummies* comes in. In fact, this is a book many of us could have done with years ago as we nagged parents to tie on hooks, or sat with furrowed brows over bewildering textbooks. Above all, we hope to give you a friendly head start in a hobby that could give you a lifetime of enjoyment and discovery.

About This Book

You have in your hands the UK edition of *Fishing For Dummies*. Some things in fishing are pretty much universal (where trout like to sit in a river, how to hook worms, corny jokes), but others have a more regional flavour. Hence I

(Dominic) have been given the task of revising the successful US edition to produce a book tailor-made for British anglers. It's a team effort however, which is why you'll find 'we' used often, or an 'I' followed by one of our names in parentheses. In a nutshell, you'll still find the best and wisest words from our American colleagues but the book now has a distinct UK bias. For example, you won't find out how to fool a largemouth bass, but if you're setting up a waggler float, choosing a beachcaster or tricking crafty carp you'll quickly find the answers.

Like all *For Dummies* books, this one gives you all the information you need, with clear, easy-to-find entries. You don't have to read it from start to finish; it's not a textbook and you can pick out any section from the contents that piques your interest. Rather than confuse you with dense or confusing text, our aim is a user-friendly guide, packed with useful tips and easy-to-follow advice. Whether you're a raw beginner or already know about fishing, you'll learn plenty on all kinds of fishing and have fun along the way.

Conventions Used in This Book

We use the following conventions throughout the text to make things consistent and easy to understand:

- New terms appear in italic and are closely followed by an easy-to-understand definition.
- Bold highlights the action parts of numbered steps and key words in bullet lists.

What You're Not to Read

We intend for this book to be a pleasant and practical read so that you can quickly find and absorb the fishing material you seek. However, we sometimes can't help going a little bit deeper or relaying information that expands on the basics. You might find this information interesting, but you don't need it to understand what you came to that section to find.

When you see a Technical Stuff icon or a sidebar (a grey-shaded box of text), know that the information next to the icon or in the box is optional. You can lead a full and happy fishing life without giving it a glance. (But here's a chance to make your fishing life even fuller and happier.

Foolish Assumptions

Before we could write this book, we had to make some assumptions about who you, the reader, might be. We assume that you

- ✔ Have either fished before or want to start Want to have fun while fishing
- ✔ Are curious to know more about fish
- ✔ Desire to develop skills to fish in a variety of places
- ✔ Would like to know how to catch more than one kind of fish Seek to better understand the gear available
- ✔ Crave new information about fishing but don't have endless time to devote to the hobby

How This Book Is Organised

The upcoming sections give you a sense of our coverage of fishing. You might notice that the parts of this book follow a natural progression from getting ready to fish, to actually fishing, to dealing with fish that have been caught. You might want to start at the beginning, as you acquire some gear, or maybe you're ready to get a fish in the hand. Either way, don't be shy about casting into the book at whatever part intrigues you.

Part 1: Before the Bite

Fishing trips can be spontaneous and fun, but a little preparation goes a long way. Here, you find information about how to prepare for a fishing trip. We offer advice on how to dress, explore the water once you find it, and we even show illustrations of the fish swimming there! We also want you to stay safe while fishing, so we present a chapter on safety.

Part II: Gearing Up Without Going Overboard

You need some equipment to go fishing, starting with a rod and reel. But there's a lot of gear out there, and some of it costs quite a bit. This part explains what you need, what you don't need, and what you can wait to acquire later. We cover everything from hook types to fishing from boats.

Part III: The End of Your Line: Enticing Fish with Bait, Lures and Flies

The rod and reel matter, but the fish sees only what you present on the end of your line. This part walks you through your options, from completely natural livebait to synthetic lures. Bait can be presented in different ways; fish have different tastes, not every lure should be retrieved the same way, and not every fly imitates every insect. This chapter helps you decide what to use, and when.

Part IV: Now You're Fishing

This part is where the water meets the hook. We tell you how to rig your line to present your offering naturally, and how to make effective casts. Then we help you land the fish that can't resist your tempting offer. This part helps you tie on the hook, hook the fish, and then release the fish back into the water.

Part V: After the Catch

If you want a decent photograph of your catch before you let it go, this part gives you advice on how to do that. If you decide to keep the occasional fish to eat, we tell you how to clean and cook the fish. We even include a handful of classic recipes..

Part VI: The Part of Tens

This part provides some final, inspiring 'Top Ten' lists. This includes great fishing reads, as well as ten things we wish someone had told us when we started fishing. There's also a rundown of worthwhile fishing organisations the UK angler can learne from.

Icons Used in This Book

One of the great things about a *For Dummies* book is the interactive icons used to highlight or illustrate a point. Here are the icons we've used throughout this book to draw your attention:

Some points are worth hammering home. When we reference a concept that we've discussed elsewhere or that is particularly important to your fishing experience, we use this icon.

We try to keep the information in this book light, but when we can't resist delving deeply into a technique or piece of equipment, we use this icon to let you know that the information is skippable.

This icon sits next to any information that saves you time, money, or frustration in your quest for better fishing.

Some actions can hurt the fish, your equipment, or you. We mark those with this dangerous-looking icon.

Where to Go from Here

We've organised this book so that you can either read it start to finish or dip into it here and there to find whatever specific information meets your needs. If you think you're ready to pick out a new rod and reel, turn to Chapter 7 for advice on how to choose a good one. If you'd rather get tips on how to evaluate a lake you've never fished before, check out Chapter 3. If you want a memento of that first catch, you'll find out how to take the perfect picture in Chapter 18. If you prefer traditional angling and traditional reading, turn the page and read this sucker straight through.

Enjoy *Fishing For Dummies,* and go fishing!

Part I
Before the Bite

In this part . . .

The chapters in this part introduce you to the concept of fishing and many of the species of fish – both freshwater and saltwater – you'll attempt to catch. Covering both the basics, such as simple fish anatomy, and more complex principles, like how to evaluate fishing water you've never seen before, this part provides a lot of what you need to know before you begin fishing. A prepared angler is a successful one, and this part gets you ready.

Chapter 1

Getting Hooked on Fishing

· ·

In This Chapter

▶ Seeing the positives of fishing

▶ Figuring out where to fish

▶ Meeting common fish

▶ Gathering the basic gear

▶ Exploring fishing techniques

▶ Catching fish and taking the next steps

· ·

Everyone knows someone who fishes. After all, over five million anglers walk among us in this country. Maybe you're already an angler. Maybe you're just curious. Maybe you have a son, daughter, grandson, granddaughter or friend's kid who needs a hobby that doesn't involve a screen.

Because I have been fishing almost since I could walk, and fascinated by fish from my first memories (even an accidental dunking in the River Thames aged four didn't put me off), people often ask why I'm so captivated by fishing. Even though I think about fish every single day, it's not an easy question to answer.

But I think I fish for the same reasons so many others do: It's a chance to get outside, to be a small part of something bigger than my own schedule or routine for a while. I fish because I like hanging out in the places where fish live. Fish don't always behave the way I think they should, or follow my plans for them. The weather doesn't either. I like that unpredictability because it forces me to react, to plan, to ponder. I like angling because I like spending time with fellow anglers. When I have a disappointing fishing trip (and what they say is true – there is no bad day fishing), I can't wait to go again. When I have a great fishing trip, I can't wait to go again.

We hope you can find something in fishing that sustains you, too. In this chapter, we give you an overview of this sport we love, from the motivation to get out there to an idea of where you should go to give it a try. Because there's some gear involved, as well as skill and technique, we introduce you to these topics as well, so that you're prepared to fish successfully.

Why Fish?

Fish are alive, and although the latest studies suggest that they do not feel pain, at least not in a capacity anywhere near the way we do, they do not jump at the chance to be caught. Using your gear and more importantly your mind, you must outmanoeuvre the fish. This presents an interesting, constantly-shifting challenge.

Obviously, fish live in an environment much different from ours. Understand, though, that they're well-suited to that environment. With a few exceptions, they're cold-blooded and possess a good sense of smell. They live in the water (you already knew that), have backbones, and pull oxygen from the water through gills. They are shaped to move efficiently through water (many like torpedoes), using fins to navigate, and most are covered with scales. All fish are also covered with a slime-like mucus that protects them from disease and injury. (This is why you should only handle fish with wet hands – dry hands or a towel will remove this valuable slimecoat.) Fish don't have external ears, but they do have internal ones and are highly sensitive to noise like the thudding of a boat hull. Fish possess a lateral line, running from tail to head, that they use to detect low-frequency vibrations. They use this organ to locate prey and evade predators, while also gathering information about water temperature and current. So fish might not share many characteristics with humans, but they're more than able opponents when it comes to people trying to outsmart them. They know their surroundings as well as you know your living room. Figure 1-1 shows a typical fish, with some of the traits described here.

Every angler has a particular reason for pursuing the sport, and after a few trips out to the water you're likely to figure out what it is you appreciate and enjoy about it too. From a little one-on-one time with Mother Nature to the calm and peace of the pursuit – or the thought that your very next cast could produce that reel-screaming monster fish – fishing has something for everyone.

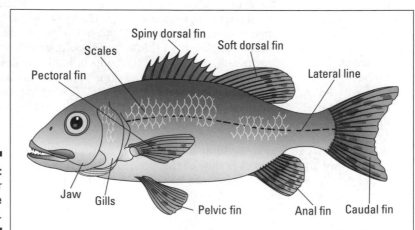

Figure 1-1:
Meet your average fish.

For the outdoors

You probably already know this, but fishing is an outdoor activity. So the first reason to take up fishing is that it requires you to go outside. Some of us think that there's something good for the soul about being outdoors, especially in those places that are natural. Fishing gives you the perfect excuse to spend time in beautiful surroundings.

For the enjoyment

Take up fishing because you need some time spent quietly by yourself. Or take up fishing because you want to spend quality time with others. Two anglers fishing in a boat, or wading their way quietly upstream, won't be distracted by scrolling news programmes, honking cars or instant messages. Mobile phones can be turned off, and Facebook can be ignored for a while. Whether you're alone or in a small group, fishing quiets the mind.

This is not to suggest that all fishing is quiet! When a monster fish bends your rod double, or goes airborne trying to throw the hook, the adrenaline rush the angler feels rivals that of a footballer scoring a goal, or a racing driver taking a dangerous bend. It's a physical sensation. (See Chapter 18 to find out how to land that huge carp.)

What fishing provides us might be one thing. You, too, will find a way to make fishing work for you. If you crave excitement, fish in a way that offers it. If you seek peaceful, introspective time, fishing can give you that, as well. And no one will make you commit to one kind of fishing all the time. Your fishing can evolve as you do.

For the table?

Our ancestors fished for food, but most UK anglers fish purely for sporting reasons. Indeed, most of our freshwater fishing is strictly catch-and-release, usually by law. The reasoning is simple: with a limited amount of water and many keen anglers, the fishing must be protected. Once killed, a fish cannot produce young, or grow bigger to give a future angler further pleasure. Fish can and do survive capture perfectly well, provided we are careful (for catch-and-release tips see Chapter 17).

If you do want fresh fish for the table, sea fish or stocked trout are both excellent options. Species such as mackerel and pollack are plentiful from our shores, while the fly fisher can take rainbow trout home for family and friends. Fish are great tasting and good for you, as well. Chapter 19 tells you how to prepare fish for the table, and we even offer you some proven recipes, allowing you to make wonderful meals of your fresh-caught fish.

Where Should You Fish?

Chapter 3 discusses this issue in detail, but the best advice we can give you is to fish wherever you can. (Later, we also advise you to fish whenever you can.) Big fish come from both large and small waters. Beautiful places to fish can be found locally. Pop down to a local canal and you'll be surprised how wild even your city waters can be. Many ponds and canals are stocked, and some of them face very little fishing pressure. Beaches, piers and estuaries offer a range of fish species too.

Part of the joy and challenge of fishing lies in finding your favourite spots. Fish move seasonally, especially in rivers and the seas, so catching a particular species of fish all year long will often involve moving to follow their migrations. You'll also learn to go to different areas to catch different kinds of fish during certain times of the year.

Fishing freshwater

Not all freshwater fishing is the same, and almost every area of Britain offers a wide range of fishing possibilities. The West Country, for example, offers everything from trout streams to wild beaches; the Midlands is famed for its canals and gravel pits; Wales and Scotland offer secluded rivers and beautiful, natural lakes. Even those places far from giant bodies of water boast rivers of varying sizes and both natural and man-made lakes. Your gear, and your approach, will vary quite a bit from place to place, but this too is part of the fun of fishing.

Much freshwater fishing boils down to current: You're fishing either moving or still water. And there are a lot of fish – and a lot of techniques to fish for them – in both kinds of water. Wherever you live, you are close to good freshwater fishing. Chapter 3 will help you learn how to seek it out.

Sea fishing

Sea fishing possibilities might not always be local since we don't all live near a coast. When you find saltwater, you find an almost limitless variety of fish.

Many of the techniques used in freshwater carry over to saltwater; however, the game changes a bit when you're dealing with the fast, strong fish of the sea.

For this reason, tackling saltwater can be intimidating. But if you limit your initial forays into sea fishing to the inshore waters – places like estuaries, beaches and piers – you'll find that even beginners can find plenty of exciting action.

What Are You Fishing For?

I (Dominic) once caught a large pike from the shallow swimming area of a clear lake. My younger brother quickly decided he no longer wanted to paddle there! It just goes to show that just about anywhere you find water, varied and often wholly unexpected fishing awaits.

So what are you fishing for? Both salt and freshwater bodies of water boast a wide range of species, many of which can be taken on rod and reel. Maybe you prefer to get plenty of bites from silver fish such as roach and bream? Perhaps the mackerel are in town on your local pier? Or maybe you've found a lake full of hard-fighting carp?

Your favourite species might change over time, and you can always adjust your gear and tactics to specialise. You might switch seasonally, too. Some fish stop biting enthusiastically when the water cools in the autumn, whereas others bite all winter long. When you get into fishing, we promise you're not going to exhaust the possibilities.

Common freshwater catches

Just as there are many different kinds of habitat for freshwater fish, there are many different kinds of fish populating those habitats. Trout require cooler water. Carp do well in everything from farm ponds to big reservoirs.

Big rivers hide big fish like barbel, chub and pike, as well as fish like roach and dace. Natural and man-made lakes can be home to any kind of freshwater fish, including carp, bream, and tench. Perch can be found everywhere from the largest river to the smallest pond. Freshwater fish represent a diverse collection of species, and each one of them brings something different to the angler.

Freshwater fish species are often divided into two main groups: 'Game' fish (trout, salmon and other species usually tackled with fly gear) and 'coarse' fish (all the others!) For complete coverage of freshwater fish, turn to Chapter 4.

Common sea catches

The sky's the limit, or in the case of saltwater fishing, the sea's the limit. Even fishing inshore waters, anglers could catch everything from conger eels to plaice. Winter anglers can expect flounder, cod and whiting to congregate in beaches and estuaries. Spring and summer see the return of bass and mackerel to give excellent sport to lure and fly anglers.

Flat sandy beaches and estuaries offer flatfish, mullet and other visitors. For those who dare, rock marks hold wrasse, pollack and various dogfish. Charter boats and their skippers can lead you to deep-sea fishing for powerful conger, rays and other creatures. With sea fishing, you don't really know what you're going to catch next, which is part of its great allure.

For the lowdown on the range of sea fish available to you, check out Chapter 5.

What Do You Need to Fish?

Commerical fishermen – those fishing to gather fish or shellfish for food – often use devices like nets, traps or long lines with multiple hooks to take fish. This book deals with sportfishing, which is fishing with a rod and reel. So, just as you need a few clubs to play golf, you need a rod and reel to fish in the traditional manner.

Beyond the rod and reel, your needs are relatively few. You need a hook to snare the fish's mouth, and a line to get that hook from the rod to the water. You can keep your fishing simple. But, just as a golfer probably acquires more than a couple of clubs, anglers tend to gather the equipment that makes the pursuit of their favourite fish more successful and pleasurable.

The important thing to remember is that fishing does not have to be an expensive hobby. Once you have your required rod licence, many waters provide inexpensive or even free fishing. However, if you are someone who likes to fish with nice equipment and the latest technology, well, all that awaits you, too. Anglers with deep pockets and a matching desire can fish from large, spacious boats boasting cutting-edge electronics and with an arsenal of rods and reels.

One of your first choices when you begin fishing is to decide what kind of gear you intend to use. We will divide these into coarse, sea and fly set ups in much more detail later on (see Chapter 7). Figure 1-2 shows some common set ups,

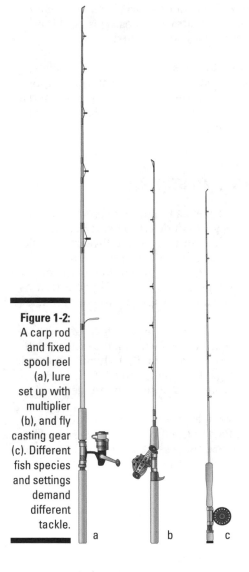

Figure 1-2:
A carp rod and fixed spool reel (a), lure set up with multiplier (b), and fly casting gear (c). Different fish species and settings demand different tackle.

a   b   c

Picking up fishing essentials

Basically, to begin fishing, you need a rod and reel spooled with line and a handful of *terminal tackle* – things like weights and hooks (covered completely in Chapter 9). Even someone who possesses one hook can probably find a garden worm somewhere and catch a fish.

Most likely, you'll want some kind of tackle carrier to carry your terminal tackle, and other *lures* (artificial, man-made baits) and flies. This could be as simple as a plastic tackle box or a fishing vest with pockets.

The right clothes will keep you comfortable and safe, as well. Anglers fishing from boats or near rapid current should wear a life jacket. Waterproof footwear may not be a necessity, but it's pretty close, at times. Sunglasses and a suitable hat make life easier while fishing, as well. Chapter 2 tells you much more about how to dress for fishing success.

Adding to your angling arsenal

Today's angler is spoilt for choice when it comes to kit. In many ways today's angler can reap the rewards of countless years of development; Hardy, for example, have been producing fishing tackle for well over 100 years. Retailers such as Fishing Republic, Mullarkeys and The Friendly Fisherman offer a vast array of tackle to order online. But the most important link in the chain is your local bait and tackle shop, and a good one will provide you with not only choice but friendly, invaluable advice and info specific to your area.

There's no shortage of gear out there. As you get deeper into fishing, you'll see the need to get various pieces of equipment. Anglers who want to start catching specimen carp need strong line and a rod and reel built to handle it. A well-crafted fishing rod can be thing of beauty, so light and supple it feels like an extension of the hand. There's nothing wrong with desiring better gear.

So, while you should start with the basics, feel free to add to that pile of fishing tackle in the corner of your garage. Part of the fun of fishing is seeing how the latest gear can help to make you a more successful angler (and trying to justify that next 'essential' purchase to your partner!).

How Do You Fish?

Fish bite an object because they think it's something to eat, or they strike out of some instinct to do so – because they're defending their territory, for example. Fishing, then, requires that you offer something with a hook or hooks attached in hopes of getting a fish to bite it. You can do this by presenting livebait that the fish are used to eating – casting a hooked minnow into a shoal of perch, for example. More often you might use a bait such as bread, sweetcorn or meat which is not strictly 'natural' but offers the fish a tasty, free meal. Or you may turn to trickery – using a fly tied to look like a beetle to hook a trout, or using the flash of a wobbling spoon to trigger an attack from a pike or bass.

Whatever you use on the end of your line, *presentation* matters. Presentation refers to the methods you use to put your offering in front of the fish. You might cast and retrieve a diving plug for zander, or use a leger rig to anchor a chunk of luncheon meat for chub and barbel. Basically, you want to present a bait or lure in a way that looks natural to the fish, and the right presentation should allow you to hook the fish after it bites.

Casting around: Basic and fly

Because fish are sometimes found some distance from shore, you need to get your bait or lure to them – and this involves the art of *casting*. Casting requires you to use your rod and reel to propel your offering to the target. When using a conventional rod and reel (a fixed spool or multiplier) casting requires you to use the flex of the rod to launch your weight, float or lure outward, and the weight of this pulls the line off your reel. When fly casting, it is the line itself which provides the weight. You use the flex of the rod to cast the line, and the fly (comparatively very light) goes with it.

Like any sport that requires you to do something with your body, casting calls for a certain amount of dexterity and coordination. However, even beginners can learn how to cast effectively. The casting motion (typically involving a swinging, overhead movement) is a simple, natural one. And not every fishing situation calls for perfect casts; many fish are found near shore or around piers or docks, and they require only short, simple casts. In fact, sometimes the best fishing can be found right under your rod tip. To find out how to cast using any of the common kinds of gear, check out Chapter 15.

Finding freshwater fish

Before you can catch a fish, you have to find the fish. That means figuring out where the fish are within a body of water. We call this process *watercraft*. Anglers will often talk about 'features' when sizing up a water. By this they simply mean the characteristics of the place, be they man made or natural. It's not rocket science, but a little detective work can go a long way. Identifying a few types of features can be helpful:

- ✔ **Structure** refers to the permanent features that mark a lake or stream – a drop-off, ledge or hole is structure. Fish relate to structure and often remain close to it.

- ✔ **Cover** consists of things like weedbeds, overhanging trees or even moored boats. Fish need shelter for various reasons – to hide from predators or ambush prey, for example.

✔ **Natural characteristics** are not always solid or obvious. On a river, for example, a 'crease' refers to where a faster current meets slower water – a good place to find fish. Even on 'still' water, currents exist and the wind affects the fish.

Knowing that fish are often found near particular features helps you figure out how to fish for them. When you know where fish are, you can decide how best to approach them. Perhaps that weedy corner would be best fished with a shallow float rig? Or would it be better to try the deeper water with a bait on the bottom?

Different species of fish respond to different presentations, and with experience and the help of this book, you'll improve at both finding the fish and then getting them to bite. Chapter 3 looks at suitable places to find the different fish species, while Chapter 16 explores popular techniques in more detail.

Basic techniques for sea fishing

Most presentations involve either static fishing – where a bait is cast out and largely left alone until a fish finds it – or by retrieving a lure or bait. Baits and lures can be presented in many different ways. Some lures are meant to be reeled in quickly, while others work better when *jigged* (hopped up and down by lifting and lowering the rod tip). Other presentations include drifting or trolling baits or lures from a boat.

Finding a fishing mentor

Many of us were lucky enough to have a parent or grandparent to teach us how to cast for fish, and more importantly, to make the time to take us fishing. But if that's not the case for you, don't despair. Plenty of ways to learn how to fish exist, and many people willing to show you a few shortcuts. We suggest finding someone who fishes for the fish you would like to pursue, and does so in a way that matches your personality. Watch others on the bank and don't be afraid to chat. You might even seek out online fishing forums. Ask questions first to get to know someone, and then see if they extend an offer to take you fishing. Most are happy to share their excitement for the sport. Fishing clubs are also a brilliant source of information and many have 'learn to fish' days for newcomers. Another option, albeit a costlier one, is to hire a local guide. Observing a guide for a day is a great way to learn about fishing from an expert. As always, don't be afraid to ask questions.

Fishing the sea means understanding tides, and how the flow of the rising or falling tides affect fish. Because tides tend to concentrate prey fish and establish feeding areas, locating your quarry becomes a matter of finding ambush points where the fish find easy pickings.

Fish On! Now What?

When a fish strikes your bait, fly or lure, the first thing you have to do is *set the hook*. This refers to the act of embedding the hook into the mouth of the fish. Many hooksets involve lifting the rod sharply overhead, using the flex of the rod to drive the hook or hooks into the fish's mouth.

After a fish is hooked, you have to *fight* the fish to the shore or boat, and this means controlling the ensuing struggle enough that the fish cannot wrap the line around a snag or do a number of other things to free itself. This is covered completely in Chapter 17, but you should always strive to keep the rod tip up, using the flex of the rod to maintain a tight line and keep the hook firmly planted in the fish's mouth.

It's not hunting: Release your fish!

When a fish is in your net or hand, assuming the fish is legal, you have a choice to make: Do you release the fish, or keep it? For most freshwater fishing situations, the rules state that fish must be carefully released. Indeed, a fishery owner would not take kindly to his prized stock being put on a barbecue! If it is a stocked trout, however, you may be obliged to take it home. Sea fish are at your discretion, but must conform to minimum size limits to be legally kept. 95 per cent of the fish I (Dominic) personally catch go back unharmed, and the sight of a fish swimming away to fight another day always gives me more satisfaction than taking it home. Coarse fish make notoriously bad eating in any case – one old recipe for stuffed bream, for example, finishes with the instruction 'throw away bream and eat stuffing.'

With practice, you can easily unhook a fish, and most fish, when fought to the bank properly, will zip off unharmed when released back into the water.

If the fight has been particularly long or gruelling, the fish might be fully exhausted, in which case the angler might need to *revive* the fish before he or she releases it. Incidentally, a good angler never 'throws' a fish back, but will hold his or her catch in the water until it swims off. Chapter 17 describes how to revive and release an exhausted fish, as well as further catch and release tips.

Releasing fish ensures that other anglers will have the chance to catch fish, and releasing a *specimen* fish (angling speak for a whopper!) is a way to keep the right genes (the kind that make big, healthy fish!) in the water. Of course, as mentioned in Chapter 18, be sure to get a picture of that big fish before returning it with care.

The occasional fish supper

Naturally, where rules permit you may want to eat your catch on occasion, and shouldn't feel too guilty about taking the odd fish. The chances are it will be illegal to do so from your local river or canal (and frankly you would have to be quite mad to do this anyway from many waters!) but fresh sea fish and rainbow trout can be excellent.

Because a fish's body is made up primarily of muscle, they are great source of protein. With practice, it's possible to clean fish efficiently and with a minimal amount of gore. Once properly cleaned, fish can be cooked in many different ways, pleasing even the most discerning palate. Chapter 19 includes a handful of fish recipes for preparing different kinds of fish in a variety of ways.

Chapter 2

Gathering What You Need to Fish

- -

In This Chapter

▶ Dressing properly for fishing

▶ Packing a foul-weather bag

▶ Making waders work for you

▶ Picking the right tackle boxes and bags

▶ Bringing a good lunch

▶ Staying legal while fishing

- -

Be prepared. That's good advice that the Boy Scouts have followed for 100 years now. Some people want their trips to be spontaneous, fun and unpredictable. Others don't get to go fishing as often as they would like (who does?) and so want every minute they get on the water to be as enjoyable and stress-free as possible. And that means being prepared for the unplanned things that inevitably happen while fishing.

Being ready doesn't mean your fishing expeditions will somehow lack spontaneity or fun. On the contrary – the more prepared you are for a trip, the more energy and time you can dedicate to the important stuff: the fishing. That's the enjoyable part, after all. No one has fun fishing in the rain, cold and hungry, knowing the waterproofs and lunch are back at the house.

This chapter gives you an overview of the basic things you might need before you hit the water. Don't worry – you won't need everything for every trip; the less you have to carry, the better. But we offer advice here for what to wear and what to carry that prepares you for most of your fishing excursions, most of the time. (If you still want to go fishing on every single trip looking like a total beginner, absolutely clueless to what's happening in the world around you, go ahead: Greg's brothers have been doing it for decades, seemingly with no ill effects.)

Dressing for Fishing Success

If you want to take up fishing because you like the idea of impressing other anglers with your latest outfit, you, my friend, are going into the wrong hobby. Or you're going into the right hobby for all the wrong reasons! What you wear while fishing isn't about impressing other anglers. But it should be about comfort and success.

You desire clothes that are comfortable, and you also want them to work for you in all weathers. Hemingway's Santiago says in *The Old Man and the Sea*: 'Anyone can be a fisherman in May.' And May fishing can be quite pleasant. It can also be cold, rainy, stormy and downright nasty. And you're not only going to fish in May, are you? You want the right clothes for all seasons and all conditions.

As strange as it sounds, you also need clothes that help you catch fish. You want to wear clothes that don't scare fish by giving away your position, and you need gear that lets you get as close to the fish as you can while being as quiet as possible. But have no fear: We're not talking about getting ready for an interview, here. The clothes you wear while fishing can be inexpensive, old and ratty. They probably should be. But you should think a little bit about what you're wearing, beyond that lucky feeling you get from your Iron Maiden t-shirt.

Wear layers and always be happy

You don't need to dress fashionably, but you need to think practical. Wearing layers is the key to adapting to changing weather conditions while fishing. Even on a calm, sunny day, you face big temperature swings on a typical fishing trip. When you start out, possibly before dawn, the day begins dark, chilly and damp. Four hours later, you find yourself under a blazing sun cooking you with 30 °C of oven-blast heat.

Of course, the weather can change beyond the normal progression of the sun, as well. Storms blow in, rain starts and stops. Winds pick up and die down. One outfit won't match all of these ever-changing conditions. Even with the latest clothing technology, which really is quite amazing, you need to dress in layers to be comfortable all day or night long when fishing.

The basic setup in the following list will serve you in most places, most of the time. Modify it when it's ultra-hot, like in the West Country during a summer heatwave or, at the opposite end of the weather spectrum, when it's cold and going to stay that way, like for instance, up north in December. Outside of those extremes, follow this list and you'll be prepared for weather from freezing to 30 °, which is the range at which most of us fish:

- **Underwear:** Don a regular old cotton t-shirt and shorts in all but the coolest weather.

- **A long-sleeve cotton turtleneck or t-shirt:** This layer provides an overall covering of your torso and protects your neck and chest from wind (which you can pretty much always count on if you're in a boat).

- **Long underwear:** Long underwear made of silk or synthetic fabrics that wick away moisture can be light, cheap and warm. Even if you don't need it while fishing, it takes up little space and you'll be glad you have it when your jeans are wet and you haven't brought spare clothes for the drive home. Long johns are a winter staple for many grateful anglers.

- **Hiking or athletic shorts (with pockets):** Have them in a spare bag in the car in case it's a warm day. This means bring a bag with a change of clothes.

- **Jeans or khakis:** There's a reason that people just naturally wear these trousers when given a choice. They're comfortable, they break the wind, they keep the sun off and so on. If you don't like cotton, wear something made of nylon, polyester or fleece.

- **Long-sleeve cotton shirt (for warmish weather):** When it's hot, a long-sleeve cotton shirt keeps the sun off. At this stage of the game, we think most of you know that prolonged exposure to the sun is disastrous on unprotected skin. And fishing is a pastime that gives you about as much sun as any human activity. Modern shirts have sun-blocking capabilities built right into the fabric, and advertise the UPF on the label.

- **Long-sleeve wool shirt (for cold weather):** Wool stays warm even when it's wet. For early spring and autumn fishing, you may prefer it to cotton.

- **Fleece pullover:** There are a lot of brand names for that soft, fleecy synthetic material. All are warm, lightweight and comfortable.

- **Hoodies:** These are also excellent and have the added advantage that they will keep your head warm should you forget to bring a hat.

- **Rain wear:** You can buy very high-tech, very expensive rain jackets that 'breathe.' That sounds good, but the only thing that we have ever found that keeps you dry in an all-day soaker is a completely impermeable rain jacket. Make sure it has a hood. Waist-high is the best length for wading anglers. Waterproof trousers are also a good idea, either the simple sort or purpose made overtrousers from fishing stockists. The latter usually have braces and also keep you warm.

- **Pac-a-mac:** For a really portable solution, these waterproofs provide insurance against unexpected showers without taking up much space.

If you forget your rain jacket, you can make a poncho out of a decent-sized bin liner, so it's a good idea to keep a couple in your car boot as well. Cut holes for the head and arms and, in a pinch, you're in business. Now, you'll look a little funny, but you'll be dry.

Pack your foul-weather bag

Given the unpredictability of the weather, a foul weather bag (FWB) containing spares and essentials is an excellent idea in case conditions turn ugly. On a fishing trip to Ireland, I recall hailstones, heavy rain and sunshine all in the same day. On days like these, a waterproof and some spare dry clothes are a godsend. Here's Greg's list for an invaluable foul-weather bag:

✔ Buy a waterproof bag, available at most tackle shops and from outdoor retailers such as Blacks and Millets. The ones I like feature a roll-down top that buckles shut. It doesn't need to be large – about the size of a loaf of bread could do, but mine is about the size of a small office wastebasket. It should be waterproof and submersible.

✔ Stuff it with clothes and gear you might need, should the weather change or an emergency erupt.

✔ In my FWB: rainsuit, woollen hat, gloves, fleece pullover, matches, socks. The rainsuit stays near the top because that's what I use most often. The fleece and the hat have kept me warm on many autumn and spring nights.

It can be kind of a hassle to drag along the FWB at times, especially if you're traveling on foot and walking a good distance. If you know you're going to be out for only a short time, and the weather has little chance of changing, leave it behind. But when it doubt, bring it along. You can always stow it in the boot of your car if you're not walking long distances. You'll be glad you had the extra clothing when you get cold or wet.

Gloves are another recommendation for cold days on the water. Many experienced anglers shun gloves, however, because they deprive their hands of the necessary 'feel' to carry out simple tasks such as tying knots and handling fish. If you do get gloves for fishing though, go for the 'fingerless' variety so that you can still fish effectively.

Predator anglers – the ones who specialise in fishing for carnivorous species – sometimes wear gloves to protect their fingers from toothy fish such as pike. Special chain gloves are available, but in most cases a gardening glove will suffice, especially for those unsure about unhooking fish with impressive dentistry. *Note:* You don't want to grab a fish by its sides with dry gloves or hands, as this will remove the slimecoat. (Wet your gloves and hands first.)

Pick a good hat

Are some fishing hats luckier than others? Well, that's up for you (and the fish) to decide. But we do strongly recommend that you wear a hat while fishing. Hats will protect you from the sun or the rain (because you're probably going to see some of one or the other on most trips), and the hat's peak or brim will help shade your eyes to allow you to better watch the water. Your hat, when worn in conjunction with a good pair of polarised sunglasses, will help your eyes cut through the water's glare. (For more on sun protection and sunglasses, see Chapter 6.) This will allow you to see what's happening beneath the water's surface.

A baseball cap works well, as does any brimmed hat, which will keep both your face and your neck cool and shaded. Some hats now come with ultraviolet protection factor (UPF) ratings, which reflect the sun-blocking capabilities of the fabric, and are ventilated to allow cool breezes to keep your brain from overheating while you ponder fishing strategies.

Winter anglers will appreciate a well-made woollen hat. Choose something non-itchy which offers good insulation and covers the ears.

Pull on waders to wander into the fish's world

If you plan on doing any stream wading or surfcasting, you need *waders*. Although you can wade in the warmest months wearing little more than shorts and an old pair of trainers, to fish in cooler water, waders offer you warmth and dryness. Essentially, waders are waterproof hipboots meant to cover at least part of your legs and possibly your torso. The first time you wade into a stream wearing waders, you'll marvel at the experience. Standing in the stream almost chest-deep, with the current gently swirling around you, is a little like becoming a fish yourself.

Waders come in a variety of styles, made from a few different kinds of materials. Waders, like tents and boots, are meant to be waterproof. But like tents and boots, waders suffer tears and punctures. Luckily, many times a hole can be patched.

Waders come in several different styles, and are available almost anywhere tackle is sold:

   ✔ **Boot-foot waders:** This one-piece chest-high outfit has rubber boots attached to the legs of the waders, making it the most convenient design for dressing in a hurry. It is also the only design for surfcasting because sand or pebbles cannot find their way into your boots.

Often, when you buy boot-foot waders, you have to choose between getting felt or rubber grips on the soles of the boots (although some have 'combi-soles' which are a mix of the two). When rocks are covered with algae, wet leaves, dead seaweed or unidentifiable slime, they are very slippery. Felt soles cling and help to counteract the slipperiness. Rubber grip soles are okay, too, but you won't get the traction on slippery rocks that you'll find with felt soles. If you fish mostly in sand or mud, rubber grip soles will work fine. *Note:* On some streams, felt is illegal because of its tendency to transfer invasive species. To counter that, some manufacturers now offer soles made of things like crushed walnut shells. Look for these eco-friendly soles, or use studded or rubber grip soles.

- **Stocking-foot waders:** Stocking-foot waders (which are also chest high) do not come with boots attached, so they require wading shoes. Many anglers prefer this style because they say sturdy wading shoes give them extra support while wading. To prevent abrasion of the stocking foot, you should always wear a pair of wading socks over the foot of the wader.

- **Thigh waders:** Great for fishing streams in the summer. These reach your upper thigh, and can often be attached to your belt with garter-type straps (insert your own joke here). You can't go nearly as deep in hip waders as you can with chest-high waders, but if the river never gets that deep, why roast inside of chest waders? You'll also find it easier to answer the call of nature while wearing hip boots.

- **Waist waders:** Another option, between thigh and chest waders, these are effectively wading trousers. Usually belted and stocking footed, these are very comfortable and cooler than chest waders.

Waders are often made of the following three materials, and vary in durability and comfort:

- **Neoprene:** The material used in wet suits, neoprene works well if you are fishing in cold waters. Walking around in neoprene waders on a hot day, you'll feel like a baked potato in a microwave oven. Neoprene punctures, like rubber ones, can be resealed. Neoprene waders keep you warm in water below 10 °C.

- **Rubber and nylon:** The least expensive of the bunch, rubber waders are basically rubber boots that 'go all the way up.' Most feature reinforced knee patches and factory-sealed seams. They can last a long time if cared for.

- **Breathables:** Made of Gore-Tex and other fancy materials, breathable waders are the most expensive, but they're ultra-comfortable. The breathable membranes of these waders allow you to stay cooler in warmer months.

Duct tape, the wader wonder

Duct tape is brilliant stuff, with a multitude of uses. You only have to ask Peter for first hand evidence: 'I have one mounted fish on my wall. He's a 6 and 3/4-pound trout. I caught him on a stream in Labrador in early August. When I hooked him, I worked my way over to the side of the stream to continue the fight where I had a chance of winning. This required me to shift my backside across a number of midstream boulders. As luck would have it, one of those boulders had a sharp edge that tore a five-inch gash in my flyweight waders. When I had calmed down from the excitement of my gorgeous brookie, reality set in. When you're in the middle of Labrador and the nearest store is over 100 miles away, you can't just hop in the truck and get a wader repair kit at the nearest tackle shop. I did have a roll of duct tape in my duffel bag. I ripped off a piece and ran it alongside the gash in my waders. I got another two full seasons out of them, and in the end, it was the seams and not my patch that gave out. Always carry a roll of duct tape.'

It's easy to have a giggle at the oldies of the angling community wearing belts and braces. These would make for pretty ridiculous streetwear, but with most waders it's a must. You wear braces to hold up your waders, and the belt keeps water from rushing in if you get a dunking. This is a serious safety precaution. You can drown if your waders fill up.

Vests: Great for wading

Vests are such a common sight on streams that it's hard to imagine wading and fishing without them. Yet until Lee Wulff had the bright idea of sewing some blue jeans pockets onto a denim vest over seventy years ago, there were no fishing vests. You can buy vests with a gazillion pockets and you can stuff every one of those pockets. And you can also make sure that you have every possible gizmo hanging off the little snaps and rings that many vests have. We know that some of you will because fishing, like every other pastime, has its share of gear freaks (*tackle tarts* in fishing speak). However, we recommend that you take as little as possible in your vest. When wading, it's advisable to travel light.

Here are the five features to look for for in a vest:

> ✔ **Two large outer pockets suitable for holding a box of lures or flies:** The pockets should open and fasten from the top. If your vest has pockets that open on the side, you'll forget to zip up one day and eventually you will lose a box of expensive flies or lures.

- ✔ **Four inner pockets:** These are smaller, and it's okay if they only have velcro and no zippers. You may put a box of split shot in one pocket, tippet or leader material in another, and bug repellent in another.

- ✔ **Four small outer pockets:** One should have a zipper for an extra car key. The rest are for a small box to carry flies, floatant and this and that.

- ✔ **A metal ring:** You can tie your clippers onto this. They do make retractable pin-on gadgets that are designed as clipper holders, but we've had bad luck with those gadgets breaking. Save old fly line for these kinds of jobs instead. Tie your clippers on with them. Fly line is also a free alternative to a lanyard for holding your sunglasses when you want to keep them handy.

- ✔ **Outside back pouch:** Put your rain jacket in here, or maybe your lunch, water bottle, extra reel and so on.

Now that you have a vest, here are ten things you should always carry in it:

- ✔ **Sunscreen:** Use it for all daytime fishing.

- ✔ **Insect repellent:** For obvious reasons.

- ✔ **Clippers:** For cutting leader and trimming knots, clippers are preferable to teeth because clippers don't need to go to the dentist.

- ✔ **Thermometer:** Many tackle shops sell inexpensive thermometers designed to withstand being tossed about in vests and tackle boxes. With a thermometer, you can tell what species of fish may be most actively feeding.

- ✔ **A plastic bin bag:** You may not keep fish as a rule, but every so often you will want to, and who needs a vest full of fish slime? You don't need a family-size laundry bag; a wastebasket liner is more like it.

- ✔ **Forceps:** They help remove hooks more easily. This is good for the catch-and-release angler who wants to get the fish back in the water in a hurry. Some models will also crush barbs to render flies more fish friendly. Long forceps are essential for dealing with fish with sharp teeth, such as pike.

- ✔ **Rain jacket:** It doesn't take up much room and it makes a big difference, especially when it rains!

- ✔ **Spare car key:** Everybody loses the car key sometimes. It's a bummer if this happens when it's dark and cold by the side of a trout stream 20 miles from home. If you have a key with electronics, keep it in an airtight plastic bag.

- ✔ **Torch:** They make small torches that you can clip on and aim so that you have two free hands for knot tying, removing hooks and so forth. Then, on the way to the car, you can see where you are going.

- ✔ **First aid kit:** It's easy to find a compact first aid kit. Buy one and keep it in your vest at all times. If you're allergic to bee stings or other insects' bites, make sure you have something to treat severe allergic reactions.

Carrying Just What You Need to Fish

Okay, maybe it seems like we're loading you down with gear here. Admittedly, to be totally prepared for everything that can happen while fishing, you'd have to carry a truckload of stuff. You can't, and you shouldn't have to. Do this: Have what you need available, and bring the gear that a particular trip calls for, as well as you can predict. With experience, this process of choosing what to bring gets easier.

Bringing stuff also gets easier if you have the right tools to carry the stuff. A good fishing vest is one such tool (check out the previous section). A favourite tackle bag or box is another vital tool. Of course, an angler who shows up at the lake with his vest, foul-weather bag and tackle box but no rod and reel looks like a plonker.

Start with your rod, reel and net

Everything you need to know about choosing a good rod and reel for you is covered in Chapter 7. You can choose a set up that best matches the kind of fishing you do, and most likely you'll end up someday owning more than one or two and having the classic 'what do you need another rod for?' debate with your significant other. Most beginners start with a simple float or spinning rod and a fixed spool reel. Aim for a light outfit that transports easily.

As your fishing evolves to match your tastes, your rod and reel are also likely to change. With any rod and reel, remember that you have to get it to wherever you're fishing. The rod's most important job, of course, occurs on the water. But before it gets to the water, it has to survive inside of your car's trunk. Or a boat compartment. Or the mile-long trail down to the stream. Most rods 'break down,' meaning that they can be separated into sections. This makes packing easier. Some rods are one-piece, so think about your travel issues before you purchase a rod. Although you won't need them for basic fishing, rod carriers or 'holdalls' are available. Some are made from tough plastic to protect your gear while in transport, usually minus reels. Others are padded and will take rods set up and ready to go, which can be a real time saver on the bank. 'Quivers' are similar but hold rods externally and are ideal for the roving angler. Most of these handy luggage items also have space for your bank sticks and even a brolly.

The vast majority of freshwater anglers will also need a landing net. Otherwise you may have no way to bank that star catch. Some are collapsible and fold neatly for carrying. These are less practical than a model with a detachable head and a long handle – be optimistic and select a net that will comfortably handle the best fish you hope to catch. There's nothing worse than losing a big fish because your net wasn't up to the job. A soft unhooking mat is an excellent idea to protect your catch and many waters now insist on them. More on nets and mats in Chapter 17.

Pick a tackle carrier and load up

In the old days, tackle boxes were metal and looked like miniature tool boxes. Today's anglers can choose from tackle containers that are as varied as the selection of suitcases in a luggage store. Tackle bags and boxes house your lures, flies, hooks and other terminal tackle, and maybe a spare spool of line. Most have varying compartments to keep gear organised.. As there are different kinds of fishing, there are different kinds of bags. (Some are built to hold many lures, for example. Others, spare reel spools and accessories .)

Anglers can still buy the traditional tackle box, although plastic has replaced metal. These are a good choice because they are waterproof when sealed, available in many different sizes and styles, and tough as nails. Some feature drawers with compartments to hold things like lures and hooks, others have removable utility boxes that can be filled with your stuff. Others offer trays that fold out when you open the box. A good tackle store will have a range of boxes available, and there are even more options online. Shop around and handle a few before you buy. They come in hundreds of different sizes and styles. Some are difficult to carry for long distances; others work better on the floor of a boat.

Soft-sided tackle bags are increasingly popular now. These come in different sizes, as well, and can be filled with plastic utility boxes that you can mix and match for different trips. You might have one box of carp leads and rig materials; another box might hold a selection of lures for pike. Some of these bags have handles that double as shoulder straps, allowing you to wear the bag as a backpack. Most bags come in suitably subdued colours such as dark greens or browns.

A word on size: You need a tackle box or bag big enough to hold your gear, but the bigger the carrier is, the clunkier and heavier it gets. My advice is to buy a bag or box that feels right for your current needs, then sell it or give it to a friend when and if you outgrow it. Lugging around a tackle box half full is like seeing a stadium half full of fans. There's a lot of wasted space.

Are you sitting comfortably?

Some anglers such as lure or fly fishers who roam the banks have no need for a place to park their backside. The rest of us, and especially bait anglers in search of coarse fish, require something to sit on other than wet grass or stinging nettles. The model you choose will depend on your own style of fishing, but there are four basic types.

- ✔ **Stools**: They may be basic, but there's nothing wrong with a good old fashioned fishing stool. These are basically just a two folding halves and a canvas seat panel. Some even have a compartment to stow some gear.

- ✔ **Seats:** These are a more expensive but more comfortable option. Besides comfort, remember that you also have to carry the thing. The best fishing is seldom the flat, convenient area by the car park, so go for a light model with adjustable legs and add a carrying strap. You get what you pay for, but a dependable model will give years of service.

- ✔ **Seat Boxes:** Loved by match anglers but also useful for the general coarse angler, these combine ample tackle storage with a comfy seat. Basic models are cheap and hold a lot of gear. Posher versions have padded seats, adjustable legs for dodgy banks and lots of cool features and places for all your odds and ends.

- ✔ **Bed Chairs:** You would struggle to carry a bed chair far, but for long stay anglers who may have a long wait in store for a big fish, these are the ultimate in comfort. Carp addicts and night fishers wouldn't be without a cosy bed chair to chill out or even take a nap on.

Don't forget food and drink for yourself

We cover the importance of drinking a lot of fluids in Chapter 6 because staying hydrated is both a safety issue and a comfort issue. You need to pack a lot of drinking water or sports drinks (say, a bottle every couple of hours or so, because it's never a good idea to drink from the water from where you're fishing). Drinking plenty of fluids (that you brought from home) will keep you sharp and clear-headed. If you pack a cooler, freeze some water in plastic bottles. It will keep your food cold, and as it thaws, you'll have nice cold water to drink.

But you don't want to go hungry, do you? Bring a sandwich or two, and some apples, bananas and nuts. A plastic container of peanuts can be tipped to your mouth without having to handle the goods.

Some of the more hygienically challenged might have no problem with grabbing a sandwich with their mitts covered in smelly bait or fish slime. For the rest of us, a hand towel or anti-bacterial wipes are a good call. Another useful option is a small bottle of the alcohol-based hand wash gel found in hospitals and other work places, which kills bugs but requires no soap or water.

Some sandwich thoughts from Peter: I'm taking it for granted that you already know how to make a sandwich. Over the years, I have found just a few common-sense things that have resulted in better sandwich eating or at least less sandwich disasters in the bottom of the cooler.

- **Wrap it small and tight.** A hulking great sandwich looks great, but you will not normally eat it all at once. Then you are in the position of having to rewrap it, which hardly anyone ever does properly, and the result is a lot of ham, lettuce and tomato bits rolling around the cooler or the back of your vest. Cut the sandwich into smaller pieces and wrap each piece individually. I use greaseproof paper or cling film for wrapping and then I put everything inside a plastic bag.

- **Dry is good.** Although soggy bread may be good for bait, it's lousy on a sandwich. Remember that a sandwich to take along on a fishing trip is not the same as a sandwich that you make at halftime while watching the match on TV. Often, you are not going to eat your fishing sandwich for a few hours. That mayonnaise that tastes so good on a ham sandwich in the den is going to squoosh right through the bread when you unwrap your sandwich at the stream. Sliced tomatoes will soak through the crustiest, freshest roll. My solution is to cut down on the wet stuff, and if I absolutely need some, then I put it next to the meat and cover it with a piece of lettuce or a slice of cheese.

Tucking Your Fishing Licence in a Safe Spot

Before setting out to fish it is vital that you are licensed to do so. Sea anglers do not require a licence; everyone else does. To tackle any fresh water you need a licence from the Environment Agency (EA). The EA monitors and protects waters across the land, as well as policing against poachers and others who threaten the sport. You can buy a day or week fishing licence (£3.75 and £10 respectively), but the vast majority take a season permit (currently £27), which runs twelve months exactly from March 15. The good news for youngsters is that under-twelves fish for free, and under-sixteens can get a season ticket for just £5, while OAPs and the disabled save a third of the price on season tickets. All the more reason to take your younger and older friends and relatives fishing.

Anglers who wish to use more than two rods (usually carp specialists) require two licences. If you want to target salmon or sea trout as well as the usual suspects, you require a special licence for migratory game fish at £8 per day or £72 season, adult rates, but still just £5 a season for under 16s and a third off for OAPs and disabled anglers.

This is your basic legality covered and on some waters, typically urban rivers and some public reservoirs, fishing is 'free' to any EA licence holder. However the majority of places require an additional day or season ticket from the fishery owner. This could range from £5 to fish a farm pond, to several hundred pounds for access to an exclusive big fish 'syndicate' water for the year. Fees go towards vital running costs, from water maintenance to stocking fish. It can be tricky to decide where to try, but the best value of all comes from the many angling clubs and associations all over the UK. Many provide a variety of fishing for as little as £30 a season. You'd struggle to get into one Premier League football match for that amount, let alone buy a season's worth of action.

EA licences are available online at the Agency's informative site (`www.environment-agency.gov.uk`) or from any Post Office branch. Most tackle shops sell day and season tickets for local club waters. Private fisheries and so called 'commercial' or day ticket waters have their own ticket options. Often these can be bought on the bank, but some venues insist on payment before you tackle up.

Carry your licence in a waterproof container, or place your licence in your wallet and your wallet in a sealed plastic bag.

Like anything governed by rules or laws, in fishing there are those who knowingly break the laws for their own gain. Most often this involves an angler illegally removing fish, or by catching fish using illegal methods. The EA has a 24-hour number printed on your licence to allow you to report this sort of activity. We recommend you do just that if you see someone wantonly breaking the fishing laws in your area. After all, a poacher is taking fish illegally – fish that you and other law-abiding citizens will no longer be able to catch. The more info you can offer the better (exact location, details, car registration etc.). You should also report pollution, and a prompt phone call could make a big difference to the future health of a fishery. Fishing clubs have their own bailiffs to take action when something is wrong. Remember, anglers are the eyes and ears of our waters. If something is wrong, make that call.

Seasons in fishing

Different fish species and waters have specific fishing seasons. This is to protect fish at spawning time and give the natural environment a healthy break. Always check if in doubt, but the following norms should be observed:

- ✔ **Coarse fishing:** Once upon a time, fishing for coarse species (anything except trout and salmon) was only allowed from June 16 to March 14 the following year, with a closed season over the spring and early summer in between. Indeed, some folks still get that twinge of excitement as the magical day of June 16 arrives and they can return to their favourite sport. Today rivers and wilder waters still enjoy a rest from mid-March, but many lakes and canals remain open all year round.

- ✔ **Game fishing:** Trout and salmon have a different season in rivers and wild lakes, with the fishing usually running from March 15 to September 31. Savvy types among you will quickly spot that during the coarse fishing closed season, those itching to wet a line can turn their attention to fly fishing. Trout reservoirs also tend to follow this pattern, but many other stocked lakes are open all year round giving sport with rainbow and brown trout right through the winter.

✔ **Sea fishing:** No closed season. This also extends to estuaries, although you'll have to leave any coarse species present alone between March 15 and June 15.

Rules for good reasons

Various rules govern fishing in the UK. The EA has its own national and local byelaws which apply to all fresh water (see the EA website). Others are put in place by clubs and fisheries. A common example is that many day ticket venues insist on barbless hooks and unhooking mats, which help protect the fish from damage.

There are too many other examples of rules to list, but do always check. The vast majority of rules are there to protect the fishing and ensure you have a safe, positive experience. Antisocial types who litter the banks or harm the environment can quickly find themselves banned.

The most important rules of all surround catch and release. On virtually all coarse fisheries it is illegal to remove fish, other than possibly a limited number of small ones (under 20 cm) for use as live or dead bait. Game fish are also frequently fished for on a strict catch-and-release basis, with the exception of fish such as rainbow trout which are stocked specially for the table.

Catch and release makes perfect sense: it ensures that fish populations remain healthy and are not exploited to the detriment of the sport. It also means that the fine specimen you land today could grow even bigger for next season or give another person the same pleasure. As one wise soul put it: 'A fish is too precious to be caught only once.' More on safe catch and release can be found in Chapter 17.

Sea fishing is another matter entirely with the 'keep or let go?' question. Nobody 'owns' sea fish. However, minimum size limits apply, preventing anglers from taking undersized fish which haven't had the chance to spawn yet (for a full list of minimum sizes go to `www.sea-fishing.org/nfsa-size-limits.html`). It's your call, but if you're not going to eat it put it back carefully.

Chapter 3

Finding and Evaluating Water for Fishing

Simply put, every decision made about how and what you're fishing for follows the first, crucial decision: the location you've chosen. You don't fish streams the same way you fish ponds. Big rivers aren't lakes. Public piers jutting out from the beach aren't exactly like a muddy estuary. So begin your fishing adventures by studying the body of water you intend to fish. Anglers call the business of sussing out this puzzle *watercraft*. When you know the water, you'll begin to know the fish in it. And then the fun – the catching – begins!

Wherever you fish, pay close attention to the world around you. Watch the water. Every swirl and splash tells you something. The fish's world is largely hidden from you, but if you pay attention, you'll find that every body of water provides hints about what's happening below the surface. Watch the prey (flies minnows and the like) and fellow predators like birds, and they'll tell you where the fish are.

All fish, in any body of water, relate to what anglers call *features*. These are simply the characteristics of any given body of water and we can divide them into two basic types: *structure* and *cover*. Structure refers to what lies beneath the surface of the body of water; a sharp drop-off or a *point* (a finger of land jutting into the water) is structure, for example. Think of structure as permanent features. Cover could be things like a weedbed or a sunken log.

Man-made cover, like docks or piers, hold fish just as natural cover does. Be aware of structure and cover and you'll find – and catch – more fish.

This chapter helps you figure out where to fish and then how and when to fish that location. There are a lot of variables at play when it comes to finding and sussing out fishing waters, but we do our best in this chapter to call out some typical conditions for both freshwater and saltwater locations.

Knowing Where to Go

As Chapters 4 and 5 make clear, there are many of species of fish awaiting you. While they prefer a variety of habitats, some of those fish invariably live close to you. Although no two waters are exactly alike (and that's part of the fun of this whole adventure!), streams in the Southwest share some things in common with streams in the east or anywhere. Farm ponds are alike wherever you go. What you learn in one spot will add to your understanding of how to fish the next.

Fishable water is where you find it. Train yourself to look for water with the following two characteristics:

✔ **Access:** Fishable water is either open to the public or privately owned. Public water, such as the banks of a canal or river, is governed by rules and your first step is to investigate and learn those rules. These will often be set by a fishing club which looks after the water. Almost all will have a booklet available when you buy your permit, if not a website you can look up. Is fishing allowed only during certain hours? Are there rules regarding hooks, baits or any other practices?

If the water is privately owned, then you must have that owner's permission. Many waters operate on a 'day ticket' basis. In other words you pay a daily fee to the owner for the right to fish. Many of these places are advertised and you can simply turn up when you like and either deposit some money and fill your details when you arrive, or pay the owner in person. If in doubt however, find out before diving in. Never fish first, intending to ask later! It's not only rude, but illegal. However, many landowners will grant you permission if you ask politely and this can be a good way of discovering new and untapped fishing locations. Common sense rules apply: Ask in a courteous manner; take rejection if it comes; be honest about your intentions; and don't bring all your friends. In other words, it's a lot like asking a father for permission to date his daughter. If you're fishing in a farm pond, remember to shut all gates behind you – you don't want to let any animals out!

✔ **Fish:** Sometimes giant bodies of water hold only stunted populations of scrawny fish. Occasionally the little pond on the golf course yields a twenty-pound carp. The only real way to know is to study the water. Private landowners often know what fish have been stocked in that body of water. Some public places will post notices about the fish available, too. Better still, carry out your own research in person or online. Fisheries depend on permit sales and you may well find listings and info available with popular fishing areas as well as the fish you can expect to find there. Ideally, you should seek water that carries a healthy supply of your favorite kind of fish in an aesthetically pleasing environment. How do you find such a paradise? This chapter helps you locate it.

Fish the one you're with: Finding fishing water close to home

Familiarity breeds success when it comes to fishing. Show me a person with a shack on the river, or a lakeside house with a boat, and I'll show you someone who can catch fish when others cannot. The more time you spend on a body of water, the more you get to know it, and the better you understand its personality as seasons pass. Living along a stream will acquaint you with the length of time it takes to return to normal flow after a flood. Visit a lake every weekend for a year and you begin to understand when roach gather in the shallows and when tench spawn. Fishery owners and guides know their home water because it's their job: They see it on a daily basis.

But you can get to know a piece of water, too, even without quitting your day job. Just give the water time; even if you can only fish for an hour after work, every hour adds to your understanding. Now, I know some anglers only fish a particular place for a particular species, even if this place is far away: say, fishing for salmon on a remote river. These anglers save up and go once a year, and that's the sum of their fishing. Fine, but that's not the way to build up a greater understanding and really enjoy fishing to the full.

Locate a fishing spot close to your home or work, study and fish it regularly. You could even throw in a helping of bait at the end of each trip to get the fish used to it. Keep your eyes and ears open every time you visit. Take note of the fish you catch: What bait did it take? Where was the fish when it hit? What was the water like? The weather? Every fish you catch helps you complete the puzzle. Fishing a place regularly – and throughout the seasons – helps you become a better angler.

Investigating fishing waters on Google Earth

By now, you've probably seen your house from space. That's certainly cool, but what about putting that technology to better use by using satellites to plan your next fishing trip? A program like Google Earth makes it possible to follow streams and rivers, seeking public access landings. You can also find hidden coves on big lakes, or small ponds hidden from the public eye. You'll still need permission or a licence to fish these finds, of course, but finding the water is the first step. Visit www.google.com/earth to download the application.

Finding fish when you're on the road

A big part of the fun of angling is fishing in new places, for new and different fish. If you travel with a packable fishing rod, a handful of lures or flies, and a small collection of terminal tackle, you can be ready to fish anytime, anyplace. (Just make sure you're fishing legally! See the section on licences later in Chapter 2.) Perhaps you could steal away during the next family holiday for a visit to the beach. Maybe you travel with your work and find yourself with a spare hour or two in a tempting location. If your travels bring you closer to new and exciting fishing, even a short foray could make a great angling memory! You don't need bags of time to catch fish. Just resist the temptation to plant your backside in the nearest available spot; travel light and search out the fish.

You won't know this water well, and you won't have time to study it hard. But bodies of water share characteristics. Also, techniques that work in one stream will work in another. (See Chapter 17 for more on techniques.) And local tackle shops can suggest the best baits and methods for that area, as well as giving helpful advice.

Even without local help you can catch fish. Certain lures, like small spinners, tend to work everywhere. Baits such as worms and maggots will tempt almost any fish that swims. Fishing far from home challenges you. You're not likely to match your catch totals from your home waters, but there's always that chance . . .

Getting the Scoop

Okay, so you find some fishable water. You fish it a few times, and try to pay attention to what the water tells you. But you still can't catch fish, or catch enough of them. There's no shame in asking for a little advice. Every angler has done this a few times and exchanging information is very much part of the sport. Some anglers seem to enjoy talking as much as fishing!

You'll probably find that everyone has advice when it comes to fishing. Everyone! Some old guy at the petrol station who hasn't fished since before colour television will tell you to dangle a worm under the bridge along the canal to catch a record perch. Then he might tell you about the price of fuel or what the government is doing wrong. You need advice you can use, and you don't have all day. There's fish to be caught! This section takes you on a tour of reliable places to gather information.

From tackle shops

Local tackle shops are a tried-and-tested source of fishing insight. Tackle shops probably came into existence not long after the discovery of the fishing rod, and good ones carry an established reputation along with rods, reels and hooks. Tackle shop owners (and your fellow customers) often know the water nearby. They can refer to the handy map taped to the wall, or even mark the copy they sell you. They stock lures, flies and bait that work for local waters, as well as advice on how to use them. They can also put you in touch with, and sell permits for, local fishing clubs, another excellent source of information.

The tackle shop is a business, and that business isn't Free Advice. They need to sell items to keep the doors open, so buy something (even if it's just a packet of hooks) to get people talking. Another tip: Study the fish pictures tacked to the walls. Just knowing what fish are out there helps you plan your approach. Now, if all the fish pictures look as old as your school photos that's telling you something else.

From online forums

People say all fishermen are liars and there might be some truth to that. But they can also be surprisingly forthcoming in online forums. Often dedicated to a particular species or region, forums and Websites can save you a lot of time on the water. And unlike tackle shops, they're open all night long, allowing you to do your research at night and your fishing during the day. Use a search engine to find and bookmark the best ones for your area or your kind of fish. Forums are often broken down into different regions and styles of fishing (coarse, sea, carp, fly etc). Within each section are countless threads about what's being caught and through what methods. Often members will offer to take strangers fishing. Like all things online, it's good to be cautious, but it's a pretty amazing resource when you think about it.

Don't ignore the traditional printed media either for catch results and interesting leads. Publications such as the *Angling Times* always have notable catches and 'where to fish' sections. Local papers also regularly have a weekly angling section worth keeping an eye on.

From guides

Guides are anglers who get paid to take you fishing, and the best guides are equal parts anglers and teachers. A good guide will know the water and a great deal about the fish within it. You can find guides online, in classified ads in the press, or through word of mouth at the tackle shop or fishing lodge. Most can be hired for either half- or full-day trips, and in return, you can expect the guide to do most of the work for you.

What do you do as a client? Pack, sunscreen, rain gear, a camera, and a good attitude. (Ask if lunch and drinks are included; if they aren't, pack those too.) Pay attention and ask questions. Guides fish their home waters five or six days a week, and that kind of experience is invaluable. Most guides will offer advice on technique, productive areas and the right fly or bait. Costs vary from location to location, but plan on tipping a bit over the initial charge if your guide works hard for you. (Don't punish a guide for the morning's cold front that shut the fish down. Even the best get stumped sometimes.) Remember, even at a fair price a guide can offer great value in showing you techniques and local knowhow it might have taken years to learn unassisted.

When no one knows: Walk the bank

Suppose you find a fishing spot no one has seen before. Let's say it's on another planet. There's no local tackle shop; no online forum mentions it. Can you still figure out this lake, and what lives within it? Of course you can. It comes back to paying attention: Walk the banks and watch the water. What's the water clarity like? Cloudy or stained water means fish probably aren't feeding visually – you might select a big, smelly bait such as luncheon meat or a loud, noisy lure like a spinnerbait. Are weeds prevalent? Lilies? Fish of all sizes will hide under lilies and in weedbeds, which means predator fish will patrol nearby. See schools of small fish? Can you identify the species? If there are babies, there will be adults to catch, of course. Be on the lookout for dead fish or skeletons because these, too, will tell you what species live here. Without wetting a line you can learn a lot about a body of water and the fish that live there.

Evaluating Freshwater Sites

From a tiny southern stream to the grandeur of Scotland's lochs, how can an angler approach such varying freshwater? First, he or she realises that only knowing one approach won't work. Different kinds of water call for different techniques (see Chapter 16), different gear, and different mindsets. Sure, all fishing has a lot in common, and your angling knowledge is transferable from one situation to another, but great anglers adapt to the situation and habitat they're facing.

Ponds and commercial fisheries

Natural and man-made ponds dot the landscape. They range from farm ponds made as a source of drinking water for animals, to flooded quarries and clay pits. Some of these places, such as the classic lily-infested carp ponds of England, are truly idyllic. Most prevalent of all however, are the burgeoning number of so called *commercial fisheries*. These range from small clusters of ponds to bigger pools that can hold dozens of anglers. They might not always be the most natural looking settings, but these purpose made waters are often packed with fish.

Ponds can support a lot of fish if carefully managed, and they provide a safe fishing environment for millions of anglers. Some ponds have fish populations that are carefully monitored by humans, others have wilder, more natural populations that self-regulate. Contrary to popular belief, birds don't spread fish eggs from pond to pond.

Who's home?

Carp, tench, roach, rudd and perch are the classic choices for pond stocking, along with possible bonuses such as crucians and bream. A murky looking pond is often the sign of a good head of carp, which churn up the bottom as they feed.

If a pond has good quality water that stays cool enough year round, trout can also survive and there are some delightful spring-fed trout fisheries of this type. Trout thrive especially well in old quarry ponds, for example, where the water is deep and clear. A well-managed pond will feature all the habitat of larger natural bodies of water, with plenty of features (such as trees, islands and weed beds), good water quality, and a healthy balance of fish populations.

There may be more wild and natural looking places, but many commercial pools offer a reliable fishing fix for less than ten quid a day. They also provide safe places for youngsters to fish and plenty of bites for beginners.

Commercials also appeal to those who value creature comforts such as working toilets and a place to buy some bait or a coffee.

How to fish the water

Ponds suit themselves perfectly to float fishing methods from the bank. It would be daft to use several rods and heavy tackle in most instances, and by using simple, light tackle and introducing a regular trickle of free bait such as maggots, corn or pellets you may well enjoy bites all day. You could also try a much larger bait to single out something bigger. Trout pools can be tackled with a leisurely stroll around, casting a fly to any visible fish or likely looking areas.

Most ponds have access points where you can get near the water and cast. Because there may not be a lot of structure to a pond (they are often bowl-shaped), one spot may be about as good any other. Still, a visual inspection will usually call your attention to a few key spots – cover like fallen, partially submerged trees or islands draw fish. If the pond has a *dam* or *levy* (the earthen bank built across the lower end of the valley to hold back the water and form the pond), the water in front of it is often the deepest, and that might hold fish too, especially in the winter. Corners or coves often attract fish and carp love to feed close to the bank in these areas.

Canals and Drains

Originally created to transport goods by boat, canals offer diverse and affordable fishing for all. *Drains* fall into a similar category, cut into the landscape for irrigation and water management, particularly in low-lying wetland areas. From the canals of the Midlands to the Fenland drains, there are countless miles of surprisingly good fishing available to all. Some of these waters are rustic and pretty, others are grey and urban; all have fish.

Angling clubs have long cherished these lengthy channels, where you can often fish for a pittance. They are usually characterised by shallow sides and a deeper centre or *track*. The *shelf* where the bottom slopes away is often a key fish holding area.

Who's home?

Don't be deceived by the sometimes uniform, humdrum nature of some drains and canals; they can hold a terrific head of fish and not just small ones. You might catch almost any of the coarse species. Roach, bream and perch are the commonest fish, but pike will also be present. Many of these man-made venues also contain carp, rudd and tench. In some areas they are also a refuge for some of those unusual and less widespread coarse fish, such as zander.

How to fish the water

Canals and drains can be fished with a vast array of methods. Float fishing with a rod or pole and small baits can be excellent for roach, rudd and bream. You could also try legering corn or boilies for bonus fish like carp and tench, and there are monsters present which seldom see a hook! Lures and fish baits will catch pike and other predators. If the water clarity is good, fly fishing is a thrilling and effective way to pick out many of these species. Check out Chapter 16 for more on these techniques.

With miles of water, it is important to be mobile. Some of these places look very uniform, but the fish can be quite concentrated. Pay special attention to any deeper or wider areas such as boat basins, as well as bankside features and junctions with other waterways. If stuck for clues, a good walk wearing polarising glasses is a good starting point.

Streams, small rivers and big rivers

Small rivers and streams often feature everything that makes for a great fishing trip: interesting fish, an ever-changing environment and beautiful scenery. Unlike small ponds, which usually start with an introduced population of fish, streams run wild and may carry wild populations of fish.

The majority of streams and rivers follow a pattern known as *riffle-pool-run*. A riffle is often visible – the water will churn as it flows over a harder bottom. Riffles are shallower than the surrounding water, and mark the beginning of a pool – the area where the current carves away the bottom after tumbling through the riffle. Pools are the deepest parts of the river. Runs or *glides* occur where the river assumes a fairly stable depth until the next riffle. (Although the depths of a pool might range from a foot or two in a stream to many feet in a large river, the basic pattern remains.)

Who's home?

Trout favour cool, stony streams and the narrower, faster parts of rivers. You'll also find fish such as chub and dace present in these flows. As the river gradually slows and widens many coarse fish species start to occur, including roach, bream, barbel, pike and perch. The largest rivers are deep enough to hide some of the biggest fish in freshwater. Many rivers also contain carp, whether introduced by accident or design. Streams and rivers allow for fish mobility, so fish can move up and down rivers seasonally. Many fish move upstream in the spring (often seeking spawning sites) and downstream in the autumn, seeking deeper holes for wintering. That varies from place to place and by species, but you should see the river as a highway with no roadblocks – it flows from place to place, and unless there's a dam to stop them, fish can move freely up- and downriver. Hence anglers should stay mobile too.

How to fish the water

What makes a stream different from a pond is its current. A stream's current influences a fish's life about as much as work and rest affect yours. Fish in streams make most of their decisions based on the current, so you need to understand how current works. Start with this nugget: Fish face into the current, so they can see food being swept downstream toward them. This is especially notable in trout. Therefore, you should present your fly, lure or bait so that it looks natural: In other words, cast upstream of your target and retrieve your offering downstream. Now, this doesn't mean always casting straight, or directly, upstream every time, but do try to use the current to your advantage and to present your tackle and bait naturally. Casting just upstream of an overhanging tree, for example, will let the scent of a smelly bait carry to the fish hiding underneath. *Trotting,* a classic float fishing method, is another good example of using the current, in this case to let the bait drift downstream naturally to the fish.

Fish often want to be near the current (to take food from it), but they don't like expending more energy than necessary to maintain a position. For this reason, fish will often hide behind a large boulder, submerged branches or other obstruction, so they can be near the current but out of it. A *crease* is another classic area, meaning the spot where faster and slower water meet. (You can find more on how to fish currents in Chapter 17.) Learning about individual fish species will also help. Some fish will tolerate a fairly strong current (barbel, roach, trout), others are lazier and prefer slacker water out of the main flow (pike, bream, perch).

Fishing large rivers is sometimes difficult without a boat, as fish are not spread out equally along the length of the river – most of the fish are usually in the steady glides and deeper holes. If you have shore access to one of these spots, you could be in luck. But on a large river, deep pools might be miles apart.

Lakes and reservoirs

Lakes are natural and range widely in depth, age, and fish populations. Reservoirs are man-made lakes, formed when a river is dammed. Because reservoirs quite literally grow out of rivers, they feature a *channel,* which is the now-flooded river. Gravel pits are another type of lake – former excavation sites which become a rich, clear-water environment where fish thrive. Other stillwaters are completely natural. Lakes and reservoirs range in size from a few acres to thousands, and can feature all kinds of structure and cover within that space.

Who's home?

Lakes and reservoirs offer the size needed to grow large fish. Almost any freshwater fish could be found in these large bodies of water, provided the water offers the temperature, food base, and so on that a particular species of fish requires. Because reservoirs are still connected to a river, and because many lakes have streams draining into them, fish populations vary as fish move in and out of the waterway. Fish are also frequently stocked (in other words reared and introduced by man); trout or carp are common additions which can grow big in these rich environments. Check with tackle shops and any printed or online resources to see what fish species are present in a particular lake or reservoir.

How to fish the water

The size of any large body of water is intimidating. Don't let it be. Whereas boats offer anglers the advantage of covering more water, most lakes and reservoirs offer shorebound anglers bank access. Fishing any lake or reservoir calls for ruling out the fishless water. The fish population won't be distributed equally over the acres, so whether you're fishing from boat or bank, seek out features in the form of cover or interesting structures. A point will attract fish, especially if it provides cover, too. A bank with a rocky ledge will usually lure fish. A bridge over a lake will often appear in a narrower area where the banks are closer together and may feature banks reinforced with large stones or chunks of rock to control erosion. Pay attention – the land above the water line provides clues about the bottom. A sharp rising bank usually means the water is deep below the surface, because the bottom will fall away just as steeply. Fish will be drawn to edges, or differences – where one bottom type meets another (say where a sandy bottom becomes rocky, where there is a gravel bar, or where a weedbed stops). It might be worthwhile casting about with a lure or sinker and counting down how long it takes to reach the bottom, to get a rough idea of depths.

Generally, fish will be in shallower water in the spring, seeking warmer water (the sun warms shallower water faster) and potential spawning sites. As the summer passes, fish move into areas offering the right structure and cover all over the lake, and as autumn approaches, fish tend to move to deeper sections of the lake or reservoir. Usually, the closer you are to the dam, the deeper the water will be. Plan your location around the season and you're on the right path.

Unless you're positive you've found the fish, don't spend too long in one spot. Be mobile and learn more about the water.

Underexplored hotspots

Sometimes success is about fishing where others aren't. Constantly seek underfished water. Often, this means making more effort than other anglers are willing to expend. Humans are naturally lazy. Many anglers simply aim for a nice flat spot, not too far from the car and out of the wind – things the fish couldn't care less about. Walk further than other anglers. Ask permission to fish the tiny pond others simply drive past. Cast around the docks in the bay behind the packed tourist hotels. You never know where a big fish will appear. (And if your local water is packed with anglers on the weekend, fish when others aren't.)

Evaluating Saltwater Sites

Sea fishing can be intimidating due to the vastness of the ocean. Chances are, though, if you're reading this book, you're going to do most of your saltwater fishing within three miles of shore, in water less than 100 feet deep. To fish the deep blue of the sea, you need a serious boat, gear, and experience. You may not have those things yet, but you can always hire a boat and skipper to get a taste of fishing the biggest water. A professional skipper will have the proper gear and knowledge, which takes the pressure off you. You can relax and enjoy the trip! But fear not – even if you fish on your own, closer to shore, plenty of adventure awaits the coastal angler.

Approach saltwater fishing as you would freshwater – seek access and any information on resident fish. Pay attention to your surroundings and watch for clues about what's happening beneath the surface. Saltwater species often come closer to shore to pursue prey because the shoreline offers the habitat that creatures like crabs, shrimp, and small fish need. In a feeding frenzy, larger fish chase huge schools of prey fish to the shore and, once the trap is set, feed voraciously and fearlessly. You can catch feeding fish if you understand the saltwater fishing basics of tides, structure, and cover.

Tidal estuaries and bays

To fish saltwater, you need to understand tides. Tides affect all oceans, of course, but the *tidal range* varies from place to place. Sometimes the tidal range can be relatively small But with irregular coastlines with inlets, bays and streams, the tidal range can be much greater. Tides affect fishing just as current does in any stream: The fish understand that tides move small fish and other prey and they respond accordingly.

Tides are basically predictable and you can find charts informing of you of the *high,* or rising, tide, as well as the *low,* or falling, tide. Most regions offer a handy little booklet of tide times, which is well worth buying. But even predictable ones can be very affected by storms and other natural events many miles away. When the tide is neither rising nor falling, it's known as a *slack* tide. As in a river, where too little current often makes for difficult fishing, a slack tide tends to slow or stop the bite (there are few rules that don't have exceptions).

Who's home?

Fish can't survive without food, and tidal estuaries and bays offer a smorgasbord of prey fish, crabs, shrimp, sandeels, and the like. Bass love these places, moving in with the tide and chasing shoals of sandeels. Flatfish such as flounder and plaice seek out mussel beds and shrimp. In the warmer months, many other visitors such as bream, plaice and rays will also venture into estuaries to feed. Mullet are another staple, perhaps the most numerous of all the bigger fishes present.

How to fish the water

In places like muddy,river mouths and brackish streams, a high tide offers fish a chance to chase prey in prime habitat. But a low tide will force fish back into deeper water, so time your trips to coincide with moving tides. Predators such as bass will often be either rushing out or rushing in with the rising tide, chasing the displaced bait. Fish inside harbours and river mouths during high tides, as fish will be moving into shallow water, and outside these shallower areas as the tide recedes (shown later in Figure 3-1).

All tides can consolidate and move fish. Look for ambush points like rock outcroppings that game fish use (just as freshwater fish do) to jump prey being carried by the tide. Look for variances in structure – reefs, sandbars and drop-offs – and watch for signs of fleeing prey fish. Birds won't help you as much in most freshwater fishing situations, but in saltwater, they're a valuable aid. Watch birds like cormorants and seagulls – they'll respond to schools of prey fish, and if the birds are following the food, you can be sure the fish are as well. Sightfishing can be excellent fun when casting flies or lures for bass and other predators. Those who fancy a different challenge may want to grab some coarse fishing gear and try for mullet with bread or small worm baits. Polarised sunglasses, which we recommend in Chapter 6, will help you see the fish.

Surf fishing

Waves shake things up and attract everything along the food chain. Stirred up sand displaces everything from zooplankton to crabs, which attract small fish, which of course attract bigger fish. Surf fishing allows you to fish from the beach or shore, capitalizing on the feeding frenzy triggered by breaking waves.

Who's home?

Bass are popular quarry, but anglers catch everything from cod to flatties, dogfish and rays while surf casting. Rocky areas yield wrasse, conger and pollack. It may also be worth investigating the prospect of night fishing, as even more species will move inshore under cover of darkness. Understanding the seasonal movements of particular species of fish will help you understand when and where to cast from the surf. Some species make what is called a *run*, or migration, up and down the coastline, sometimes traveling hundreds of miles. Ask the locals or in tackle shops for information about the local runs of various species.

How to fish the water

Although a good portion of shore fishing can be done with your more robust coarse tackle, surf casting usually requires a longer, more robust gear. A 12-foot plus beachcaster allows you to cast heavy weights out beyond the breakers. In a heavy swell you may need a tool capable of handling 5 ounces or more of lead in the tide. Peeler crab, fish and worm baits are standard fare, although it could be worth trying with lures where fish venture closer to shore.

Watch the water to see the subtle differences in a long stretch of breaking waves. Running roughly parallel to the beach is what's called the *outer bar,* essentially a sand bar that's higher than the bottom on either side of it. Fishing cuts and dips in the outer bar can be effective, and fish may hold in the drop-offs in front of or behind it. Scanning a mark at low tide might tell you more about the features present, or you could take to higher ground such as a cliff top walk to study the water. Look out for darker patches in the sea, which mark those weedy or rocky places fish are attracted to.

As with all fishing, the more you observe, the more you learn. Experience trumps anything we can say about surf fishing here. Many anglers wade and fish at night while surf fishing, so know your limits before you imitate more experienced anglers.

If you use your freshwater tackle to fish in saltwater, be sure to rinse it thoroughly after you're done. If you don't, the saltwater will corrode the inner workings of your reel. If you plan to fish saltwater regularly, buy gear rated for saltwater use, which will feature higher-quality bearings and better seals. Rinse saltwater off all equipment, regardless of the type or quality!.

Fishing piers and breakwaters

Fishing piers and other man-made structures may lack the beauty and serenity, perhaps, of chasing your quarry on a wild beach. But it makes up for any shortcomings with convenience. Piers provide a high, stable vantage point for shorebound anglers (including those who are young or physically disabled), and offer a safe, inexpensive opportunity to pull fish from the ocean. We should really include harbours and any substantial sea walls such as marinas and breakwaters into the bargain here. Such places also offer deep water without the need for hefty, long distance casts.

Who's home?

Although it's hard to imagine a cleaner, easier way to fish, fishing from piers, harbours and other structures isn't just for lazy anglers catching baby fish. Some excellent catches of codling and even the odd big bass or conger are made from such structures. There could be many species on offer, but the most common summer catch will be mackerel, followed by pollack and wrasse. Depending on the season and location, it's possible to catch just about anything.

How to fish it

Many fish move in and out of the protection offered by the pilings of the pier itself, meaning that good fishing is literally underfoot (see Figure 3-1). You'll often find wrasse and pollack here, as well as bigger bonuses at night. You may want to use bottom rigs here, but where nasty snags exist, savvy anglers attach weights on a link of weaker line, so that they can land a hooked fish even if the sinker becomes stuck and needs to be broken off.

Float fishing is a fun way to catch all sorts of fish and light tackle (such as a carp or spinning rod) offers even better sport. Try a fish strip for mackerel and garfish, or ragworm for wrasse and pollack. Perhaps the most efficient way to take mackerel, however, is to use a team of feathers (a method known as 'chicken chucking' in West Country slang!) but a more enjoyable way is to use a light spinning rod and suitable lure, which may also catch you pollack and the odd bass.

It pays to be prepared when fishing piers and other structures. Where there is a long drop to the water, a drop net (like the end section of a keepnet, but fastened to rope) may be required to bring a big fish in without getting smashed up. Another must if you're planning on keeping a few fish to eat is a well-iced cool box.

Figure 3-1:
Anglers
bottom-
fishing
from a pier.

Finding the Right Time to Fish

This one is simple: Fish whenever you can. Sadly, the fish don't always feed at conveniently sociable hours, but by trying different times and you'll find that patterns emerge for your favourite waters and species. In the heat of summer, for example, carp can be lethargic in the day. Night fishing can be excellent for that big fish which only wanted to feed when most anglers had gone home. Crucians, on the other hand, will often happily feed on a sunny afternoon. By winter you'd hardly see these golden fish, although other species will be on the feed. Pike are a typical example and if you're keen (or mad) they can even be caught through the ice. Cod are another winter example – a species for those with thick jumpers and stout hearts! At any moment, year-round, some fish are biting somewhere. Go and experiment until you catch them. Over time you'll be able to predict which is the best option for your next trip.

Of course, some times are better than others. Low-light periods of dawn and dusk encourage most fish to feed. Spring and autumn, often marked by heavy rainfall and wild temperature swings, can make for unpredictable fishing. (Although it can be as good as it is bad!) The *spawning season* (time for breeding, eggs and nesting) of each species of fish will definitely affect the angling for that species. While spawning, some fish become almost impossible to catch, whereas others become aggressive. There are ethical issues to consider when fishing for spawning fish, as well.

All fish are affected by lunar cycles, too. Traditionally, the three days on either side of a new or full moon make for better fishing. (Although it will alter night fishing and daytime fishing differently. Some anglers swear by fishing a full moon – others feel like it's impossible to catch fish at night then.) Lunar cycles also change the tides – a full moon marks an especially high and low tide.

In rivers, a steady rise of the water level can excite fish. The water may be badly coloured in times of heavy rain and resulting floods, but as the river settles back down and visibility clears the fish often feed very well. A big rain can also raise a lake or pond level, and this activates fish.

There's a lot of opinion out there about the right time to fish. The bottom line: Fish when you can. Let's face it – your work and family schedule will dictate your fishing time, anyway. But if you begin to notice a pattern, like a new moon triggers a hot period of dawn fishing on your favorite lake, you may need to schedule some leave.

Watching the Weather

Everyone knows that the weather affects fishing. Beyond that, there are no agreements regarding the two subjects. Much of what you hear about fishing weather patterns will be discounted or contradicted elsewhere. Most anglers agree that a cold front makes fishing tough, as fish go deep and grow sluggish. (Although fishing before the cold front arrives can be super.) High pressure, bluebird-sky days look like the perfect fishing days, but they can make for very slow going as oxygen levels drop and fish bask in the sun rather than feeding.

Planning a trip around the weather

It won't take you long to notice how weather patterns affect your kind of fishing. This summer, I had my biggest ever perch on a blue, clear day – exactly when I expected to struggle. As a rule, though, cloudy, overcast days make for better fishing than sunny, bright days. Some anglers are uncomfortable fishing in the rain, but a steady rain can trigger feeding.

If you're planning a trip a week or two in advance, how can you predict the weather? You can't. Just go and make the most of it. You might find, though, that shifting a day trip by a couple of hours in either direction could make a big difference on that day.

Reacting to changing weather while fishing

You often hear anglers complaining about the weather. After all, what is office small talk to others can affect their favourite pastime critically. We're often quick to declare that the weather is too cold, too hot or too bright if bites are not forthcoming. But you always know the weather will change, and sooner or later, a fishing trip will be affected by a sudden development overhead. Will this turn the fish on or off? It's impossible to say, but you need to be prepared. Your safety should come first. Some anglers have found that an approaching storm triggers the best bite of the day, but don't get struck by lightning because you can't tear yourself away from that hot spot. Be prepared for weather changes because although you can't predict what it will do to the fishing, you know it will affect you. (For advice on how to prepare a foul-weather bag, turn to Chapter 2.)

Chapter 4

Putting a Face on the Fins: Common Freshwater Fish

In This Chapter

▶ Revealing the most popular freshwater fish

▶ Understanding the different coarse and game fish.

▶ Discovering the different habitats of popular species

*W*herever you are, chances are you're close to some fishable water: canals, farm ponds, reservoirs, drains, small streams or mighty rivers. Freshwater fishing is so popular in large part because of this incredible wealth of habitat, which is home to some pretty amazing fish.

You probably have – or will soon have – a favourite species of freshwater fish. And you might already have a favourite place to pursue that fish. Although traveling long distances to fish is one of the greatest joys and challenges in angling, most people usually fish in water close to home. Either way, getting to know various species of fish (and their habitats) is the first step toward discovering your favourite quarry, or your next piscatorial challenge. Anglers find themselves drawn to particular fish for various reasons – they like the way a tench fights when hooked; they love wild streams where trout live; they enjoy the challenge of tricking a big, wily carp; or they simply like the excitement of casting lures for pike. The more fish you know, the more fish you begin to understand and appreciate, the longer your list of options for fishing on any given day.

Coarse Fish

Coarse fish may be summarised as all the freshwater species other than trout, grayling and salmon. Where does this division spring from? It is partly tradition, partly a case of different habitats. Coarse fish tend to be caught with bait, game fish with the fly. Such arbitrary rules certainly help us classify the fishes but we should always remember that fish don't read the same guide books. Frankly, they couldn't give a monkey's and a trout or grayling will happily take a worm just as coarse fish will readily accept an artificial fly. Angling clubs are usually divided into one or other of 'coarse' or 'game' factions however.

Silver Fish

For many anglers, roach, bream and their relatives make up the staple catch of many a good day's fishing. Anglers talking of 'silver fish' mean a handful of traditional favourites – not outsized, stocked creatures but those shiny fishes which thrive in so many different types of water, from small canals to big, powerful rivers.

These are species which, though widespread, many never tire of catching. They provide youngsters with those all important bites, but equally the challenge of catching an old 'specimen' sized fish that dwarfs all the tiddlers is one which captivates others for a lifetime.

Roach: Old red eye

Amongst the most adaptable of all the coarse fishes, roach remain a favourite catch for many anglers. An attractive species, roach have gleaming silver flanks with bright red fins and eyes. The little ones are cute, the really large samples are nothing short of beautiful.

The key to the success of the roach is its sheer adaptability. Whether the water is still or flowing, crystal clear or muddy, you'll find roach just about anywhere. The angling methods to catch them are no less diverse, from pole fishing to specialist leger rigs.

Common the roach may be, but this dainty feeder demands a degree of finesse, shying away from thick line and large hooks. The roach takes all kinds of bait, but maggots, casters (fly chrysalises) and bread are classics. Any roach bigger than a pound is a fine catch and a two-pounder is a specimen to delight even the most experienced angler.

Bream: Slabs and skimmers

Another widespread species, bream often represent the best chance of catching a real net sized fish on many canals, lakes and slow flowing rivers. A broad sided, hump backed fish they like to gather in big shoals which graze the bottom for food. They are renowned as lazy, ponderous fighters but are lots of fun on light tackle.

Small bream, up to about a pound, are silvery and often called 'skimmers' perhaps because of the ease with which they can be skimmed across the surface to the landing net. As the fish mature they take on a more bronze colour and become the weighty 'slabs' match anglers love to catch. A typical adult bream weighs three to five pounds. When you consider that a shoal could number over fifty fish you could be in for a big catch.

Bream are not ultra difficult to catch if you can locate a shoal and give them what they want, that is, food and plenty of it! Float or leger methods work, but the bream prefer their grub right down on the bottom, usually in calm, deep water. Worms, maggots and corn are all great bream catchers. Evening or night fishing can bring the best results.

Rudd: Golden wonders

Of all the coarse fishes you might encounter, rudd are one of the most strikingly handsome of all. They look rather like roach, sharing their red fins and general body shape with one or two key differences. Rudd are more golden in colour, from a tinge of colour to spectacularly so. The other main difference to roach and a useful clue to identification and lifestyle is the rudd's upturned mouth. Note the protruding bottom lip which gives away the species' preference for looking up in the water to feed. They will take slow sinking or buoyant baits well on light float tackle, but are also superb fun for the fly fisherman.

Big rudd, and by big I mean those golden giants of two or even over three pounds, are increasingly rare. This is partly due to the species love of the kind of wild, unspoiled habitats which are disappearing. Rural canals, overgrown lakes and wild places such as the Fens are prime places, although many commercial fisheries stock them too and you may even encounter the wildie's even more brightly hued ornamental cousin, the golden rudd.

Spot the difference: Roach or rudd (or hybrid)? Figure 4-1 can help.

- **Roach**: Eyes are a true red, and the dorsal fin is set almost midway down back.
- **Rudd:** Slightly deeper in the body, with an upturned mouth and the dorsal fin set slightly further back.
- **Or Hybrid?** The above are all good pointers, but there is also the possibility you might have caught a hybrid. Bream, roach and rudd all interbreed to produce these odd pick 'n' mix style crossbreeds. If you catch a fish which looks rather roachy but is too big and has a bream's profile and humped back, for example, you've probably caught a roach-bream hybrid. These are often still attractive and fun to catch, they just might take some head scratching to identify!

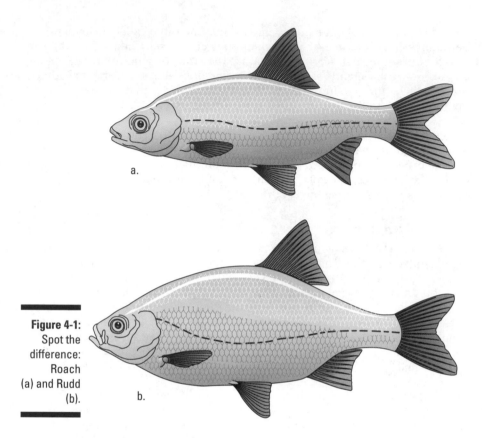

Figure 4-1:
Spot the
difference:
Roach
(a) and Rudd
(b).

a.

b.

Carp and friends

Many of the common coarse fish are part of the *cyprinid* or carp family. But while it's fun to catch the likes of roach and bream, we should also distinguish some of the larger family members. Carp, tench and crucians are fish which thrive especially well in slower, weedy waters such as ponds and lakes. They have wide ranging appetites and anglers rate them highly for their beauty and fighting prowess.

Commons and mirrors

Carp have rapidly become the most highly sought after of all freshwater fish. Their appeal is undeniable: Carp grow big, fight hard and look impressive. They are also wily customers and can be a real challenge to tempt on rod and line, making devotees spend many days and nights in the pursuit of a monster.

Carp come in two varieties, mostly: Common and mirror carp, which derive from the same species. Commons are fully-scaled fish, often golden in colour and wilder looking; mirror carp are fatter variants bred originally for the table with far fewer but bigger 'mirror' scales, hence the glamorous name. Occasionally, you might also find mirrors with no scales, sometimes called 'leather carp'. Both kinds of fish are recognisable not only by their great size and deep, chunky build, but by their distinctive whiskers or *barbels* which they use to taste and probe the bottom for food.

The range of habitats and diets for carp is vast. They can be found everywhere from small ponds right the way through to reservoirs, big rivers and many canals. 'Commercial' fisheries well stocked with carp of all sizes are now very popular and an ideal place to start, whilst the fish in bigger and more demanding waters can grow to huge sizes but require dedication. Carp feed naturally on a vast array of living things – from pondweed to bloodworm, insects and snails. Anglers tend to prefer trusted baits from old favourites (bread, sweetcorn, maggots) to special high protein offerings, most often boilies.

These days carp are fished for year round. In the summer float fishing in shallow margins or using floating baits are excellent fun. In the cooler months legering comes into its own. Carp of up to and over 20 pounds are common today, specimens of over 30 or even 40 pounds are achievable to the dedicated specialist. Figure 4-2 shows a carp.

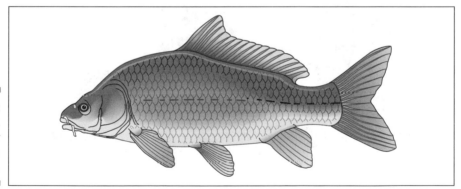

Figure 4-2:
A chunky, muscular common carp.

Crucian Carp: Cute and crafty

Besides the big, bullish specimens carp anglers dream of, crucians are another kettle of carp altogether. Distinguished by their smaller size, a lack of carpy whiskers and a delightful buttery-gold colouration, crucians are the cheeky little cousin in the family.

Unfortunately for the crucian, it crosses rather easily with other species such as common carp and goldfish. Hence in many places, strains of 'true crucian' have been all but eradicated.

Crucians are classic summer fish of weedy ponds and lakes. They have much smaller mouths than the other carp and a well-founded reputation for giving tricky, playful bites that often result in anglers striking at thin air. They fight surprisingly well though, and are great fun to catch on light float tackle with small hooks and baits, such as corn or maggots.

Tench: Tenacious T

Tench are frequently found in the same environs as carp: weedy ponds and stillwaters where they browse the bottom for food. The species has similar barbules to the carp, albeit just two rather than four. Tench are handsome creatures with olive sides, rounded fins and cute red eyes. Don't be fooled by appearances however, tench are muscular, powerful fighters that battle with a bold tenacity, often diving straight for sanctuary amongst heavy weed.

Tench are very much a fish of the summer, being most active in the milder months when you might spot the telltale sign of feeding fish, trails of little bubbles erupting from the bottom of the water. Tench specialists swear by early morning and late evening sessions. Float or leger set-ups work, and while the tench will accept many baits, among the favourites are worms, corn and luncheon meat. Figure 4-3 shows a tench.

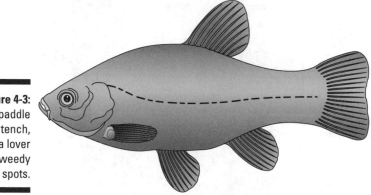

Figure 4-3:
The paddle tailed tench, a lover of weedy spots.

River residents

Some fish species thrive in many environments. Roach, bream and pike, for example, are found almost everywhere. Others are designed for running water. On the coarse species side of things we have some of the most sought-after species of all in running water.

Barbel: Whiskered missiles

Barbel are muscular, torpedo-shaped fish found in many river systems. From their body shape and downward pointing, whiskered mouths you quickly recognise a bottom feeder designed for flowing water.

Barbel are strong for a good reason. They use their power and profile to negotiate strong currents, grubbing for food such as caddis and fresh water shrimps amongst stones and debris. These same characteristics dictate the way you fish for them; strong tackle is a must and baits should be presented close to or dead on the bottom.

Above all, barbel anglers relish the stupendous power of a hooked fish. They are tempted using baits such as sweetcorn, maggots, boilies and luncheon meat and the trick is to get them feeding well by introducing lots of free offerings. Legering with heavy tackle is most often used, although float gear works too and some enthusiasts even fly fish for them. They commonly reach six pounds in weight, and a ten-pounder is a specimen you won't forget in a hurry.

Chub: Big mouth strikes again

A fish of contrary nature, the chub has a big mouth but a wary eye. They are great eaters of almost any prey item or bait you care to name (minnows, mayflies, bread, maggots, meat and so on) but are also easy fish to scare if you are anything but ultra-careful.

Chub can be found in rivers everywhere and show a special preference for the spots anglers hate. Areas of snags, undercut banks and overhanging trees are all prime habitat, although you may also find them in streamier, more open water.

Methods for chub are as varied as their diet. You can leger or trot a float for them but equally they'll take a small lure or dry fly beautifully. Whatever you do though, you can't be too careful to avoid spooking them, so tread gently.

The Dace: Lightning slim

Different fish species give very different bites, from bold as brass to downright shy. Knowing when to strike is one of the challenges of fishing. No species is quicker than the dace. This dapper, slim and silvery fish, found mainly on rivers, is truly a fish to test the angler's reflexes.

Dace don't grow big, and the large ones (over half a pound) can be confused with small chub. Look for a smaller, sharper mouth and bright silver colouration.

Tackle up for dace with light gear and keep your eyes peeled. These pretty fish like a steady flow of water and form good-sized shoals. Float fishing with maggots on tiny hooks is excellent – as is casting a suitably small artificial fly. Be ready to react in an instant however, or you may find yourself striking at thin air!

It's spot the difference time: Is it a large dace or a small chub? When in doubt, look for the following clues.

- ✔ **Chub**: Are often way bigger than dace. Other differences include a bigger mouth, blunter head and a convex dorsal fin.
- ✔ **Dace**: Aside from smaller size, look for a daintier mouth and concave dorsal fin.

Figure 4-4 shows you the key pointers in telling chub from dace.

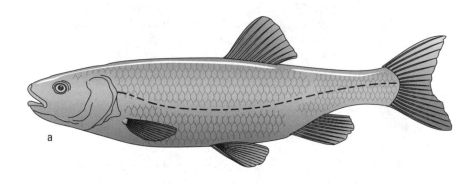

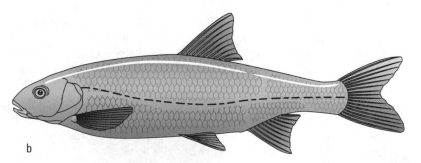

Figure 4-4: A big-mouthed Chub (a) and a Dace (b).

Predators on the prowl

Some fish lead fairly docile existences, browsing for food in groups. Predators, by contrast, make their living by active hunting, adding a flavour of murder and intrigue to your fishing. Besides bait, these fish will take lures and flies designed to look like prey fish or intruders. Witnessing an attacking predator first hand is one of the most exciting experiences in fishing, but these hunters do require a special approach. They also need care on the bank; in spite of bad teeth and an even badder attitude, predatory fish are fragile and require care when handling and releasing, for the sake of fish and angler alike.

Pike: Water wolf

Pike are nearly always the top predator in our waters, a fish with a striking appearance and a mean reputation to boot. No species has fuelled so many scare stories, myths and old wives' tales as old 'Esox'. They thrive in a wide variety of waters, wherever there is ample cover and a good supply of food. In a rich water, pike can reach weights of over 20 pounds (around 10 kg), the benchmark weight for a very special fish.

Pike are clearly designed to attack and devour. All kinds of fish (and even young pike), ducklings, rodents, frogs and anything else it finds within striking distance can find its way into a pike's belly at one time or another. It is a misconception that pike 'eat everything' in the water, however. In reality they survive in close balance with prey populations, removing the sick and the stunted to maintain the health of our waters.

You are likely to find pike in weedy shallows (especially if the water's cool) where they wait to ambush their prey. In the chill of winter or summer heat, they retreat to the deeps. As stealthy as a lion in wait, or as swift as a springing panther, pike stalk and pursue their prey. They will also scavenge, however, and perhaps the most popular way to fish for them is with a dead bait, whether this is a small native species such as a roach or an oily sea fish. Live bait is another option, although increasingly shunned in modern times.

Lure fishing is another excellent and active approach gaining in popularity, in which artificial baits are used to entice an angry strike. They'll also take large, specially designed flies. In spite of their formidable appearance, pike are surprisingly fragile creatures which require careful handling and release. More than any other coarse fish they require special gear – wire traces stop them biting through line, and foot-long forceps to remove hooks. A large landing net and unhooking mat are also essential. Figure 4-5 illustrates a pike.

Figure 4-5: The pike: handle with care.

How to unhook a pike

There is a definite knack to unhooking pike safely. The first step is not to be afraid. Pike will thrash about on the bank, but won't try to bite you. Once netted, put your fish onto an unhooking mat or at the very least, soft grass. A mat is better because you can now hold the fish down without risk of damage if it struggles.

If you can reach the hooks easily, simply pick them out with forceps. If they are further down, you must open the fish's mouth. Do this by reaching your hand underneath the pike's head and finding the slit at the side, where the gills open.

Avoiding the red 'gill-rakers' which are sharp, run your index and middle fingers inside this this ridge till you get to the chin. You'll come to a 'sweet spot' here with no teeth. Holding on here, the pike's mouth should open easily. There's a knack to this which comes with simple practice, but it could help to watch an experienced angler or join the Pike Anglers Club (PAC). The PAC site (www.pacgb.co.uk) has great pictures and sound advice on handling pike. Gloves are another insurance for the beginner, but better 'feel' comes from fingers alone.

When handling any fish, you must be firm but gentle. Always wet your hands – not only does this prevent the fish losing its protective slime, you'll also find your catch wriggles less. One effective way to handle small-to-midsize specimens is to grab the fish gently but firmly across the back, just behind the gills – although do be careful with spiny fish such as perch.

Perch: Handsome devils

With bold stripes, crimson fins and a big, spiny dorsal fin, the perch is an attractive killer. His huge mouth leaves you in little doubt about the lifestyle of this versatile predator. Perch are found in most waters and fare best where there is a rich supply of dinner in the form of roach, bleak and other small fish.

Small perch can be child's play to catch on worms; the real monsters of over two pounds can be a much greater challenge. Besides areas where small fish are concentrated, the species also shows a marked preference for structures both natural and man-made, whether this means bridges, boat yards or overhanging bushes. In the autumn and winter, prime perch times, see if you can find such areas where the water deepens off; the slack underneath an old tree is a classic.

Perch are caught on various methods. Worms and maggots work, but a small dead or live fish can be better still if you're after a monster. Lure and fly fishing are also excellent, especially useful for exploring a new water where you're not sure where to start.

You could say it was an almighty fluke but the tale beautifully illustrates that anything is possible in fishing. We all love to attribute our successes to skill, but luck plays a big part and one of the joys of the sport is its unpredictability. You never quite know what the next bite will bring. Figure 4-6 shows a perch.

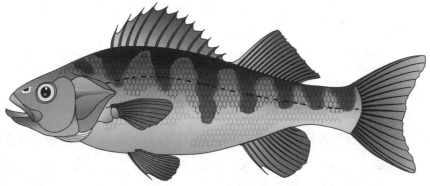

Figure 4-6: A perch, easily recognised by the bold stripes and spiky fin.

Zander: Spiny like a perch, toothy like a pike

Once called the 'pike-perch', the zander is no hybrid but a species of its own. Besides native territories in Europe, the species has been introduced legally and illegally in many new waters. Aside from local controversy, it has quickly become a favourite with predator anglers.

Zander, and especially the smaller ones, are often found in schools, hanging out around underwater structures, and usually locate themselves near drop-offs. Large rivers, drains and canals are ideal habitat. It eats any small fish available, with roach and bleak as typical staples. Despite having pretty mean teeth, it lacks the laughing gear of the pike and thus smaller baits tend to be used. Lure fishing is gaining in popularity too, with deep diving plugs and soft jigs both effective.

A true fishy tale

On a small lake in April 2002, schoolboy Dean Rawlings was fishing for anything which came along. Using a simple float, thick line and an oversized hook crammed with maggots, nobody could have predicted that he was about to make history in spectacular fashion.

As the boy was impatiently bringing in his bait for another cast, an unseen monster reacted to the movement of his maggots. Big jaws opened and in a flash a huge perch was hooked. His rod heaved over and after a few tense moments the giant came to the net. At 5 pounds, 9 ounces it was not merely an incredible fish but a new British record, making Dean the envy of not only schoolboys but specialist anglers all over the country.

The zander is a very light-sensitive fish, so although you may take one in shallow water, chances are that you will do so when light levels are low. The zander has a preference for murky water, and fishing during the evening or even overnight is the classic method. You won't require shark tackle, but a wire trace is important to stop those mean-looking fangs, as well as any pike which intercept the bait.

The zander is a torpedo-shaped fish with big eyes, a greyish silver-greenish brown colour, and sometimes dabs of camouflage marking along the flanks. Zander reach just over 20 pounds, but anything over 10 pounds is a monster.

Your mother wouldn't like 'em: Oddballs

Some fish are certainly more conventionally attractive than others. Or is beauty in the eye of the beholder? It takes a special kind of fanatic to spend weeks in pursuit of a big eel or catfish, but the sport of fishing is only richer for these unusual monsters. Whether you fish deliberately or not for them, it's useful to know how to deal with fish such as eels too.

Eels: Slithery and mysterious

Spare a thought for the eel. Many fishers would rather catch an old boot, but the species is a fascinating one. A great deal of the eel's life cycle is a mystery. What we do know is that eels are great scavengers and nomads, being the only fish in these pages that will gladly travel over land in rainy conditions. They can (and do) turn up anywhere, thriving especially well in lakes with dense shoals of stunted roach and rudd.

From a fishing perspective, lobworms and small dead fish make suitable baits, usually legered on the bottom and cast into a suitable area. Eels like snags and deep holes, feeding best on mild nights or dull days. They can be awkward to unhook, although eel specialists use a curious trick of calming them by stroking their sides as they lay flat.

The casual eel captor would be advised to strike bites early and use barbless hooks to avoid damage. If a small hook is well gorged, cutting the line as close as possible will do less damage than prodding about and handling the creature excessively. Show some respect though – the species is currently in decline, and a really big eel, say four pounds plus, could be over sixty years old!

Wels Catfish: Killer kitties

You wouldn't exactly call it pretty but a big wels catfish is an awe inspiring creature. These bottom feeders will eat anything and feed best at night. They have poor eyesight but a keen sense of smell, so anglers favour smelly baits such as dead fish, large oily halibut pellets or chunks of meat.

They are hardly widespread at present, but a number of stillwaters now stock 'moggies', which are growing fast. A twenty pounder would be a small one! Catfishing brings its own demands, least of all adequately strong tackle to cater for this powerful beast. An extra large net is another must if you ever hope to get one on the bank. Cats have sandpaper-like teeth and a gardening glove is a good idea for unhooking.

Game Fish

Game fish are traditionally the preserve of the fly angler. The distinction is arbitrary, but remains in place. Once upon a time this meant that the 'game' fish were the preserve of the upper crust only. Thankfully this is no longer true and perhaps the biggest development in recent years has been the increase in affordable game fishing for all, with day ticket waters open to all and numerous excellent projects emerging.

Rainbow trout: High jumpers

The colourful rainbow trout is one of the most sought-after gamefishes in the world. They originate in the cold rivers of the USA and Canada, but are now found all over Europe as stocked fish, usually triploids (that is, non-breeding fish). It's fair to say that rainbows have transformed stillwater trout fishing in the UK. They reach good sizes, adapt superbly to a semi-wild existence and give a thrilling fight on light tackle.

The rainbow often has spots over its whole body (although in some locations, the larger rainbows are more often an overall silver). A much more reliable sign of 'rainbowness' is the pink band or line that runs along the flank of the fish from shoulder to tail.

The fish vary in fly preferences: freshly introduced 'stockies' are aggressive creatures that will savage a bright, lure-style fly. Longer term residents quickly adapt to natural food and perhaps the biggest single food item on the menu is the buzzer, imitated by a host of artificial flies. They will also happily take a spinner or worm where rules allow. Rainbow trout are commonly taken around the two pound mark. The ultimate prize on reservoirs, however, is an overwintered fish which may have survived several seasons and grown large and fit on nature's spoils.

Who was Izaak Walton anyway?

Without question, the most famous book ever written about angling is *The Compleat Angler*, published by Izaak Walton in 1653. Since that time, it has been through more than 300 editions and is probably the most widely read (or at least widely owned) book after the Bible and the Koran. Because *The Compleat Angler* is an all-around handbook for fishing in England, people who are not familiar with Walton have an idea that it is only for purist fly fishing snobs. It isn't.

Izaak Walton was primarily a bait fisherman who came late to the fly. He was a self-made businessman who retired in his 50s and wrote the book that would earn him immortality at the age of 60. His prose is so simple and clear that most people today could read his book with much less difficulty than they could read the plays of, for example, Shakespeare.

Much of the best advice in the book was actually written by Charles Cotton, a young man of leisure who was a remarkable fly fisher. It was Cotton, not Walton, who wrote 'to fish fine and far off, is the first and principle rule for trout angling.' In other words, use a light leader, and keep your distance from the fish so you don't spook it. This advice is as valuable today as it was three-and-a-half centuries ago when Walton and Cotton filled their days fishing and talking. What a life!

Brown trout: Wildly spotty

The brown trout is a fish almost purpose-designed for the fly angler. It often feeds on the surface. It rises to a properly presented fly. It fights like stink. The brown didn't acquire a reputation as a 'gentleman's fish' because it had particularly good manners and went to the right school.

It is anything but dull 'brown' as the name might suggest. The back is dark, the sides can be anywhere between deep bronze and light gold. As shown in Figure 4-7, the brown trout is covered with spots everywhere but on its tail. The majority of the spots are dark brown or black, but you'll also find red and even blue spots. Most stream-bred fish average less than a pound, but bigger individuals that feed on fish as well as bugs attain much greater sizes. The species is long lived and in prime habitat such as fertile lakes can reach weights of over ten pounds.

Atlantic salmon: The leaper

The Atlantic salmon is regarded by many as the aristocrat of fishes. Perhaps it has this reputation because you have to be an aristocrat to be able to afford a few days on one of the choice salmon rivers. Not surprisingly, with something that has become the sporting property of upper-class gentlemen, one is usually required to fish for Atlantic salmon with a fly rod; and on many rivers, one also has to rent a guide. Don't hold any of this against the salmon. He had very little to do with all the tradition surrounding him. On the plus side, the number of affordable places to catch salmon beyond the private estates is increasing.

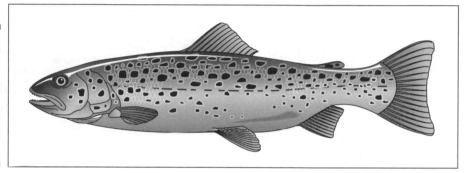

Figure 4-7: The brown trout is a wily and rewarding fish when taken on rod and reel.

Known for its acrobatic jumps, the Atlantic salmon is a cousin to the brown trout but spends most of its time at sea (although a salmon's infancy is passed in a river, and it is to that river that it returns to spawn). Classic spots to try are the pools and sanctuaries where salmon linger on their journey upstream. They eat nothing in fresh water, but will still snap at a fly or spinner. If plenty of action is what you crave, salmon fishing is not for you: Just one fish a day is a very good average on most streams.

Sea Trout: A salty brownie

Almost all species of trout, if given the chance, drop downstream to the ocean, where they usually grow to much greater size than trout confined to streams and lakes. Sea-run browns (those that forage in the ocean and return to spawn in freshwater) are called sea trout. These fish have usually lost the distinctive colouration of the freshwater browns, and take on a brighter, more silvery coloration.

Sea trout are sometimes caught in the day, but traditionally after dark is the time to go. Anglers will seek out a likely pool on the river and intercept fish on the move. Particularly thrilling is the art of using large fies to 'wake' the surface of the water, where they are liable to be grabbed in no uncertain terms.

Like salmon, sea trout have declined somewhat and you'll find catch-and-release is obligatory in many areas. The rivers of Wales and southwest England are your best bet for healthy sport with this highly prized trout.

It's ironic to think that once upon a time this king of fishes was so plentiful it formed a staple food for the poor of London. These days the salmon is under threat and needs all the protection we can give it. Even where salmon fishing doesn't cost a king's ransom, do check local and national byelaws. Some methods (such as spinning or bait fishing) may be restricted, and catch-and-release is often a legal requirement. Figure 4-8 shows a salmon.

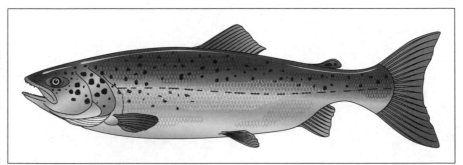

Figure 4-8: The Atlantic salmon is prized for both food and sport.

Grayling: Shady ladies

The grayling is a fish which could be said to straddle the divide between coarse and game fishes. It can be caught on maggots or sweetcorn, but more latterly it has been reclassified by many as a game fish. Grayling love the same river stretches as trout and chub, take a fly well, and – since they share the same season as coarse species – also offer sport through the winter months when trout fishing is off limits.

Nicknamed 'the lady of the stream', the grayling is a graceful, silvery-grey fish with faint stripes and tiny dots on its flanks. Its unique feature is the exotic looking crimson to purple sail-like fin on the back. In males, especially, this fin can be huge, and is draped over the female during courtship.

Grayling are less easy to spook than trout but are excellently camouflaged and tricky to spot. They like steady glides of shallow, well oxygenated water. They rise well for dry flies but the specimens of two pounds and over tend to fall to nymphs and wet flies.

Chapter 5

Familiarising Yourself with Common Sea Fish

In This Chapter

▶ Getting to know popular sea fish species

▶ Understanding which baits work for each species

▶ Figuring out what fish are accessible to shorebound anglers

'There are many fish in the sea', they say, and this time, they're right! Anglers face a tremendous array of options when it comes to pursuing sea fish. And habitat? Saltwater fishing offers anglers the opportunity to fish everything from quiet harbours to rocky beaches and deep water wrecks. Sea fish tend to be faster and stronger than their freshwater cousins, simply because their environment demands it. Some of them also grow to impressive sizes. Add to this the fact that, unlike with coarse fish, many sea fish are tasty and can be taken home to eat and you can see why sea fishing is a terrific experience anywhere you find it. To walk along the shore with the surf crashing, gulls wheeling overhead and hungry fish moving inshore on the tide – that's a great place to be!

We lack the space here to detail all the species you might catch. This would take a book in its own right. However, you'll find many of the best loved species, as well as a few genuine monsters to excite the intrepid sea angler.

Flatfish

The scientific grouping and naming of fish can be a confusing business, but in this case, it isn't – fish in this family are flat. Flatfish share common features, such as a thin body that is white on one side and brownish on the other. This allows flatfish to lie on the ocean floor and blend into their surroundings.

Both eyes of the flatfish species are on one side of the body – either the left or right side, depending upon the species. These fish make for delicious food.

Flounder: A winter staple

A common target for anyone who lives near an estuary, flounder make for fun shore fishing even on cold days. They don't grow especially big, with a fish of over two pounds a good one, but are widespread, and you won't need long casts or special tackle to get amongst them. Their colour matches the bottom, usually a brown or sandy hue, and they sometimes have a few red spots.

Flounder fishing is usually carried out in sandy or muddy estuaries where these bottom dwellers thrive on food such as crab, small shellfish and shrimp. As the tide rushes in, the flounders move with it to explore new areas, often coming into shallow water to feed. Peeler crab on a smallish hook is the finest bait and many anglers use brightly coloured beads in their rigs to help attract this inquisitive flattie.

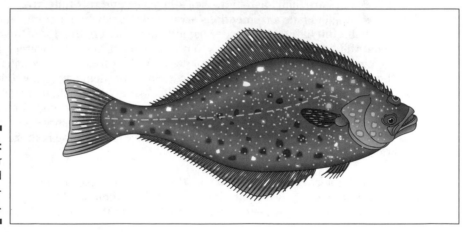

Figure 5-1:
The flounder is right-eyed and right-mouthed.

Plaice: Spotty and highly prized

There's only one thing better than plaice and chips and that's a fish supper when you caught the plaice yourself. The more delicate appearance and bright orange spots distinguish the species from the flounder. Targetted from sand and shingle beaches in summer, a long cast with the right bait can be vital. The other option is to boat fish, with many charter skippers offering trips from spring onwards.

With increasing commercial pressure, bin-lid sized plaice are a thing of the past sadly. A three pounder would be a decent boat fish, or the catch of the season from the shore. Worm baits, often tipped with squid or fish strip, are amongst the most popular bait options.

Dab: Small but tasty

Dabs are one of the smallest flatfishes, a cute creature that takes on the hue of its habitat, usually a sandy brown. What they lack in size they make up for in taste however and can be found in many sandy locations year round, often no more than a short cast away. They are not especially fussy feeders, but do require small hooks because of their little mouths. A dab of over a pound would be classed as a big one and usually they're barely half that size.

Cod Family

The cod family is made up of numerous fishes popular with anglers. Unfortunately for these fishes, their excellent white flesh and ease of capture has led to chronic overfishing in some areas. Nevertheless, for both shore and boat anglers they represent a challenging, fun and highly palatable target.

Cod: Monster mouth

Cod seek cold water, and for this reason, they are prevalent in Northern seas, before making an annual migration south in the cold of the winter months. Commercially fished to the point of decline in spots, cod are extremely valuable as a food fish.

Cod angling is pretty much of the meat-and-potatoes variety: simple bait fishing or jigging just off the bottom over wrecks. A sturdy boat rod or a stout beach caster are the preferred weapons of most cod anglers. Cod have huge mouths hence the best cod bait is a generous helping of lugworms or peeler crab. Mussels or whole baby squid work well in some locations too. Another ruse is to bait up with a small pout or other prey fish. This is certainly more sporting than my father in law's old navy method of using depth charges.

From the shore, smaller codling of up to six pounds dominate catches. For the chance of a monster, boat fishing offers the chance of a double figure fish, and in the past fish to 200 pounds have been netted. Today a twenty pounder would be remarkable in most areas. Figure 5-2 shows an Atlantic cod with the telltale single *barbel* (whisker) hanging from its lower jaw.

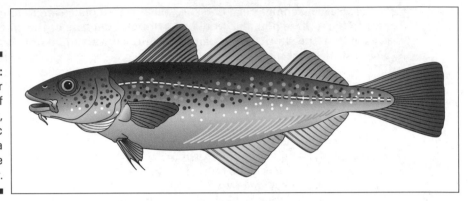

Figure 5-2:
Like other members of its family, the Atlantic cod has a goatee-like whisker.

Pollack: Don't call me Colin!

A fish of reefs, wrecks and rock marks, the pollack is a powerful, predatory member of the cod clan. With a colour ranging from silver gray to greenish gold, you'll quickly notice that this cod family member has a protruding lower lip and no 'beard', marking it as an active midwater feeder. The smaller pollack are common on rocky shores and sea walls whereas the big boys generally favour deeper reefs and wrecks accessible by boats only.

Pollack can be caught by presenting live prawn or fish baits on float tackle. Another fun method is to lure fish. From rocky shore marks lures such as rubber eels, spoons and plugs all work well. By boat, jigged soft shads, rubber eels such as the Redgill and the good old fashioned pirk all catch their share of bigger fish. Figure 5-3 shows a pollack.

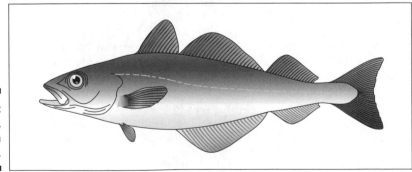

Figure 5-3:
The pollack, also known as 'Colin'.

Occasionally confusion can arise with the pollack's very similar cousin, the coalfish. The 'coalie' has a more even mouth, however, lacking the protruding lower jaw of the pollack. The species makes good eating and with cod stocks in decline, one food company decided to rebrand pollack as a more sustainable substitute. 'Pollack' rhymed with the slang name for part of the male anatomy however, so the fish was given its French alias 'Colin'. All well and good, but of course in English 'Colin' is a male forename. To punters, the marketing ploy must have seemed akin to renaming the haddock 'Geoff'. Never mind the pollacks, anglers still use the p-word.

Pouting: Common as muck

A good deal smaller but still possessing the goatee-like chin barbel, the pouting ('pout' or 'bib' for short) is one of the commonest fish in the sea. These brownish bronze sided fish are often thick on the ground around piers, wrecks and reefs. They tend to be small, usually well under a pound, and will take just about any scrap of bait you throw at them.

Whilst related to cod, pout are not a highly rated eating fish, partly because they lose freshness quickly. When quickly gutted and kept cool however, they make decent fish cakes or boullabaise. The tiddlers also make a good bait for big predators such as bass, cod or conger eels.

Whiting: Ravenous hordes

The whiting is essentially a miniature, pale type of cod, but an important winter visitor all the same. When the mercury plummets, these light coloured fishes turn up in their droves on many beaches and will snaffle any worm or fish bait on a smallish hook. Smartly shelving shingle beaches are often productive.

Aside from their pale colouration, look for the usual whisker on the chin and fine teeth. Whiting bite well and are highly edible if nothing else. Like pouting, the gathering of these critters en masse can also attract the attention of bigger visitors such as cod. In other words, if youre catching bags of whiting, you could try a bigger bait or even use a small whiting on the hook.

Sea Bass: The silver surf king

The bass is probably the best loved of all the sea fish, and what's not to love? They reach a good size, can be caught on a variety of methods and fight valiantly. The bass is also beautiful in appearance – a bold, powerful profile not unlike a large perch with its large spiky dorsal fin, but brilliant silver in colour.

Bass are highly predatory and angling methods reflect this. Their location and diet can be highly localised. Sandeels, crabs, prawns and small or juvenile fish are all common prey the angler can use for bait. Lures and flies are another exciting option. Prime time is from spring onwards and both boat and shore anglers have plenty of options, from rocky coves and estuary mouths to offshore reefs. Bass can often be caught close to the shore and this is especially true at night. A thirty yard lob might be adequate on a beach, or you may find them right under your feet from a vantage point on the rocks. In less rough conditions where heavy leads aren't required a carp or spinning rod is great fun to use.

Bass make good eating, but remember that populations are localised and these commercially pressurised fish grow very slowly. Minimum size limits currently allow anglers to kill fish which have yet to spawn, a daft situation. Male bass only breed after 3-6 years and females take 6-8 years to reach maturity. We'd recommend you release all the bass you catch, but if you must keep one, make sure it's over three pounds in weight. Figure 5-4 shows a bass.

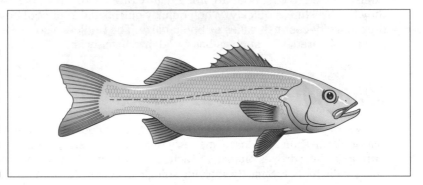

Figure 5-4: The bass is a hand-some, powerful sea predator.

What bass really want

Bass have such a wide range of habitats and food preferences that some local detective work can save you a lot of guessing. A good general rule once you've found a suitable area is to suss out what the fish are eating. In sandy estuaries where you spot masses of small sandeels, for example, you can be sure a suitably sized rubber eel or fly will work. On rocky coastlines, search the gullies for clues. If you find good numbers of prawns it's a safe bet that the bass will accept one on a small hook. Boat anglers catch some huge bass on small 'joey' mackerel when the shoals are about. Finally, look for dramatic weather patterns; in the aftermath of a heavy swell or stormy conditions bass will move close in to mop up all the food dislodged in the commotion.

Wrasse

A fish so vibrant in appearance it wouldn't look out of place in the tropics, that's the wrasse. The biggest and most important member of the family for sea anglers is the ballan wrasse. Colours range from marbled green and black hues through to brilliant reds and white spots. These strong customers are common around rough ground, harbours and man-made structures, using their powerful build and teeth to pick their dinner from rocks. Besides shell-fish, they also like prawns and crabs.

Wrasse are willing biters in the summer months that will take any suitable bait including rag or lugworms, live prawn or crab. Float fishing is fun, but legering catches the bigger fish which can run to over five pounds. Tackle losses can be high in typical wrasse spots, hence 'rotten bottom' rigs are popular and thrifty types use cheaper lead substitutes such as old spark plugs or even stones.

Hooking your wrasse is perhaps the easy part of the deal; wrestling a good one from rocks is no job for the faint-hearted and calls for strongarm tactics and stout gear. They make for bony, poor eating and should be quickly released. Debarbing hooks is a sensible move as they can wolf down baits.

There are also several brightly coloured but smaller wrasse species such as the corkwing and the cuckoo wrasse, but only the ballan regularly reaches over a pound in weight.

Mackerel

Depending on your mindset, the abundant mackerel is either just a fresh source of bait or one of the most underrated sea fish that swims. These ravenous, shoaling predators are easy to catch and offer sport for all in the warmer months. Some dismiss them as too easy, but on slow days the mackerel is a godsend. They're not fussy by any stretch and in fact one old timer I know used to catch them as a boy by dressing hooks with the foil tops from milk bottles. Mackerel bite anything shiny and for their size they fight like tigers.

Mackerel can be caught from a boat easily enough, but shore anglers should look for deep water close in: Piers, harbours, breakwaters and steeply shelving beaches are ideal. Methods are simple. For pure efficiency a team of feathers (which mimic small prey fish) can be trailed off a boat or hurled out with a beachcaster. Far more fun, however, is to use light tackle such as a spinning or carp rod. Float fishing is one option, with a pike sized float and a strip of fish for bait. Lure fishing also works well with a small casting spoon or spinner – the

Dexter Wedge is perhaps the best mackerel taker of them all. Fly fishing is another exhilarating option to feel the power of these athletic fighters.

The key is often to find the right depth, which is frequently twelve to fifteen feet from deep shore marks. If they're present you won't struggle to catch them. Look for groups of fleeing fry and the culprits will usually be mackerel. Plentiful they can be, but don't take more than you need for the table. They usually average around half a pound, with the bigger mackerel showing later in the summer. To keep this tasty, oily fish fresh, bring a bucket or cool bag full of ice and gut your catch immediately. Figure 5-5 shows a mackerel.

Figure 5-5: Mackerel are common in summer, and make good eating.

Garfish

Genuinely odd but very sporty, the garfish is a welcome presence amidst the summer mackerel shoals. It's a weird looking creature: if the elongated body and long, tooth-filled beak didn't freak you out, just try cooking one (it's bones are green, although it's perfectly edible).

Garfish come close inshore, like mackerel, to terrorise shoals of small fish. They like to hang higher in the water than the mackerel however, usually at less than ten feet down. The best method is float fishing with a thin strip of mackerel. Because of their odd beak, they can be hard to hook properly, so let the float really bury before striking. They leap gamely in the fight and punch above their weight, just as well because one of two pounds would be a big one. Small, debarbed hooks are recommended for catch-and-release, although gars can be eaten or used to make lovely, shiny strips of bait.

Grey Mullet

If there's one fish that could be said to blur the boundaries between fresh and salt water fish, it's the grey mullet. These fish are equally at home on the open coast or rubbing shoulders with coarse fish on a tidal river. They are easily spotted around many harbours and jetties in the summer. If only it was as easy to catch one! Coarse tackle is better suited than heavier sea gear due to their frustratingly finicky nature.

The grey mullet are divided into two main sub species, thick-lipped and thin-lipped mullet. Distinguishing between the two isn't easy, but one difference is that the thick lip has a more substantially developed upper lip with bumps on it. There is also a third, less common species called the golden grey mullet, distinguished by a golden marking on the sides of the head. All three types are bony, top heavy looking fish with odd, almost oval mouths and striped silver-grey sides.

Both types are easily located and mix readily, although the thick lips grow bigger, to about eight pounds, and are even more fiendishly hard to catch than the thin lips. The test is getting this wily fish to take your hookbait. Not always easy, as it feeds mainly by grubbing for minute food items in the mud. Bread is the best all round bait, although maggots or small ragworms can also work. In some areas fly casters have also had some joy with shrimp or bait patterns.

Hooking a mullet is only half the battle, however. Pound for pound they are amongst the strongest of all fish. Hence if you tackle up too light, you may be smashed with ease; tackle up too heavy and they won't bite. Lines of 5 to 6 pounds are usually about right, along with a quality reel which will smoothly yield line when the fireworks begin. Borrowing coarse angling rigs is the best strategy and regular helpings of groundbait help to wean the fish onto your hookbait. Other than dynamite or a net, the only other strategy is to use a spinner baited with a piece of ragworm, which can be excellent for thin lips.

Sea Bream

Sea bream are a highly prized catch, not to be confused with their freshwater namesakes. They're much more silvery customers, as well as stronger fighters. You probably wouldn't want to tuck into a lazy old bream from your local canal either: They taste like old boots, unlike the highly palatable sea species. Much of the best bream fishing is by boat, unless you get to know a special shore fishing spot, which are the locals often prefer to keep quiet.

Black Bream: Pretty and palatable

Sea bream look nothing like the muddy bronze fish of rivers and lakes. If anything, the black bream is more like a perch, with a spiny dorsal fin and a thumping, headshaking fighting action. They are not black, but have silver flanks attractively marked with several thin bars. Fish are commonly taken around the pound mark, with two pounds a good fish and three pounds a specimen.

For a sea fish, the black bream has a fairly small mouth and a curious nature. Small hooks (size 2-6) work best, therefore, often baited with fish or squid strip. Beads add further attraction and canny skippers and anglers get good results by lowering a mesh bag or metal bait dropper filled with groundbait, which seems to work exceedingly well for these fish.

Gilthead Bream: Silver slabs

Gilthead bream are easily distinguished from the black bream by their more angular, less rounded shape which tapers away to be thinner towards the tail. They also have a tell-tale black patch on both sides of their heads. Like their other sea bream cousins, they have smallish mouths, feed on shellfish and other small items and, sadly for them, are very tasty to humans.

Giltheads are mostly caught by boat, with sandy or mixed ground areas rich in shellfish a favourite location. The shore angler may find them in estuaries or off some beaches in the spring and summer, however, where they will come close to shore and take a suitably small bait such as worm section or prawn presented on a similarly small hook. One pounders are common, but fish well over this size to five pounds plus are possible. All give a thumping good fight on light tackle.

Rays and Skate

Besides the usual suspects, part of the fun and mystery of sea fishing is the presence of bigger, weirder monsters. They don't get much more strange or intruiging than the rays and their larger brethren. Some can be caught from shore or estuary marks, but the real beasts tend to fall to boats.

All rays are marked by their flat, almost kite-like profile and a slender, sometimes dangerous tail. They are more closely related to sharks than the flatfishes, however. These highly specialised fish are camouflage experts and deadly predators, part submerging themselves on the bottom to ambush unfortunates such as prawns, sandeels and other small fish. They also have an uncanny ability to detect the electrical pulse of other living things. Indeed, some enterprising anglers have even used rigs incorporating batteries and electrical circuits. You needn't go that far, but some knowledge of their habits is a must.

Thornback Ray: Watch those spines

Probably the most likely ray the angler will encounter is the thornback, so named because of the thorn-like growths on its back and tail. These are not poisonous, but worthy of respect all the same. At an average size of five to eight pounds, thornies are well worth catching from boat or shore marks.

Thornbacks are a viable target from spring to autumn, when they move closer inshore and use their mottled backs to blend with the bottom. They don't often come tight to land, so cast long or find a steep beach which shelves quickly into deeper water. Peeler crab is an excellent bait, or try mackerel strip or sandeel later in the summer from June onwards. Evenings and just into darkness are the best time to try. Figure 5-6 shows a thornback ray.

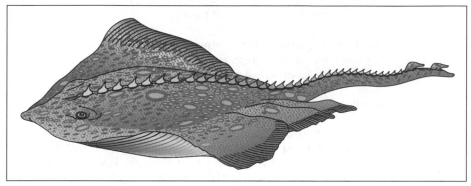

Figure 5-6: Thornback ray.

Blonde Ray: Fair game

Another relatively common ray, the blonde can be confused with the thornback as it also has bumpy growths on the back. It has a less sharp head profile and wings than the thornie however.

Comparing its lifestyle with other rays, you might say blondes have just as much fun. They like gullies and depressions in sandy or sometimes mixed bottoms where they lie low to ambush small fish, crabs and other creatures. Bait choices are the same as for thornbacks. The bites also follow the same pattern, a few little taps before the rod slams over as the fish moves away. Better keep an eye on that beachcaster!

Common Skate: Flat and dangerous

If you thought the rays were a mean bunch, skate take us into the realm of monsters. These bigger relatives are usually found in deeper water and grow huge, eating bigger prey, notably flatfish and crustaceans.

Some huge specimens have been landed by shore anglers in Ireland and Scotland, but these are exceptions to the general rule and boat fishing is your best bet. Tackle for these monsters must be robust and baits on the large side; this is a fish capable of eating a group of flat fish as if they were party nibbles.

Conger Eels

Conger eels are like marmite. You either love them or they make you screw your face up in terror and/or disgust. We happen to think they're awesome. Wreck fishing from a boat yields the real monsters which can exceed a hundred pounds. Shore anglers can get results with smaller eels (which could still be over thirty pounds!) by presenting a large dead fish or squid bait around rocky, snaggy water at night.

Wherever you fish for them, conger demand tough tackle. A minimum of 50-pound line is sensible even from the shore, along with a strong rod. Curiously, bites can be quite gentle. Once a conger is hooked, however, you must pull up promptly and prevent the eel from grabbing hold of any snags which could spell game over in an instant.

Sea fish such as conger, tope and larger dogfish require tough tackle not just because of their strength, but due to formidable teeth and the habit of twisting and grinding against your line. For this reason, thick and abrasion resistant mono of anything up to over 100 pounds strength may be required to land that monster fish. Wire is another option, but some feel this can damage not only the fish, but the angler landing it as the catch thrashes about. It's a good idea is to try with an experienced angler first, or at least bring a friend! The message is simple though: Be prepared and have the right gear. You wouldn't hunt tigers with an air rifle, so tackle up tough!

Sharks and Dogfish

Sharks are popular in large part because they're, well, sharks. The fascination with sharks runs deep and is well-earned. They're often called 'killing and eating machines,' and are among the most impressive of any predators on land or sea.

In British waters angling usually focuses on the smaller members of the shark family in the form of the different types of dogfish. These are still not to be sniffed at though, offering impressive strength and the chance to catch a real rod-bending fish. Like the rays, there are too many types to detail here, so we'll deal with a handful of those you're most likely to encounter.

Of the larger beasts, blue sharks are perhaps the most common, although mako and porbeagles are also sometimes landed. These razor-toothed killers are no casual afternoon sport and for those keen to try, the answer is to hire the services of an experienced skipper. Who knows what you might catch; in the warmer seas of recent years the odd great white has even been spotted!

Lesser spotted dogfish: Down boy!

The most widespread of all the smaller sharks, the lesser spotted dogfish is so plentiful that in some areas that anglers consider it a nuisance. They are great scavengers, seizing any bait with a strong smell whether or not it was cast for their attention.

By shark standards, these spotty, sandy coloured sharks are just puppies. At an average of a pound or two they still liven up slow fishing trips though, and are especially active at night. They have sandpaper-like skin and demand careful handling. The best grip is to take the tail in one hand and grab the back of the head firmly in the other, thus stopping the fish from curling around your hand or arm. Like any unruly dog, you must show it who's boss! Debarbing hooks will also help with pain-free unhooking. Figure 5-7 shows a lesser spotted dogfish.

Figure 5-7: The lesser spotted dogfish, a common night scavenger.

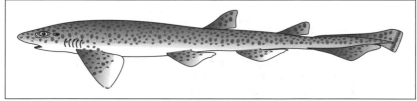

Smoothhounds: Night brawlers

A bigger and stronger mini-shark, the smoothound is another night feeder that likes broken ground and steeply shelving beaches. He makes a living on the bottom through both scavenging and active hunting on just about anything unlucky enough to get in his path, from hermit crabs to small fish.

Again, boat anglers tend to find the bigger samples, which can get to over twenty pounds. Deep or coloured water produces fish in the day, but shore anglers have their best chance at night. Wherever you encounter these tough dogs, their strength and rasping teeth make a mockery of light tackle and demand heavy, abrasion-resistant line. Whole calamari or fresh fish baits are common offerings.

Tope: Seriously strong

Amongst the smaller sharks the tope is most definitely 'top dog' around much of the coast. You can do battle with one from a boat, but the real bonus is that shore anglers with local knowledge can also tackle up for an almighty tussle. A summer night casting a big bait could lead to the kind of battle to make grown men tremble at the knees.

Tope are even more formidable than their doggy relatives. Brutally sharp teeth make short work of prey such as dabs, whiting and sole. Factor in a powerful body potentially longer than your own and the need for strong tackle is a no-brainer. Like all sizeable doggies, large smelly baits are recommended, and if you value your rod, don't leave it unattended!

Several sea fish species have hazardous characteristics. Some have spiny fins (for example bass and bream) or sharp growths (rays). Others have rough skin and/or teeth that could make mincemeat out of a human finger. It can pay to make a trip or two with an experienced angler if in any doubt, but a protective glove is also a good idea. Crushing the barbs on your hooks will also aid unhooking, and some sea anglers also use a 't-bar' disgorger, a device which removes hooks without the need to put your fingers at risk.

Blue Shark: Cold blooded killers

For bigger sharks, those true hunters of the open sea, boat fishing is the only serious option in British waters. Blue shark are perhaps the most viable target, especially from the south west.

This job calls for steady nerves and expert help in the form of an experienced skipper. A bloody trail of fish guts or 'rubby dubby' is used to draw in sharks which are then tempted on a whole mackerel or a chunk of bloody bait. It could result in the biggest fish you've ever seen, let alone caught, with blues reaching in excess of 100 pounds.

Chapter 6

Staying Safe on (or Near) the Water

Fishing is one of the safest, most enjoyable outdoor pastimes available to you – especially when compared to hobbies like mountain biking, skiing, or rock climbing. But like any passion that brings you into the natural world, fishing has its own inherent dangers. You need to be close to the water to fish, of course, and it's possible to take a dunking or worse. And good, sharp hooks practically wait with keen anticipation for a chance to hook their owners. Fishing from a boat increases the risk of something going wrong because you could fall into deep water, and it may be harder to get help should something happen. Like any outdoor sport, fishing also puts you at the mercy of the weather and all its challenges.

You'll also find that fishing, like a family sized bag of crisps, perhaps, is something that you'll stick with a little longer than you should. You want to catch one more fish, explore one more bend in the river. Stay out just a little longer before the storm hits. These traits – which all good anglers share – sometimes get us into trouble.

Still, you can make your fishing experience safer. Safety begins with you being prepared for the bad stuff. A prepared angler is not only a successful one, but one who comes home just as healthy as he or she left. Planning for a trip should reflect the level of adventure. For a short afternoon session, for example, on a familiar water, you might bring little other than something to drink and a sun hat. If you intend to venture several miles, stay out all day or explore an unknown place you should always be well prepared. Admittedly, there are always anglers who seldom venture far from their cars. It's more fun to be adventurous, however; you see more and you often catch more, but you do need to think ahead and be ready.

Planning Ahead for Your Trip

An angler on foot is like a soldier. You have to carry equipment for fast-changing weather, food and water, and (after you get to the scene of the battle) fishing gear. To carry all of this, you have to balance two variables:

- **Pack light:** There's a law of physics (or at least a law of the physics of anglers) that every pound that you pack to go fishing feels like two pounds coming back. Take only what you need.

  Regardless of your feelings about the solitude of nature, bring a mobile phone. Turn it off if you choose, ignore it all you want, but carry it for emergencies. Don't forget to put it in a plastic bag first! Mobile phones have a nasty habit of jumping into the water.

- **Pack completely:** If you aren't comfortable, you'll be miserable. The cold feels colder, the wet feels wetter, and hunger and thirst seem more insistent. Think of what you'll need and make sure that you take it with you.

Leave a note or a message with a friend about where you're going and when you expect to return. Be specific – you might say, 'I'll be on the west side of Shipley Lake,' or 'I'll wade downstream from the landing at Heron's Point.' If you don't have any friends, leave a note at your home. If a search party is involved later, directions like this will make the searching easier.

You look at the map and it shows two miles to the stream you plan to fish. So you reckon "Two miles in; two miles out: No big deal." But it is a big deal if those two returning miles are on an uphill grade, in the dark, on an unmarked path with landowners who like to do the rounds with a shotgun before going to bed. Also, after you get to the fishing spot in the first place, you have to fish. Often, this means a good deal of wading, stream-crossing, and rock-hopping, all of which can be very tiring. Bottom line: Think about how far you can reasonably walk – then cut that distance in half. Then see how it all works out. The worst thing that can happen if you follow this advice is you will have more time to fish.

If you are in a new place and the path is so-so, don't wait until dark to start the walk back. One of these times, you may lose your way, and being lost in the woods at night will remind you of what it was like to be a scared four-year-old in a strange, dark house. Make a mental note of how much time it took to get to the stream, and leave that same amount of time to get back while it is still light.

Water, Water Everywhere: Bringing Food and Drink

Regardless of where you fish, don't let the water you're fishing in touch your lips. Sure, you might drink from a pristine wilderness river and be fine. Or you might contract something nasty. When bacteria from tainted water enter your body, the results can be severe. (As in severe diarrhoea and vomiting. But are those things ever not severe?) Even accidental contact, such as eating a sandwich after rinsing your hands in the river, should be avoided. You don't need to be paranoid about it, but you should be smart. A little bottle of alcohol-based hand wash takes up little space, but will quickly clean and sterilise your fingers – or indeed any cuts or scrapes you get on the bank.

Bringing plenty to drink is a necessity, but don't overlook your body's need for food, too. You may get too involved in the fishing to remember to eat much of the food you've packed, but it's better to have it and not need it, then to need it and not have it. Hunger makes you ditzy and irrational, and prone to making mistakes. Come to think of it, my (Greg's) brothers must be hungry all the time.

A small cool bag, well packed, can carry all you need for a trip. Keep your food sealed in a bag.

Dehydration hurts

Ironically, sports involving the water often tend to dehydrate people faster than other activities. The sun's rays reflect off water, increasing the effects of light and heat. Wading in current or walking with gear burns energy. For these reasons, anglers need to drink plenty of fluids, and drinking water is best. Just remember to drink it throughout the day! Bring about twice what you think you'll need, and drink it all. Once, on a fishing trip in South Carolina, Greg's cousin grew more loopy and foggy-headed than normal. He couldn't string together a sentence and could hardly stand. We'd been fishing hard for days, and he had simply got dehydrated. With plenty of water and rest, he returned to his normal levels of foggy-headedness. Dehydration is nothing to play around with.

Alcohol kills

People often connect angling with drinking alcohol, and it's true that nothing goes better with fried fish than a cold beer. But beer and the hard stuff pairs better with the end of the trip than the beginning. Drinking alcohol exacerbates the effects of dehydration, and the alcohol tends to take hold sooner. Drinking while operating a boat is illegal and especially stupid. Drink, if you choose, to celebrate a good trip, but don't use it to kick one off.

Don't forget the bait for yourself

I find that I fish smarter when I'm comfortable. Most of us fish to get away from work, so make your time on the water as hassle-free as possible. In addition to plenty of water, I also bring a chocolate bar or two and a couple of sandwiches. The food not only makes the day more comfortable, but if something were to happen and I was forced to spend the night on the water, I'd have plenty of energy to survive.

A big doorstep sandwich looks great, but you will not normally eat it all at once. Then you are in the position of having to rewrap it, which hardly anyone ever does properly, and the result is a lot of salami, lettuce, and tomato bits rolling around the cooler or the back of your vest. Cut the sandwich into smaller pieces and wrap each piece individually. Otherwise those small clip locking boxes are also good for ensuring your lunch doesn't become a dog's breakfast.

Although soggy bread may be good for bait, it's lousy on a sandwich. Remember that a sandwich to take along on a fishing trip is not the same as a sandwich that you make at half-time while watching the footy on TV. Often, you are not going to eat your fishing sandwich for a few hours. That mayonnaise that tastes so good on a ham sandwich in the den is going to squish right through the bread when you unwrap your sandwich at the stream. Sliced tomatoes will soak through the crustiest, freshest roll. My solution is to cut down on the wet stuff, and if I absolutely need some, then I spread it right on the meat and cover it with a piece of lettuce or a slice of cheese.

Serious Safety: First Aid Kits and Sun Protection

You can always make and pack your own first aid kit, but I prefer to buy prepackaged kits and store them in both my boat and tackle bag. That way I have the basic supplies I need, whether I'm afoot or afloat. Available at most sporting goods stores, first aid kits list their contents on the packaging, and you can pick the one that matches your needs. This may seem excessive for shorter fishing trips, but for those who go on longer trips, especially into wilderness areas, a first aid kit is a sensible idea.

I like kits in waterproof packaging, and I don't even open it when I buy one: I simply stow it away, sealed. A good first aid kit will have what you need to address the most common scrapes, cuts and stings a trip might bring. Likewise, my tackle bag has a bottle and a stick of sunblock, as well as a bottle of insect repellent.

Making your own kit

You know your medical needs better than anyone, so you may be more comfortable just making your own kit to bring what you need. If you're highly allergic to bee stings, bring your EpiPen. Chronic sinusitis sufferers should bring sinus relief medicine. You're prone to heartburn? Pack the antacids! Bringing these common medicines sounds obvious, but many anglers forget them in the morning's rush. Don't let a minor affliction ruin your trip. A small plastic container, such as a small tackle box or a plastic kitchen container, makes a good miniature medicine chest that can be tucked into your vest or tackle box. One more thing to include: Bring a tube of superglue. Use it to mend both torn plastic lures and minor repairs or adjustments to other tackle items.

The sun is a fair-weather friend (sort of)

When you're on the water, sunlight gets you two times – once as it comes down, and again when it reflects back up off the water. Sunscreen is a must. Spread it on before you begin fishing and reapply once or twice. Serious sunburn is no joke. Covering exposed skin with clothing and a good hat really helps, too.

Why polarised sunglasses make a difference

I (Greg) started wearing contacts simply so I could wear nice sunglasses. I wasn't worried about their appearance, though – I just wanted a great pair of polarised sunglasses to cut the glare from the water's surface. On bright days, you'll be grateful for any pair of shades. Polarised lenses, though, cut through the shiny glare on the water's surface, allowing you to see deeper into the water. This will help you spot cruising fish – like carp or trout– or spot underwater cover you might have missed. When boating, seeing more might make the difference between a missed obstacle and a busted prop.

Safe Wading

Even though wading is just walking, it requires much more skill and care than walking down the street does. First, you are often dealing with the force of moving water. Second, you can't always see the ground in front of you very well (or at all). And third, underwater rocks and plants can be slippery. For all of these reasons, there is one cardinal rule of wading: Take it slow!

Come to think of it, there is a second cardinal rule: Test the footing in front of you before you take the weight off your back foot. Drop-offs, unseen rocks, and current surges are often invisible, so you need to wade slowly and cautiously, one foot at a time.

In addition to these cardinal rules of wading in any body of water, this section gives you some additional advice for staying on your feet as well as what to do if you take a tumble.

Thy rod and thy staff, and thy friend, too

I (Peter) do most of my wading without a staff, but there are times when one really helps, either as a probing device or as a third leg.

Although a stick lying around on the ground may make a serviceable wading staff, what do you do with it after you're in the middle of the stream? For greater convenience, many people like commercial wading staffs that can be tied to a belt. If you can't find such a staff, a cheap and easy alternative is a ski pole with the little rubber circle cut off of the bottom. I say cheap because in the summertime, ski poles are not a hot ticket, and you can often pick up a bunch at bargain-basement prices.

You would think that if one person can easily slip and fall in a stream, then linking two people is a sure recipe for a dunking. But the opposite is true. By linking arms together, two anglers can actually gain strength and stability. If one of you is a stronger wader, that person should take the upstream position because that is the more difficult one. (This is also a good way to get a new angler a little more used to handling moving water.)

Handling the current and the occasional mishap

When a fish is hooked and it wants to use the force of the current to fight you, it turns broadside to the current. This may work fine for a fish trying to escape. For an angler trying to wade, it's precisely the wrong thing to do. You want to present the thinnest silhouette possible. In other words, stand sideways. I realise that some of us older anglers may have a shape that looks more like a soup spoon than a steak knife, but sideways is still the most efficient way to deal with the physics of moving water.

Suppose you see a nice fish rising behind a midstream rock. Inch by inch you begin to wade across the treacherous stream. It's slow going, but you're slowly getting in position for that perfect cast. And then the bottom drops sharply and you realise there's no way you're going to make it. Whatever you do, don't turn around and wade out! This action simply presents the broadest part of your body to the flow, and it's a great way to get knocked off your feet. Just take your time and back out slowly, inch by inch.

Still, one of these days, you are going to take a tumble into the water. If you are careful, you will tumble much less often than you think. In 25 years of angling, I (Peter) have fallen into the stream exactly twice. I've come close to falling more often than that, but in terms of bona fide butt-soakings, that's it. That makes me lucky. If you fall in, you should be able to right yourself pretty quickly. It helps if you keep your waders tightly cinched with a belt. If the current does take you, don't fight it: The river always wins. If possible, keep your feet in front of you so that if some part of you strikes a rock, it probably won't be your head. Although taking an involuntary ride is a little scary, try and remember that most dunkings will leave you in calm water in less than half a minute. And if you just can't manage to stay safe and hold on to your rod, let the rod go. After all, you can buy a new rod easier than the rod can buy a new you. For this reason, you might also wear a life jacket.

Danger Amplified: Boating Safety

You can get into trouble while wading or walking the bank, but as soon as you climb into a floating vessel, you assume more risk. Boats (even self-powered vessels like canoes and float tubes) allow you to move faster and over deeper water. And while there's nothing more peaceful than floating in a little jonboat on a shallow pond, a high-powered charter boat can power out to an offshore wreck double quick..Whether you own a boat or fish from a friend's, you need to be smart about your own safety.

It starts with life jackets

State and federal agencies come up with different slogans to encourage you to wear a life jacket, including "It Only Works If You Wear It!" and "A Life Jacket is an Expensive Seat . . . It Could Cost You Your Life." A phrase that worked for me (Greg) came from a conservation officer after a body was recovered from a local river. He said, "We never find a corpse wearing a life jacket."

When we talk about life jackets, you probably picture the classic orange, upside-down U yoke that fits over your head. Well, life jackets have come a long way in terms of comfort. Figure 6-1 shows different styles of life jackets, including belts and vests that inflate only when they hit the water. Modern life jackets are comfortable to wear, cool in the summer, and unobtrusive, so you can wear one all the time while boating. The fanciest life jackets are quite pricey, but others are equally effective and inexpensive. Besides, isn't your life worth it?

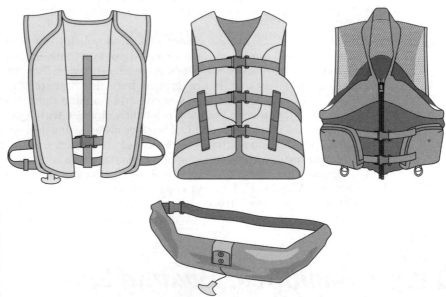

Figure 6-1:
A range of
modern life
jackets.

Your call, Captain

If you own the boat, you're in charge. That's a lot of pressure: You need to ensure that your boat is seaworthy, legal, and equipped. Any guests will have varying amounts of on-the-water experience, and before you worry about getting everyone fishing, you need to make sure they know the rules of the boat. After all, if an accident occurs, you might be held responsible.

The first thing the owner of a boat has to do is make sure everything is legal. The bigger a boat is, the more regulations it has to follow. Rules vary from state to state, but make sure you have a proper license. This will probably require stickers placed on the hull to mark your boat, as a license plate identifies a car. Your boat will also bear a metal tag that limits the number of persons it should carry. Obey that limit.

A safe boat is properly equipped. You need a good accessible life jacket for everyone on board. A flotation aid such as a life ring is also a good idea, especially if you have a passenger who isn't the most confident swimmer. Make sure the boat has the proper lighting, bow and stern, and that it works. You might also be required to carry a horn or additional safety devices. Weather or marine radios are a must for sea anglers. Fire extinguishers rated for marine use are too. Figure 6-2 shows a safely equipped boat. Check with your local authorities for specific rules: The Royal National Lifeboat Institution has further sound advice for boat users (www.rnli.org.uk).

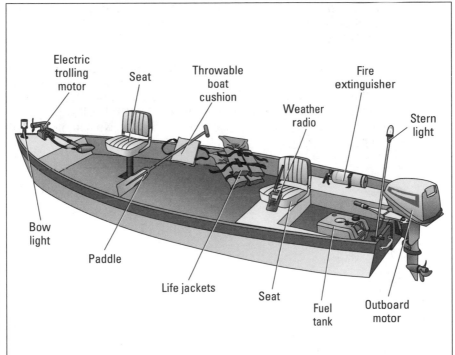

Figure 6-2: This fishing boat carries the necessary safety gear.

In any boating situation, you want to ensure two things: that the boat maintains its power, and that the boaters stay aboard. To ensure the first, I (Greg) follow the three-kinds-of-power rule: Every boat needs to have three methods of movement, should one or two fail. In most cases, this will include a petrol engine, an electric trolling motor, and a paddle or two. Check before each trip to make sure your boat has three kinds of power, and that each is in good working order. Boaters need to stay aboard for obvious reasons – when in the water, anyone could fall victim to drowning or hypothermia, or risk being hit by another boat. Even on mild days, someone treading water could succumb to hypothermia quickly because the water sucks the heat from a body. Make sure life jackets are worn and people remain seated when the boat is moving. As a captain, avoid making sharp turns and excessive speeds. If someone does go overboard, keep an eye on them while you turn around and position your boat between the man overboard and any nearby vessels. Pull them to safety as soon as possible.

Of course, you also need to know the rules of the water. Unlike drivers, boaters aren't usually required to pass a test to operate a boat, and this can be a scary thing when you're on a big body of water. You may feel like you're surrounded by nincompoops! And you might well be. Some regions offer courses, often online, that you can take to learn boating safety. Take the course. Boat with experienced captains first. And stick to smaller waters (and avoid popular boating times, like the weekends) until you learn the ropes. Or, in this case, the buoy markers.

Owning a fishing boat is a source of tremendous pride for me and millions of other anglers. But, like a car, a boat brings with it some additional responsibility. Know your guests before you take them out in your boat. If the trip isn't going well, make an excuse and cut it off early. If you're on someone else's boat, and you feel unsafe, cut it off early. No fishing is worth risking your life for.

Part II

Gearing Up Without Going Overboard

In this part . . .

You uncover all you need to know about the gear of fishing: everything from the different styles of reels, to all kinds of terminal tackle, to the latest in sonar units. While fishing doesn't have to be complicated, the latest technology offers a lot to the contemporary angler, helping him or her catch more and bigger fish. Fishing line has evolved. Rods are lighter and more sensitive than ever. Even the classic fish hook has a new twist. This part helps you decide what kind of gear you need, and what you can live without.

Chapter 7

Hot Rods and Cool Reels

· ·

· ·

*Y*ou can still catch fish with a cane pole. Find a long bamboo shoot or willow branch, tie a string to the end and add a hook and a float. Flip over a stone or two for some worms, get your grandfather, and head down to the river. Catch a few fish and have fun. The iconic cane pole of yesteryear has been replaced many times over though. Today's rods are constructed of everything from graphite to carrot fibres (no kidding). Modern reels now feature everything from one-piece aluminum or magnesium frames, up to a dozen bearings, and titanium parts. But in spite of all the innovation, the price of quality fishing tackle has come down to a level anyone can afford.

As advanced as rods and reels are today, there remain a few distinct types of equipment anglers use to store line, cast a lure or baited hook, and fight fish. Sadly no one outfit is perfect for everything; a light quivertip rod would be hopeless for big pike, just as a pike rod would be way too heavy for catching roach. Some rod and reel set ups will make a passable job at doing several jobs and we'll look at these as we go, but it's usually best to go for tackle that feels just right for your chosen style of fishing.

This chapter tells you how to distinguish between different kinds of gear, as well as the advantages and disadvantages of each. You gain a good idea of what you need in your first rod and reel, but also some of the more special-ised gear you may need as you evolve as an angler. Do buy gear with care. The Internet is fine, but there's no 'virtual' way to pick up and bend a rod or see how it balances with that particular reel. The wise move is to get to a tackle shop where you can handle the gear yourself and get some friendly help into the bargain.

Getting a Handle on Fishing Rod Basics

A rod is used for catching fish. To do this, it must be stiff but supple, strong but delicate. If fishing were just a matter of cranking them in, you could use a broom handle. But angling for a fish is a three-part job that requires three different tasks of your rod:

- **Getting the bait, lure or fly to where the fish is:** That is, your rod needs to deliver the goods.

- **Setting the hook:** Because not every take is a visual one, a rod has to be sensitive enough to let you feel the fish as it takes your worm (or lunges at your lure) and strong enough to set the hook.

- **Fighting the fish:** The rod is a big lever that transmits a great deal of force; and because of its ability to bend, it transmits variable force as required, acting as a shock absorber when the fish suddenly turns or bolts off again.

The way in which a rod accomplishes these three tasks varies. Sometimes the delivery has to be as light as goose down. In other situations, you need to heave your bait into heavy current and hold it there. To accommodate the key tasks as well as the differences between anglers, many kinds of rods are available. In time, if you fish enough, you will discover how to feel the differences between rods. You may like some but not care for others. Your personal fondness for a particular rod doesn't mean that one rod is necessarily better than another (although there are both winners and stinkers out there). It just means that one is better for you and the kind of fishing you want to do at any given time.

Unlike reels, all rods share many of the following common features, as shown in Figure 7-1. For more on reels, see the section 'Catching Up with Reels' later in this chapter.

- **Butt:** The bottom half or third of the shaft, or *blank,* of the rod. As with the tip, on some rods, the butt really bends, while on others it doesn't.

- **Ferrule:** The joint where the rod blank can be separated. In the old days, this was a metal connector that decreased the rod's sensitivity. Now, the smaller section of the blank is made to fit inside a larger section, with little effect on performance.

- **Grip:** The handle part you hold onto. It can be made of cork or synthetic materials. Grips come in many shapes and sizes. The main point is that it should be comfortable for the way you fish.

- **Guides:** Small eyes often called *rod rings* that direct the line on its journey from the reel to the tip ring. On a spinning or float rod, in particular, the guides get progressively smaller as you go from reel to tip top, channeling the large coils that come off the reel into a straight line to your target. Guides, often formed of stainless steel or other metals, might be lined with ceramic or some other material to allow the line to slide smoothly through the guide. Check your guides frequently to ensure that they are nick-free, as a chink in the lining of the guide will damage your line.

✔ **Reel seat:** Usually a set of screw-tightened washers or rings that fit over the base of the reel and attach it to the rod.

✔ **Tip:** The last foot or so of rod. Sometimes, as with a quiver tip, the rod's tip may be used to spot bites. It can bend a little or a great deal and is critical in determining the action and sensitivity of the rod. See the later section 'How slow can you go?' for more on how rods bend.

✔ **Tip ring:** The uppermost guide, the point where the line leaves the rod on its way to the fish.

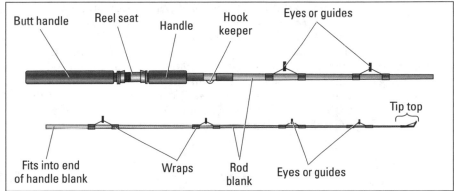

Figure 7-1: Rod anatomy.

The writing on the rod

Fishing rods usually have the following information printed right above the handle:

✔ **Action:** When you apply force to rods, they bend quickly or slowly. Some flex only at the tip, although others bend all the way down to the butt. How fast and where a rod bends determines its *action*.

For the record, tackle manufacturers classify their rods as *ultrafast* (or *extra-fast*), *fast, moderate* and *slow*. Which one is right for you? It depends on what fish you pursue and the kind of methods you use. Moderate or slow rods, often described as having a *through action*, are probably the best bets for beginners, as they're more forgiving and flexible.

✔ **Length:** The length of the rod is usually expressed in feet and inches. Printing the length right on the rod prevents the social awkwardness of having to hold the rod against your forehead in the tackle shop to determine how long, or tall, it is.

Shorter rods work better in tight spaces, like when you're fishing under overhanging branches, but in general longer rods allow for longer casts and better control. And a longer rod acts like a shock absorber, making it easier to maintain a tight line while fighting a surging fish.

✔ **Optimum lure/line weight:** Manufacturers also classify rods by how much weight they can optimally cast, listing the preferred range in grams or ounces. So '1–4 oz.' printed on a beachcasting rod, indicates that this rod works well when casting weights between one and four ounces. A spinning rod marked '10–40 g' tells you that the rod will cast small to medium lures in quite a broad weight band. In addition, rods often print the preferred line test, usually labeled as such and in pounds, as in 'Line 4–8 lb.'

✔ **Power:** In addition to a rod's action, most manufacturers will print the rod's *power,* the amount of weight required to bend the rod, on the blank. Words like, *light, medium* and *heavy,* or some combination of these terms, such as ultra-light may appear. Others use *test curve,* often abbreviated to *T.C.* This indicates the weight required to bend the tip over to a 90° angle; 1 lb would be a fairly light rod, whereas a 2.5 lb rod would handle large carp. Don't worry too much about these distinctions just yet, however; the overall feel of the rod is what counts, and whether it matches the job you intend to use it for.

How slow can you go?

As shown in Figure 7-2, a rod can bend a little or a great deal. Fast rods bend in the tip, whereas slower rods (or those described as having a *through action*) bend through the whole length of the rod (from the tip to the butt in a gentle arc). In general, a fast rod casts well when distance is a priority. It is punchier than a slow rod. It is also sensitive in the tip, so that you can feel a bite or even a tiny nibble right away. A slower rod generally allows for a more delicate presentation. Whereas a fast, or *tippy,* rod may have a tendency to tear bait off the hook, a slower action will give a nice even heave.

If you're doing a great deal of fishing with jigs and lighter lures, for example, the stiffness and feel of a fast, tippy rod are desirable. On the other hand, if you're looking for a rod to play carp at close range, a slower, through action rod would be ideal for containing the weighty lunges of a hooked fish. Although a fast rod can be more sensitive than a slow rod (with a fast rod, you can feel the tiniest tap-tap of a fish), a slow rod acts as a better shock absorbed when you're battling big fish.

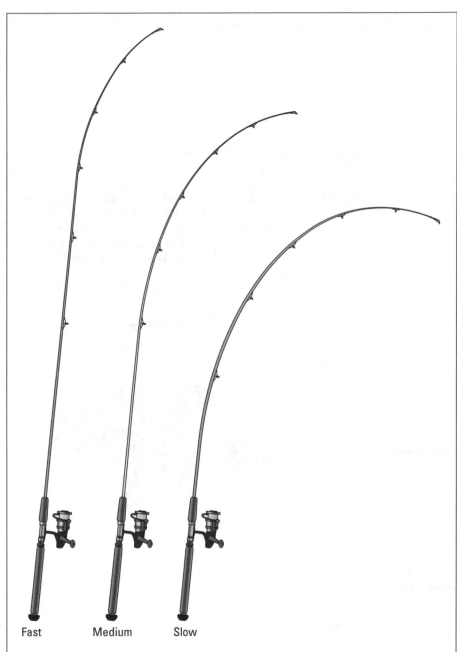

Figure 7-2:
Fast,
medium,
and slow
rod actions.

Fast   Medium   Slow

Catching Up with Reels

Saying every reel works the same is akin to saying every car works the same: It may be true on a basic level, but everyone knows the difference between a Landrover and a SmartCar. The common kinds of reel range widely in performance and function. But all reels, like all rods, share a few features in common. Figure 7-3 points out the basic parts that reels share.

✔ **Anti-reverse:** This lever can be found on virtually all reels, and when switched on, this device prevents the crank from turning in reverse. Some anglers leave the anti-reverse off so they can wind line in, or give line out (by turning the handle anti-clockwise). But most find life easier when the anti-reverse is on because, while fighting a fish, you can take your hand off the handle and not worry about the fish taking line off the reel. Put simply, with your drag properly adjusted, you're better off with the anti-reverse on. You'll certainly get fewer tangles if the handle only turns one way.

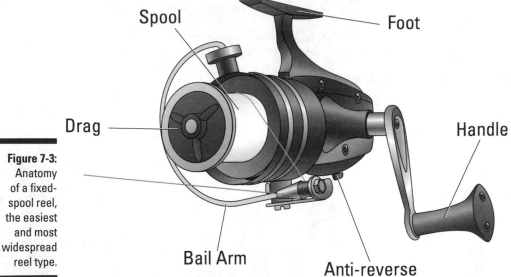

Spool   Foot

Drag   Handle

Figure 7-3:
Anatomy
of a fixed-
spool reel,
the easiest
and most
widespread
reel type.

Bail Arm   Anti-reverse

✔ **Bail arm/line release:** Every reel except the fly reel features a button, lever, or device that allows the release of line. On the fixed-spool reel, as pictured, the bale arm serves this task and is flipped over to allow the line to come off freely when casting. Because every reel completes two basic jobs – sending line out or bringing it back – a reel is either *disengaged* (allowing line out) or *engaged* (bringing line in).

✔ **Handle:** This is the part of the reel you turn. You see single-grip handles, double-grip handles and handles with grips so soft your fingers rejoice when they touch them. But they all turn to bring line into the reel. On most fixed-spool reels, the handle can also be switched over for left handers (who will want to crank with their right hand).

✔ **Drag:** A knob on the front of the spool or right at the back, that tightens the spool to control the fight of a fish.

✔ **Reel foot:** This part connects into the *reel seat* of the rod.

It's a drag, but it works

The *drag* on a reel works with you to control a fighting fish. A fixed-spool reel sometimes features a knob in front of the spool, although more of them have a rear-mounted drag on the back of the reel's body for easier access. A fly reel's drag is often a knob right on the axis of the main spool. On a multiplier reel, you might find a star-shaped knob inside the handle.

All drags work to control surging fish by controlling the speed of line leaving the spool once *engaged*. You might wonder, but if a reel is engaged, line can only come in, right? Not quite. A strong fish could pull a reel out of your hands if there were no give. (More likely, it would break the line first.) Drag lets a fish take line out, while leaving the reel engaged. A big fish, in its strongest moments, might take out some line against even a tight drag. (One of the sweetest things to happen in all of angling!)

You 'set' the drag using the knob on your reel. With the drag set too loose, you can't even pull in your weight or lure. You turn the handle and nothing happens. A hooked fish could simply swim away, towing your line. But make the drag too tight and a big fish might break the line or tear the hook free. So do the following before you cast the first time on any trip: Engage the reel, then pull the line off the reel with your hand. (Grab it right in front of the reel.) If it comes off easily, tighten the drag a bit. If it appears to be locked down, loosen it up a bit. Adjust again once you begin fishing, and after you catch (hopefully!) a few fish. All we can say is, you get a feel for your drag. So many anglers don't bother, but wish they had when they lose a big fish.

Know where your drag is *before* a big fish catches you off guard. You should be able to reach down and adjust the drag (just a little now!) while fighting a whopper.

The writing on the reel

Reel manufacturers make your life a little easier by telling you a reel's *capacities* right on the reel itself. Most reels are stamped with a series of numbers, and, like the numbers on the side of a car's tire, knowing what they mean can help you understand more about what you need.

The first number refers to the size of line a reel can hold. This is usually given in pounds, referring to the *pound test* of the line. The second number refers to the amount of line the reel's spool can hold. This number is usually given in yards. The bigger the reel, the more line it can hold. Incidentally, rods, reels and indeed most angling gear use the abbreviation 'lbs' for pounds.

As reels get bigger, they also get heavier, bulkier, and often costlier. It's easy to overestimate the amount and size of line you need. Start smaller, and if you discover you need more or heavier line, you can upsize later.

Suppose a reel is stamped '12/200.' This means the reel likes 12-pound test line, and it holds 200 metres of it. I say 'likes' because reels are built to utilize a particular range of line tests, and you can fudge that range a bit, but don't be surprised if your reel no longer works as well. A reel that likes 12-pound test can hold 20-pound test, but it may not cast as far or as smoothly. (And it won't hold as much of it.) Sometimes, reel manufacturers give you several sets of numbers, allowing you to choose the line that fits your fishing: 4/245, 6/200, 8/150. See how it works? The heavier the line, the less you can put on the reel. Many also come with one or two spare spools so you can easily switch lines. Tench fishing close to the bank? Sure, go with 6-pound test. Casting across the pond for rudd? Drop to 3-pound line. (Chapter 8 covers line in detail.)

Which reel: Fixed-spool, multiplier or centrepin?

If you're confused by different reels, the good news is that with the exception of fly reels, they all fit into three basic categories. For the vast majority of anglers, a fixed-spool reel is the best and easiest all-round choice. Whether you're casting a float or a leger rig, a little spinner or a large plug, the fixed spool is a reliable tool to use. Just make sure you match your reel to your rod sensibly. Small fixed-spool reels, for example, are ideal for float fishing or light spinning; at the other end of the scale, large fixed spools are designed to carry many yards of strong line – useful if you need to cast a hundred yards from a beach, for example, or fish at distance for big carp or pike on a gravel pit.

The stronger and heavier your rod, the more substantial the reel you're likely to need to balance the outfit properly and carry lots of thicker line. If you had to pick one reel however, it would probably be a mid-sized fixed-spool reel that will handle lines from 6–12 pounds.

Ordering online may be convenient, but remember, nothing beats actually handling tackle yourself and in a shop you can physically attach reel to rod and see how they feel together.

Another common variant of the fixed spool worth mentioning is the *baitrunner*. These are just like regular reels but feature a a special switch towards the back which puts the reel into *free-spool* mode. This means that the drag won't kick in and the spool will turn freely to give out line to a big fish (and prevent your rod being pulled in!). A turn of the reel handle will engage the drag again and it's business as usual. These reels are particularly useful for carp, which can tear off at a rate of knots and make your prized rod do an impression of a water skier if you're not careful!

Multiplier reels are usually the preserve of the sea or lure angler. These sit on top of the rod, rather than beneath it like a fixed–spool reel. They offer good control over large fish, but can be more problematic and easy to tangle when casting (you can find more on the intricacies of casting in Chapter 15).

Finally, we have the centrepin. It looks rather like a large fly reel. This is a more traditional reel, usually only used by river anglers. You can't cast far with one, but a quality 'pin has a spool that turns incredibly freely, hence it is ideal for *trotting* which means using the current to take your float and bait to the fish as naturally as possible. They're also fun for fishing close in on lakes however. It's not a tool for the beginner, but if you love river fishing you may eventually want to invest in one.

Coarse Fishing Gear: There's Nothing Coarse About It . . .

Many ways exist to tackle freshwater fish, so when it comes to the gear you use there is no such thing as 'one size fits all'. Coarse tackle, contrary to the name, can be highly refined gear suitable for all the common freshwater species you target with bait or lures. The more experienced you become and the more challenging the fishing you find, the more specialised the gear becomes.

The names of modern coarse fishing rods are awash with buzzwords and the names of species: A tribute not only to marketing but also to the tremendous diversity of methods you can use. Fear not, however, because we're about to break down coarse tackle into clear categories. For every ultra-specialised tool, other outfits will catch various species, so it makes perfect sense to start with the all-rounders.

Apart from poles and whips, just about every coarse fishing rod that follows is best matched with a suitable fixed-spool reel. *Multipliers* (or *baitcasters* as the Americans call them) are best left to sea anglers or lure addicts.

No reel, but really deadly: Poles & whips

'Simple is best' is a phrase you often hear in fishing, and this statement is certainly true of the pole. In a sense these lengthy rods take fishing back to its roots, when reels were absent and anglers simply fastened their lines to the tip of the rod. Don't be fooled by their simplicity though, because today's multi-section poles are lightweight, strong and deadly in the right hands. The World Championships are won time and again by skilled pole anglers, and they aren't the only contest of which that's true.

Poles might be the choice of champions, but with no reel to tangle they're also well suited to beginners. The pros use featherlight carbon models that can cost as much as a small car and extend to over 16 metres in length. A sensible starter model would be half this size and, thankfully, a small fraction of the price.

A pole breaks down into *sections* when in use. In other words, you have your line, float and hook matched up to the first three metres or so of pole, and then further sections are added to extend it to greater lengths. To land a fish, you remove sections to shorten the pole back to a shorter, manage-able length. Pole anglers fish right under the rod tip, which makes for both a sensitive and super-accurate method. Not only does a pole allow you to use almost weightless floats to fool the shyest fish, it's also brilliant for drop-ping your bait tight to fish-holding features. Short of positioning your bait by hand, nothing could be more accurate.

Poles are not just for small fish either. In fact, many poles are now designed to handle carp. They take a length of special elastic internally, which stretches out from the tip of the pole to cushion the fight of the fish. Look for a sensible length which won't break the bank for your first pole. For around £60 you might find an 8 metre pole ready-elasticated. Elastics themselves are graded by number: A number six would be ideal for bream, roach and chub whilst a twelve would handle carp and tench.

Whips are also poles, but even simpler. They have no elastic and are usu-ally found in shorter lengths of 4-5 metres. Suited to lines no greater than 3 pounds strength they're not ideal for big fish, but are excellent value and terrific fun for catching lots of roach, perch and other fish. These are great for kids and beginners who want lots of bites with minimum complication. As with longer poles, you can store the rigs on little plastic winders so that you're set up and ready to fish in seconds. Obviously with any pole you can only fish the length of the one you own. Then again, good fishing is often found close to the bank, which is a worthwhile lesson in itself.

Fun and finesse: Float rods

A float-fishing tool is often the first serious rod an angler buys, and with good reason. They're light, offer good control and will catch you all kinds of species from tiny dace to runaway carp. You'll see these rods sold under various titles, most commonly as *match rods*, but also *waggler* or *Avon* rods. All are designed specially for float fishing, so they tend to be around twelve feet long for good line control, with enough flex to handle fine lines and sufficient lightness to be comfortable to hold all day long.

Short rods are often recommended for beginners but something of at least 10 feet (3 metres) is far more practical, even for a child. The version you choose should reflect the type of fishing you seek. For general fishing on lakes, canals, rivers and ponds where you may catch any one of several species, a standard match rod will do nicely. Combined with a small fixed-spool reel filled with 4 pound line you can have excellent fun with many species and stand a good chance of landing the odd bigger fish too if you play them with care. Other rods, often labelled as 'power match' or with 'carp' or 'commercial' in the name, represent stronger rods designed to tame small to medium carp with heavier lines of, say, 6 to 8 pounds. The Avon rod is a further option: These are also a little stronger than a typical match rod, with a softer through action that will handle hard-battling fish like chub and tench.

You see a lot of pre-packaged starter kits aimed at beginners. The rods are brightly coloured and include random bits of tackle. They might appear to represent good value, but the vast majority are horrible. Even an expert would struggle with a garden gnome rod, thick line and crude hooks. The better option is to seek a starter deal from a reputable tackle dealer, explaining your fishing needs to a friendly expert. Quality tackle isn't especially costly, but you definitely get what you pay for.

Top Tips: Quiver Tip Rods

Besides float fishing, another commonly used and effective method is legering, which means fishing on the bottom. Big fish such as bream, tench and carp are especially susceptible to a bait presented on the deck with a bomb or swimfeeder to hold the bait on the bottom (more on these methods in Chapter 14). You detect bites via a thin, flexible and brightly-coloured quiver tip section – the clue is in the title! Most of these rods come with two or three different tips which range from the most delicate affair for shy-biting roach to beefier sections aimed at carp and barbel. Most tips are made of carbon, although some river experts still swear by the softer action of a fibreglass tip.

Like float rods, you'll find quiver tip rods in various guises, with names including words such as *feeder, quiver tip* or *bomb*. A short rod of 8 to 9 feet (2.5 to 3 metres) would be ideal for small rivers or canals, while the longer 11-foot-plus beasts are for bigger waters and long casts. Another common variant is the *method* or *carp feeder* rod. These are specially designed to launch heavy, bait-packed swim feeders and to cope with rip-roaring bites and powerful fish.

Big ideas: Carp & specimen rods

There comes a time in the life of any keen angler when the appeal of bigger fish is hard to resist. The real zoo creatures such as colossal carp, pike or barbel demand stronger tackle. You wouldn't hunt tigers with a pea shooter, now would you? Rods for outsized specimens need extra power for various reasons: To control a surging barbel in a fast current; to cast a whole sardine and set the hook in the bony jaw of a pike; to prevent a 20-pound carp from smashing you up in a snaggy corner.

Carp rods are now extremely popular. But do you absolutely need one? If you're stepping up to waters where the fish come in bigger sizes and you may wait a long time between bites, the answer is probably yes. For those many waters where carp average under 10 pounds, however, a power match or feeder rod is more effective and you'll get a much better fight. In fact, the only time when two or three heavy rods and bite alarms are required is on a water where the fish are big and bites harder to come by.

Carp rods vary in strength according to their test curve (often abbreviated to TC) which we discussed earlier in this chapter. It's worth noting that you don't need a broom handle of a rod to land big carp. Fishing legend Richard Walker caught his one-time record 44-pound carp on a rod of 1.5 pounds test curve, less than half the welly of today's average brute. Common strengths are between 2.25 and 3 pounds TC. In lighter strengths you have a rod with more flex that will handle lighter lines, say down to 8 pounds. These are the tools to use for fishing at short to medium range, say up to 50 metres. Not only is the extra flex more fun, it's more forgiving for when you have a carp powering around at close quarters.

For greater distances and heavier demands, for example casting a heavy lead plus a PVA bag full of free bait to the horizon, a more powerful beast of 3 pounds TC or greater is the answer. If you fish a reservoir or gravel pit for big fish, such a rod could be essential. If you were to try lighter lines with such a weapon, you could easily be broken off, but they will handle braid or mono line in strengths of 12 to 15 pounds or greater should the situation demand (For more on the subject of different fishing lines, see Chapter 8). Whatever your needs, the market is crammed with carp rods. Various companies are competing for your business, so thrifty anglers can shop around for some excellent deals.

A carp rod will also serve for some pike fishing, although if you do a lot of piking, dedicated rods do a better job. These have similarly high test curves and a lot of poke, not only because big pike are strong but because you may need to cast large baits. Equally, with the species possessing a supremely bony mouth you need enough power to set the hooks on the strike. Predator tackle is no longer the realm of broom handles, however, with companies such as Greys producing excellent rods for the pike enthusiast. Lighter blanks of 2.25 to 2.5 TC are great fun for float fishing and for use on smaller waters such as drains and canals. A monster stopper of 3 to 3.5 TC will launch a whole fish bait the greater distances required on big waters.

Naturally, *specimen* fishing doesn't always mean enormous fish. The term simply refers to winkling out the bigger samples of one particular species. A two-pound roach or perch is as much a noteworthy 'specimen' as a hulking great carp. Lighter specimen rods come in strengths from as little as 1 pound TC and these are ideal for those who seek big bream, perch and other species. Some canny tackle makers also produce 'twin tip' or 'multi-tip' rods. These are usually two piece weapons where you get two entirely different top sections (1 pound and 1.5 pound TC for example) which gives you a handy versatility. Barbel rods are another example of this, with some possessing different top sections for different scenarios. For example so you could fish either a standard tip section to trot a big float, or switch to a brightly coloured quiver tip to try a heavy swimfeeder without needing to buy two rods.

Predator catchers: Spinning & lure rods

From solid, all-round performers to ultra specialised tools, spinning rods fall into a class of their own. All are designed to cast and retrieve artificial lures such as spinners, spoons, plugs and jigs in search of predators like pike and perch. However, beyond the usual coarse suspects it's worth mentioning that sea and game species like bass and trout can also be caught on spinning or lure tackle. They are also used widely in some areas for salmon fishing (although this is only permitted at certain times of year, so do check).

The perfect all-rounder?

The perfect set up for every fishing situation is something which, strictly speaking, doesn't exist. Looking at rods is a bit like looking at different athletes; they all excel at what they do but there is a world of difference between a heavyweight boxer and a marathon runner. Which is better? That depends on whether you want a race or a punch up! There are also those who are good at lots of tasks but not top dog at any one event. The same is true of rods.

If you had to pick just one rod, it would probably be either an Avon or a spinning rod. Many Avons come with both normal tip sections and quiver tips, making them suitable for both float fishing and legering. I (Dominic) have a friend who regularly catches big carp on his trusty Avon, but also takes roach on it. For the coarse angler the Avon must be close to the ideal all-rounder.

My own choice, however, would probably be a light-to-medium spinning rod of around 10 feet, capable of casting up to around an ounce and a half (40 g) in weight. You can catch coarse, sea or game fish on lures with such a rod, but at this length it will also perform other tasks. It works for float fishing with various coarse or even sea species. It also works well free-lining a floating bait for carp. It must be close to the best all-rounder for the roving angler and I've caught everything from 20-pound pike to sea bass on my trusty 10-footer.

A mid range spinning rod makes a great casting tool for many different fish. Short rods as little as 6 feet long can be used for boat fishing, but for the bank fisher something of 9-10 feet is way more practical, offering much better control over a hooked fish and leverage around bankside cover. Most will offer a recommended casting weight in grams and since most plugs, jigs and other common lures fall into the 10-40g weight bracket, a rod of similar rating makes perfect sense. Aim for a model with generously sized rings and a slim tip section (that is, the last two feet or so) which will allow you to really feel your lures working. 'Feel' is of great importance to the lure angler, who wants to be able to tell when a fish knocks the lure, or when they've hit the bottom, weed or other features. For just about any lure fishing, braid is the best line to use to get maximum strength and sensitivity (for more on different types of line, see Chapter 8).

As far as rod ratings go it's true that you can also cast lures which are outside a rod's recommended casting weight. Heavy lures might give a sloppy feel, however, whilst you may hardly feel a tiny spinner. A more satisfactory answer for those who favour lures that fall well outside the average is to invest in a more specialised tool. At one end of the scale we have *ultralight* spinning rods which are slender customers that work beautifully well with tiny lures. Those who prefer great big artificials such as jerkbaits would be better suited with a *jerkbait* rod or lure rod labelled 'heavy'; these tend to be shorter, meatier beasts and also present one of the few scenarios in coarse fishing where multiplier reels are a good bet.

Spinning rods cross all the fishing categories (coarse, sea and game), so it's also worth considering the needs of the sea or game angler. Fishing a windy beach for bass, or a big river for salmon and sea trout, the best option might be the extra length and power of an 11–12 footer. Where conditions allow, however, a lighter rod with more 'feel' is excellent fun.

Making Waves: Sea Fishing Rods

The sea is a wild and sometimes rough environment which places special demands on fishing gear. Sea fishing rods clearly have to cope with factors you won't find on the average pond. Strong fish, crashing waves and rocks all put an extra burden on tackle. Add in the fact that heavy weights may be called for to put a bait a hundred yards or more into the surf and you're looking for a very different beast in a rod.

There are exceptions to every rule of course, and in calm conditions or sheltered locations such as piers and breakwaters coarse tackle may suffice for some fun sport on light tackle. Mackerel, pollack and bass are nothing short of sensational on a spinning or carp rod, whilst float or feeder gear is spot on for mullet. But for anyone who regularly tackles the sea by beach or boat, a dedicated set-up is the only answer.

Taming the tide: Beachcasters

Faced with rolling waves, an onshore breeze and fish that you can only reach with a long cast, a beachcaster is the best choice. These rods are typically 12 to 13 feet (4 metres) long, although some go to 16 feet (5 metres) plus. They're robust and capable of slinging a good sized weight right out there where it counts. Check just above the handle for a weight rating in ounces. A sensible all rounder will cast from around 3 to 6 ounces, although those who frequent really rough, exposed shorelines or aim to wrestle big, ugly fish from the rocks may want something that will handle even heavier weights.

Look for a model which feels comfortable to grip and has a distinct tip section (usually white or yellow) which will help you spot bites. Beachcasters are made differently for either fixed-spool reels or multipliers. Many distance casting experts swear by the multiplier, but a fixed-spool set up is far more user-friendly for those newer and less salt-bitten anglers. As with any set up, it's important to find a reel which balances well together with your beachcaster, usually a large reel capable of taking 200 metres or more of strong line.

Many tackle shops offer rod and reel deals, which can represent good value for money. Do explain your needs to the dealer carefully, however, and avoid short rods and cheap or suspect tackle; it's always worth buying the best you can afford. You'll probably also want to invest in a tripod style rod rest, unless you fancy holding a formidably long rod for several hours.

Saltwater with a twist: Specialist shore rods from bass to the pier

Just like coarse and fly rods, besides the solid general-fit models you'll also find sea fishing rods that cater for a particular niche. Bass and flatfish rods are typical offerings; these often have lighter casting weight specifications and a more sensitive feel. There are several reasons for this: Fish like bass and the flounders of estuaries come close to the shore and don't always give stupendously hard bites. It's also much more fun to play the average sea fish on a rod with more bend. Such tackle might not cope with the rigours of a storm beach on a rough tide, but for those who frequent estuary mouths or are addicted to a particular species these rods offer a good fit.

Another common variant on the beachcaster is the pier rod. These are slightly shorter than the average surf slayer, at around 10 feet, to cater for fishing close in to man-made structures. Again, they are no substitute for a beachcaster on the open shore, but for those whose regular haunt is the pier or harbour these offer an affordable starting point. They also suit youngsters who might struggle with lengthier, more formidable casting tools.

Catching afloat: Boat rods

When you're dropping baits just over the side of a boat, possibly in the company of several anglers, the last thing you want is the awkwardness of a 12 foot rod. Start waving a beachcaster around and you might quickly lose your friends! Boat rods hence tend to be short, usually no more than 8 feet in length. The likelihood of battles with heavyweight species in deep water also requires something with plenty of power. It's for the same reason that the vast majority of boat anglers use multiplier reels, which are unbeatable when it comes to cranking up a big fish from the depths.

Boat rods are often classified by *weight class* or *line class*, which describes the power of the model much like test curve does in coarse gear. A rod in the 8–12 pound class would be a sporty little number for playing bream or bass. One in the 15–20 pound bracket would be more of an all-rounder, suitable for battling powerful cod and pollack from reefs or wrecks. But if you seek the real heavyweights such as conger or tope, a 50-pound class rod wouldn't be overdoing it.

TIP

Breaking down any rod

No matter which rods you own, very few will fit in a car unless broken down into sections. The exception is a fairly short, one-piece spinning or boat rod, which can be taken anwhere already set up and ready to fish. Most of us will have to break rods down, however, and most of today's models come in two or three pieces. The current trend is often towards two, since it's easier to carry a rod folded in half and ready set up (either in a quiver or just in your car boot) in this manner. If you're careful you can simply separate and fold the two halves down together whilst reeling in any slack to leave your kit tackled up and ready to go. Some quivers and holdalls have special compartments for this, but *rod wraps* (Velcro fastening bands) are a useful alternative for keeping everything tidy when transporting single rods. For more limited spaces and the rigours of longer distance travel, you'll also find multi-section 'travel' rods of various kinds which will pack away to a length as little as 18'.

This leads to the larger question of *ferrules* (the joints where two pieces of a rod fit together). The old wisdom has it that the more ferrules you have, the more strength and action you give up in your rod. But this wisdom hardly applies to most modern rod designs. Instinctively, I (Peter) like the look of fewer ferrules; but as a travelling fisherman, I can tell you that you can't fit a nine-foot rod in the overhead luggage bin on a plane. Travelling rods that come in four or five pieces are probably less smooth than one- or two-piece rods, but I don't think that you really

notice that much difference. For most fishing, most of the time, a multipiece rod works perfectly fine, and it has the advantage of being handy anywhere you go.

Although one-piece rods are neat, 99 per cent of the readers of this book have (or will have) rods that break down into two or more pieces. Going on the time-honored principle of 'If something bad can happen, it will,' you can count on a pair of ferrules getting stuck together someday. When this happens, remember the following do's and don'ts.

Don't use pliers. A blank is usually a hollow tube, and pliers are *guaranteed* to break your rod. It may not break right then and there — although it usually does — but take my word for it: You will injure the fibres in the rod, and it will break one day.

The same goes for twisting the stuck ferrule apart like a screw-top bottle. First, this technique probably won't work; and second, you could easily snap one of the guides. Use a gentle twisting motion when you disassemble a rod; but if that technique doesn't work, try applying ice to the joint. If you don't have any ice handy, try running cool water (such as from that stream behind you) over the joint. Wait a moment and then try again to separate the ferrules.

Before you assemble the rod the next time, apply some wax to the joint. Wax will prevent the rod blanks from sticking in the first place.

Another variant on the boat rod is the *uptide* rod. Uptiding is a method where short casts are made from a boat (rather than just lowering your bait over the side), to let the bait settle in a tidal flow. These tend to be longer (9–10ft) and are well suited to inshore boat anglers especially.

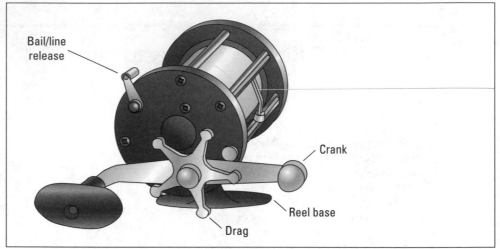

Figure 7-4: Multipliers take some getting used to, but are favoured by many sea anglers.

Bail/line release

Crank

Reel base

Drag

Flyfishing Gear: Artful and Effective

The various kinds of gear discussed so far all work in similar ways, and they all have one thing in common – they require the presence of the weight, lure or bait to pull the line off the reel. (This is why heavier lures cast further.) Flycasting is different. Because flies used for fishing weigh next to nothing, flyfishing gear is designed to cast using a different system, with the fly line itself providing all the necessary weight for casting. With flycasting, the reel has less work to do, so the rod picks up the lion's share of the work.

Just like with sea or coarse tackle, fly rods and reels are designed to perform at their best with particular lines. These are classified by numbers, with recommended lines found printed on rods or reels alongside the letters AFTM or the # symbol. A typical stillwater trout rod would take a 6 weight line. For more on fly lines and what these numbers mean, Chapter 8 reveals all.

When it comes to reels, the fly reel often has the simplest mechanism of all those discussed in this chapter. Its first function is for storage of line. Action, gear ratio, drag, and the like are secondary considerations in flyfishing. The basic fly reel is a *single-action reel,* which means that one turn of the crank handle equals one revolution of the spool. Figure 7-5 illustrates a basic reel. It has a spool, a housing for the spool, a handle and, sometimes, a drag adjustment. Like a fixed-spool reel, a fly reel is mounted below the rod. With most reels you have a choice of buying a reel for either winding with the left hand or right hand. Because I (Peter) cast with my right arm, I like to hold the rod in my right hand and reel with my left. This way, I don't have to complicate my life and change hands to fight a fish using the strength of my more powerful arm to assist the rod during the struggle. Some switch hands after a cast, and this becomes second nature to them. However, most right-handers will naturally feel most comfortable reeling with their left hand. If in doubt, check with your tackle dealer to make sure you have the reel that suits you. Some can also be switched from left to right hand wind.

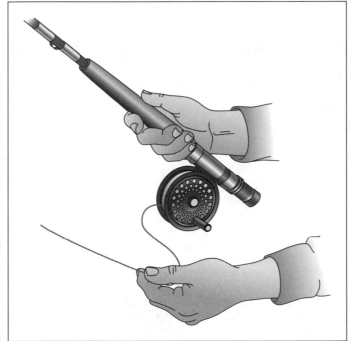

Figure 7-5:
The fly reel
is a very
simple
machine.

Don't forget to oil your reels. Because reels are made with moving metal parts, they need to be lubricated. Manufacturers often include oil with their reels, and many stores sell reel oil and grease. Check with the manufacturer's reel instructions to see where to apply oil or grease. Oil works well for gears. I (Peter) like to lubricate spools and spool posts with silicone lubricant, which holds up under a wide temperature range.

Advantages and disadvantages of flycasting gear

So the flycasting reel is a simple machine. What makes casting a fly rod such an art, then? Part of the challenge lies in the fact that the reel, while it doesn't hurt you with complicated mechanics, doesn't help you much, either. The reel is basically just a device to store line. This keeps the cost of flycasting reels relatively inexpensive (although, like anything, it's certainly possible to spend a pretty penny if one is so inclined!) and relatively easy to maintain. The reels are light and unobtrusive. Landing a fish on a fly rod is not like landing a fish on other tackle, though. Gone is the anti-reverse and the cranking power of a strong multiplier reel. Much of the time you might not use the reel at all, but simply play fish by trapping the line between your fingers, as you usually would when retrieving a fly, and bringing it in a foot or two at a time.

Fly rods: Choosing the right one

Although fly rodding is steeped in tradition, fly rods aren't. In Izaak Walton's day, there were no fancy split-cane bamboo rods – only solid pieces of pliable local woods like willow and ash. Bamboo technology came along only in the last century and only dominated for about a hundred years. Bamboo is fun to cast, and there's something pleasurable in using material that was once living. No question about it, when fiberglass came along, many more people could afford to get into fly fishing. And now, the successor to fibreglass – carbon fibre – is the most high-performance material so far. Casting is the name of the game in fly fishing. Much of the pleasure of the sport comes from laying out a good cast.

Casting a fly is kind of like throwing a ball: Almost everybody has a slightly different style. I (Peter) have a kind of three-quarter, sidearm kind of cast that is miles away from the classic English style of straight-up-and-down cast with the elbow held tight against the chest. Some rods that more-traditional casters love give me a problem. Some rods work for me at short distances; but when I really want to lay the line out there, a 'dead spot' appears that probably has more to do with my casting motion than it has to do with the rod. So when people ask 'What rod is best for me?' I can make recommendations, but in the end, you are going to have to feel your way into this and get the rod that feels best for you. If no one had said it before, then I am sure that some fly rodder, somewhere, would have come up with the saying 'different strokes for different folks.'

The following sections cover the best options for different fishing situations.

Small streams, small rods

In general, fishing in small streams with overhanging branches often leads to a tangle of rod and line. Watching anglers fish in such a setting is almost like watching people in an old slapstick comedy: the angler looks in front for obstacles, and then, with equal care, looks behind. Then he or she very carefully casts and — boing! — the line is hung up in a tree somewhere behind Mr. or Ms. Fly Fisher. Apart from being very conscious of where your line is going to go when you cast, using a short rod with a fast tip enables you to aim casts beneath trees and obstructions with very little line out of the guides.

A typical smaller stream tool would be in the 7-8 foot range and handle three or four weight lines. Not only is a daintier rod good for gentle presentation, it will also provide a cracking bend in the fight with even a smallish brown trout.

Fast rods for most trout

Most trout rods – and especially those for typical stillwater fishing on lakes and reservoirs – fall into a comfortable middle bracket. 9 to 9 and a half feet is a comfortable length and typical line weight ratings are in the 5–8 bracket. A 6 is perhaps the ideal sporty middle weight to handle a wide range of flies; 7s and 8s are useful for casting a longer line in breezier conditions or for bigger flies such as lures. Something a little lighter, say a 5 weight rod, will offer a more delicate presentation for dry flies and light leaders. As with coarse fishing gear, the lighter and more flexible the rod, the lighter the final few feet of line (or '*tippet*' to a fly fisher) that can be used without the risk of a break.

The majority of modern fly rods have what you would describe as a fast action. A fast tip makes for a tighter casting loop, which is good, especially with small flies. But you need to be careful when setting the hook with a fast rod, especially when using a light tippet. If the rod doesn't have much give, you will break right off. To avoid this situation, you need to learn to strike with firm, but not explosive, pressure. Quite often a measured lift is enough.

As you gain more experience, certain situations in fly fishing call for more niche rods with slightly different characteristics. For example, boat fly fishers tend to favour slightly longer 10-foot rods for their excellent line control. Nymph fishers on flowing water also like a longer blank; those who target trout and grayling at close range are especially drawn to the extra reach and control of a 10-foot rod for methods such as Czech Nymphing, in which the angler presents their flies just off the rod tip with a minimum of fly line out.

Rods for salmon fishing

Salmon fly rods are very much tools for the experienced angler. They tend to be long and powerful (13–16 feet, or 4–5 metres, usually), and one from a reputable manufacturer could cost an arm and a leg. This goes with the territory: strong fish, big rivers and often a high premium for the best fishing. These are not cast in the quite same way as trout rods, but with special Spey casting techniques. Those who wish to pursue this branch of game fishing would be best served by expert tuition in the field.

For smaller rivers, however, and for those who wish to sample salmon fishing without remortgaging the house, you can also try for salmon with a heavy-ish single-handed trout rod (say an 8 or 9 weight). A quality spinning rod will also suffice, where rules permit.

Slowing down for pike and sea fish

Taking on powerful fish in testing conditions, whether this means pike on a wild lake or sea bass from a rocky shore, demands a different breed of fly rod. Fly casting has a great deal to do with *line* speed (which many anglers, unfortunately, confuse with *arm* speed). When you're fishing with big, air-resistant pike or saltwater flies (and when you add to them the amount of line you need to carry in the air for distance-casting in saltwater), you don't want to do a great deal of hurry-up casting with a load of false casts. Fast trout rods tend to reinforce this tendency to speeding up, and the one thing I (Peter) tell trout fishermen when they begin saltwater fly fishing is to slow down. A slower, somewhat softer rod encourages an angler to let the fly line have that extra second or two in the air to load up (flex) the rod fully. The result in your cast is less false casting and longer distances. Ideally, I like a fast tip with slower action through the body of the rod.

A nine-foot, nine-weight rod is a good pike or saltwater all-rounder, and an increasing number of tackle companies now produce rods specifically for these branches of the sport. Pike rods have the extra power to deliver big flies and set the hook in bony mouths. Fly rods for salt water are similarly stepped up weapons, often with special fittings which won't corrode as badly in salt water. You'll still want to rinse your prized caster off after a trip to the sea though.

Chapter 8

The Bottom Line on Line

Your fishing line forms a crucial link between you and the fish. It's easy to match it to the kind of gear you use and the fishing you do. Some anglers routinely cast line that won't break under 50 pounds of pressure. Others use line that you could easily snap with a light tug. The lines we discuss in this chapter are made from things like nylon, Dacron, and microfilaments. Fishing line, regardless of what kind it is or what it's made of, has two jobs to perform:

✔ It must deliver your lure, fly, or bait to the fish and present it in a natural manner.

✔ When a fish bites, the line should help you land the fish without breaking.

The concepts are pretty simple, and although you have choices to make, our guess is that you're going to end up using good-old-fashioned monofilament line. But just in case, this chapter also introduces you to the other basic types of fishing line and what to consider when buying your line, as well as how to care for it and attach it to your reel.

Fly line is a whole different kettle of fish, but even with fly line, the leader at the end of the line is usually made of nylon monofilament, so much of what we say in this chapter about the lines you use for lure and bait fishing also holds true for the last few feet of your flyfishing set up as well.

Getting to Know the Three Kinds of Line

Fishing line companies work tirelessly to improve their product. Many of the improvements take place on a microscopic level – what looks like just another line to you may feature a revolutionary new way of blending things like copolymers, alloys, fluorocarbon crystals and other fancy fibres. That's all well and good, but what you really need to know is that three basic types of fishing line exist: monofilament, braid and fluorocarbon. We fill you in on all three in the next sections.

Monofilament: Best for beginners

Monofilament line (often called just *mono*) is really just a single strand of nylon line, and it's the line you should start with if you're a beginning angler. Mono has been around for a long time and for good reason. Mono possesses the following characteristics:

- Knots well
- Comes in a wide range of pound tests, colours and varieties
- Matches almost every fishing style
- Is relatively inexpensive and quite durable
- Stretches (which can help you hook and fight a fish smoothly)
- Casts well off any kind of reel, provided it's properly matched

Braid: For those who don't like to stretch

Braided line consists of strands of fibres intertwined or braided. It's extremely strong for its diameter, a characteristic that allows you to put more line on a spool. This is important if you're fishing deep water for big fish. Pike and lure anglers in particular like its great strength and low diameter. Braid also

- Has very little stretch (meaning you feel every bite)
- Is super strong
- Works well on multiplier reels

Fluorocarbon: For serious anglers

Fluorocarbon line, a monofilament nylon alloy, is a more expensive line that essentially disappears from sight in the water and is used by serious anglers fishing in situations where precision and extreme sensitivity count. Fluorocarbon line is

- ✔ Super sensitive
- ✔ Easy to cast
- ✔ Dense enough to sink
- ✔ More resistant than mono to ultraviolet rays
- ✔ Better suited to multiplier reels than fixed-spool reels

Buying Line 101

Finding the right type of line for your rod, reel and needs is pretty simple, provided you take the time to gather some basic information before heading to the store. Of course, you also need to consider a few important characteristics of line when you're standing there in front of your options. If you don't, you may come home with the wrong line and have to waste time returning the undesirable line when you could've been fishing.

Like anything else, as you gain experience, line shopping becomes second nature. After you cast a lure a thousand times or catch a hundred fish, you know what you like. Then buying line is just like buying socks: You know what size and style fits you best.

Information to get before you leave home

Virtually any tackle shop will have an area filled to the rafters with colourful boxes of fishing line. Usually, the boxes are marked with jumping fish, flashy graphics and a handful of numbers. It's a lot to process. But just as you shouldn't go grocery shopping on an empty stomach, you really shouldn't shop for line until you do just a little homework. Here's a breakdown of the important information you should find out before you ever set foot in the store:

> ✔ **Your reel's size limitations:** The manufacturer built your reel (and labelled it) for a particular size of line, and if you don't know what your reel is made to handle, you won't know what line to buy. (If you buy your reel as part of a combo deal, it may well come prespooled with line – meaning that you won't need to buy line for some time.) So check your reel first and see what size of line it recommends.
>
> ✔ **Your rod's size limitations:** Also check your rod – it, too, is marked, right above the handle, for a particular size of line.
>
> ✔ **Where you fish and what you pursue:** Line comes in a wide range of styles and sizes, but it's not complicated if you know your quarry. Is it a lake mostly open and free of snags like sunken trees? Are you fishing a river lined with sharp-edged rocks? Are most of the fish in the pond under ten pounds? Often, line of the same size can be bought in either extra tough (more abrasion resistant) or extra limp (better castability).

Be realistic about what you need for your conditions and buy the line that best fits your equipment and fishing situation.

Factors to consider when you're at the shop

Even if you have a rough idea of what you need in a fishing line, you can get confused at the store. Some line is expensive but lasts a long time. Some line is cheap and fishes like it: It kinks readily and breaks easily. Other spools may promise great strength but cast like a length of garden hose. Some line sacrifices strength for sensitivity. It's easy to get confused, but understanding the numbers on the spool will help you make the right choice.

Although you can buy line at almost every place you buy tackle, some staff are more knowledgeable and willing to help than others. Don't be afraid to ask for advice. But even if you're left to your own devices, you can choose a good line by following the advice in this section.

Most spools of line carry about 300 yards of line – that's plenty. (Your reel may only hold 100 yards.) You can save money by buying a bigger spool (allowing you to respool your reel many times over from one spool), but you may not want to commit to a giant spool of line until you're sure it delivers the performance you're seeking. And if you ask nicely some shops will even fill your reel for you. This is especially handy if you're unsure and avoids the hassle of having to do the job yourself.

Breaking up is never easy

It's inevitable that you'll get snagged from time to time when fishing, so what can you do? The first step is to try walking a few yards and changing the angle of the line, which might free the hook. If you're stuck fast however, you're going to have to grit your teeth and pull until something gives. Point the rod tip directly at the snag first: At least this way you won't break your rod by bending it obscenely hard. Apply some pressure and shake the rod tip up and down; sometimes this bounces the hook free. If not, it's time to bite the bullet. Clamp down on the reel spool and pull steadily, turning your face away in case anything should ping free in your direction!

Pole anglers cannot pull for a break like this, as pointing the pole straight at a snag could result in sections of rod shooting into the water. Instead, stretch the elastic until you can grab it. Now turn your face away and keep pulling, with a towel or other protection over your hand in case the hook suddenly shoots free.

Test

The word *test* as it applies to fishing line means that somebody tested the line and guaranteed it won't break if you apply a specific amount of force to it. In other words, if you apply anything less than 12 pounds of pull to a 12-pound test line, you *should* be fine. Apply more than 12 pounds of pull, and the line may part. A line made for ultra-light gear can be 2-pound test, and a line made for heavy duty work can be 100-pound test (or more!).

Line test isn't an absolute measurement. The give or stretch in the line, the kind of knot you use, how many fish you've caught with that line and other factors all figure into the equation, often to the advantage of the fish, not the angler. On the other hand, most manufacturers play it on the safe side when they list the line test, the same way that the weather people on TV do: They leave a little room for error.

After you learn how to play a fish, you might be surprised at how heavy a fish you can subdue with a relatively light line. Notice we said 'subdue.' Line isn't designed to *lift* fish. Most of the time, a large fish will be lifted out with a landing net (see Chapter 17). Just because the fish weighs 6 pounds doesn't mean you need 6-pound test line.

Look at it this way: Suppose you weigh 140 pounds (about 65 kilograms). If we stuck a hook in your lip, we bet you it would take a lot less than 140 pounds of force to lead you around. In fact, human beings are so wimpy that a pound or two of pressure should have you following along quite nicely. Fish are a little tougher, but still, we've caught 20-pound carp on 5-pound test. We've also lost 3-pound trout on 6-pound test. And remember: Sometimes you need to break your line by choice. If you snag on the bottom, you must break or cut your line. The heavier that line is, the harder this task becomes. Trust us – when you get snagged, it's better to have 6-pound line over 20-pound line.

Thickness

In fishing line, thin is usually better. Thin line cuts through the air with less resistance and likewise cuts more easily through the water. You can fit more of a thinner line on your spool. It throws less of a shadow in shallow water (a big consideration with spooky fish like trout or roach). It also usually knots more easily. For any given line material, the thinner product has a lighter line test rating: 6-pound test mono is thinner then 12-pound test mono of the same brand and style. But 12-pound braid is thinner than 12-pound mono. Again, it's all about balancing out your needs for a particular fishing situation.

A little quarter-ounce lure has a hard time pulling 20-pound test line off your reel. On the other hand, a two-ounce lure might snap off or give you a royal backlash if you try to cast it with 6-pound test line. Many lure manufacturers recommend a line weight and you can always ask the person at the tackle shop for a recommendation. But understand that it may be impossible to match your line to one exact lure, as you're sure to fish more than one kind of lure. Still, if you know you fish most of the time with lures or baits weighing less than an ounce, you can spool up line accordingly. You'll learn quickly what lures and rigs fish well on what kinds of line.

Flexibility

Flexibility, or limpness, is a good thing when you're fishing with bait, or lures with a delicate action. Heavy or stiff line can interfere with the action of the lure. (Sometimes anglers say that heavy line 'clotheslines,' meaning that it drags the bait or lure through the water with a very unlifelike action.) Generally, lighter, thinner line is limper than heavier line. Nylon monofilament is not as flexible as braided line.

Hook lengths

Many anglers finish their rigs with a short length of slightly finer line to tie their hook to. This *hook length* is there for two very good reasons: First, finer and more supple line presents the bait better. Secondly, should you get snagged or broken off, you'll only lose a hook and a few inches of line, rather than your whole rig and several yards of line (or that favourite float you couldn't bear to lose!).

Balance is the key with hook lengths. If your main line is 6-pound test, for example, a 4–5 pound hook length would be sensible. Attaching 3-pound line to 15-pound main line would be too much of a mismatch, posing a big risk of breaking the finer line.

Many companies sell ultra-thin hook length materials, which give great finesse for their strength. These are especially useful when you're targeting shy-biting fish (roach, crucian carp and skimmers, for example) with fairly small hooks and baits. The bait will behave more naturally and you'll get more bites. Whichever species you target, however, the last foot or two of line are vital and you'll seldom catch sly, big specimens with crude, conspicuous tackle.

The exception to this rule comes with meaner, bigger fish, however. When sea anglers tackle tope or conger, for example, a really tough abrasion-resistant *trace,* frequently made of wire, is often used to counter their abrasive mouths and dirty fighting tactics. Pike and zander require a length of wire at the business end of rigs because of their sharp teeth (more on this subject in Chapter 14).

Stretch

If you have a tendency to set the hook really hard, you should probably stick with monofilament line. Many newcomers, as well as a lot of longtime anglers, rear back the minute they feel a bite, sometimes yanking the hook right out of the fish's mouth. For the record, a positive lift is often all that's required. Thankfully for those who get a bit excited, most mono lines stretch.. In fighting the fish, mono absorbs more of the shock of any sudden twists or turns.. For all these reasons, monofilament is a good line for beginners.

On the other hand, stretchy line isn't ideal if you're the kind of person who has really sensitive fingertips and who can feel that tiny bump when a big perch plucks at a lure. If you're in this group, you probably want a line with less stretch in it so you can set the hook with a single, firm stroke. Braided line has almost no stretch, and fluorocarbon has just a little, so both types offer more sensitivity and control. Just know that they're less forgiving than monofilament, so you may need to adjust your techniques, such as trying softer hooksets. You may also need to adjust your gear to fish with braided or fluorocarbon line, such as using a longer rod and less drag on the reel.

Visibility

Almost all kinds of line can be found in different colours, including bright fluorescent ones. Some lines are made to literally glow when seen under an artificial light source such as a torch, which is helpful for anglers fishing at night for fish like cod. But what do these colours mean to the fish?

Working out the kinks

Line, especially monofilament kind, has a habit of coming off the reel in pesky coils. This is doubly true when you pick up your rod and reel for the first time after a winter lay-off. Look at it this way: You have a hard time straightening out right away after an hour or two's nap on the sofa, so it's not surprising that fishing line acts the same way after three months in the cupboard. Fixed spool reels are major offenders in the line-curling department.

One way to straighten your line is to take a good few yards off the reel and either attach a heavy weight or tie it to something fixed. When you've fed out the line, pull firmly. ('Firmly' doesn't mean a violent yank: Use steady, medium pressure.) Now wind the line back onto the reel under some tension. Don't use brute force, just enough to keep it tight

A good way of keeping uniform tension on the line is with the thumb and forefinger of your non-winding hand. (You also can hold the line with a towel, between the reel and the first guide, which will prevent friction burns on your hand.) Applying steady pressure assures that the line goes evenly onto the spool, which makes for smoother casts.

How line appears in dry air varies from how it appears underwater. Fluorocarbon line practically disappears underwater, although it can be seen above it. Some fluorescent line shows up nicely in the air but becomes pretty invisible in the water (especially at night). If you need a little extra help in seeing the above-surface part of your line, then fluorescent or brightly-coloured line can be worthwhile in detecting those subtle bumps that mean a fish has picked up your bait. They also make tangles easier to unpick. Such lines are usually the preserve of the sea angler.

Many anglers fish in ways that require the line be watched closely, as this is primarily how they detect bites. But as a general rule, you don't want the fish to see the line. Opaque or gaudy lines, as well as thick lines, put you at a disadvantage in clear water. The cloudier or dingier the water, or the less sunlight overhead, the less this factor comes into play. Bottom line: If you need to see your line, get line that you can see. But if your style of fishing isn't dependent on seeing the line, you're better off with fluorocarbon or neutral-coloured mono or braided line. For the majority of anglers, the best line colours are those that don't scare the fish, which means clear line, or lines in subtle green or brown shades.

Spooling Up: Attaching Line to a Reel

A reel must be spooled correctly, or your new line won't function as smoothly as it should, and it might twist. Follow the instructions included with the line, but the basics are as follows:

- **For fixed spool reels:** Attach the line to the reel's spool (see Chapter 14 for the correct knot) and lay the filler spool on the floor. Remember to run the line so that the bail arm is engaged first. (Don't worry if you forget; you'll officially be the one-millionth person to do so! *Tip:* Rather than retying your knot, remove the spool, run it around the bail and reattach it.) Holding the line in your free hand to apply some pressure, turn the handle with the other hand and begin to fill the reel's spool. Stop when it is halfway full, disengage the reel, and pull some line back off the reel. Does it twist and spin wildly? If so, flip the filler spool over on the ground. Remove the twist and resume filling the reel's spool. (Note: a reel filled almost to the *lip* or edge of the spool will cast far better than a half-filled reel. Do leave a gap of 2–3 mm to stop the last few metres spilling off, however.)

- **For multiplier reels:** Attach the line to the reel's spool (refer to Chapter 14 to find out which knot to use). Now ask someone to hold the filler spool by threading a pencil through the center of the spool. Your helper should hold the filler spool so that it is parallel to the reel's spool. This will allow the line to come off of one spool and smoothly go onto the other. Applying pressure to the line by pinching it a bit with your free hand, crank the reel slowly and proceed to fill the reel's spool. (***Note:*** Leave 5 mm or so of the reel's spool showing.)

Caring for Your New Line and Knowing When to Let It Go

You need to take care of your line. Great line that's worn out is still worn out line. After all, you only get so many chances at a dream fish, like the big carp that I (Dominic) once caught from a snaggy canal. As soon as the fish got up a head of steam, it made a berserk dash for the sanctuary of dense weeds. It's during moments like this that you suddenly think about the last time you checked and changed your line. With a large, stubborn fish, plus several pounds of dense undergrowth, the presence of nearly new 15-pound mono probably saved me a heart attack as well as allowing me to land the fish safely – a specimen I had waited for several nights to hook. Of course, a huge part of keeping your fishing line in good condition is knowing when line is past its prime. It doesn't matter how classy your rod, reel and all the rest of your tackle is if your line is a weak link. The sections that follow help you care for line and get rid of it when the time comes.

Protecting your line from wear and tear

The most common type of wear and tear is *abrasion,* weak spots in the line that can appear when a fish drags your line over rocks or against an over-hanging bank. (Think of an abrasion on your line like the nick you get on your knee when you trip over on concrete). The newest lines are extremely resistant to nicks and scuffs, but all lines eventually abrade to some degree. Braided line abrades fairly easily; monofilament lines less so. Damaged line will fail, sooner or later – usually, later, as in, later when a big fish is on your line.

After catching a fish (and sometimes after losing one), run your fingers along your line, especially that last 20 feet or so. If you feel a nick or rough spot, cut your line above the nick and re-tie your rig or lure. (Check out Chapter 14 for more on tying rigs.) In fact, after you've caught several hard fighting fish with the same setup, it might be a good idea to re-rig anyway. Many times, your line will develop invisible fatigue or stress points. It's better to take five minutes out and make the change than kick yourself for days later on.

Note: Most of the time, when you lose a fish, your line breaks because of a poor knot or structural failure of the line. Although it's true that the fish has to win sometimes, it's also true that many anglers (ourselves included) lose fish because they just don't take the time to re-rig.

You also need to watch out for damage caused by the following:

✔ **Sunlight:** Sunlight can affect your fishing line, especially if it's mono. So can heat. Like wine, fishing line should be stored in a cool, dark place. For most folks, storing means stacking a bunch of rods together in a corner of the basement or closet. Keep lines in a drawer or container, or alternatively a football sock makes a suitably dark place to store spools.

✔ **Saltwater:** If there is one chief enemy in the war against fishing tackle, it is salt, as in saltwater. It rusts and corrodes metal, dissolves synthetics, and in general, does the same number on your tackle as it does on all those corroded old cars you see when you're on the coast. Rinse all your tackle after fishing in saltwater, and that includes your line. You shouldn't let it sit for even a day.

Saying goodbye to old line

How often should you replace your line? Well, it depends on how you use it. If you fish once a week in an open lake, your line may well last you all summer. If cared for, line retains its strength for a long time. But certain factors speed up the wear and tear process: Fishing around snags hurts line, as does salt-water or sunlight. Catching a lot of fish will wear out a line. So inspect your line visually and with your fingers before every trip.

If your line has been on the spool for over a year (or even if you're not quite sure that it has), replace it. To remove line from a reel, just disengage the reel, pull the line off the spool and cut the line-to-reel knot (see Chapter 14 for the scoop on this knot.)

After you take line off your reel, you're left with a handful of line that is really of no use to anyone. Some stores keep a box for old line – it can and should be recycled. (Greg stores his old line in a grocery bag until it gets full and then takes the whole bag in to be recycled.) At the very least, throw used line away in a proper waste receptacle. Line litter is an eyesore and a serious hazard to birds and other wildlife. Many anglers take the step of cutting their old line into short fragments before they bin it, so the line won't tangle or harm anything.

Setting Your Sights on Fly Lines

A fly line is a totally different animal from all other fishing line. When legering, float fishing or spinning the weight of your terminal tackle pulls the line off the reel and carries it to the fish. Fly fishing is just the opposite. The weight of the line carries the relatively weightless fly to the fish.

Back in the not-so-good old days, fly line was made from braided horsehair. If you wanted a heavy line, you braided more hairs. The modern fly line is a smooth plastic coating around a core of braided nylon or Dacron. Most lines are 30 to 40 metres long and are spliced to another hundred yards or so of thinner backing line (usually braided Dacron). The backing line is purely there in case you hook a big fish which takes you well out into the river or lake; obviously if you have no more line to give out the chances are you'll be broken off. When you buy line or a reel, see if the store put the backing on and splice or knot it to your line. You can also do this yourself.

The sections that follow fill you in on some of the basics about fly lines, as well as their ever-present companions, leaders.

Looking at the types of fly lines

For most of the time, fly fishers use floating lines. In fact, some who regularly visit shallow lakes and rivers may use nothing but a floater all season, even when they use flies which sink. All well and good, you might say, until a you encounter a situation where the need arises to present a fly deeper. Hence fly rodders use different kinds of lines for different fishing situations. Often, this means using some kind of weight to get down to fish that aren't surface feeders, such as trout cruising well below the surface on a reservoir, or, pike hugging the bottom of a deep river.

These days, you have the choice of using sinking lines where the front of the line is weighted and the rest floats for easy casting. A couple of types of sinking lines exist:

- **Intermediate line** sinks very slowly so that it can be fished as a floater or a sinker. This is a very versatile line for when you might need to search a little deeper to find the fish. It also cuts through the surface chop and keeps you in contact with your fly. So called 'fast intermediate' lines are similar, but get down slightly quicker still.

- **Full sinking (FS) line** gets down fast and deep. The best are the really thin lines that have come on the market in recent years. They are slim, so they cut through the wind, and they aren't so hellish to pick up and cast as the old lead core.

  You often see a rating on the line such as Di-5 or Di-7. This simply refers to how quickly the line sinks in inches. A Di-7 would sink at around seven inches per second – pretty quickly, in other words. This could be really useful if your chosen fishery is a real bottomless pit of a lake.

Sensible anglers take more than one line with them to prepare for the unknown. The floating line is the one you'll probably use eight or nine times out of ten, but most fly reels come with spare spools enabling you to carry other lines if you need to switch. A floater, an intermediate and a fast sinker would cover almost any eventuality.

Considering the weight and taper of fly line before you buy

Buying fly line is a little different than buying line for other types of fishing. Instead of looking at characteristics such as test and stretch (see the earlier related sections), you're more concerned with the weight of the line and the type of taper, as explained in the following sections.

The weight of the line

The weight of the line is what bends the rod, allowing the rod to spring forward and shoot the line towards the fish. Fly lines come with different ratings according to their weight, and rods are rated according to the weight of the line they throw. A One Weight is a very light line that is used with an extremely delicate rod. As the numbers go up, so does the weight. Most trout fishermen prefer something in the Four to Seven range. Salmon, pike and bass demand rods of at least an 8 weight and often higher if you are to exert any control over big flies and formidable fish.

Although there are no hard and fast rules, Table 8-1 lists some recommendations for line (and rod) weights for common fish. Don't forget that coarse fish will also take a fly; some favourites are included here along with the game species.

Table 8-1	Fly Line Weights and Common Game Fish
Line Weight	**Type of Fish**
One, Two and Three Weight	Brown trout on small streams, dace
Four Weight, Five Weight	Brown and rainbow trout, grayling, chub, roach and rudd
Six Weight, Seven Weight	Brown and rainbow trout
Eight Weight, Nine Weight	Reservoir trout, salmon, pike, bass, carp
Ten Weight, Eleven Weight	Large pike and salmon, adventure fishing for big saltwater species

With graphite rods, you can usually go up or down one line weight from the recommended number and still be able to cast reasonably effectively. For optimum performance though, stick to the recommended ratings.

The type of taper

Most fly lines have a *taper;* that is, they are fatter in one part then another. The most common taper is *weight forward* (often shortened to WF). It is heavier in the head, which is the first few metres of line to come through the guides of your rod. The principle behind this is that you want to get a lot of leverage on the rod to develop momentum quickly, and then, when you have rapid line speed, the weight of the head will carry the rest of the line. In other words the weight-forward line is ideal for *delivery* of the fly.

X marks the tippet spot

If you ever catch a nice trout – make that *when* you catch a nice trout – you will be asked, 'What did you take it on?' This is actually two questions. The first is 'What fly?' and the second is 'What tippet?' Tippets are rated according to their thickness, which is directly related to their strength. Where the spin fisherman might say 'I caught it on 12-pound test,' the fly rodder's answer might be '1X.' Confusingly enough, the higher the number before the X, the lighter the strength of the line; 4X would typically be around 5 pound test. 6X or 7X would be super fine stuff for shy fish in clear water.

Tippets perform a similar task to the coarse angler's hook length; they form a more delicate final length of line which is often knotted to a stronger leader. Having finer line at the end not only makes for a subtler presentation, it also means that should you snag up the chances are you'll only lose a short section of line.

Why X? In the old days, leader tippets used to be made out of silk worm gut. They were sized by being passed through a die that shaved down the thickness of the gut. If you ran it through the die once, it was 1X; twice gave you 2X; and so on. The more shavings it got, the thinner the leader. So the higher numbers represent thinner, lighter leaders.

You will see some fly lines marked with a saltwater taper or pike taper. These, too, are weight-forward lines with a more exaggerated taper which help to cast the large flies used by pike and sea anglers.

Less common these days than it used to be is the *double taper* (or DT for short). This design is thin in the head, gradually fattens out, and then slims again. The idea is you have a good amount of line in the air to develop momentum, yet the line that lands nearest to the trout does so more delicately than the weight-forward variety. You have to be a pretty sensitive angler to be able to appreciate double taper; when you want more delicacy of presentation, it may be easier to just go to a lighter rod and line. They are good for river anglers, however, and DT lines have the added advantage that they are the same at each end, meaning you can reverse the line when one side gets old, saving you the money you might have spent on a new line.

Threading your fly line

Usually, when you thread line through your coarse or sea fishing rod, you pick up the end of the line and thread it through the guides. When you try to do this with heavy fly line, it will find a way to slip back down and make you start all over again. The easy way is to pull off about six feet of line, double it over, and pull the doubled line through the guides. That way, when you accidentally drop the line, the loop catches on the guides and doesn't slip all the way through to the reel.

Be kind to your fly lines

A little TLC goes a long way towards making your fly line not only last longer but perform better. Grit, dirt and general use can all make lines a little tired, so the occasional clean in warm water (without detergent) is a good call. If left unused for a while, fly line can also form coils, so after a lay-off you might want to carefully stretch it as you would conventional fishing line. Finally, floating lines work best when they sit crisply on the surface. When the final few feet start to sink you might risk missing bites as well as spooking fish, so treat your floating fly line to a quick smear of mucilin (sold by most tackle shops in small tubs with a fabric pad to apply it evenly).

Throwing leaders into the mix

After the *fly* (your offering, often a tiny hook covered with feathers or yarn and made to look like an insect or other prey), the most critical element of the fly fishing setup is the *leader*, meaning the nylon monofilament line that connects the fly line to the fly. A fly line is big and thick, and a fly is delicate and small. The leader must also be light; otherwise, it will overpower the fly, giving it a lifeless action. A big, fat fly line landing next to a spooky fish is guaranteed to send it straight for cover. A leader that makes as little disturbance as possible increases your chances of connecting with a fish.

As you can see in Figure 8-1, the thick section of the leader that joins to the fly line is called the *butt*. What happens between the butt and the fly is a gradual *taper* as the leader gets progressively thinner and lighter. The result is a smooth and even transfer of force from the rod to the line and down through the leader. The last section of the taper is also known as the *tippet*.

Figure 8-1:
The sections of the leader are the butt, taper, and tippet.

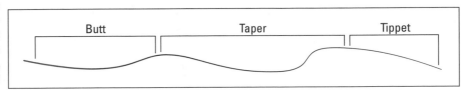

Leaders are usually between 7 and 12 feet (2 and 4 metres) in length. You can buy them knotted or knotless (look for them sold as 'tapered leaders' by tackle shops). The taper of a knotted leader is made up of progressively lighter lengths of monofilament line knotted together. The knotless type, is just a single strand that smoothly tapers.

When you change flies a lot, you end up cutting off and replacing tippet. Using a knotted leader is a handy way to remember what thickness you are fishing. On the other hand, if you are just starting out, knotless is pretty simple, so keep it simple. You can always go with a knotless, tapered leader and tie your own 2–3 foot length of tippet to the end. Tippet material is sold in tiny spools, which makes it convenient to replace.

Chapter 9

It's Terminal (Tackle): Hooks, Weights, Snaps, Swivels and Floats

A t first glance, this may appear to be one of the most boring chapters in *Fishing For Dummies*. It lacks the illustrations of the fish ID chapters, and the excitement of the fishing techniques chapter But wait , there's more here that you need to know, in fact – what we cover in this chapter is both interesting and crucial to your fishing success! *Terminal tackle* refers to the equipment that accompanies your line on its way to the fish. Although rods and reels matter, and it's hard to overstate the importance of line, your understanding of terminal tackle will greatly influence the number of fish you catch. In fact, those last few feet and inches of tackle are the most critical of all.

Hooks: What They Do and Why They Matter

Put simply, the invention of the fish hook changed history. More effective than spears or bare hands, fish hooks allowed humans to fish deeper water and opened the door for so many things, including, many centuries later, the thick catalogues of fishing gear we get through the post. Of course, those first anglers were crude, smelly individuals, speaking in grunts and barely capable of thought outside of what bait to try next. Come to think of it, they sound a bit like some of my friends.

The first hook-type devices, called *gorges,* were used during the Stone Age. Gorges were small pieces of wood or bone sharpened on both ends, with a line tied to the centre. When embedded in bait, the entire gorge could be swallowed by a fish, and when the line jerked tight, the gorge would lodge across the throat of the fish. (This is handy to know in a survival situation – it's hard to carve a hook, but you can easily make a gorge.) Later, the traditional fish hook was carved from bone. The invention of metal made for better fish hooks, and after centuries of progress, today's hooks are sometimes chemically sharpened and surgical in their effectiveness. But the basic shape of the hook remains the same.

Thanks to improved hooks and hook-setting techniques, along with the growing use of barbless hooks, it's now possible to release virtually all the fish you catch. (I don't think catch-and-release fishing was as popular in cave man days.) Whether you're using a single hook on a bait rig, or a lure with three treble hooks, your hope for landing a fish lies with that curved steel. Hooks are the key. Buy quality hooks, inspect them often, and don't cast them unless they hold your utmost confidence.

This section covers many types of hooks. Most of these have the classic J shape, but otherwise vary quite a bit. We have small, delicate hooks for shy-biting fish and we have large powerful hooks intended for big baits and monster fish. Like rods and reels, there is no 'one size fits all' hook. It's very much a case of horses for courses: you wouldn't kill a house fly with a machine gun, just as you wouldn't go into battle armed with a fly swat.

Apart from the classic J-hook, some other styles are also worth mentioning. Treble hooks are commonly used either on lures or when fishing for bony-mouthed predators such as pike.. Circle hooks are another very different looking type of hook, used mostly by sea anglers. Since they seem to hook fish cleanly in the side of the jaw they are good for catch-and-release but require the angler to tighten up steadily rather than striking in the usual fashion. Circles are probably best left until you've mastered the J-hook. Figure 9-1 shows the main types of hooks.

Figure 9-1:
The standard J hook (a), circle hook (b) and treble hook.

a   b   c

Following are the most important parts of a typical hook (see Figure 9-2):

✔ The *point* is where tackle meets fish. As in many situations in life, the first impression is an important one. If you don't have a good sharp point on your hook, you can have the most expensive rod in the world, but you won't catch fish.

✔ The *barb* is a type of a reverse point that is designed to keep a fish on the hook after the fish bites. Bigger is not better with barbs. Big barbs can make setting a hook difficult when the hook meets up with a tough-mouthed fish like a pike. A severe barb can also damage the mouth of a fish, so many tackle companies have switched to far kinder, smaller *micro barbs*. Better still, you could use barbless hooks, and indeed many fisheries now insist on their use.

One way to help speed up the catch and release process is to *debarb* (remove the barbs from) your hooks. Simply take a pair of pliers (needlenose work best) and crimp the barb against the hook's tip. Remember that you're not using a wire cutter here, and you're not trying to take the whole point off the hook. On most hooks, a small amount of pressure on the barb does the trick. Both J hooks and trebles can be debarbed. (Debarbing also makes it much easier to remove a hook from your skin if you happen to hook yourself. And you probably will – it happens to the best of us.)

✔ The *bend* is the curved part of the hook, and all those fine-sounding hook names, such as Limerick or Sproat, have something to do with the bend. Actually, such hook names have to do with two parts of the bend: the throat and the gape. Think of the *throat* as the depth that the hook penetrates. Think of the *gape* as the width of the hook, from point to shank. A relatively wide gape may be the best option with certain baits that can clog up narrower hooks making the hook point less efficient. For example, a big chunk of luncheon meat or peeler crab might easily mask the point of a narrow hook; time to go for a wide gape.

If the hook straightens out, you are using a hook that is either too light (referring to the *gauge* of the wire) or too big in the gape for the amount of pressure that you (not the fish) applied. Losing a fish this way happens to everybody; but still, developing a sense of how much pressure your tackle can take is part of becoming an educated angler.

✔ The *shank* connects the bend to the eye. A shank can be long or short. As with gape, a longer shank means that a hook is easier for a fish to bend. So why aren't all hooks short-shanked? The answer has to do with what goes on the hook. A short-shanked hook isn't very effective for threading on a worm (see Chapter 12), but a longer-shanked worm hook is. A longer-shanked hook makes it easier to unhook a fish, too. Sometimes the shank of a sea fishing hook has a barb or two to help hold bait more securely. These are called baitholder hooks.

✔ The *eye* of the hook (the loop through which line passes) may be turned up, turned down, or straight. Some hooks have no eye at all, but just a flat section where the eye would usually be. These are called *spade end* hooks and are tied on with a spade end knot, in which the line is whipped around the shank of the hook. These are best left for when you gain more experience, although some swear they present a small bait more naturally.

✔ The *gauge* refers to the diameter of the hook's wire. Heavier gauge hooks resist bending even when embedded in the mouth of a big fish. Smaller gauge hooks are lighter and easier to hide. The heavier the gauge, the stronger the tackle required to set the hook on the strike.

✔ The *finish* refers to the coating on the hook. Some hooks wear a finish to protect them from saltwater, others are even finished in colours such as gold or red. It adds to the options you have in selecting hooks.

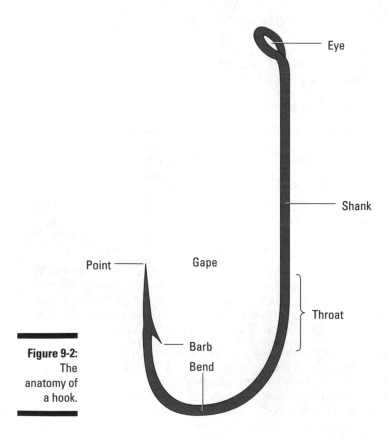

Eye

Shank

Point

Gape

Throat

Barb

Bend

Figure 9-2:
The anatomy of a hook.

Keeping a range of hooks

Look at the display of hooks in a tackle shop and you'll meet with a whole host of names and key words. These tags are not there to bamboozle you but to provide helpful clues as to their intended use. Hooks with 'match', 'fine' or 'silver fish' would usually be intended for small baits and delicate presentation for example. Words like 'power' 'specimen', or 'specialist' denote greater strength for bigger species. Some hooks are even named after the baits they're designed for ('maggot', 'corn', 'crab' and so on) or particular methods or species ('feeder', 'bass' and so on).

Beginners often get bogged down when selecting hooks, but it doesn't have to be complicated. Know this: Some hooks work better than others with particular baits or methods. A small, fine wire hook would be spot on for catching roach on maggots, for example. If you wanted to target big carp on the other hand, you would need something stronger and larger. But you can't predict from one trip to the next exactly what hooks a situation will call for.

Suppose you like fishing in the local river, and you always carry a packet or two of hooks ideal for maggots.to catch roach and dace. But one day you find some big perch that like a large worm. After digging up some big, juicy lobworms for your next trip, you find that your existing hooks are miles too small; they just get swamped by a worm and you miss bites.. But if you carry a range of hooks, you can easily tie on a larger hook that presents a lobworm perfectly. A good angler is ready for new baits or new fish.

The solution is an easy one: Buy a range of separate hooks that will work for your fishing location. If you fish a rocky sea mark, for example, you may want some small hooks to fish worm or prawn baits to catch anything that comes along, but equally, you may also want some bigger hooks to try for bigger species with a meaty mouthful such as a whole peeler crab or a small fish. Manufacturers often package hooks in species-specific packets, and sales staff will help, as well. But the bottom line is this: Begin assembling a range of hooks like the ones in Figure 9-3, from tiny to large, and in a few styles. You want to be ready to fish for whatever fish presents itself, with whatever bait is available and needed. Using a hook too small will result in missed bites or, worse still, swallowed hooks – making the hook difficult to remove and endangering the fish. A hook that is too large will look unnatural and may be avoided by the fish.

Although hooks come in a variety of shapes and styles, they also come in a tremendous range of sizes – from hooks bigger than your thumb to tiny hooks smaller than the word 'to' in this sentence. The classification system for hooks confuses some people, but here's what you need to know: When you use the word 'size' before you give the number of the hook, you are dealing with smaller hooks (as in, 'I caught it on a size 6 hook.'). The *higher* the number, the *smaller* the hook. A size 6 hook is much bigger than a size 20 hook. And by the way, hook sizes are counted by twos (14, 12, 10, 8 and so on) with no odd numbers until size 1. Actually, the measuring system changes at 1 when zeroes then appear (written 1/0, 2/0 and the like) In the zeroes or 'O's', the higher the number, the bigger the hook. So a size 28 is tiny, a size 1 is bigger, and a 2/0 is bigger still.

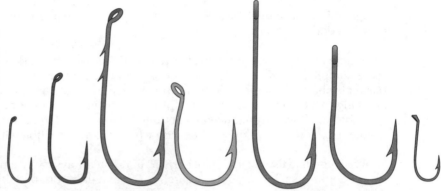

Figure 9-3:
A typical range of hooks the general-species angler should carry at all times.

As a very rough guide, it's worth mentioning that sea anglers tend to use bigger hooks (typically from size 2 and right into the zeroes). This is because sea baits tend to be larger and the fish have bigger mouths and are less suspicious (many are only caught once!). Coarse anglers tend to use hooks in the 6–20 range, with big baits such as boilies and meat at the thicker end of the scale, maggots at the other. Fly fishers use quite a wide range; a 3/0 would make a decent pike fly, but a size 20 would be a more likely size for a trout angler's tiny black gnat fly.

Making a point

Dull hooks rarely catch fish. Whichever type you use, only sharp hooks get the job done.

Some anglers think they have a sharp hook as long as the hook's point pricks the skin. But a hook is more than a needle. Even though the point of a hook is relatively small, the point has some area and edge to it. That edge, just like the edge of a knife, needs to be sharp to cut into the fish beyond the end of the barb. Driving the hook home to this depth is called *striking.* How to do this, when to do this, and how hard to do this are all-important elements of angling technique. But you'll never get a chance to show off all your mind-blowing techniques with dull hooks.

The smaller hooks are inexpensive (often not much more than 10p each) and so it is false economy to use the same one for several trips. In fact, competition anglers quite often change to a new hook mid-match to ensure they maintain top performance. Freshen up regularly, at least at the start of each session, for best results, or you'll *bump* fish. By bumping, anglers mean those times you feel something on the strike but the hook doesn't penetrate.

With larger hooks, and especially those on flies and lures, a hook sharpener is a good idea. You sharpen a hook just as you would sharpen a knife, with a file or sharpening steel. Special hook hones and files are made expressly for this purpose. How often you check and sharpen hooks is your call, but punishing environments such as a rocky river or snaggy sea bed could take the edge off a hook fairly quickly. If your experience is like ours, you'll neglect sharpening *until* you lose a good fish. However, before you put on a lure, it's always best to run your file along the edge of your lure's hook to get it good and sharp.

Some manufacturers use chemical sharpening now, which means that hook points are honed in the factory not with a file, but with the application of various coats of chemicals. The result is a scary-sharp hook. But it's hard for you to re-sharpen chemically sharpened hooks. I've (Greg) noticed with my chemically sharpened hooks that the extra-sharp point can roll over itself when the point snags or hits a rock or something. Assuming I free the hook after it becomes snagged, I inspect the point. If the point is rolled, the hook goes in the bin. I could never get it sharp enough again with a file. It may seem like a waste of money, but I consider it part of the cost of doing business. I want confidence in my hooks, so I invest in plenty. Sooner or later, every hook gets lost or has to be replaced. Love your hooks, but be ready to let them go.

Spark plug files (which you can find in any car parts shop) make good hook sharpeners. This makes sense when you consider that spark plug points (like fishhooks) are small, have a narrow gap, and are made of metal. Fly fishers who find themselves out in a stream with a dull hook and no file may try using the striking surface on a matchbook cover to touch up their hooks. For the sake of five to ten quid though, it's well worth buying a hook sharpener, especially if you're a lure or fly angler.

J hooks: Some things never change

By a J hook we simply refer to any commonly found hook with the shape of that letter (most of them in other words). J hooks work because they fit into a fish's mouth and then catch on something on the way out, and they've worked that same way for a long time. Not every J hook is the same, though, and many styles put a twist (sometimes quite literally) on the standard. Any fish that swims can be caught on the right J hook.

Buy J hooks that match your intended target. What's the typical mouth size of the fish you hope to catch? Crucian carp, for example, have small mouths; even a big specimen would have to open wide to bite the tip of your thumb. So using giant hooks to fish for crucians is only likely to result in choice language and hooks stripped of bait. Then again, other fish are the opposite; cod, for example, have huge mouths and like big, meaty baits. Hence cod fishers like a large, wide-gaped hook.

Striking with J hooks

When a fish bites a baited hook or lure, you've been successful: You've seduced that fish into making a connection with you. But that connection – through the rod and reel, down the line, across any terminal tackle your rig consists of, and culminating in the sharp hook you've selected – is a tenuous one. You need to act quickly and wisely to ensure that the fish stays connected to you. This is called *striking*, and it's the process by which the hook passes from merely being in the fish's mouth to being through the fish's mouth. When fishing with J hooks, setting the hook means tightening the line, and lifting the rod decisively back toward you, driving the hook into the fish's mouth.

Different species call for different hooksets, and different baits call for different tactics. For example, fish such as conger and pike have bony mouths and so a firm strike is best to drive the hook home. Carp are bulky and big mouthed fish which often give decisive bites, hence a measured lift is better than a solid yank, which could break the line. Some fish are lightning quick; dace and small trout need a fast, decisive strike, for example. Others, like bream and perch, may work free if you set the hook too hard. But the following tips should work for you most of the time, with most fish caught on most rigs.

- ✔ **Keep a relatively tight line between your hook and your reel at all times.** When fishing with a float rig, for example, slack line can form between your rod and the float. When a fish bites and the float sinks, that fish is ready to be hooked, but the slack line can prevent you from driving the hook home. By the time you furiously crank up the loose line, the fish may have ejected the bait and moved away. Avoid too much slack line, and be ready to set the hook at any time.

- ✔ **Let the rod help you.** As you sweep the rod overhead, the rod should bend. This bend is providing the force that sets the hook. If your rod isn't bending on the hookset, you're not providing enough force. The other possibility is that there remains too much slack in the line. If that happens, quickly reel up the slack and set the hook again. The fish may still be on the line!

- ✔ **Strike quickly.** We don't usually advise waiting to set the hook, unless it's one of those odd situations. Look at it this way – if you feel a fish tap your bait, or your float goes under, that fish has your hook in its mouth. A fish can't move your bait with its hands! If the bait is in a fish's mouth, then the hook should be able to find purchase. Some folks will tell you to wait, to 'make sure he has it' or something, but most of the time this pause results in a *deep-hooked* fish. A swallowed hook can lead to an inadvertent fish death, and is usually the result of waiting too long to set the hook. Your goal should be to land every fish that bites, but also to be able to release every fish you land.

✔ **Go the distance.** There is a big difference between striking a fish under your feet and hitting one sixty yards out. At close quarters, a hefty strike could be overkill and you may even break the line on a heavy fish. Fishing at long distance is the opposite – there will often be more slack line to pick up, and if you're using mono there may be quite a bit of stretch to contend with, hence a more powerful, sweeping strike may be required. Braid has far less stretch than mono and therefore you don't need to strike as hard.

Keeping J hooks organised

As we explain in the earlier section 'Keeping a Range of Hooks,' you really can't avoid accumulating more than a few styles and sizes of hooks. Having a good variety of J hooks on hand will find you ready for about any fishing challenge. But although you may lump all your floats together or carry a box of assorted weights, you should keep your hooks divided.

Special magnetic hook boxes or containers with lots of little compartments are readily available and very handy to stay organised and keep your hooks dry. Separate your hooks in your tackle carrier by placing different sizes in different compartments. Sort by size and function. Put small hooks for maggots, casters and the like in one place, larger hooks for meat or boilies in another. Hooks have a nasty habit of tangling together when stored in proximity, making it harder to remove the hook you need when you need it. Picking a tiny hook from a snarl of hooks is like reaching into a bag of needles.

Treble hooks: Extra points

Treble hooks are a more specialised beast than simple J-hooks, but quite widespread in their use by anglers using lures or targeting predators such as pike and zander. As the name suggests, these hooks are effectively three in one, and those additional points are worthy of caution and respect.

So why use three points? Usually the reason is because the single point of a J-hook is easily lost against a large lure or bait (say a six-inch plug or a whole sardine cast for pike). Anglers using whole fish baits often use a pair of trebles; one of the points of each treble goes into the bait to hold it in place, the others stand proud. Several companies now make *semi-barbed* trebles. These are trebles where only one point is barbed – the one intended to stick into and hold the bait, the other points are barbless. These are a great idea, because a pike can engulf a bait greedily, and the last thing you want is several barbs to contend with as well as all those teeth (more on pike and predator rigs in Chapter 14).

Just like other hooks, trebles need to be looked after. The treble hooks on lures, in particular, may be used many times and if you don't check them for wear and tear, the fish certainly will! Use a hook sharpener regularly on the trebles of lures, and if they show any signs of rust they should be replaced.

Barbed, barbless or 'bumped' hooks?

There is some debate amongst anglers as to whether barbed or barbless hooks are better. You might think that more fish are lost on barbless hooks, but as long as you keep the line tight when playing fish, losses are surprisingly few. A barbless hook will actually penetrate more easily on the strike too. The biggest advantage of a barbless hook is how easy it is to remove from a fish; you can often just stroke one backwards with your index finger and it will slip out effortlessly. This ease of unhooking also equates to less handling and less time out of the water for your catch, definitely a good thing.

Some maintain, however, that the sticking power of a small barb is best. Certainly, for large fish a barbless hook can shift during a longer fight, perhaps doing more damage than a barbed hook which stays put. The large, brutal barbs found on cheap hooks are inevitably bad news for fish, but most modern hooks have small micro-barbs which do minimal damage. If you're fishing for just one or two bites a session, using big hooks for big fish, you could even break the hook in half to remove it from your catch with no damage.

A third solution, and perhaps the ideal compromise, is to use a 'bumped' hook. To create this effect, take a pair of pliers and apply steady pressure to the barb. Use enough force to remove the sharp profile of the barb, but not so much that it is squashed flat. You are now left with a bump rather than a barb; a hook with some staying power but still easily removed without damaging your catch.

Dehooking yourself

If you fish, someday, somewhere, you will hook yourself. You may reach up to pull down a tree branch where a fly has snagged. You start to disentangle the fly. Then the branch springs back, and you have a fly right in the meaty part of your finger. Or maybe you have pulled in a nice pike that you caught on a professor spoon. You grab the beast under the chin (just like the book says to do), and the pike decides to give one last shake that leaves you semi-permanently attached to a lively pike. In both cases, you have the same reaction: You want to get that hook out of you!

You have a number of choices. First, if the lure is still attached to the fish you have landed (or anything else for that matter), cut the line to free the lure. Sometimes you can continue to push the hook all the way through the wound and out again. This action is somewhat painful, but sometimes doable. You can then break the hook with a suitable tool. Pike anglers often carry wire cutters for the purpose of removing awkwardly caught treble hooks without damaging the fish, but they are also useful for emergencies in which you are the one hooked!

Another method, favoured by many anglers, looks as if it shouldn't work, but it does, as long as you have a J hook imbedded in you. You need to have some confidence in this method, or you may not do very well. You could even try practising this on a piece of raw meat until you understand what you are doing. After you get the idea, it all makes sense.

The following steps, which are illustrated in Figure 9-4, show you how to remove a hook that is embedded in some part of your body.

1. **Take a two-foot length of at least 25-pound test line and tie the ends together so that you have a loop.**

   If you do not have 25-pound test line, then double a few strands of 10-pound or 12-pound test line.

2. **Loop the line over your wrist, and form a small loop between your thumb and forefinger.**

3. **Take this small loop and put it around the hook in the centre of the hook's bend.**

4. **With your other thumb, press down on the eye of the hook.**

   This action should open the wound enough for you to gently back the barb out of your flesh. Getting the barb clear of the flesh is *very* important. If you do not get the barb clear, you should not continue with this procedure.

5. **Finally, pull on the small loop with a sharp jerk.**

   The hook should come free with relatively little pain to you.

Of course, prevention is the best practice when it comes to hooking injuries, and you can deflect many wandering hooks with a hat and a pair of glasses. Wear them. Indeed, most fly fishers see polarising sun glasses as essential to avoid the risk of a wayward cast or sudden gust of wind directing a fly into an eye! Prevention is better than cure, but accidents do happen and so it's a good idea to bring that first-aid kit, stocked with antiseptic and bandages, that we recommend in Chapter 6!

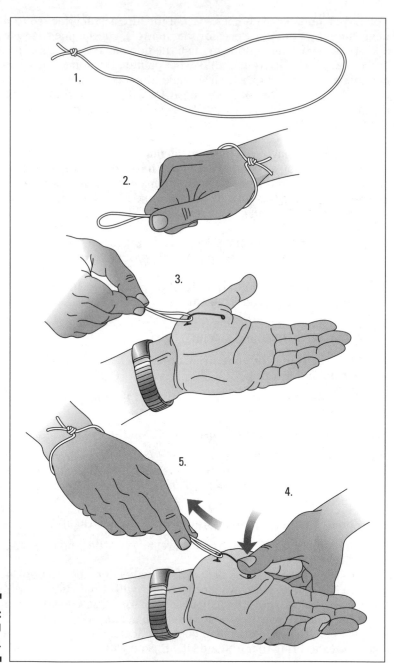

Figure 9-4:
Getting a J
hook out.

Leads and Sinkers: When You Need To Get Down to the Fish

Weights or *sinkers* are used to pull your baited hook down to where the fish are. They also serve as casting mass should you need to throw the bait well out from the bank or shore to reach the fish. Sinkers are traditionally made of poured lead (in fact they're often simply referred to as *leads*), but they're increasingly being made of other heavy substances due to concerns about the environmental and health impacts of lead. Whatever they're made of, sinkers vary a great deal in shape and function. Similar to hooks, weights are your friends and can be used to present your bait effectively.

When using weights, sometimes just a split shot or two does the trick (we describe these in the next section). At other times (for example, when fishing in a moving current), you need much more lead. Otherwise your bait could be swept helplessly along the bottom, picking up weed and snags on the way.

Other types of weight do far more than simply let you cast out and stay on the bottom. *Swimfeeders* (often just referred to as *feeders*) are weighted devices which hold ground bait to attract fish to your hook. Other weights are designed for use with only a short length of line between hook and lead, the idea being that the fish try to move off with the bait, feel the weight of the lead, and hook themselves in the process.

Selecting the right range of weights

Fish are not usually bothered by fishing weights. The important part is the bait and the presentation of that bait. So think about weights and sinkers in this way: Their only purpose is to help you present your bait. If you can present your bait in an effective way without a weight, by all means do it! In fact, one of the simplest and most effective ways to fish is with just a line and a hook, often called *free lining*. But if your bait is not reaching the fish due to current or the fact that your bait is not sinking deep enough, employ a weight. Various weights are available at any store that carries tackle, and the different styles are labelled with their weight in grams and/or ounces.

In sinkers, shape influences function. As shown in Figure 9-5, a number of sinker choices are available.

The following are the most common types of weight:

- **Bombs** are standard, pear- or roughly oval-shaped leads with an eye at the top. These are commonly used for *legering* which means presenting a bait on the bottom with a lead. Both coarse and sea anglers use these often.

  Some of these leads or bombs come in special shapes. For example 'distance' or 'torpedo' leads are streamlined for long casts.

- **Watch leads and grip leads** are designed to hold better on the bottom in strong currents or tides. These are either flatter and/or more contoured for better grip. A sea angler's grip lead has wire arms which dig in to the bottom for added stability

- **In-line sinkers** work differently to regular leads. They have a central hole drilled through the middle and are made to slide on the mainline. These are often used for carp fishing *bolt rigs* in which the fish picks up the bait and hooks itself against the weight.

- **Drilled bullets** are small in-line sinkers that are used with sea or pike floats. Some are simple drilled balls or ovals, others are labelled as 'pike' or 'egg' sinkers and have rubber sleeves to fit snugly on the line.

- **Swimfeeders** are clever devices that not only provide weight, but attract the fish. The mass is provided by metal, while a frame holds bait to attract the fish. These come in several types and various sizes, from dinky little things you might sling into the local canal to heavyweights designed for big rivers.

- **Maggot feeders** are little weighted containers you fill with maggots before sealing with a lid. On the bottom, the maggots crawl out and attract fish, which will then happily chomp the maggots on your hook.

- **Open-ended or groundbait feeders** are tube-shaped devices into which you squeeze groundbait. When you cast out, this disperses in an attractive cloud which draws the fish in like nobody's business.

- **Method feeders** are a newer invention. They work like in-line sinkers, but unlike other feeders have a hard frame to which you attach sticky groundbait. Your own hook bait is presented on a very short length of line, either buried inside or just outside the mix. The fish (most often carp) attack the sticky ground bait on the feeder before grabbing the hook bait and hooking themselves against weight of the feeder.

- **Split shot** are most often used to *cock* a float, which simply means to make it sit correctly in the water with just the tip showing. They also serve to make little adjustments to other rigs. They were once made of lead, but now all shot is non-toxic to avoid danger to swans and other wildlife. Split shot come in various sizes, with a system of letters and numbers. The biggest are denoted by letters with SSG being the biggest followed by AA and BB. The other shot sizes go from a size 1 to a size 10, the higher the number the smaller the shot. The tiniest are often called *dust shot*; these are used to make subtle adjustments to float rigs.

✓ **Tungsten putty** is another simple way of adding weight to various rigs. It comes in small tubs and you mould it onto your line. This is brilliant for a quick fix way of adding weight. For example, a little pinch on the line could help you balance a carp rig, or make a wet fly sink a little quicker. It's handy stuff.

Figure 9-5: Several weights.

Start your collection of weights by picking up a variety pack of split shot. The best way to buy them is in a circular dispenser which holds a variety of shot from small to large sizes. These will serve you well in a variety of situations, and they're the kind you're most likely to need.

A few sinkers or bombs are also a must – especially if you intend to fish at longer distances or target moving water. Get a range of weights in sinkers, all the way up to several ounces, because you never know how fast and strong the current will be. Sea anglers, especially, demand large leads commonly in the 3–6 ounce (85 to 170 gram) bracket, and it's worth taking a few wired grip leads too. Coarse anglers needn't go so heavy, but a few sinkers from half an ounce to two ounces (15–60 grams) will be useful, with perhaps a few heavier models if you're after carp, pike or barbel.

If you start with a few sinkers of various types and carry a range of weights, you should be ready for most situations. If you find that you can't fish the way you want to, you'll know what kind (or weight) of sinker to pick up next time you're in the store.

The shocking truth about shock leaders

For obvious reasons, casting a heavy weight with light line is a bad idea. In fact it's a sure recipe for what angler's refer to as a *crack-off*; not a city in Poland but that horrible (and potentially dangerous) moment when the line goes snap and you kiss goodbye to your lead while all your mates either take cover or fall about laughing. For this reason, anglers try to use balanced tackle which is up to the job.

So how strong does your line need to be? If you cast smoothly and without undue force, you can get away with somewhat lighter line, but a general formula is that for every 1-ounce of weight, around 10-pounds of line strength is required. Sure, you'll manage 2-3 ounces of weight on 15-pound line if you cast sensibly. You will have little bother casting a one ounce feeder on 5-pound line with a flexible rod. But if you really want to hit long range with a good punch, tackle must be strong enough. The trouble is, thick line doesn't exactly fly effortlessly off the reel. Hence sea anglers especially like to use a *shock leader*. This simply means a length of stronger line (usually two rod lengths or so) attached to the end of the reel line to provide a shock absorber. If you routinely heave out 4 ounce leads therefore, a shock leader of 40-pound test line would be sensible ($4 \times 10 = 40$ pounds).

Storing your weights

A collection of weights can be quite heavy! Sea anglers especially might find themselves using a lead of 4–5 ounces for every rig and ample spares are a necessity. Weights can be a disruptive force in your tackle box and don't mix well with delicate items such as floats. Store your weights in a plastic container or cloth pouch. A small tackle box with a few good-sized compartments is better still. You can keep this in the bottom of your tackle bag. Keep your split shot weights handy because these can be added quickly to a lure or rig as needed. (To see examples of popular rigs incorporating sinkers and swimfeeders, see Chapter 14.)

Buying lots of spare lead weights can be expensive, especially if you lose a lot of tackle. Sea anglers fishing in rocky locations are especially prone to the wrong sort of 'weight loss'! Therefore, thrifty anglers come up with cheap alternatives. Once upon a time, spark plugs or rough sections of lead piping were favoured. Stones work well too however, and are a popular option. Find a suitable sized stone of an acceptable weight and you can either whip some elastic or cord around it before attaching a swivel or mono loop – or better still drill one end and use super glue or strong epoxy to embed a swivel into the gap.

Carp anglers also like using stones. This isn't because they're cheapskates, but because carp are crafty; where the water is heavily fished, the carp sometimes learn to avoid suspicious looking objects such as bombs and feeders.

Adding On Swivels and Snap Links

A *swivel* is a small metal device with two eyes designed to spin independently (see Figure 9-6a). Swivels come in different sizes and feature different materials and construction. The best swivels use ball bearings. The cheapest swivels (those with twisted wire eyes) barely work. A swivel is used when the action of the lure, bait, or sinker has a tendency to twist the line. The swivel spins instead of the line, so everything stays tidy. Some rigs will mercilessly twist your line unless you incorporate swivels into the arrangement. Line twist is no fun, but swivels can be a weak link the chain. They add knots to your rig, for one thing, and knotted line is always weaker than unknotted. But, again, some rigs demand them (often for adding leaders of various lengths and uses). Our advice is to buy a package of high-quality swivels. They will be rated in pound-test increments, just like line. Get swivels with a heavier pound test than your line, so they don't fail before your line does. See Chapter 14 for rigging advice, and use swivels as and when you need them. Swivels are also important for attaching different line materials together, for example when pike fishing and you want to attach a tooth-proof wire trace to a mono reel line. Knotting braid or wire direct to mono is a massively bad idea because these materials cut through mono easily, hence a swivel is the answer.

A *snap link* (often just referred to as a 'snap') is most useful when you need to change lures or weights quickly (see Figure 9-6b). A snap might be just a little shaped piece of wire that can be opened or closed to attach lures. When tied to your line, this can make switching lures a breeze. It's certainly better than tying a new knot every time you fancy switching lures, or stepping up to a heavier lead. A few lures are also shaped in such a way that makes tying them on tricky. With such lures, snaps can make life easier. Sometimes a snap incorporates a swivel into its construction, to help prevent line twist.

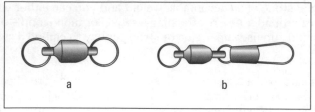

Figure 9-6:
Examples of
a swivel (a)
and a
snap (b).

a   b

Floats: Dipping Delights

All anglers have, at one time or another, fished with a float. *Floats* work well
and are fun. Watching the little taps as a fish starts to nibble at your bait and
then seeing the float go under are two of the most exciting experiences in
fishing. Watch a skilled float fisherman and you'll also see that float fishing
can be a real art form, as well as something deeply enjoyable.

Apart from those types of fish confined to really deep water, almost any species can be caught with float tackle. Hence the range of floats is huge. Some
are attached bottom end only through a little loop, on others the line passes
through the body or is fixed in place with little rubber sleeves.

The advantages to floats are numerous:

- Floats are the best way to present your bait suspended, which works
  especially well for fish that come up in the water to feed like roach, rudd
  and chub – or even mackerel and pollack on the coast.

- The bottom of a body of water tends to be the snaggiest place, and a
  float will keep your line above the worst of it, even if your bait itself is on
  the bottom. Weedy areas can be a nightmare with heavy leads, but not
  with a float.

- A float can sometimes be used to drift with the current or wind, presenting your bait to more fish.

- Floats serve as great bite indicators and offer good sensitivity. A float
  also makes far less splash than a heavy sinker and will scare fewer fish.

- All this, and they're fun to watch!

Below we list the main types of float along with their uses. Figure 9-7 shows
you a few of the most common.

- **Pole floats** are the ultimate in sensitivity. Because a pole angler doesn't
  need to cast but simply lowers their bait into the water, it's possible
  to use a really light, fine float. This is an excellent ploy, not only for

smaller, shy biting fish like roach, but for canny bigger bullies like carp and tench. Pole floats are shown in Figures 9-7a and 9-7b.

Pole floats usually comprise of three parts: a wire stem, a rounded or pear shaped body and a brightly coloured tip to spot bites. They are threaded onto the line by a little wire eye on the body, while little rubber sleeves attach the stem of the float to the line.

✔ **Stick floats** are designed for rivers and ideal for *trotting,* which means presenting a moving bait with the flow. A stick float is attached by two or three rubber sleeves that keep the float fixed to the line. They come in various sizes and designs. A small one would suit a stream, the larger beasts are for stronger, deeper flows and larger baits. Figure 9-7c shows a stick float.

✔ **Wagglers** are perhaps the most commonly used floats for the coarse angler. These come in various sizes but all are straight lengths of plastic or wood, attached by the bottom end only through a small eye. To keep the waggler in place, it is trapped with split shot at either side. Figure 9-7d and 9-7e are wagglers.

Some wagglers have a thinner top called an *insert.* So called *insert wagglers* are very sensitive and give excellent bite detection. Other wagglers are thicker and better for longer casts, windy conditions or presenting bigger baits.

✔ **Pike floats and sea floats** are sometimes referred to as *sliding floats.* This is because they aren't usually fixed to the line like other floats, but slide freely on the line, sitting upright against a *float stop* (a little rubber bead that is threaded on the line) or a special knot. These floats tend to dwarf the rest because they are intended for use in rocking waves or for big, toothy fish. They are sometimes attached through a swivel at the bottom end, or sometimes the line runs through the body. Figure 9-7f and 9-7g show these chunky monkeys.

Some pike floats are relatively slim and cigar shaped. These are for using with static bait on the bottom. Others are more rounded and sturdy, suitable for live baits or baits suspended off the bottom. Some floats have vanes on the top like dart flights. These are handy because they cast well and can be easily spotted even at long range.

Like pike, sea fish tend not to be terribly shy when biting, so bigger floats work well. Some are designed to take up to over an ounce of weight (usually a drilled bullet) should you need to cast fifty yards or more to reach the fish.

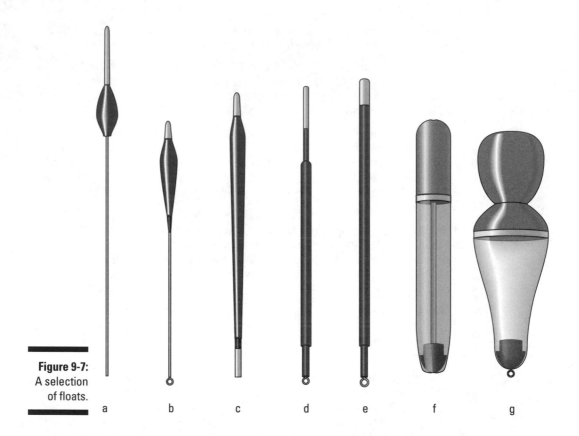

a   b   c   d   e   f   g

Many floats, such as wagglers, stick and pole floats, are attached to the line with shot or rubber sleeves. You can easily change the depth by sliding the float up or down the line. This is all well and good, until the water gets deep and you end up with an ungainly length of line that is a nightmare to cast tidily. *Sliding floats* are the answer. With sliding floats the line slides through the float until it hits a *float stop,* which you can easily place and adjust on your line. You can readily buy float stops made of rubber, or you can tie a *stop knot* with a spare piece of line. The float stop has to be small enough to fit through the rod rings (so you can cast the rig smoothly), and large enough to stop the float. To facilitate this process, a *small plastic bead* is often added between the float and the float stop. This helps prevent the float stop from going through the float. The baited hook and a few split shot or a drilled bullet help pull the line through the float until it hits the float stop. Now you can fish any depth you want, merely by adjusting the placement of the float stop. This is an ingenious way of taking float fishing to another depth.

Sliding floats are most commonly used for pike or sea fishing, but you can also use a large waggler in this fashion. Special wagglers usually called *sliders* are available for this, featuring a swivel at the bottom end. Whichever type of sliding float you use, however, be sure to test the depth carefully: Too much line between float and hook could result in poor bite indication. A badly set float catches few fish, and could also result in deep hooking. For more on all kinds of float rigs, as well as the right way to test the depth with a float, Chapter 14 has all the answers.

If you use wagglers, the best all-rounders of the lot, you can attach the float by a little device called a *float adapter*. These handy widgets are little silicone sleeves which thread onto the line and grip the bottom of your waggler, holding it in place but allowing you to switch to a lighter or heavier float in seconds. Figure 9-8 shows a waggler float fitted with a float adapter.

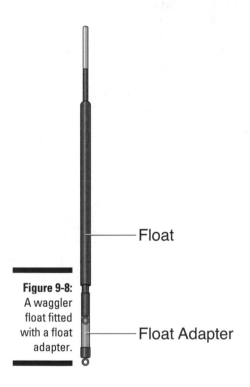

————— Float

Figure 9-8:
A waggler
float fitted
with a float
adapter.

————— Float Adapter

As you quickly start to notice, floats come in many shapes and sizes to adjust to a variety of bait and water conditions. Some floats are built to handle heavy currents and bold biters. Others are thin and fine, perfect for calmer waters and sly fish. Some are tall to be seen from great distances. Others, designed for night fishing, either glow in the dark, have notches for glow in the dark isotopes, or feature battery-operated lights that appear as tiny beacons on the dark water! The options are endless.

The best float for the job is often a bone of contention for anglers. The answer starts with the fish you're trying to catch and the conditions of your chosen location. A dinky little waggler or pole float would be ideal for fishing close to the bank on a pond; a much longer, thicker tipped model would be better if you needed to cast further out into the wind.

Many fish, and coarse species on stillwaters especially, don't like a big, crude float. If they feel too much resistance they may well drop the bait. But as a rule, it's always easier to cast with a slightly heavier float, and preferable to flailing away and tangling with one that is too diddy.

One rule for all float fishing is to try to set your float so that only the coloured tip is showing. If half the float is standing out of the water only the stupidest fish is likely to take the bait properly. Match anglers trying for wily species, for example, will sometimes dot their float down to the tiniest dimple so that a fish only has to breathe on the bait for a bite to register.

Fishing with floats is a game all its own, but, like all things fishing, experience and time on the water will open your eyes to the possibilities. Know this: Almost every fish in the water – from the perch to the shark – can be taken on a float rig, if it's presented properly. And sometimes, a float allows you to present a bait in just the right way.

Chapter 10

Going the Extra Mile: Boats, Gadgets and More

*B*esides all the essentials of angling such as line and hooks, the modern angler has never had more additional items to choose from. But do you need boats, fishfinders, bite alarms and all the rest? The short answer is no. But that said, as your fishing develops you may want to consider some additional extras. Just remember, there is no substitute for knowledge and experience and a smart angler will always outfish a lazy one no matter how impressive the gear on display.

These days all manner of gadgets and extras are on offer to assist the angler. Bite alarms signal takes from fish, while fish finders help find them in the first place. But if there is one item which truly changes the way you might go about your fishing more than any other it is a boat, which is where we begin.

Taking Advantage of Boat Fishing

Okay, so Captain Ahab probably would have been better off if he'd stayed on shore. Maybe we shouldn't use him for a model! For many anglers though, and especially those who take on the sea, fishing from boats provides more flexibility, excitement and success. Although boats can be expensive, afford-able models exist, and even simple vessels can increase your catches.

Don't buy a boat solely for fishing if you're a beginning angler. Learn how to fish first, and see how much you like the hobby. While fishing from the shore, you can better learn the habits of fish, perfect your casting technique, and practise catching and landing fish.

Would having access to a boat change the way you fish local waters? For anglers fishing small rivers or lakes, boating may be impossible. Even anglers fishing big waters sometimes choose to stay on the bank for a variety of reasons. There's nothing wrong with that. It's quite possible the kind of fishing that best suits you doesn't require a boat. Certainly, most coarse fishing is done from the bank and on many waters boats are either banned or only provided on a hire basis. Sea anglers are perhaps the exception, as they welcome the freedom a suitable vessel affords..

But if you feel ready, and if your water allows it, another angling world awaits. Fishing from boats, even non-motorised vessels, takes you into the fish's world. No longer are you observing this world from dry land – when you're floating, you become something like a fish yourself. Some things become much more complicated in boats (you have to ensure your boat is sound, watch out for obstacles, and so on), but other things are simplified (now, instead of trying to make that long, impossible cast, you can simply lower your bait . . .).

Boating isn't for everyone. And one kind of fishing isn't superior to other kinds. But knowing what boats offer anglers can help you decide if you're ready to leave the solid footing of the shore. You can always hire a boat first to see if you enjoy fishing afloat. Many bigger lakes hire out boats to anglers at a day rate, and similarly many coastal towns have local skippers who will take you out fishing for a reasonable fee, giving you a taste of boat fishing with a great deal of the hassle removed.

Fishing is fishing, whether you're leaning against a railing on a public pier or casting for sharks. Boat fishing calls for many of the same techniques utilised by bank anglers. (There are exceptions – shorebound anglers can't troll, for example.) For more on angling techniques, turn to Chapter 16. Fishing from a boat, though – whether it's a 14-foot canoe or a deep sea charter boat – provides several advantages that shorefishing cannot.

More casting angles

Really, understanding how to fish well from a boat means visualising angles. But don't worry – no need to brush off that old geometry textbook from school. Just think about the angles your lure and line takes as you retrieve a cast to the bank. For one thing, every cast you make from one position returns eventually to that same position. But retrieving a bait or lure to the bank means pulling that lure back to the surface near your feet – so the angle of the lure in the water looks similar, too.

When boat fishing, you can *jig* (a technique that requires lifting and lowering your offering) a lure straight below the boat, sometimes 100 feet below your shoes. You can retrieve a deep-running plug into the deep water below the boat, eventually cranking it to the surface. You can maneuver a boat along a bank, casting to different targets along the shore. This, too, varies the angle of the lure as it is retrieved. So boat fishing allows you to work different angles on both a vertical and horizontal axis.

Fishing places shorebound anglers can't reach

Any lake, river, bay or inlet will have some places more accessible to foot traffic and some places that are hard to reach. For example, bank fishermen often fish lakes near public landings or ramps, which provide safe parking areas and a bank with less underbrush. But does that particular area hold a lot of fish? Maybe. Maybe not. In all these situations and more, fishing from a boat allows you to go places far from the angling crowd.

Sometimes, finding this under-fished water makes all the difference. Fish living in commonly fished areas learn quickly to avoid certain lures. (Or they get caught and become more wary!) Certainly, if you take on large waters such as wild lakes or the sea, mobility is a great asset and Kayaks and other small craft are increasingly popular with anglers wanting to explore more water. Even fishing the far shoreline of a bay or lake can make a difference.

When fishing from a boat, remind yourself – you're not limited to waters with easy bank access. Take advantage. Fish the areas bank anglers cannot.

Finding bluer water: Humps, points, and channels

Shorebound anglers can only fish as far as they can cast. In certain situations, the wind or current may take an offering farther offshore, but for the most part, fishermen are limited by the lengths of their casts. Anglers in boats, though, don't need to cast as far because they can move closer to the target. Boats really earn their keep when they allow you to fish offshore concentrations of fish.

Many fish live near shore because that's where a lot of the cover is. But cover and structure can be found far from the bank, too. Electronic devices like sonar and GPS units make this easier (see later in this chapter for more on these tools), but even the naked eye can spot potential offshore spots. Islands provide structure and shoreline cover that's inaccessible to many anglers. Submerged humps and channels draw fish, and with a boat, you can hover right over them. Often, these humps get enough sunlight to trigger weed growth, which attracts all kinds of prey.

Choosing a Boat That's Right for the Way You Fish

After you decide to get off the bank, your first choice is simple: Do you get a boat that's motorised or non-motorised? Of course, cost is an issue that limits almost all of us. Beyond cost, you need to think about storage and upkeep. Safety and your overall comfort level with boating must be on the top of the list of things to consider.

But all of those things come later. First, examine your fishing water and the kinds of fish you like to pursue. What kind of boat would allow you to fish your water better? If you fish smallish, wild lakes or lochs for trout, a large boat would be overkill. That situation begs for a float tube, which would allow you approach wary fish silently, and also carry your own vessel to a lake hundreds of yards from any road access. If you intend to fish inshore waters or an estuary for bass and mackerel, a kayak could be fun, but if you want to go further out a larger, motorised boat is the only safe option.

Check local water's regulations, too – many lakes and rivers have speed limits. Other lakes allow only trolling using electric motors. If the water you fish most often only allows small boats, don't waste your money on Cleopatra's barge with rod holders. The following sections look at the most common offerings in non-motorised and motorised boats for anglers.

Great non-motorised boats for fishing

You don't need a boat to catch fish. You don't need a motorised boat to catch fish either. Non-motorised boats boast qualities like affordability, silence, and ease of use. For small waters, non-motorised boats may be the only option. Unfortunately, such vessels usually can't cart your whole family. For the most part, boats in this category carry one or two individuals and not a lot of gear beyond that. They don't go anywhere too quickly (unless you're a champion paddler or oarsman), and they don't work well for anglers with some physical limitations.

But fish don't care about fast boats, and many of us carry too much gear, anyway. Non-motorised boats force you to streamline your presentation, and when you couple that with a silent approach, it's no wonder anglers catch a lot of fish from boats of this type. You also avoid many of the hassles and costs of larger boats such as registration and insurance. Regardless of where you fish, the following options showcase the range of non-motorised boats. One of them may help you fish your home water more effectively.

Rowboats and Punts

A classic that deserves mention, rowboats are *semi-V* boats (meaning that the *hull,* or part of the boat that touches the water, forms a shallow V when viewed from the front, or bow) with pointed bows that use *oars* for propulsion. Oars, unlike paddles, connect to the boat in *oarlocks,* and you use this fulcrum point to swing the oars and move the boat forward. They will also take a small motor should you want to use one. Rowboats can be car-topped or carried in a trailer and make for a stable fishing platform. Typically 14 feet (4 metres) long or less, rowboats are a bit clunkier than the other boats in this section, but they can carry more weight. A metal one is also virtually indestructible, which means there's a good chance your grandfather still has his in the garage. Punts have a boxier but highly stable shape and are often also powered simply by oars. These are another common hire choice on day ticket lakes and usually very comfortable for a pair of anglers to fish from.

Canoes

Although some canoes feature a square stern made to allow you to mount a small motor, true canoes are pointed at both ends and designed to handle current. Two people can paddle a canoe with ease after they get the hang of it, and it's possible – though difficult – to take three anglers or go it solo. Canoes can handle calm or flowing water and are at home in small rivers. They also travel well on the top of a car. Be warned, though: on many rivers other anglers will not take kindly to you paddling through their *swim* (the stretch of water they're fishing) and in some places canoes are banned.

Kayaks

Kayaks are the faster, sleeker siblings of canoes (see Figure 10-1a). Kayaks primarily carry one or two anglers, and you sit atop or inside the hull, depending on the design. Kayaks love fast current and are good for rivers. Sea anglers enjoy kayaks too, and some amazingly large fish have been hooked by anglers pursuing saltwater fish from their relatively tiny vessels.

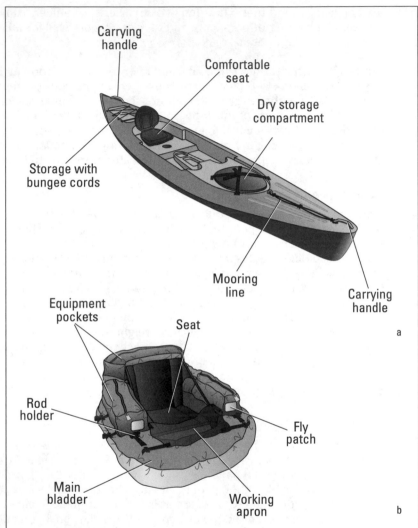

Figure 10-1:
Popular non-motorised boats: Kayak (a) and float tube (b).

Similar to canoes, kayaks are easy to customise and transport. Kayak fishing is a rapidly increasing hobby, and manufacturers offer a range of models and angling options to meet the new demand. Kayaks are typically propelled with a two-bladed paddle.

Float tubes and kick boats

You paddle canoes and kayaks with paddles, for the most part, but you propel float tubes with your feet. Also called *belly boats,* float tubes originated as innertubes (yes, like the innertubes you used to float in as a kid) rigged with a seat in the middle. Most float tubes now feature two parallel inflated tubes, which allows an angler to move around, half submerged, and cast to fish quite literally at his or her feet (see Figure 10-1b). In hot weather you can paddle in swimming shorts using surf flippers. For cooler conditions, chest waders can be worn, along with special flippers that fit over your wading boots.

Float tubes come in various, often very affordable models and work best in lakes or other still waters – strong current or heavy winds could be disastrous in a float tube. For sheer portability however the float tube is a brilliant little craft and most will fit into a suitcase deflated. Do check local rules however, because float tubes can fall victim to the health and safety jobsworths; a shame because they are pretty safe and create minimal disturbance. That said, many reservoirs now have special days for float tubers and enthusiasts even have their own club, the British Float Tube Association (www.bfta.org.uk).

Ideal motorised boats for fishing

The motors on some boats move them across the water at speeds more typical of cars on a main road. For most anglers, though, motorised boats offer them the chance to pursue fish in a quiet, leisurely manner that offers dependability and safety. Whereas some might think small, non-motorised boats are inherently safer, going on big water in a small boat is much more dangerous than going in a properly equipped large boat. And although some motorised boats are blazingly powerful, most are powered by simple two-stroke outboards generating less than 40 horsepower. Motors aren't cheap but small motors make a good investment. For elderly anglers or those with disabilities, motors allow them to get out on the water more easily.

Electric motors can complete a boat. Even boats with petrol engines often also have an electric motor, not just as back up but because they are quieter and scare fewer fish when you move around. You can buy these electric motors in different sizes, and, depending on the size of the motor, they run on a purpose made battery, or often a car battery. While the motors and batteries aren't cheap, they're reliable, long-lasting, and quiet. Think of it this way: You move spots with your petrol motor, but many times you actually do the fishing with your electric motor. They are ideal for trolling or simply idling along and casting as you go.

Jon boats and wheely boats

Jon boats are small, aluminum, square boats that look like floating tubs. Wheely boats are similar: also sturdy, a little boxy looking but flat, spacious and often provided by fisheries for disabled anglers. Square across stern and bow, such boat types don't slice through the water. Rather, they float along on top of it. (They're called *flatbottoms* for a reason.) What they lack in grace, though, they make up for with stability. You'll most often find them used on lakes or stillwaters.

The open floorplan of a jon or wheely boat makes it ideal for carrying lots of gear. Because they're aluminum, these boats are easily customised: You can bolt rod holders to the *gunnels* (the edges of the boat), fasten lights to the bow, add soft seats to the benches – the options are endless. Jon boats can be trailered or carried on a car. They come in small sizes – like 8 feet long – all the way up to over 20 feet. Manufacturers design them for a variety of waters and uses.

Purpose built fishing boats and cuddy boats

For the real boat enthusiast, the ultimate recreational fishing investment is a purpose made fishing boat that holds anything up to four or so anglers. These traditionally shaped boats are sometimes referred to as "V" boats, earning their name from the shape of their hull. When viewed from the front, the bow forms a V shape, and a deep-V features a hull with high sides that offer wave protection (see Figure 10-2). Another common feature is a *cuddy* – the small cabin or raised structure at the front of the boat which often affords you some storage space and protection from the elements.

Such boats can handle rough water and are ideally suited to big lakes and rivers, or indeed inshore sea fishing. You could pursue any species from a deep-V, but these are often heavy, expensive boats best matched with big-water fishing. They are often 16 to 22 feet long, and are paired most commonly with an outboard motor (although an inboard motor is also a possibility). Again, the size of the motor greatly influences the price of the boat.

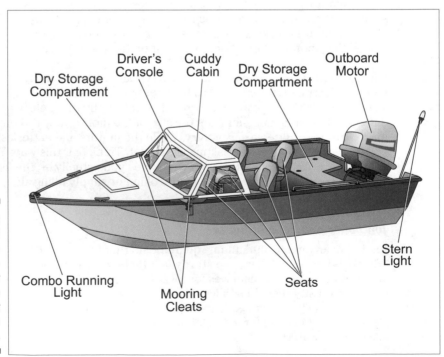

Figure 10-2: A typical purpose built fishing boat for use in large waters or inshore sea fishing.

Considering the Costs of Watercraft

The old adage goes like this: The two happiest days of a boat owner's life are when he buys his boat and when he sells it. Bah, I say, the two happiest days of a boat owner's life are when he buys his boat and when he buys his second boat. Thousands of people invest in watercraft and never regret the decision. A little forethought will help you become one of those people.

As with anything, research before you buy. Shop around and look for deals. Timing matters too – some say the best time to buy a boat is in winter, when manufacturers are looking to secure sales to get the factory churning out units. Talk to dealers, attend boat shows, shop online – but don't be pressured to buy. Make sure you know exactly what you want – and what's a reasonable price for that – before you sign on the line.

Used boats appear along roadsides and in want ads every day. Certainly good deals are possible. As with buying a used car, check out any boat before you buy it. If you're buying a motorised boat, know that most of your investment is in the motor. You can check the *hull* – the outer part of the boat that touches the water – pretty easily, and you can inspect the interior, as well. But have a mechanic check the motor if you're not sure what you're looking for.

Start small. Your first boat probably isn't your last. My (Greg's) first boat was an inflatable dingy. A canoe came later. Before long a jon boat with an electric motor followed me home. Then I added an outboard motor. Then a bigger outboard. Finally, I bought an 18-foot deep-V with a four stroke outboard delivering 115 horsepower. I researched every purchase beforehand, bought high quality for the lowest price I could find, and enjoyed every day with every one. Some added expenses to owning a fishing boat are detailed in the next sections, but let us start by offering a mild caution: Like any hobby, boating can get expensive if you let it.

Licensing, safety and fees

Check your local laws concerning the registration of boats. Mooring fees apply just about anywhere you plan to keep a boat on the water. Boating around the coast requires no licence, but on inland waterways you will usually need one. Almost all of freshwater bodies in the UK fall under three organisations: British Waterways, the Environment Agency and the Broads Authority. Fees vary according to boat sizes and private or business use. Much like a car has an MOT, many areas insist that a registered boat must pass a test under the Boat Safety Scheme (www.boatsafetyscheme.com) and you may well also require insurance. If your boat has a trailer, the trailer will need a licence plate of its own.

Although expenses such as mooring and registration fees add to the overall cost of boating, a portion of the funds collected should go toward upkeep of boat facilities and management of the waters themselves. In other words, you'll get some of your money back through fishing and facilities.

It should go without saying that every boat owner should own lifejackets and pay attention to safety requirements. This may seem less exciting than talking about fishing, but it is the most important consideration of all and starts with careful preparation (for more on safety see Chapter 6).

Upkeep, storage, and maintenance

The bigger your boat is, the more work you have to do to keep it in running order. Big boats call for bigger motors, which require periodic service and can be costly to repair if something breaks. Small, non-motorised boats, though, can cost almost nothing in maintenance. Keep a fibreglass canoe clean with a little elbow grease and it should last about forever.

All boats require storage space, however, and that can vary from the rafters in a garage to rented space. Before you buy, think about the boat you have room for, and think about the annual costs of maintenance and possible storage fees.

Trailering

Some boats come with fully rigged trailers. Other small boats, like small rowboats, are often priced for the boat only. Of course, the best advice is to know exactly what you're buying. Some boat dealers have trailers for sale as well, and they'll often adjust it to fit your new boat. Whereas some small boats can be attached to the top of a car, a decent-sized vessel needs a trailer. This means another expense for you, and additional maintenance. However, a good trailer lasts a long time without a lot of upkeep, and you won't miss having to muscle your boat onto the top of your car.

Don't cut corners on the trailer. You need one that's adequate for the weight of your boat, plus any gear that stays in the boat. In fact, it's a good idea to buy a heavy-duty trailer that can handle your boat and then some. Because you will add some more gear to your boat, we assure you.

Boat trailers need licence plates. For safety, they need working lights and dependable straps to hold the boat securely. Inspect the straps often, make sure the lights are in working order, and ensure the tyres are properly inflated. Keep the wheel bearings greased, too.

Towing a boat takes a little practice, and I (Greg) recommend you do that in your driveway or a large flat space, as opposed to the slipway at the lake on Sunday. You can learn how to back a boat trailer – a lot of us do it, and we're not all geniuses – but you will need to practise. And learn to rely on your side mirrors, too, instead of having to twist your back to look over your shoulder.

Before launching at a busy ramp, load your boat with your gear first and attach a line to the bow. Back your boat trailer into the water (usually, until the tops of the trailer tires are at the surface of the water), set the hand brake of the vehicle, and push the boat from the trailer. Using the bow line, guide the boat away from the ramp and attach it to the bank or a dock. Park your vehicle and return to the boat. Having a partner along helps – he or she can board the boat before you launch and motor the boat off the trailer.

Fishing in the 21st Century: Gadgets Galore!

The technology that shapes our daily lives has accelerated in recent years. For proof, look no further than the mobile phone in your pocket. In the span of a few short years, mobiles evolved from small, reliable phones (you know – just phones, like in the old days) to touch screen, web surfing devices.

Before we discuss any modern gadgets, we should begin with a disclaimer: You can catch fish without using a single high tech item. You might even be able to outfish someone with a boatload of these tools, and you certainly can have as much fun. So, if you want to keep your fishing simple, forever or just for now, by all means, cast away.

On the other hand, new technology does have its uses. Fishfinders help you locate your quarry and measure depths, whilst GPS allows you to mark structure and cover. Bite alarms aid night fishermen in the pitch black whilst bait boats allow crafty carp anglers to position baits with uncanny accuracy.

Technology helps only if you know how to work it. And it's there to help you fish, not distract you. Even the best technology can't make fish bite. It might help you find them, but it won't hook them for you. And if you get so obsessed with your gadgets that you're no longer fishing, you might as well stay at home and play computer games.

Fish Finders: Can They Really Find Fish?

Yes, they can. And they can do it surprisingly well. But in truth, much of the time they don't find fish, but features. In other words, they give vital clues about depths and underwater features that are key to success. Anglers who fish small ponds and streams will find no use for a fish finder – your eyes will serve you much better. As a rule, if a body of water is too small to fish from a boat, it doesn't beg for a fish finder. But for anglers fishing big water – say a giant Loch – the hundreds of acres of water defy mere visual inspection.

As you can imagine, fish finders are primarily used in boats. As anglers in boats move around a lake or inlet, their fish finders show them what is under the hull. Many fish finders are permanently mounted to boats, but portable models allow you add a fish finder to small vessels like kayaks and float tubes. Some can also be cast out and retrieved and these are very handy for bank fishers mapping out big waters such as gravel pits.

How fish finders work

Fish finder is a common term applied to *sonar units,* and sonar stands for SOund, NAvigation and Ranging. Sonar units are used by millions of anglers today, but the technology first had to find something more important than a cod or pike: enemy submarines during World War II. Any sonar unit has four components: transmitter, transducer, receiver and display. The transmitter sends out an electrical impulse, which the transducer converts into a sound wave. These sound waves are sent into the water, where they bounce off of objects and return to the transducer as echoes. Those results are converted back into electric signals and shown on the display.

On boats, the transducer is often mounted on the lower hull of the transom. The transducer often rides in the water, and the display is mounted somewhere in the boat where the angler can see it. The castable fish finder lets you attach the small transducer to your line while you keep the display on your person (often wearing it as a watch). You can read the depth and look for fish under the spot of your cast!

Transducers emit these sound waves in a cone shape, spreading out as they leave the transducer. Usually this cone is broadcast directly beneath the boat. The bottom is shown as a line near the bottom of the display, and as fish move into the cone, they appear on the screen, as well. Some units allow you to project this cone to the side of the boat, too. All objects that enter the cone – fish, schools of prey fish, tree branches, sunken cars, rock structures – show up on the display. Learning how to interpret the marks on the display takes practice, but every object in the cone should appear. The display will show the current depth and often the water temperature, as well.

All of this sounds confusing, probably. It is! What you need to know: the biggest sonar manufacturers (Lowrance, Humminbird, Garmin) have great, interactive Web sites, and tackle shops often have displays of live units that feature tutorial modes. You can examine fish finders closely before you buy, and the best tackle shops will often have one or two experts among the staff.

Do you really need a fish finder?

The majority of coarse and fly anglers do not need a fish finder. Some traditionalists would go further, claiming that such devices rob the sport of a certain mystery. If you're bank fishing or fishing from a small, non-motorised boat in shallow water, you probably don't need a fish finder. While small, portable sonar units help you interpret the water around you, they don't add much to the picture your other senses can paint for you. Any electronic device can serve as a distraction if you let it, and in my experience, time spent messing with portable fish finders would be better spent fishing and observing your surroundings.

Having said that, fish finders are amazing tools. People often assume sonar units find fish only. More often this is of secondary importance to telling you things about the water body in general: the depth, temperature, constitution of the bottom (whether it's hard or soft, rock or sand), presence of cover, and the appearance of structure – things like channel drop-offs and ledges. That information is crucial to your fishing success, and it might help you even if you never mark a fish.

Cost is the other issue. You don't need a top-of-the-line model, however. There are very good fish finders on the market for less than £200. More cash outlay brings you a more powerful transmitter, a sharper display, colour screens, and more features. But even quite a basic fish finder will give you important details.

Large boats need sonar units for safety, if for no other reason. Vessels running in big, wild waters or at sea need the information sonar units provide to avoid running aground.

Where to find fish finders

Our best advice is to push the buttons on a fish finder unit before you buy it. Although you can order them online (along with everything else), you probably want to interact with the various models before you choose one. Research fish finders online, and maybe even purchase one online, but visit a tackle shop to examine the units before buying.

Many bigger stores that sell a decent selection of rods and reels will also sell electronics. They probably have a display case with all of their sonar unit models connected to a power source and in display mode. Spend some time browsing the different units and ask questions of the sales staff. If you buy a boat from a marina, often they will install a unit for you. Other stores may or may not be able to install units for you, but they should be able to recommend someone who can.

GPS Units: Finding Yourself

GPS operates on this rock-solid, easy-to-understand system: there are 24 satellites positioned above the earth. Just like the SatNav in your car, GPS works out your position in relation to three or more of these satellites. Modern GPS receivers can pinpoint your location to within a few feet. So how can GPS help anglers?

Well, GPS can help you find your way to and from a fishing spot. It can also help you mark fish or likely locations of fish. You can begin to take advantage of GPS while fishing in one of two ways: You can either add a GPS unit to your boat (many fish finders now come with built-in GPS), or you can purchase a handheld unit (to be used either from the boat or while bank fishing). Either can help you fish more safely and effectively, regardless of where or how you're fishing.

A GPS unit will show your location and a trail of where you've been. Anglers, though, tend to find great value in the *waypoints* – saved spots that remain on your GPS map. These could be access points, for example, boat ramps or fishing hotspots, and most units will let you customise the symbols to make your own key.

Waypoints seem unnecessary on small locations; on a trout stream for example, you will more than likely remember that lovely pool where you took the best fish of the day. With boats and large waters, they are more useful though. You could mark down productive areas, mark where you trolled or even add in where bait fish were shoaled up, or where you caught fish.

Look for patterns in your waypoints. As with any kind of fishing, by paying attention to the fish you catch, you can begin to ascertain a pattern. Seeing a pattern allows you to tighten your approach, leading to more caught fish. If you drift along a shoreline and make a waypoint for every caught fish, and then notice that most of your waypoints are clustered near a drop-off, you know where the most active fish are feeding.

Bite Alarms: Racket or Asset?

Perhaps the most common of all the gadgets seen in coarse fishing today, the bite alarm still divides opinion. Originally devised by Richard Walker for night fishing, when spotting bites proved tricky after dark, bite alarms are hugely popular amongst today's anglers. These alarms fit on a bankstick, and the way they work is simple: your rod is positioned on top of the alarm, in the same way as in a rod rest, with the line sitting in a little grooved wheel. When a fish moves with the bait and takes line, the wheel turns and the alarm sounds. Alarms are used in conjunction with another bite indicator such as a hanging bobbin. These are important because they keep just enough tension on the line to make everything work properly, even if the fish runs towards you rather than away from you. You could happily use a bobbin or other indicator without any gadget with it; all the alarm does is make bites audible as well as visible.

Bite alarms vary from ultra-swish models with long guarantees to cheap-as-chips models that basically just beep and that's it. We'd recommend you make sure you go for one of a reputable make (for example Chub, Fox or Nash). Spend a little more and you can be sure the alarm is properly water-proof and you also want volume control (because a screeching alarm is a sure way to give your fellow anglers a headache on a peaceful afternoon).

The golden question remains: do you really need them? In many situations, they are unnecessary. A venue full of medium-sized carp, for example, demands no such device because you are unlikely to have to wait long for a bite, and you might well irritate those around you if your gear is continually beeping. They can also make you lazy, and you'll hit more bites by sitting close to your rods and watching closely, than by lying back half asleep. Alarms are called for when fishing is tough and you may wait a long time between bites. They spare you the ordeal of staring at indicators for hours on end. They're especially useful at night, when it's difficult to spot bites by sight alone. For more on specialist carp set-ups using alarms, see Chapter 16.

Bait Boats: Smart Thinking or Cheating?

Today's anglers could almost be split down the middle. There are those who are suspicious of new fads and stick to traditional common sense, but also those techy types who look for any new dodges that will put more fish on the bank. The bait boat is either genius or sacrilege, depending on your view point. These devices are essentially radio controlled boats which are used to deliver your baited rig, often along with free bait, and drop it into the water with pinpoint accuracy. You could, for example, position your rig right under that overhanging bush fifty yards away without the usual very risky cast.

To many anglers it's just not cricket, and detracts from the skill of fishing. Why not just learn to cast accurately in the first place? Some waters even ban bait boats. After all, fishing should be at least partly a game of skill and chance. If you push technology to its conclusion you might end up with a pastime of very little human input, where rigs are automatically positioned, the fish hook themselves against clever rigs and all the angler does is reel in. Why not get a robot to do that for you as well?

In truth however, the angler still needs a grasp of watercraft and no amount of clever gadgets or rigs guarantee success. To draw a random parallel, you could give an exquisite Fender electric guitar and a plethora of funky devices to a novice and they still couldn't play a tune. A bait boat costs every bit as much as a quality guitar, for the record, but it won't teach you a single thing about fishing. Should you learn your craft patiently however, and find yourself regularly fishing a snag-infested water where the fish are cute and casting is a nightmare, the dreaded baitboat might just prove to be a real asset.

Part III
The End of Your Line: Enticing Fish with Bait, Lures and Flies

"The fish seem very confident in this part of the river."

In this part . . .

You'll find three chapters covering the three basic kinds of offerings you'll present to a fish: bait, lures and flies. Here you'll get advice on gathering and storing livebait, choosing the right lure and matching the hatch on a trout stream. Each kind of offering has its advantages and disadvantages, and that's all covered here.

Chapter 11

Real Food for Real Fish: Using Bait

Think about it this way: Fish still eat when you aren't there, fishing for them. As they go about their fishy lives, they seek shelter and protection, reproduce when the time is right, and look for something to eat. All fish do some combination of those three activities year-round. So, when you show up at their home with a fishing rod in your hands, you're simply stepping into a world in progress.

When you offer fish a hook baited with something they're used to eating, presented in a way that looks natural, you have an excellent chance of catching fish. But equally, fish have no problem accepting less natural baits introduced by anglers. Indeed, on waters where fishing is regular, the fish quickly accept offerings such as maggots or pellets as 'natural'.

Over decades of trial and error, anglers have discovered that fish will eat all sorts of baits. Bread, sweetcorn and cheese are just three examples which are hardly 'as nature intended' but catch plenty. Many far stranger baits have also worked, from sweets to chunks of liver. Indeed part of the fun is in working out which baits work and which don't for each place you fish.

Part III of this book covers what you can offer on your hook in an effort to catch fish, and it makes sense to start with bait. After all, bait is easy to obtain and use, and it often works more effectively than anything else. Some species of fish (like catfish) can be caught reliably only with bait. Almost every fish in the world can be caught with some kind of bait.

Assessing Your Bait Options

Bait, by popular definition, is any natural (think worms) or processed food (say, cheese) used to catch fish. Over the years, the term *lure* has come to mean any artificial offering made of plastic, wood or metal to mimic a moving, living thing. Lures, covered in Chapter 12, typically imitate fish, and they come in a dazzling variety of styles. But bait, too, can be divided into different categories and styles.

- **Natural baits:** Anything that a fish finds and eats in its habitat is considered natural bait. Minnows, crabs, insects, slugs, sandeels, worms, prawns – you name it. Fish eat what's available, and using the same natural bait is an effective technique. Some baits we class as natural offerings may not often be found in nature, maggots for example, but are so universally accepted by fish that they also fall into this category.

- **Processed and man-made baits:** Manufacturers produce a variety of baits designed to attract fish. Often made with real or processed foods, processed baits are sold alongside fishing tackle in convenient packaging. Pellets and boilies are two typical examples, both packed with protein and fish attracting flavours.

  Many foods that humans eat also take fish. Sweetcorn, bread, cheese and meats of all kind can be used to catch fish. The most convenient of all kinds of bait to use, food baits are accessible, cheap, and often less messy than other kinds of bait.

- **Livebaits and deadbaits:** The term livebait most often refers to fishing a natural bait, almost always a fish, while it is still alive. For example, hooking a minnow through the lips and allowing it to swim freely. These are very effective for predatory species such as pike, perch and bass. For reasons of convenience as well as ethical concerns and regional bans however, many anglers in search of predators now shun livebaits in favour of other offerings such as deadbaits or lures.

  Deadbaits, as the name suggests, are dead fish that offer your quarry an easy meal. This could be a freshly killed roach, or half a mackerel. Species such as catfish, eels and pike respond well to the potent smell of a smaller fish that has kicked the bucket. Equally though, sea scavengers such as dogfish and rays will also accept a free fish supper in this manner.

Gathering and Keeping Bait

Some anglers have a gift for fishing; some anglers have a gift for bait. Catching natural baits like lobworms or prawns takes a degree of skill. Figuring out which baits to use on which days also requires some thought.

Greg's younger brother, on most days a mediocre fisherman, is a dedicated baithound. He would rather pursue bait than go fishing. Other anglers are known for concocting their own, deadly home-made baits such as boilies and special pastes. A friend who always has top quality bait is a useful accomplice!

Support your local tackle shop

Occasionally you might find a garage or small store that sells some bait to visiting anglers. Nine times out of ten however, the best bet is your friendly local tackle shop. Besides a range of useful baits you can also usually count on finding interesting characters who know the local waters. Not only can you buy baits that work in the surrounding areas, you can gather advice on how to use them and where to fish. You may be able to order processed baits such as pellets and boilies on the internet, but you don't get the same useful clues and personal service into the bargain.

Forget your wallet: Gathering free bait

You need quality bait, but you don't have to go broke obtaining it. The enterprising angler can find a supply of bait at minimal cost. With natural baits, you can fish with bait you caught with your own hands. You can gather lobworms from lawns at night; trap or minnows using a fine meshed landing net; and go rock-pooling for fresh prawns to catch bass and pollack. In a sense, gathering natural baits becomes its own fishing expedition. And if you seek out bait from the water's edge where you will be fishing you can be pretty sure that the fish will accept it. To take one example, sea anglers heading out for a day on the boat will quite often start by fishing for mackerel. Not only is this fun in itself but ensures they'll have a supply of perfectly fresh bait to use.

Ideally, natural bait you gather should come from the area immediately surrounding the area you intend to fish. Minnows caught in a stream will look and taste just right to the perch in that stream. Sandeels taken from an estuary will be readily accepted by the resident bass.

Remember to look on dry land, too. Baits such as slugs and grasshoppers may be unfashionable, but drop one into tree cover where chub lurk and the result could be explosive. Worms and grubs often reside under rotting logs and stones; the family compost heap is also an excellent source of wriggling bait. Be observant and seek out free bait. You'll save money and often outfish those using more expensive offerings.

Supermarket baits

If the tackle shop is closed and you don't have the time or energy to gather your own natural bait, you can buy effective bait right where you do your food shopping. Canned sweet corn, sliced bread, tinned meat – many groceries can go straight from your trolley to the water. Dog biscuits from the pet section make great floating baits for carp, and those sardines on the fish counter could work a treat for pike. Mackerel is a good back up bait for sea anglers.

What you need depends upon the fish you're after, but many species of fish, from roach to carp, will take corn. Tench will take beans or chickpeas. Many barbel have been caught on meatballs. Experiment and try out different recipes. We don't know why fish like corn – it's not likely they could ever find it in their habitat – but someone discovered that it works. Your next crazy brainwave could be tomorrow's killer bait.

Storing and transporting bait

Different kinds of baits call for different storage and transportation techniques. Generally, though, most baits should be kept cool and they shouldn't be kept for long. If you're married or live with a partner, allow us to save your relationship with this nugget: Don't forget that tub of worms in the boot of the car. Or this one: Don't put maggots in the fridge in a container without a really good lid – and don't forget to label it as a courtesy to anyone else who may be scouting your fridge for a snack.

When transporting bait of any kind, make sure the container is securely packed and airtight, if possible. (Of course, some baits, like maggots, require air holes.) Check to ensure the lids are on tight. Many a fishing trip has been derailed after a tub of maggots released themselves, one by one, into the darkness under the car seats.

Coarse Fishing Baits

At one time or another, somebody, somewhere, has tried just about everything to catch coarse fish: bacon rind, cereals, leftover cuts of meat, dead (and sometimes not dead) goldfish from the aquarium, you name it. But through centuries of trial and error, anglers have narrowed their bait choices to a few favourites. The next sections cover a selection of reliable baits wherever you fish.

Worms: Great bait by the dozen

Wherever you find them, worms catch many kinds of fish. Long before todays processed baits were invented, fish were being caught on worms, which are still an excellent bait. The two most useful kinds are the *lobworm* and the *redworm*.

Redworms, named because of their reddish hue, can be gathered in numbers in virtually any compost heap. Fished whole or in pieces they wriggle beautifully and are loved by many species but are especially good for bream, tench and carp.

Lobworms are the biggest you'll find and hence a more selective bait. Perch, carp and other big-mouthed fishes love them and they're also less likely to be stolen by tiddlers.

The most common natural bait in the country, worms should accompany you on your next fishing trip for several reasons:

✔ You can buy a dozen almost anywhere bait is sold.

   Make sure to check the bait before you pay. Open the carton carefully and look for casualties. If things haven't gone well in that container, you'll smell it pretty quickly.

✔ With practice, you can gather your own. See the next section for advice on catching your own supply.

✔ They catch fish. Fish that have never seen a worm will attack one when given the opportunity. Many other creatures that look like earthworms appear in the fish's environment: eels, leeches and aquatic worms, and fish feed on them readily. It's also true that earthworms do get washed into the water as well: A big mud-producing rain can wash a decent number of worms into the water, where it's fair to say that 'a worm in a stream is like a fish out of water.' In other words, it's easy prey.

Get him! Grabbing a fistful of worms

If you have access to a big compost heap or a pile or rotting leaves, redworms can be easy to gather in good numbers. A garden fork, a bait box and a low regard for cleanliness are all you'll need! If you have outdoor space but no compost heap, be sure you start one; rather than exchanging your hard earned cash on worms you can get them in return for potato peelings and other food waste.

You may be lucky enough to find the odd lobworm in the compost too, but for any serious quantity you need to find a good-sized area of grass, whether that's the local park, playing fields or a friend's lawn. Grab a torch too, as they are not often found in the day (hence the American name, 'nightcrawler').

Lobworms live in tunnels that run quite far beneath the ground. However, a deep, soaking rain can bring them to the surface, even during the day. When that happens, you can often gather them easily from the edges of any grassy area – the street-lit edges of a park are ideal. Store lobs in a cool, dark place in container with loose soil mixed with wet moss, leaves, or grass clippings.

Even without rain, you can catch lobworms at night provided the grass is moist (although rainy nights are miles better). On a warm summer evening, look for a lush lawn that hasn't been overly treated with chemicals. Using a torch that isn't super bright (if your light is too garish, cover the lens with a red balloon skin or a thin cloth), step softly and scan the ground for worms. (Some bait hunters like to use headlamps, which free up both hands.) When you see one, odds are good that part of the worm is still in its burrow, and with a jerk, the worm can disappear back down its tunnel. So you have to be quick, but soft at the same time. Holding the flashlight in your non-dominant hand, crouch and position your other hand near the worm. Grab it as close to the tunnel as possible, pinching the worm firmly, but not so firm that you break the thing in two. Holding the worm firmly, slowly and steadily pull the worm from its hole.

Yes, it gets easier with practice. But, as with all forms of gathering bait, some people are just naturals. Our advice? Teach your kids to grab worms and then pay them five pence per bait.

Hooking a worm

There are a few standard ways to put a worm on your hook. Be sure to use a hook large enough to hold the bait, but small enough for the fish you're targeting.

- ✔ The simplest method is to push the hook through the smooth or *collar* section of the worm, as shown in Figure 11-1a.

- ✔ It takes a little more finesse, but another method is to put the point through the top of the head and then out through the collar, as shown in Figure 11-1b. It gives the worm great action when you move it through the water.

- ✔ There's no rule that says you must use a whole worm. A little section of head or tail is ideal for smaller mouths and also gives out more scent. Figure 11-1c shows you how to hook a worm section.

When using a barbless hook, worms tend to wriggle their way free rather easily. Smart anglers solve this by sliding a little piece of rubber band or a single maggot onto the hook after the worm. This acts as a handy stopper, ensuring also that the hook point remains clear and you connect with the fish.

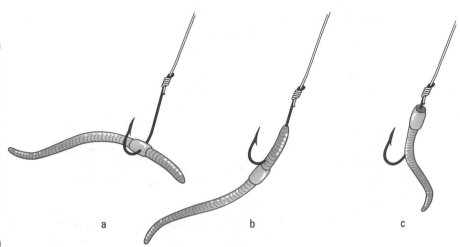

Figure 11-1:
Three ways to hook a worm: through the collar (a), through the top of the head (b) and using a worm section (c).

a   b   c

Further ways with worms

A plain old worm is a great bait on its own, but other tricks can make this classic bait even more effective. It's a grisly job, but chopping a few worms up with sharp scissors and throwing them in around your hook bait is a great way to draw fish into the area. You can also add chopped worm pieces to your groundbait or put them in a swim feeder.

As for the most ingenious of all worm tricks, you can make a lobworm even more easy for the fish to find by carefully injecting it with some air. A split shot a couple of inches from the bait anchors it in place – great for weedy waters where the worm can wriggle into cover and not be found. Always do this carefully, with the syringe pointed down on a flat surface, *never* your hand, as injecting oxygen into your blood could be fatal.

Maggots and casters: Grub's up

If you asked many fishermen which single bait they would choose if they could only pick one, the most common answer would be maggots. As the larval stage of flies, maggots may make squeamish types cringe but they catch fish of virtually all kinds and sizes, from tiny rudd to huge carp. They are a brilliant bait, easy to use and available from virtually every tackle shop in existence.

Maggots are usually bought, like beer, by the pint or half pint, although we hope you wouldn't drink a pint of maggots. When you consider just how many hundreds of these grubs would fit inside a pint glass this represents excellent value. They are often dyed different colours too. As well as natural white grubs, you'll often find red, amber and even fluorescent-coloured baits which are also useful.

Maggots come in sawdust, which keeps them clean and soft. You can use them as they come, but many anglers like to use a *riddle* (a sort of bait sieve) to remove the dust and often replace it with another medium. Some even flavour maggots with turmeric or curry powder. This may seem odd, but then again anglers have always had an alarmingly close relationship with maggots. On bitter winter days you might find hardened match anglers slipping a couple of maggots into their mouths briefly before they see the hook, warming them up so that they continue to wriggle in the cold!

As well as normal-sized maggots you might also find two smaller varieties in your local tackle shop. *Pinkies* are daintier maggots, ideal for fishing canals and anywhere the going is tough and shy fish like roach and skimmers are the target. *Squats* are even smaller: tiny little critters that are ideal for mixing into groundbait or on the hook for small fish.

Whichever maggots you decide on, they are best stored in a sealed baitbox with a perforated lid. Unless you're going to use them right away, store them in a fridge where they should keep for around two weeks. Be warned, however: that forgotten tub of maggots could land you in the doghouse if left to fester or, worse still, turn into a pint of flies!

Hooking maggots

Because of their small size, maggots are best suited to fairly dainty hooks. They can be fished singly on a size 20, or as doubles on a 16 or 18. Having said that, big fish hunters sometimes use a whole bunch on a larger hook.

The trick with maggots is to only nick them on the hook lightly, so that you don't puncture them and lose that deadly wriggle. To do this hold the maggot between the tip of your thumb and index finger so that the blunt end of the grub points upwards. Nick the hook carefully through the skin. If you do it right there will be no mess and the maggot will happily still wriggle away. Two maggots are best presented back to back.

Bonus time: Casters

When maggots are left to their own devices, they eventually undergo a transformation. They stop wriggling and darken, becoming *casters*. Far from being useless at this point, casters have an uncanny knack for picking out bigger fish and bream and big roach in particular love them.

The trouble with casters is that they quite quickly turn from light to dark brown, in which state they begin to float and are no good for most fishing. Hence once they 'turn' casters should be kept in airtight conditions such as a sealed plastic bag. This keeps them in stasis until you want to use them, although you need to air the bag every day or so to prevent them from dying.

On the bank you should keep them from darkening in the fresh air by submerging them in water within their container.

Some anglers make their own casters out of a pint or more of white maggots, removing those which have become casters at regular intervals for separate storage. A much easier solution is to buy ready prepared casters at your local tackle shop, although you may have to request these in advance.

Casters can be hooked like maggots, just nicked in the blunt end on a small hook. If the fish are fussy however, another way is to push the hook point into the caster and gently feed the hook inside it, sneakily hiding the evidence so that a big, wily fish will take it without suspicion.

Feeding time: Catch more fish with loose feed

You might be lucky and catch a fish by casting out a single maggot or piece of corn, but you will achieve far better results by getting the fish going with free helpings of bait. Anglers call this process *loose feeding*. The aim is to get the fish feeding confidently so that by the time they reach the bait on your hook, they think it's just another freebie and take it without a second thought.

You can simply throw helpings of loose feed short distances, or use a catapult if fishing further out. If you can keep this to a tight area with accurate feeding, so much the better as you'll concentrate the fish in one spot. Do this regularly and the fish will begin competing for the bait, often drawing in bigger ones in the process. It's a bit like feeding the ducks. If you keep throwing bread more will arrive, perhaps followed by some great big swans which then bully the smaller birds away.

How much and how often you feed is where the skill comes in. Feed too much and the fish may be put off or have too much choice; feed too little and they might lose interest. A good general rule is 'little and often': in other words keep them interested but don't overdo it. Smart anglers and the match-fishing stars in particular may feed two or more areas in one session, so that when one spot goes quiet they can switch and keep catching.

Groundbait: Super crumbs

The term *groundbait* generally refers not to any substance you put on your hook, but to bait that is mixed and thrown into the water to attract fish and encourage them to stick around and feed. Sometimes confusingly, anglers interchange the terms *groundbaiting* and *loosefeeding*. Both mean the practice of putting out free bait to draw in the fish, but groundbait usually refers to a mixture made by combining breadcrumbs, fishmeal and other powdered ingredients with water. Once mixed to a nice consistency this can be moulded into balls to be thrown in or introduced by a swim feeder, a device which you can check out in Chapter 9.

Grabbing your groundbait

Groundbait can be bought from any tackle shop in bags of dry powder sold by the kilo. The most basic kind is simply brown or white crumb, but various other groundbaits exist. Some smell sweet, others might turn your stomach, but they all attract fish. The names and packaging are usually a giveaway, usually listing the intended species whether that's roach, bream, carp or any other species. Most anglers save cash by mixing these more expensive groundbaits with plain old crumb. For example a bream angler might make a 50/50 mixture of brown crumb and specialist flavoured groundbait.

Mastering the mix

To mix groundbait, a large round bottomed container is best. Special collapsible *mixing bowls* are sold in tackle shops, but a bucket will suffice otherwise. First of all dry ingredients are mixed thoroughly together by hand. Next take a little water in a bait tub and add a little at a time whilst mixing together with your fingers. Avoid adding too much water at this stage but mix in just enough to moisten the ingredients. The groundbait is then best left to settle and fully absorb the water for a few minutes; for this reason many anglers make this the first job when they arrive by the water, letting the mix settle while they tackle up. After five or ten minutes, keep adding a little more water, working the mixture thoroughly between your fingers and breaking down any big lumps to achieve a smoother consistency. When it's ready, you'll be able to squeeze it into little balls but it will still break up relatively easily. This is why it's important to add water sparingly: you can't take out what you've added and a stodgy mess is less than ideal. A dry mix will break up easily, dispersing in the water attractively; a stickier, heavier mix is better for deep or flowing water. When finished, cover the mix with a towel or lid to keep it from drying out.

Groundbait is particularly good for shoal fish like bream and roach, making an attractive cloud as it breaks up in the water. How much you throw in depends on your aim. If a big catch is expected, a big shoal of bream for example, an angler might throw in six or more tennis ball sized helpings. If the fishing is tough, just a walnut sized ball at intervals may be all that's required to keep the fish interested but not give them too much. Remember you can always add a little at first and add more when bites are regular; whereas if you pile it in there's no way of going back.

Sweetcorn: Yellow and deadly

Sweetcorn, often just referred to as corn by anglers, is another timeless bait with wide appeal. Is it natural? Strictly speaking no, or at least we haven't met many fish with tin openers. That fish such as carp, tench, chub and grayling love it is undeniable, though, and even fish which have never tried it before can soon get a taste for sweetcorn. Being yellow, it is easy for hungry fish to locate. It has a potent, sweet scent as well, and you can also buy special fishing corn boosted by other flavours and colourings.

In many ways corn is the perfect convenience bait. You can store a tin or two in your tackle bag or car boot for ages. To avoid the frustration of forgetting the can opener however, you may want to go for tins with a handy ring pull. Corn works best on a smallish wide-gaped hook such as a size 12, nicked on gently so that the hook point is well exposed. You could use a single grain, but sometimes anglers use two or three grains on a bigger hook or hair rigged.

Working up an appetite: Prebaiting

Savvy anglers know the value of loosefeeding free bait to get the fish going, but some take the process a whole step further. What if you were to throw bait in the day before you fish, or even repeatedly over days or weeks? It may seem a lot of effort, but the results can be awesome. Not only does this get the fish used to eating your chosen bait, it can also keep them in a particular area and make them easier to catch once you arrive with a rod.

Prebaiting is ideal if you live near to a particular water or pass one regularly in your daily goings on. It's also great for long or large waters where fish such as carp roam long distances and you might struggle to find them on your day off. How much should you put in? Enough to keep their interest, certainly, whether that means a few handfuls each visit or more. In the latter case it may be worth buying a bulk supply of bait or finding cheaper ingredients to bulk out your freebies.

Bread: Flaky food

Another of those baits which probably caught plenty of fish for your great-great-grandfather, plain old white bread is just as effective today. It can be used in various forms and roach, rudd, bream, chub, carp and tench all love it. For most angling a cheap sliced white loaf will do nicely.

The size of the piece of bread you use depends largely on the size and type of fish you're after. *Flake* refers to a fingernail-sized piece pinched onto a hook such as a size 10, a lovely bait for a tench or carp. Anglers in search of roach and other daintier feeders often use smaller baits using a tool called a *bread punch.* Placing a bread slice on a hard, flat surface, you push one of these devices down on the slice to punch out a little round pellet of bread, usually fished on small hooks from sizes 14-20. Punched bread is a terrific winter roach bait.

Next on the list we also have *bread paste* which is made by kneading white bread together with a little water to form a paste stiff enough to be moulded around a hook, from a tiny pea-sized bait to a walnut-sized lump depending on your target species.

Perhaps the most exciting way of all to try bread is to use a piece of floating crust, and proper bakery or French bread works best for this. A chunk of the crust makes a fine carp bait on a large hook, perfect for targeting surface feeding carp in the summer.

Bread is also great to use as groundbait, thrown in to attract more fish. For roach and shyer species, a few slices of white bread reduced to fine crumbs in a food processor make a suitable groundbait which works well with punched bread on the hook. This can be squeezed into little balls to feed, usually with a touch of water to help bind it together. Indeed, you can also buy ready powdered *punch crumb* which is very similar and just requires mixing with water.

The more traditional way to draw fish in, however, is with *mashed bread*. This is a stodgier mix, ideal for bigger fish in conjunction with a thumbnail-sized piece of bread flake on the hook. To make this, grind up bread and mix it with water to make a sloppy, stodgy but very attractive mix. You'd struggle to throw this any great distance in balls, but it works nicely in a swimfeeder.

Figure 11-2 shows a selection of coarse fishing baits.

Figure 11-2:
A selection of coarse fishing baits: Maggot (a), caster (b), sweetcorn (c), bread flake (d), luncheon meat (e), hempseed (f) and a pellet (g).

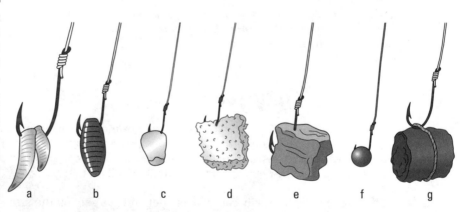

a   b   c   d   e   f   g

Meat Baits: Savoury specials

Various types of processed meat can make highly effective baits. Luncheon meat such as Spam is perhaps the classic, cut into cubes or chunks of a suitable size. A tiny piece on a size 18 might be best for crucian carp, whereas a great big chunk on a size 6 wouldn't be overkill for big, greedy carp or barbel. It can be rather soft for longer casts, so anglers sometimes fry it to give it a slightly tougher 'skin' to keep it on the hook.

Other meats are also worthy of experimentation. Sausage meat, small meat-balls, cat food and even pepperami have all had their moments in fishing. Salty or spicy offerings seem especially useful in murky water as the strong flavour helps fish find the bait.

Boilies: rolling with flavour

Fishing baits have come a long way since somebody put a worm on a hook. Boilies are baits which offer big fish, and especially carp, something rarely found in nature: addictively tasty, highly nutritious treats fit for a big mouth. They are made from countless ingredients but always utilise a powdered food substance bound together with eggs. They come in many flavours. Some are simple classics such as strawberry or fishmeal. Others are totally bonkers, such as lobster thermidor, white chocolate or mint and otter (okay, so we made the last one up). Why a big carp should care for such extravagant flavours is anyone's guess, but they seem irresistibly drawn to potent-smelling, protein rich mixes. Most hardcore carp fishers have their own favourites.

Boilies can be bought in convenient bags ready for use. *Shelf life* boilies keep for ages and are the ones you can find in virtually any tackle shop, sold by the kilo. Some believe that frozen boilies are better still; when thawed out they're certainly a little softer and stinkier, perhaps easier for carp to break down. The other answer of course is to roll your own, but this specialised area is best left for those carp nuts who demand lots of bait.

Boilies also offer a significant advantage over many other baits in that they are boiled into solid balls. This means that the tiddlers in the lake cannot manage them, leaving the bait intact for the moment a great big pair of lips arrive for dinner. To that effect they come in various sizes, always measured in millimetres. The real gobstoppers are perfect for monster carp but the smaller versions also have their moments for good-sized bream, tench and other fish.

Hair-rigging boilies and other baits

Carp can be crafty fish, adept at avoiding suspicious rigs and quickly ejecting baits. For this reason anglers have developed various little dodges to outfox them and perhaps the greatest of all time is the *hair rig*. Whether it is the extra weight or different feel of a hooked bait, carp have a maddening knack of avoiding food with metal in it. Rather than simply hooking the bait, therefore, savvy anglers came up with hair-rigging. This means threading the bait onto a flexible 'hair' so that it sits just off the hook. Not only does this allow the bait to move more freely and be picked up with less suspicion, it also ensures the hook point is always clear to penetrate – even if a whacking great bait is employed.

The hair itself leads below the hook and finishes in a little loop. The bait is impaled on a special needle which fits onto this loop. The bait is then slid onto the hair and a little plastic tag called a *boilie stop* or *bait stop* is placed in the loop to keep your offering in place. Figure 11-3 shows a typical boilie rig.

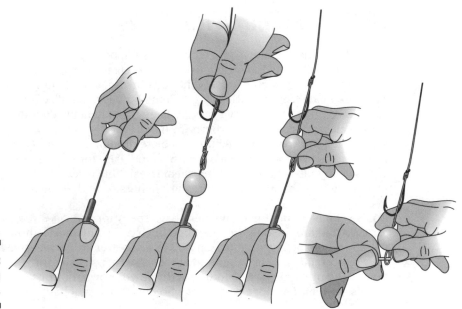

Figure 11-3:
Hair rigging
a boilie.

Pellets and paste: Fishy treats

A great many of the fish stocked in our waters are raised on pellet feed. The pellets used by anglers are an offshoot of this, and indeed, the whole craze began when it was discovered that carp went crazy for handfuls of the rich, oily pellets used on trout farms. Nowadays, all sorts of sizes and flavours of pellets exist for fishing. The little ones of 5 mm or less are much loved by match anglers catching large bags of small carp and tench. Great big pellets make a more selective bait for large carp, barbel and catfish.

These modern baits may not appeal to traditionalists, but do possess several key advantages. They are fairly cheap and because they're dry can be stored for ages, unlike maggots. Their appeal isn't just to stocked fish such as carp, either, and many wild fish such as chub, tench and barbel also eat them with gusto. Each pellet slowly breaks down when immersed, giving off attractive smells to fish. In fact some anglers dampen them before use to speed up the process and make them easier for fish to eat.

Pellets can be ideal to make a carpet of free bait over which you present a boilie or other bait. They work on the hook too, though, if you can find a way to do this. Most sold in bulk are too hard to hook, unless you use a *bait band* or *pellet band*, which is a little rubber ring which stretches around the bait, allowing you to slide it onto a hook. But perhaps the easiest solution is to buy special soft, hookable pellets and you'll find these in all sorts of sizes and types. You can then feed the regular pellets and present a softer one on the hook.

Some anglers also use special paste on the hook to go with their pellets, which uses similar fishy ingredients. You can buy this ready made, or make it yourself, which is simple enough. Paste is made from powdered pellet or fishmeal powder (sold in bags) mixed with a raw egg and kneaded so it is stiff enough to stay on the hook. You can always add water on the bank to soften this deadly bait, which is excellent for carp and tench.

Particle baits: Vegetarian killers

Of all the baits that catch fish, particles are amongst the cheapest of the lot. It's true that you might have to prepare them yourself, but this only adds to the fun and satisfaction. *Particle baits* is a term that covers a broad range of nuts, seeds, pulses, grains and the like. Some of these you can buy in dry form or tinned and ready to go from the tackle shop. Ready prepared is convenient, but it's much better value to buy such baits in bulk and prepare yourself. You may find even better value at pet shops or organic food suppliers. Nuts, seeds and other raw baits should never be used without soaking first: They can be dangerous if not properly prepared as they will swell up inside the fish. For this reason some fisheries ban particles, so do check local rules.

The list of successful particles is a long one, including wheat, chick peas, peanuts, tiger nuts, kidney beans and butter bean to name just a few. Tackle shops sometimes sell these, but you'll also find excellent value fodder at pet stores and health food suppliers. They are mainly used for species that will happily feast on such veggie fodder, such as carp, tench, roach and bream. Besides being used on the hook such baits can be used to make a carpet of food over which you can then present a different bait, miles cheaper than doing this with commercially prepared bait.

Black magic: Hemp seed

Hemp seed is an absolute classic when it comes to catching solid roach, but is also very effective for attracting and holding the interest of carp, tench and barbel. It can be bought in a tin ready to use, but otherwise must be soaked overnight and then stewed in a saucepan for at least an hour. You know it's ready when the seeds go blackish, split and reveal their white insides. As a quick word of warning, avoid using a posh saucepan and do open a window. Hemp can be conveniently frozen in suitable quantities for future trips.

Sweet and selective: Tiger nuts

Carp love the taste and protein content of nuts, pulses and other natural baits. Tiger nuts (which are actually tubers, not nuts!) are a particular favourite. These are a sweet mouthful that have the added advantage that tiddlers can't handle them. Tiger nuts must be soaked for 24 hours, like many other particles, before being stewed in a pan for an hour or more. When prepared like this, they develop into a sweet, sticky bait which carp in particular love.

Dog biscuits: Floating food

When the summer heats up and carp everywhere bask high in the water, it's time to break out the chum mixers. Carp love them and the fishing is highly visual and exciting. They're also a great value bait that can be fished very simply, just using a hook and nothing else.

Plain, roughly round biscuits are the ones to buy, although some of the larger, chewy ones also get results and have the advantage that they can be hooked. The dry kind need special treatment. You can soak them in boiling water to make them rubbery enough to hook or hair-rig, or you could bring a few superglued to fairly large hooks such as 8s.

Full flavoured fishing: Using bait flavourings

As well as all the baits available to the coarse angler, you will also find various liquids, powders and potions on sale. These extra additives are intended to boost the appeal of baits, as the packaging often loudly boasts. Naturally, the million dollar question is: Do you really need them?

The short answer is no. Plenty of anglers catch lots of fish with no such additives. However, there are times when flavours are useful, in a muddy pond or flooded river, for example, where extra scent might really help the fish find baits they struggle to see.

The choice is yours, but should you decide to pep up your bait, the process is hardly rocket science, Powders can be mixed directly into groundbait, or liquids combined with the water you add to your dry mix. For hook baits such as corn, meat or particles, the best way is to place a helping of bait into a sealed container or plastic bag. Next add a dash of flavouring and blow some air into the bag before sealing and giving a good shake. Freezing the results can also help the bait really draw in the flavour. Do remember though, that it is possible to overdo strong flavours and moderation is often better than excess.

Fake baits: Tricky treats

As well as the 'real thing' it's also worth mentioning the now wide range of rubber and plastic hookbaits on offer. It's quite possible to buy rubber maggots, corn or various others. Which leaves one glaring question: With all these lovely fresh baits at our disposal, why on earth would anyone want to use a piece of plastic?

One plus point is that a rubber bait is durable and isn't going to be pulped by minnows. The bigger answer is to do with presentation however. Many fake baits float, and whether you fish in a weedy water where your hooked offering could get lost, or you just want to make it easier for fish to eat your bait, a substitute can be very useful. Using a small shot one or two inches from your hook, it's simple to get a fake bait to sit just off the bottom. Anglers call such morsels *popped up* baits. Better still, you can combine a real piece of bait with a fake one so that you have the advantages of both – say a real piece of corn with a buoyant plastic piece of corn.

Fish for dinner: Predator baits

Fish are by no means all alike in their eating habits, so anglers need a range of baits. Offering a predator a piece of sweetcorn would be a bit like trying to get a vegan to eat a bacon sandwich. The true predators, such as pike, zander and catfish, are primarily fish eaters and hence a suitably fishy bait is required. This could be something they find naturally – a small bleak or dace, for example – but equally seafish baits can also work. Whichever you use, predators have a habit of quickly wolfing prey down, so strike early to avoid trouble removing the hooks.

Deadbaits: Dead and deadly

For a big mouthed predatory fish, a dead prey item is the ultimate free meal. Fish such as pike and catfish are scavengers as well as hunters and will often greedily accept such a find. Any number of fish species will work: roach, rudd, dace, bleak and almost any other you can think of. You can buy these frozen for convenience or catch them yourself, but if you choose the latter do check the rules. Many waters insist you don't plunder fish above a certain size (often six inches) and remove only a limited number at a time. Baits should not be transferred between waters either, because you may spread disease.

A freshly killed coarse fish makes a good offering for any predator and the smaller offerings also work for perch and zander. However, pike and catfish will also accept sea fish. Obviously a pike is never going to hunt mackerel in the local canal, but the potent, oily smell of such a bait makes it a tempting mouthful. We discuss deadbait set ups themselves, along with other rigs, in Chapter 14, but a range of sea deadbaits will work. Mackerel, herring and sardines are especially oily favourites, but smelt, sprats and others are also effective.

Livebaits

Live fish are not a bait that will appeal to every angler. Personally, I (Dominic) tend to use them infrequently and only as a last resort. Call me soft, but I would rather use a lure or fly when the fish want a moving bait. Nevertheless, predators will readily accept a live, natural offering. The choice is yours.

Livebaiting can be a very effective method, but do check rules first because in many places the practice is banned.

Minnows are a classic bait to catch river fish such as perch and chub, but a wide variety of other species can also be used. A small roach, bleak or gudgeon, for example, will also appeal to predatory fish. One reason for this is because thoughtless types may transfer fish from one water to another, potentially also transferring diseases and threatening whole eco-systems.

Admittedly, there is something very exciting about casting a minnow or small fish into the water and watching your line as you wait for a bite. Because bigger predators often feed on baitfish, you're offering a natural bait that triggers a wholehearted attack. For this reason you should strike as soon as you get a decisive bite.

Where to get minnows and other small fish

With few exceptions, you cannot usually buy small fish to use as bait: Don't even think about bringing new diseases to a natural water by using goldfish or other alien species! .The best way is to fish maggots or another small bait with tiny hooks and a float to get a supply, or sometimes you can get a few by running your landing net under the bank.

Never transfer fish between waters. It is not only illegal but could jeopardise the future of a natural habitat for all fishing.

Live fish are hard to keep alive for very long. Usually, the water in a bucket or container heats up and runs out of oxygen, especially in warm weather. Use a large container such as a bucket and change the water at regular intervals. Be sure to release any baits you don't use.

Hooking a small baitfish

The best way to hook a small live fish is to run the point of a single or treble hook through both lips. A little plastic or rubber slip can be slipped over the point to stop the fish wriggling free. You can also hook livebait through the flank and tail. Figure 11-4 shows both methods.

Be careful when you cast. If you really muscle it, you'll rip the bait off the hook and watch it sail out over the water.

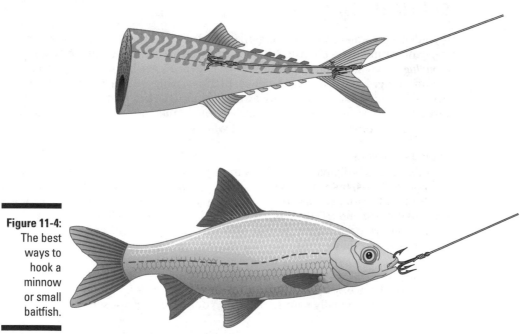

Figure 11-4: The best ways to hook a minnow or small baitfish.

Common Sea Fishing Baits

If it lives in the sea, something else in the sea eats it. Saltwater fish are oppor-tunists, which means that if they get an opportunity, they eat. Like their freshwater cousins, however, sea fish do have preferences, and the biggest bass might prefer, at times, a small sandeel or crab.

As with freshwater fishing, you have choices when it comes to baiting up for sea fish. You can either offer a general bait, such as a worm, or a specific bait meant to match exactly what your fish is feeding on. Either way, get fresh bait, keep it cool, and present it as naturally as possible. (See Chapter 14 for more on rigs.)

You can buy your bait from a tackle shop, but it's also great fun and less costly to dig or catch your own. Sea baits are often exposed at low tide, when rockpools become accessible for example. Just remember to follow all local laws concerning the capture of bait. Some areas are fair game but others, such as conservation areas, ban digging or other methods.

Lugworms: The (not so) sweet smell of success

If you've ever walked a beach or estuary and spotted those wiggly shapes on the sand or mud, the culprits are lugworms. There are two common types, *blow lugworms* and *black lugworms*. Blow lugworms are brown or reddish in colour and grow to around six inches. Blacks are bigger and skankier, growing over a foot long. Like some of my ex-neighbours, they're pretty unsavoury creatures at the best of times. They wriggle about in mud and grit. They also stink. But they're a terrific all round bait that will catch many types of sea fish.

Many tackle shops sell fresh lugworms. But if you don't mind some healthy exercise you can dig blow lugworms during low tide. They like sheltered corners on beaches, but thrive even better in estuaries. A humble garden fork is the tool for the job, along with a bucket. Each worm has a burrow with a squiggly looking *cast* and a little depression nearby. The worm will be somewhere in the middle. To get a supply, find an area with plenty of casts and dig a trench with a fork, carefully turning over the sand to spot any concealed worms.

Blow lug are best wrapped in newspaper. If you keep them cool they will last for two or three days. Forget about them and you may be greeted with a horrific stench and equally sour looks from your family or housemates.

Black lugworms are even more potent than their cousins. These are best left for the specialists to collect and prepare. Many shops sell black lug ready frozen and gutted. These sticky delicacies smell as bad as they look, but are an especially deadly bait for cod and flatfish.

Either type of lugworm is best presented on a long shanked hook of suitable size, typically 1/0 or 2/0, although sea anglers sometimes use a whole bunch on larger hooks for big fish. They should be threaded onto the hook carefully, so that the whole of the hook is covered. This prevents the bait flying off and also stops small fish stealing the worm without getting the hook.

Ragworms: Nippy critters

If you thought that lugworms were less than lovely, just take a look at the ragworm. They may not smell as bad, but besides being lined with many dodgy little legs they also have a nasty pair of pincers. That said, they make a brilliant bait for all sorts of sea fish

Ragworms can be divided into three common varieties. The *common ragworm* is the most usual find, living in wet sand or mud. These can grow over a foot long but are typically half that and reddish brown in colour. *King Ragworm* are the real beasts of the family, living in muddy, nasty places and reaching up to a metre long! On the other end of the scale is the *white ragworm*, often less than 10cm long, but a handy little bait for small species.

You might find white and the odd common ragworm when digging for lugworms, but getting them in numbers is a professional's job. Ragworm are now farmed specially for tackle shops and so it's little bother to get a supply of quality bait. They are best used quickly, although they will keep for a few days if stored in newspaper.

Like other sea worms, rags are best threaded onto a suitable sized long-shanked hook. Grab your worm behind the head to avoid the bite and pass the hook point between the nippers, feeding it up the hook shank so that at least half the body is on the hook. A large worm may require a substantial hook, unless you halve it. White rag and smaller common rags can be threaded on smaller hooks. They work for many species: Bass, pollack, wrasse dogfish and rays all like a decent helping of common or king rag. The whites are an excellent smaller bait for smaller species such as flatfish.

Peeler crabs: Soft targets

Fish eat crabs on a regular basis at sea, but the hard shelled customers make poor baits. Crabs in the process of shedding their shells, known by anglers as *peelers*, are a different prospect altogether, though. They are easily eaten by fish, loaded with potent amino acids and make a sea fishing bait par excellence.

These vulnerable creatures are found in great numbers at certain times of the year, especially in the spring. They can be found sheltering under rocks and snags, and in fact professional bait gatherers lay down sections of piping and other shelters specifically to trap them. The easiest way to check if a crab is peeling is to lift the back of its carapace (the large shield-like shell on its back) with your thumbnail and see if it comes clear. If it does you've found a peeler; if it doesn't you just have an irate crab.

The only straightforward way to get your own supply is to buy them from a tackle shop. They may not be cheap, but they're a superb bait. Bass, cod and flounders are just three species that adore a chunk of peeler crab.

Hooking up a peeler crab bait is not a job for the squeamish. First you should kill the crab by lifting off the carapace and putting a knife between the eyes. Grisly yes, but it's the kindest way. Now you have the job of peeling off all the bits of shell. This gets quicker with practice, but all of the body and legs can be shelled to reveal prime bait. Such a soft bait would never stay on the hook of its own accord so anglers use fine bait elastic to bind it to the hook. The best way is to first thread the hook through a leg socket or two and then wrap the crab squarely to the hook shank with bait elastic. Larger crabs can be cut into sections to make several baits. The legs and pincers also work and can be used to add to the main course, or fished as a bunch. A wide gaped hook is best for crab because you don't want the hook point to be lost in a chunky, messy portion of bait.

Peeler crabs can be stored in a bait tub perhaps with a little seaweed for short periods but are best used as fresh as possible. Another answer is to freeze the crabs. This softens the flesh, however, so they should be peeled prior to freezing, before being wrapped tightly in clingfilm.

Squid: Rubbery snacks

Available from tackle shops and sometimes supermarkets in convenient bulk packs, squid is another staple bait for sea anglers. Cut into strips it makes a reasonable bait for several species, although not as potent as worm or peeler crab. You'll often find baby squid or 'calamari' for sale by the box however, and one of these fished whole is where the bait really comes into its own, a decent bet for larger species such as cod, bass and conger.

Owing to the different types and sizes of bait, squid can be presented in various ways. One advantage is that it is a tough, rubbery bait and won't wriggle off the hook or come apart easily. A lean strip can be used on a small hook, say a size 1, to catch mackerel and pollack under a float. A whole small squid would require a much larger hook and some bait elastic to keep it there, or better still a two hook set up, which anglers refer to as a *pennel rig* (see Chapter 14 for more on rigs).

Make mine a cocktail

Sometimes two baits really are better than one when it comes to fishing. This way, it's possible to marry the advantages of two different offerings in one tasty package. For example, an angler might combine the wriggle of a worm with the extra scent and flash of a strip of fresh mackerel.

Cocktail baits often involve *tipping* an offering such as a worm with a smaller piece of squid or fish. This not only adds extra attraction, but adding an extra small piece of firmer bait also helps keep the worm from sliding down the hook. It can also be a cost-effective way to bulk out expensive baits.

Fish baits: Fresh is best

Almost every fish in the sea will eat other fish at some point. Even the humble flounder is a mean little predator in his own right. It's a fish eat fish world out in the surf and anglers have long capitalised on this by using small fish to catch bigger fish.

The term *livebait* is used by sea anglers in a similar way to coarse fishers and refers to the practice of using a small live fish to catch predators such as bass, pollack and even shark. Equally though, many sea species – even the hunters – are also great scavengers, hence a strip of silver flesh or a whole dead fish can also work well. The options are many, but a few key types are universal.

Sandeels

Look into the waters of any rocky shoreline or estuary in the warmer months and swarms of wriggling, elongated little fish are a common sight. These are sandeels, a major food source for many bigger species. Life is rubbish if you're a sandeel: Everything wants to eat you.

Sometimes sandeels can be bought from local netsmen or tackle shops, or even cornered in the rock pools with a fine net. If you're fortunate enough to have a supply of live eels they make a deadly bait, especially for bass, but also for pollack, mackerel and others. They are best hooked through both lips, much like the coarse angler's livebait pictured earlier in this chapter.

Sandeels can also be fished dead, however. You can buy them blast frozen in packets from many tackle shops and in this state they are still a useful bait. You can fish them head-hooked under a float, or presented on the bottom threaded onto a hook like a worm, or pennel rigged. In this state they still appeal to many fish, including rays and dogfish. As well as the common or lesser sandeel, you may also find much larger baitfish called *launce*, another effective bait.

Mackerel

With firm skin and a deliciously oily flesh, it's not only humans that consider mackerel a tempting meal. Like all fish baits, mackerel is best used fresh and can be used in a wide variety of ways. A small *joey mackerel* can be fished live to catch bass, but it is far more common to use it dead. A strip of mackerel on a smallish hook is an excellent bait to float fish for pollack, garfish and, yes, mackerel, who have no qualms about eating an oily sliver of their own kind!

A strip of mackerel can also be fished on the bottom, often as the tip of a cocktail bait. Larger helping suit larger mouths; either a small, whole fish or the head and attached guts of a bigger mackerel makes a grisly but effective bait for night feeding bass. Anglers in search of conger often use the whole darned lot – an entire mackerel cut a little to ooze scent, or with the sides cut loose but still attached, also known as a *flapper*.

Further fishes

Various other fish make effective baits when used live or dead. A good general rule is that if you find it in good supply where you're fishing, the chances are that any large predators in the area will also be eating it at some stage. Small pouting and whiting are just two examples. One of these live or dead on a suitably large hook might just get the attention of a big bass, cod or conger eel. You won't find these in tackle shops, so the usual method is to catch them with bait scraps on small hooks and save them in a bucket of seawater or suitably cool place.

Prawns and shellfish: Seafood specials

Shrimps and prawns are common all over the coast and so it should come as no surprise that fish love them. Shrimps are diddy little things, but a decent sized prawn makes a great hookbait. Forget the peeled versions from Tescos (although they do catch carp, incidentally), what a hungry fish wants is a live, juicy, kicking prawn. Some use baited nets on deep rock marks or down harbour walls, but the easiest way is to gather them from rockpools at low tide with a fine meshed net. A small, fine meshed coarse angler's landing net is ideal, along with a bucket of cool sea water to store them.

Live prawn is a brilliant bait for bass, pollack and wrasse around rocks. A small float keeps the bait in the fish's sight. They are delicate however and best presented on a small (size 4–8) hook carefully passed through the tail a couple of joints down. And if the fish don't fancy them, you can always cook them in garlic butter when you get home.

Shellfish are less useful as bait, although wrasse will accept shelled limpets and in some regions anglers catch codling or plaice using mussels. Razor fish are another option here, threaded like a worm on a long shanked hook. If nothing else all the above are free if you gather your own, and you could use them as part of cocktail baits.

Why You Can't Take It With You: Disposing of Leftover Bait

You never want to run out of bait while fishing. If you do, it often means the fish are biting better than you expected, and suddenly you reach into the bait bucket and realise you're out of bait. You'll find you never run out of bait on the slow days, when you're probably ready to head home, anyway. Instead, you'll run out of bait in the middle of a dream fishing adventure. So bring enough bait to last for your entire trip.

But what if you overestimate your bait needs? Greg's younger brother, the baithound, has to be physically pulled away from bait-gathering. He never wants to run out, so instead he tries to bury us in baitfish. But what about leftover bait?

You should always use your discretion with leftovers. Think of the impact on the water: Does that tiny pond need kilos of pellets thrown into it? If there are plenty of fish present, however, it may do little harm to put in the remaining bait, especially on a stocked fishery where the fish rely to some extent on introduced feed. One or two anglers I (Dominic) know make a killing on such fisheries at last knockings, going round and catching carp gorging themselves on handfuls of bait thrown in by departing anglers.

The other aspect of the matter is cost. It is a false economy to keep baits until they're old and past their best. However, many kinds of bait can stored away safely for next time. Dry baits last for ages. Others can be frozen. When thawed, it may work nearly as well as fresh bait. So, to sum up: Store fresh, lively bait in the refrigerator and dead bait in the freezer. (And good luck with your housemates.) As a final thought though, the best way of all to deal with small amounts of leftover bait on the day is to give it to another angler, and if it happens to be a youngster who might really appreciate half a pint of maggots or some ragworms, even better.

Chapter 12

It Only Looks Alive: Tricking Fish with Lures

- -

In This Chapter

▶ Figuring out what makes a lure a lure

▶ Understanding how plugs work

▶ Catching up with spoons, spinners, and spinnerbaits

▶ Grasping the benefits of jigs and soft baits

- -

*W*hen fishing with bait, you're offering fish a chance to eat something they can digest. Sometimes you're fishing with something they eat all the time, anyway, like using sandeels for bass, or minnows for perch. Fishing with a *lure,* though, means fishing with a device intended to merely trick a fish into thinking it's found something to eat, usually a smaller fish. Hence lures appeal to predatory fish of all kinds, whether that means a hungry pike, a sea bass or even a salmon.

Fish bite for different reasons: to eat, to defend a territory, or out of predatory instinct. Lures come in many shapes, and offer a wide variety of actions, sounds and appearances, but each one is designed to trigger a fish's willingness to bite, whether it does this on the surface of the water, a few feet down, or on the bottom. Either the lure already looks like something to eat, or you fish it in such a way that it looks good enough to eat, or provocative enough to make fish attack it.

Although fishing with bait works for obvious reasons, there are many advantages to fishing with lures. Lures can be reused many times, whereas bait is often done after one fish chomps it. Lures can be cast repeatedly more easily than bait. And bait can be messy, inconvenient or costly to buy, and hard to gather – lures allow you to head right to the water without worrying about getting bait first. Since you don't need a seat or buckets of bait, lure fishing is also a great method for travelling light, letting you explore lots of water, often with the chance of a big fish. This chapter introduces you to most of the lure categories and also helps you figure out exactly how to choose the right lures for you.

Picking Perfect Plugs

A *plug* is a lure, often made of plastic or wood that looks like a baitfish or other creature that fish want to eat. Also known as *crankbaits,* plugs can swim, dive, pop, or burble, but they are all alike in that they look and act like prey. (A few are molded to look like crayfish or even insects, but most look like fish.) Plugs cast well and come in an array of shapes and sizes. Some are coloured to look like fish, whereas others come in every colour of the rainbow. Most use treble hooks, and some incorporate rattles to attract fish. Plugs are built to fish specific areas of the water column: Some remain on the surface; others dive to several feet; and still others dive nearly 20 feet below the surface.

A whole host of companies make plugs, from American stalwarts such as Bomber and Cordell, through to the likes of Salmo, Abu Garcia and Savage Gear. You should acquire a variety of plugs, and it's a good idea to have a couple of plugs for every 'layer', or depth, of water. If you live by a shallow canal, for example, a selection of shallow runners will be handy; a deep reservoir may call for those that dive down sharply. The following sections explain the different kinds of plugs, moving from surface plugs to deep divers.

TIP

If Peter had only one lure

My favorite lure is the Rapala, which is a plug made by the Rapala company of Finland. I love the way this plug lands in the water; and even more, I love the way that it moves in the water. I've caught bass, trout, pike and even tarpon on the Rapala. *Outdoor Life* once sent me to Finland to research the story behind these phenomenal plugs that had become so popular all over America. What I found was an unusual story for a sport-fishing lure.

At the turn of the 20th century, Americans began to make a plug called a *wobbler.* The wobbler was a little wooden fish that wobbled like a distressed minnow. Some of these plugs found their way over to Finland where a woodsman and fisherman named Lauri Rapala began to fish with them. A good lure meant more to Lauri Rapala than a nice fishing trip; he depended on catching to feed his family. The plug that he devised, the one that came to be known as the Rapala, was designed for trolling behind a canoe-like boat paddled by Lauri. After a great deal of trial and error, Rapala's wobbler minnow began to wiggle and wobble behind him in a very tantalising way. It caught fish exceptionally well and the Rapala went from being a commercial fisherman's preferred tool to one of the most effective weapons in the sport-fishing arsenal.

Popping and chugging plugs: Designed for surface explosions

Popping and *chugging plugs* are designed to imitate either wounded fish on the surface or a whole host of frogs, mice, little birds, insects, and other nonaquatic creatures who find themselves out of their own element. Because predatory fish often watch the water's surface for their next meal, these plugs attract fish by disturbing this plane. Poppers and chuggers have concave, hollowed-out faces, and this scoop pops and chugs against the water when you jerk the lure. (You don't retrieve poppers and chuggers steadily – they call for more of a jerk, pause, jerk retrieve.) Fish hit these lures with abandon, and anglers love the excitement of seeing a fish strike. Sometimes a popper (like the one in Figure 12-1) can pull a nice fish from its lair even at high noon on a sunny day. They tend to work better in warmer water and when fish are actively feeding.

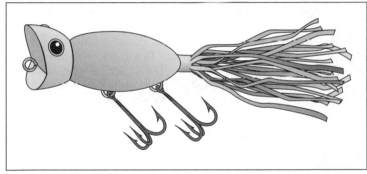

Figure 12-1:
The Hula Popper is great in fresh water.

Plunking a Hula Popper, a classic popping plug, beside a lily pad and giving it little pops or chugs has lured many pike over the years. The Skitterpop is another belter. After casting, let the lure hit the water, and wait until the concussion rings subside. Then give it another pop. Wait again. Then give it a few twitches before pausing, and so on. By using the plug that way, excited predators have time to react.

When fishing with all poppers and chuggers, sometimes the excitement of the surface strike of a large fish can rattle you. You'll be watching the plug, resting calmly on the surface while the rings of your last pop dissipate, when suddenly a fish will rocket to your lure from below. But wait! Don't set the hook until you see that the plug has disappeared, meaning the fish has the lure in its mouth. Sometimes fish miss the plug on the first attack, and setting the hook too early might jerk the lure away, preventing the fish from taking another whack at it (which they often do).

Stickbaits, propbaits and other surface specials

There are various other surface lures or *topwaters* besides the classic popper, many of which offer visually exciting fishing for sea bass as well as freshwater predators. A *stickbait,* until you do something to it, just lays there on the water like – you guessed it – a stick! Usually cigar-shaped, a stickbait needs to be jerked, twitched, and popped by the angler before it has any action. For this reason, it takes a little practice to master the back and forth pattern they call 'walking the dog.' Really, you just need to jerk and pause, jerk and pause, while holding your rod tip low and to the side. This will make the lure dart left, then right. Pike, bass and even the occasional perch or chub can't resist this wandering lure. The Zara Spook is a popular stickbait.

Propbaits, short for propeller baits, look like stickbaits with little propellers on one or both ends. Propbaits, like the Devil's Horse shown in Figure 12-2, *chug-plop-gurgle* and wobble around, all of which are good features that gain the attention of predatory fish in the neighbourhood. The propellers move in two different directions, so they don't twist your line.

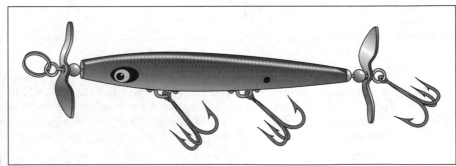

Figure 12-2:
The Devil's Horse is a stickbait with fore and aft propellers.

Floating/diving plugs: Classics that work, even for beginners

Floating/diving plugs float until you begin to reel them in. With many of these plugs, the faster you reel, the deeper they dive (although even deep-running plugs have a cutoff depth beyond which you cannot fish them). A number of fine plugs swim at or near the surface. Some plugs are designed to suspend in the water when paused, and a few sink, but many plugs fit into this floating/diving category.

When buying floating/diving plugs, you'll find that the packaging informs you of the running depth of that lure. Sometimes the depth is incorporated in the name, such as the Rapala DT, or 'Dives-To.' The model DT04 'dives-to' four feet, and so on. A Mann's 1-Minus (great lure!) runs under 1 foot deep.

Some plugs dive deeper than others. In many cases, this deep diving is a function of the angle and size of the *lip,* the angled piece of plastic on the head of the plug. The sharper the angle of the lip and the faster the retrieve, the deeper the plug dives. With this in mind, you might cast your plug over a submerged weedbed that you know lies three or four feet below the surface. Weedbeds provide a number of food sources, and predatory fish know this. As your plug travels over the weeds, you want to get it down to the level of the fish. If they don't see or sense the plug, they won't bite it. By experimenting with a few different retrieval speeds, you can see (and eventually feel) the depth at which your plug runs. Plugs in this go-a-little-deeper category include the Shakespeare Big S, the Rat-L-Trap (similar to the Rattlin' Rapala), and the Rebel Wee-R (shown in Figure 12-3).

Many diving plugs dive only when you retrieve them. When you stop the retrieve, they float to the surface (which is a good thing to bear in mind when your plug is passing over submerged rocks and stumps). Instead of reeling furiously, let the plug rise to the surface, and you will avoid snagging up on underwater hazards.

204 End of Your Line: Enticing Fish with Bait, Lures and Flies

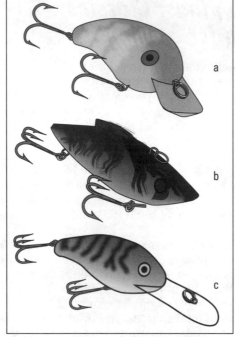

Figure 12-3:
The Big S (a), Rat-L-Trap (b), and Rebel Wee-R (c) are three plugs that work in the middle range of depth.

Deep divers: Good for hitting the bottom

Deep diver plugs are designed to dive deep quickly and stay down there. When fishing open, deep expanses of water, deep divers allow you to cover a lot of water, targeting fish near the bottom or suspended deep in the water column. Like other plugs, deep divers can be cast or *trolled* (pulled behind a boat to cover the maximum amount of water).

Depending on design, deep diving plugs work well at different depths, although no lure runs very well beyond 20 feet deep when cast unless the lure is weighted. Plug design allows them to move well through weeds and around obstacles, because the hooks tend to trail behind and under the plug. Shown in Figure 12-4 are two typical deep divers.

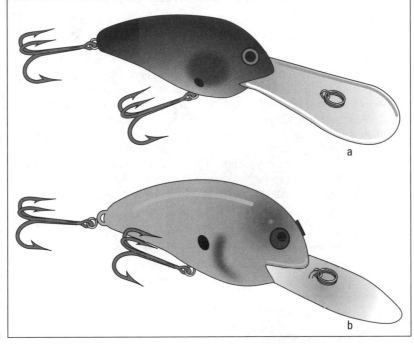

Figure 12-4:
Deep-diving plugs have long lips to enable them to dive steeply and help keep the hooks from hanging up on snags.

Suppose that the fish in the lake are *suspended* (or hanging out) at seven feet below the water surface. So you run to the tackle shop and buy a lure that says that it runs at seven feet below the water surface. Next year, you return to the lake, and you have no idea which lure in your box is the seven footer. The solution is simple: Take a fine-tipped waterproof marker and write the optimum running depth on the belly of the lure.

Spoons: Heavy Metal Time

In the old days, people fished with real tablespoons with hooks attached. If that's tough to picture, just take a look at the business end of a tablespoon. See how it's shaped somewhat like a fish? It also has some metallic sheen, and (by the nature of its design) it has shaded portions as well, so it presents that contrast between light and dark that is characteristic of many successful lures. Figure 12-5 shows a typical spoon.

A PhD in pike: The Kuusamo Professor

Of all the many spoons now in production, not all are equal and it's a case of you get what you pay for. But if it came to a straight choice, I (Dominic) would have no hesitation in turning to the Professor, a big spoon with brilliant swerve and flash, not to mention a long track record of big pike captures. How long? Suffice to say that in Northern Finland, where this king of spoons originates, such lures have been refined over many hundreds of years. Ancient models have been found made of bone, or even cut from the curved sides of copper cooking pots.

In the town of Kuusamo, Lapland, the tradition continues and these namesake spoons possess a shimmer and wallowing action that continue to drive pike wild, including the real monsters. Characterised by a sexy, distinctive curve and a red glass eye, the Professor is truly a spoon to teach any pike a lesson. You can find them in various eye-catching colour schemes, but a large silver or copper coloured beast still takes some beating.

Figure 12-5:
A typical spoon, simple but effective.

Today, fishing spoons and kitchen spoons share only the material they're made from. Spoons come in all sizes and colours, but almost all are metal and designed to sink. Spoons are usually cast or trolled. They wobble when retrieved and feature an eye for your line at one end and a treble hook on the other.

Spoons can be fished different ways, and even topped off with a piece of bait or soft plastic. Usually, a steady turn of the reel is all that's required to make them wobble attractively, although you can also fish them *sink and draw* style which means stopping every now and again to let the spoon drop and flutter before reeling in again. This is useful in deeper water. The appealing wobble and flash of all spoons make them a great lure for about every kind of fish that swims.

Spinners: Easy to Fish, Hard to Miss

Your basic in-line spinner is a metal shaft with a hook on one end, an eye on the other, and a blade rigged so that it spins around the shaft. The blade spins, and the lure spins and wobbles as well as it's pulled through the water. Quite often, some fibres of hair, red wool or rubber is attached to the spinner to give it some extra length and wiggle. A basic spinner is shown in Figure 12-6. Perhaps the classic is the Mepps, made by a French company who have made successful spinners for decades. Most spinners are small – perfect for trout and perch. But giant in-line spinners make popular lures for pike. Spinners can be cast and retrieved quickly, allowing you to cover a lot of water in a hurry, seeking out active fish.

Figure 12-6:
A typical in-line spinner.

Spinners spin, and a spinning lure that spins the way it was designed *always* twists your line. This line twisting can lead to all kinds of casting problems. The solution to these problems is simple: When using a spinner, always use a swivel tied several inches above your spinner (requiring three knots), or use a snap swivel (with one knot). (See Chapter 9 for information on snaps, swivels and other terminal tackle.)

Spinnerbaits: Freaky but Deadly

If spinnerbaits had mothers, even they would be hard pressed to say their little ones were good-looking. Made from a piece of bent wire, dressed with a few blades, some lead and a skirt, the *spinnerbait* is one of the most bizarre lures. But remember: It's not how a lure looks to you that's important. What's important is how a lure looks to a fish. A spinnerbait moving through the water looks like a baitfish or other animal doing its best to get away in a hurry. The vibrating blades also attract fish by sending out tiny shockwaves. This rapid action often triggers an attack response in predatory fish. A spinnerbait can be retrieved fast or fairly slow (as long as there's enough speed to spin the blades). With just one fairly well protected hook it's a good choice for weedy water too.

Figure 12-7:
A spinner-
bait.

Jigs, Soft Plastics & Swimbaits: Rubbery All Stars

Lures have come a long way since hunters created fish catching devices out of copper and hand carved wood. Today's lures utilise all manner of soft plastics to create supremely flexible, vigorous swimming artificials which are pleasing on the eye as well as effective.

Jigs and soft baits originated in America, where a staggering array of lures are produced to catch fish and anglers alike. Beyond the sales hype however, the new generation of soft plastic jigs and swimbaits have several key advantages in their favour. They are versatile, full of movement and dead easy to fish. Their flexibility also makes them work at all speeds, including the kind of creeping pace at which spinners or plugs stop working. It's true that soft lures lack the durability of hard bodied artificials, but they also tend to be cheaper and hence fairly kind on your pocket.

Jigs: Bouncing the bottom

A *jig* is a the common term for lures which consist of a weighted *jig head* along with a soft body. The jig head itself is a piece of metal, usually lead, with a hook attached. The original jigs were dressed with natural materials such as bucktail (as with the traditional jig shown in Figure 12-8). Nowadays most anglers attach a soft body (like the examples in Figure 12-9), which is shaped like a fish, worm or other prey item. With a vast array of jig heads and soft bodies available, a wide range of possibilities exist, from small jigs suited to perch, right through to great big monstrosities perfect for large pike or deep sea fishing for cod, bass or pollack. You can buy them as separate components, but you can also buy ready-rigged models or kits, which make a good starting point.

Jigs cast well in the wind and they sink rapidly. They can also be used directly beneath the rod, however, for example off the side of a boat or man-made structure, a practice sometimes referred to as *vertical jigging.* Sometimes fish take a jig as it drops to the bottom. Jigs can also be retrieved steadily like a plug or spinner. But more commonly the angler *jigs,* which means raising and lowering the rod tip to bounce the lure off the bottom. This motion stimulates a response in many fish, and especially those predators that like to hug the deck. Jigs come in a wide range of sizes, both in terms of weight and hook size, and in a variety of styles. Some jigheads are round, others flat or specially-shaped – each design works in a different way.

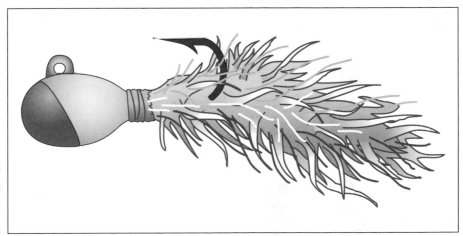

Figure 12-8:
A traditional bucktail jig.

The real advantage of jigs is that the weight is part of the lure, eliminating the need for a separate sinker. Thus, when choosing jigs, weight matters. Pick jig weights that match the conditions you're fishing. In still water, say a lake, a small 2 inch bodied jig weighing 10g or less would be effective for perch. In a big river, jigs over an ounce could be used to cut through the current. In sea fishing applications, jigs may weigh several ounces or more to reach great depths, over an offshore wreck for example.

Soft Baits: Plastic Worms and Beyond

Soft baits, generally plastic, are all the baits that aren't hard plastic like plugs, or metal like spoons. These lures look like small fish (often called *shad* designs), worms and even crayfish, eels and frogs. Ready-rigged versions are often described as *swimbaits,* dealt with in the next section. The rest you must rig yourself, which is more effort but has the advantage that you can customise your approach and use them exactly as you like. You can fish such soft plastics unweighted on a large hook, but they are more often attached to a jig head. This is done by threading them onto the hook, in a similar way to how you might hook a worm, so that the hook shank is concealed within the body. The sections that follow outline a few soft plastic baits and show you how to rig them.

Experiment with different types of soft plastic baits (like the ones shown in Figure 12-9). Depending on the kind of fish you pursue, you can probably find a soft plastic bait of a size and type that appeals.

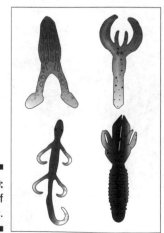

Figure 12-9:
A range of
soft plastics.

Examining three types of soft baits: Worms, fish and swimbaits

There are many kinds of soft baits available today, with more coming on the market every day. Most, though, fit into one of several categories. (And more importantly for you, they are rigged and fished primarily in one of several ways.) The following sections walk you through the three main kinds of soft baits.

- ✔ **Plastic worms and creatures:** Are fairly versatile baits, which work for perch and zander, but also sea species such as pollack. Plastic worms come in many lengths and colours, and although some could almost pass for lobworms, other oddities have crazy twisted tails, skirts and metal-flake colouring! They are usually fished on a jig head, and bounced along, or just off, the bottom. They can also be slithered off a lily pad or pulled off a log.

- ✔ **Fish:** A great many of the soft plastics available are shaped like fish, for the obvious reason that this is the main food of so many predators. Perhaps the most common is the *shad*, a classic paddle-tailed fish shape that comes in many sizes and colours but will catch just about any predator. Perch and chub will take a small one, pike, bass and even cod will take a bigger mouthful. The Kopyto Relax is arguably the deadliest shad of them all, whilst other less usual fishy shapes such as the quirkily named Skippy-fish also have their moments.

  Soft plastic lures get their action from the way that the user retrieves them: fast jerks, erratic jerks, or trolling. Make the predator believe there is an injured, easy meal on offer and there is every chance it will make a sudden grab. Shads and other soft fish are a highly versatile way to achieve this effect wherever you're fishing.

- ✔ **Swimbaits:** These days many soft plastic lures come ready to fish. Many dispense with the jig head entirely, being internally weighted. These lures are known as *swimbaits* although you still hear them referred to under the general title of jigs. These baits are often made of soft plastic, although they are sometimes hard-bodied, too, and with detailed finishes and sometimes hinged bodies they look and swim most convincingly.

  The real beauty of swimbaits is that they work in a wide range of waters straight out of the box. They can be reeled in steadily to wiggle appealingly, or retrieved with jerks and pauses to simulate a stuttering, injured fish. Storm, Savage Gear and various other brands all have their own models and it's a good policy to take a selection. A slow sinking swimbait could prove a killer on a shallow, weedy river for example, whilst a heavily weighted model may be necessary for great depths. Figure 12-10 shows a detailed swimbait.

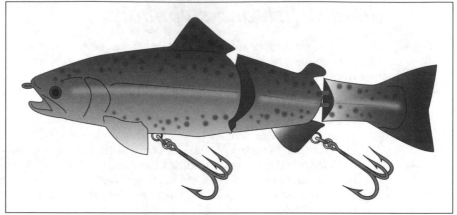

Figure 12-10:
A finely detailed and hinged swimbait.

Narrowing Your Lure Options by Asking Some Key Questions

Literally thousands of lures are available. From dual-propellered, double-jointed plugs as big as a Hummer (or at least they seem that way) to tiny leadhead bucktail jigs, and from little scale models of trout that look absolutely lifelike to salads of rubber legs and metal blades that look like something that came to life in the junkyard of a toy factory – so many lures are available that you could go bankrupt buying them all. (Some of the newest lures might cost over ten quid . . . each!) But many are just endless variations on a theme. Others have been improved upon by new technologies. Know what to buy so you don't have to buy them all.

Hybrid baits are another popular choice. These aim to combine the attraction of different lure types in one neat package, for example a lure with a hard head and a soft wiggly tail, or a hard plug with a spinner tail. Taking these many weird and wonderful creations for a swim is all part of the fun of lure fishing.

The following sections present six questions you should ask when buying and using lures.

How deep does the lure run?

If you want your lure to catch fish, you need to make sure it goes deep enough to attract the fish where they're hanging out. If the fish you're hoping to catch are suspended five feet below the surface, you're probably going to have to go to them (that is, you must fish at their level) rather than have them come to the surface. On the other hand, if they are busy feeding on the surface, a deep-running lure won't be very effective. And if you're fishing in shallow water, or over a weedbed, a deep-running lure will continually snag the bottom or the weeds – not a very effective presentation.

Where's the action?

When you retrieve the lure, think about how the lure moves. Does it wobble and shimmy, does it dive and surface, does it burble and pop, or does it chug and sputter? Any of these characteristics can serve either to excite a fish or to turn it off. A noisy, rattling plug might excite the local pike in spring, for example, but a lure with a slower, subtler action could be far better in the depths of winter when the predators feel sleepier. Different water also dictates different action. (The pronounced action that spurs a bite in off-colour water can be a real loser in clear water.) Experiment to find your own best-fit lures.

How fast is the lure designed to move through the water?

Make sure you know the optimum range of speed for any lure you're considering so you can fish at its ideal pace. Because of the advances in reel-making technology, a few turns of a reel's handle can move a lure through the water more swiftly than was possible in the old days. Many lures are at their best at a certain speed and you should aim to work out what suits each lure. If in doubt, try it out under your feet and watch closely to gauge what works best.

How big should the lure be?

Although the general rule of 'big bait, big fish' is sometimes a good one to follow, the optimum size of a lure is important and it may vary from place to place. In one area pike may feed heavily on little dace, for example; in another water the big ones might prefer a hand-sized roach. Whatever the case, you want to use the right size lure to attract them. This rule of thumb doesn't mean that your lure must always slavishly imitate the size of a fish's food. Sometimes, a little bigger lure works well. At other times, a much bigger lure works better. I can't tell you what the right size lure is in any given situation, but fish can and do. If you're not getting any bites, switch to a larger (or smaller) lure. Experiment until you start getting bites.

Does the lure raise a racket?

In the sense that sound consists of vibrations, and all fish sense vibrations through their lateral lines, then all lures produce sound. The question that you need to answer is this: What sounds turn fish on, and what sounds turn them off? As with everything in angling, no hard-and-fast rule applies, although certain tendencies apply under certain conditions. For example, in the bright light of day, a big, noisy lure (such as a Jitterbug; see the earlier 'Wobblers: Great if you lack finesse' section) may not do very much to attract fish. At night, however, the gentle chugging of a Jitterbug can be just the thing to attract a pike in low-light conditions. Some lures rattle and these can be very useful for coloured water or days when the usual lures fail to get a response.

Does a lure's colour count?

Fish respond to colour, but they don't see colour in the same way that you and I do. Take the colour red. Red is the first colour of lure that many people pick out, but after a red lure goes very deep in the water, that vibrant scarlet turns to dark grey. The thing to remember about colour is that water absorbs colour differently to air, so the brilliant hues of a lure in the air of a tackle shop may not even be visible to a fish in the water. Also, sunlight makes colours appear differently at different times during the day.

Water clarity matters when it comes to choosing the colour of your lure. If the water is exceptionally clear (you can tell this just by studying the water near the bank), naturally coloured lures work well. In other words, fish your lures that mimic real prey, like the plug painted to look like a perch (especially if the fish in that body of water feed heavily on perch). If the water is murky, try your lures painted in brighter, less natural colours that stand out. Stained or muddy water calls for bright chartreuse spinnerbaits or lurid orange plugs.

Ultimately, you always want to look at colour from a fish's point of view. Most lures are designed to appeal to anglers, as well as fish, and it isn't always the flashy paint job that gets results. Perhaps the best example of this is with black lures. When viewed from below against a light surface, black stands out beautifully, and yet when it comes to surface popping and shallow diving plugs, bright green and orange plugs outsell black plugs many times over. It is anglers, rather than the fish, who have wallets and therefore the final say in the matter.

Chapter 13

Fish Don't Fly, But Flies Catch Fish

• •

• •

*O*nce upon a time, when the only fish you fished for with a fly was a trout, a *fly* was a bit of feather and fur on a hook. It was always meant to look like an insect, such as the classic mayfly. But these days, fly fishers angle for trout, salmon, pike, carp, chub, bass, and on and on. So a *fly* no longer simply means 'something that looks like an insect.' But anglers who use a fly rod to deliver concoctions that look like shrimps, fish fry, sandeels and even swimming frogs and mice, but still refer to the thing on the end of their line as a fly.

The key thing about a fly is its weight – or lack thereof. Bait fishing rigs and lures all have some weight to them. The plug, spinner or worm and sinker that you cast out is heavier than the fishing line. The weight of the thing at the end of your line bends your rod and is catapulted to where you want to fish. A fly, on the other hand, has almost no weight. Using a heavy fly line in a bullwhip motion carries the fly to your target. The fly, when properly delivered, seems to sail to the target and land as softly as a snowflake. When stealth and delicacy are required, a fly may work well when nothing else seems to do the trick – and not just for trout.

This chapter covers many of the popular flies that work well in a variety of applications. Saltwater or pike flyfishing often call for heavier gear and larger flies. The flies detailed here work especially well in freshwater and for the most common quarry of the fly fishing angler: the trout.

Taking a Look at Where the Fly in Fly Fishing Came From

To best understand what anglers mean when they talk about 'matching the hatch,' it's helpful to understand mayflies. Figure 13-1 shows you the life of the mayfly, which begins life as a little nymph on the bottom of the stream. On the last day of its life, it sprouts wings, flies up into the bright summer sky, and, in a grand climax, mates for the first time while in midair. It then immediately dies and falls to the surface of a clear-flowing stream.

The following sections give you a look at the life cycle of the mayfly, which is of paramount interest to the trout and the fisher of trout. Why? Because terms that you come across again and again in fly fishing – wet flies, dry flies, and nymphs – all have their origin in the life cycle of the mayfly. Just to confuse everyone, anglers tend to refer only to the classic large, cream-coloured insect by the name 'mayfly'. But in reality there are many kinds of mayflies, mostly smaller, which are often referred to as *olives*. They all follow a similar sequence.

Stream born: The nymph phase

A mayfly starts out as an egg on the bottom of a stream. Soon, the egg hatches, and out crawls a many-legged little critter known as a *nymph* – or immature mayfly. When you see trout with their noses down, rooting about on the bottom of a stream, they are often feeding on nymphs.

About one year to the day from when it began life as an egg, the nymph is ready to hatch and become a full-fledged mayfly. When fly rodders talk about a *hatch,* they don't mean what happens when the egg becomes a nymph. Technically speaking, this change is a hatch, but this type of hatch isn't of much interest to trout; therefore, it is of even less interest to trout fishermen.

Time to shed some skin: The emerger phase

The *emerger stage* begins when all the mayflies of a particular species – and millions of mayflies may be in a single stretch of a stream – shed their old skin, rise to the surface, sprout wings, dry themselves off, and (for the first time) fly. This process, which takes a few minutes for each individual fly, normally takes a few days to play itself out for all of the flies of a given type on any given stream. Usually, a hatch begins in the warmer waters downstream and moves upstream, which has relatively cooler waters.

In this period of time, between when they begin to shed their skin and when they first take flight, the mayfly is at its most vulnerable. When a hatch is on, the trout know that plenty of easy-to-catch food is around, just for the taking.

Figure 13-1:
The mayfly begins at the nymph stage and then becomes an emerger, a dun and finally a spinner.

All grown up: The dun phase

When the mayfly has broken out of its old nymph case and is in the wriggling-out-of-the-wet-suit phase, it's often known as a *wet fly*. Many mayflies never make it to full-blown, flying-around mayflydom. For one reason or another, they cannot shed their cases and they just float on the surface as stillborns – stillborn, but still tasty to the trout. Most of the time, though, the mayfly does make it out of the case; and most of those that do rest for a while on the surface of the water, drying their wings and just generally getting their bearings. They're now known as *duns*.

You can easily tell if an insect is a mayfly in the dun phase because its two wings are folded back and stick up in the air like the sail of a sailboat. The mayfly may beat its wings every now and again in order to dry them, further attracting the attention of the trout. To the hungry trout, this is the sitting-duck phase. Because the mayfly instinctively knows that it may be gobbled up at any moment, it is in a hurry to get off the water. Because the trout knows this too, it will feed purposefully as long as there are mayflies on the water.

Ready to mate: The spinner phase

If a mayfly manages to survive the emerger phase and the dun phase, it is ready for one last change into the *spinner phase*. Shortly after becoming full-grown, a mayfly flies around for the first time and heads for a streamside bush or tree. After it reaches that sanctuary, its tail grows longer and its wings lose their milky translucence and become clear. Then, that evening or possibly the next day, the spinners fly over the stream and mate in midair. The male, having done his assigned job, drops to the surface of the stream and dies. The female deposits her eggs in the stream (where they cling to a rock, hatch, and start the nymph cycle all over again). Following this, the female joins her husband-for-a-day on the surface of the stream. At this time, a trout sees a huge amount of delicious mayfly meat that has no chance of escaping.

At this stage of the mayfly life cycle, known as a *spinner fall,* an angler can encounter some amazing fishing. In the case of several mayfly species – the best fishing in the whole hatch is often during the spinner fall.

Figuring Out Which Fly to Use

During any hatch, the trout may be keyed in on one phase of the mayfly's life cycle. If you can figure out what the trout are taking, you have a fighting chance to 'match the hatch.' This match-the-hatch principle is one of fly fishing's deeply held articles of faith: You try to give the trout a fly that looks like the food that it is currently eating.

Just as mayflies have different stages of life, different artificial flies represent each of those stages. We help you determine which fly to use when in the next sections.

Opting for the dry fly

For most trout anglers most of the time, the *dry fly* – any fly that stays on the surface film of water and resembles a dead or hatching insect – is the preferred method of taking trout, probably because when a trout eats your dry fly, you get to see the whole thing. If and when the trout takes your fly, it engenders one of angling's great feelings (just as the plug fisherman gets a happy jolt when watching a pike slam a popping plug; we cover plugs and other types of lures in Chapter 12). Fish won't always take a dry fly, and you need to adjust if they're feeding, say, on the bottom of a stream. But most fish, sooner or later, are susceptible to dry flies.

However, a dry fly (shown in Figure 13-2) is not always the most effective method, and it doesn't always pull up the biggest fish (although there are times when it does both). The traditional dry fly has the following features:

- The tail is as long as the body.
- The tail is usually made of stiff fibres from the *hackle* (neck feathers) of a rooster. The hackle is what allows the traditional fly to float high and dry – just like a real mayfly.
- The body is made of fur or synthetic material wound around the hook with silk thread.
- The wing is traditionally made from soft feather such as duck, but many other materials, from deer and elk hair to synthetics, work.

Not every dry fly is tied to imitate a mayfly, and not every dry fly mayfly imitation has all of the parts in the picture. For example, I (Peter) often use the Comparadun on flat, clear water. This mayfly imitation has no hackle, but it floats just fine. Of course, other fly species also have their own adult phases copied by a suitable dry fly, and this includes many flies which are simply blown onto the water by accident (like the crane fly, for example).

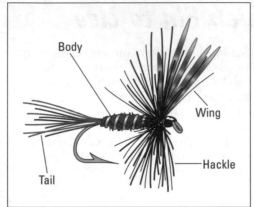

Figure 13-2:
The classic
dry fly.

The mayfly spinners fall at the end of the hatch; and for the next few hours, you may have excellent dry-fly fishing. In this case, you can use a special kind of dry fly made to imitate the spinner; this type has a less-bushy hackle and wings that lie flat out rather than upright. (I fill you in on the spinner phase of the mayfly life cycle in the earlier related section.)

The whole idea of a dry fly is that is floats on the surface just like a natural fly. But fur and feathers and other fly-making materials have a tendency to get wet in the water (no surprise here). When you also consider the weight of the hook, you are dealing with something that naturally wants to sink after a while. So you have to do something to help the fly float. You can do three things to give your fly a fighting floating chance:

- **Use a floatant.** Some *floatants* (materials designed to waterproof flies) are gloppy and some are liquid, but all floatants are designed to keep the fly on top of the surface film. You don't need to heap floatant on, but you should use it. I find that rubbing the stuff between my thumb and forefinger and then rubbing my fingers on the fly avoids saddling my fly with a large gob of goo on top.

- **Use a drying substance.** Also useful are commercial powders that work on the same drying-out, or *desiccant,* principle as cat litter. Use a commercial desiccant powder after you catch a fish, when the fly is wet and slimy, or when your fly starts to sink prematurely. Simply take the fly – no need to clip it off the leader – and put it in the desiccant bottle; then close the bottle and shake it. When you take the fly out, it is covered with white power. Blow off the loose powder. Give your fly a few false casts to remove any residual powder, and start fishing again.

- **Use the air.** Sometimes you run out of floatants and desiccants, or your floatant may have fallen out of your vest or you just plain forgot it. In these cases, swishing the fly in the air with a few crisp false casts usually dries out all but the most waterlogged fly for a reasonable float. In heavy, choppy water, however, you are simply not going to get much of a float without using a floatant or a desiccant.

Discovering when you may want a wet fly

Wet flies are called *wet flies* because, since they're submerged, they get wetter than dry flies. Back in the old days of fly fishing, wet flies served for everything: duns emergers, nymphs, and spinners. Figure 13-3 shows a classic wet fly, which has the same parts as the dry fly we describe earlier in this chapter but with a differently positioned wing. Instead of riding high and dry, a wet fly lays down on the water or sinks. Also, the hackle is softer (or *webby*) so that a wet fly rides in or under the surface film.

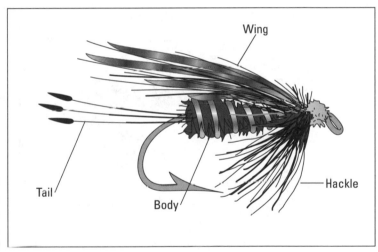

Figure 13-3: A classic wet fly.

Going the nymph route

A *nymph* imitates the nymph stage of the mayfly life cycle and usually looks more like a natural nymph than a wet fly does. The wing is gone, replaced by a wing case and nubby fur that often imitates the gills that run along the side of a nymph's body (as shown in Figure 13-4).Whether fished just under the surface or sunk further down in the water, the nymph mimics the purposeful action of a live nymph rising towards the surface and hatching into a dry fly. Nymphs are versatile flies that often score when nothing else does. Remember, even during a blizzard-like hatch, more nymphs are in the water than dries are on the surface, and trout frequently continue to feed on nymphs through the hatch.

The Brilliant 'New Zealand' Method

With nymphs and wet flies, the question is always, 'How does an angler fish it?' On a river, sinking flies can be trundled along with the current, just as the float fisherman might let a bait travel naturally with the current. Bites can be hard to spot however, so sometimes fly fishers use an indicator. This can be a little foam device that slots onto the line. But even better is to use a dry fly above as an indicator. Often called *New Zealand style* nymph fishing, this little dodge couldn't be simpler: First, tie on a fairly buoyant dry fly to the end of your leader (a Klinkhamer or caddis is ideal). Now tie two feet or so of fine line directly to the bend of the hook. Onto this you attach your wet fly or nymph, which will then be suspended neatly below the surface. When a fish takes the wet fly, your dry fly will be pulled under instantly – time to strike! This method is a good way to hedge your bets. It's an easy way to present two flies. Great on a stream, but it works on lakes too.

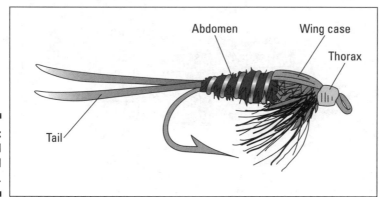

Figure 13-4:
A typical artificial nymph.

Of all trout flies, the artificial nymph looks most like the natural product (at least to the human eye). The wing case, thorax, abdomen, and tail all correspond to a stream-borne nymph.

Use the flies and methods that you are most comfortable with. In fact, this tip goes for bait fishing and lure fishing, too. If you have no confidence in a certain lure, fly, bait, or a certain technique, you cannot catch many fish. On the other hand, sometimes the 'wrong' fly, fished with style and confidence, takes the fish. Or (put another way) it isn't always *what* you fish with, but *how* you fish with it that counts.

Look at the water

You come down to a stream and see a bunch of rising fish. 'Oh, Boy!' you say to yourself as you tie on a mayfly imitation. You float a dry over the trout a dozen times. The trout continues to rise in a very splashy way, sometimes leaping clear out of the water. You are excited, but nothing happens with your fly. 'Must be taking emergers,' you say. You tie on a wet fly (or maybe you use a special pattern that looks like an emerger). You fish with great concentration, looking for the slightest twitch in your line. The trout keeps rising. You're starting to dislike this trout. It really is thumbing its nose (or maybe 'finning its nose') at you. 'Hmm, Mr. Trout must be taking a really teeny fly that I can't see,' you tell yourself as you give up on that fish and go after another splashy riser.

What went wrong? Very often a splashy rise means *caddisflies*. As the caddis pupa rockets to the surface, the trout follows it, trying to get up a head of steam that results in an attention-grabbing rise.

Remember: Next time you get to the stream, rather than casting blindly to a rise, you should study the water to see what's *really* happening.

Anglers aren't as finicky or precise about caddis imitations as they are about mayfly imitations. A typical artificial caddis has a body like a mayfly, but the caddis wing is tied in a down position, and the hackle is often wound through the body (the flytier's term for this winding technique is *palmered*). This kind of hackle breaks up the light pattern on the surface of the water and, from the trout's vantage point, gives the fly a skittering kind of appearance.

Picking meatier lures and streamer flies

Trout, especially large trout, like to eat small fish. Whether the fish is one of their own kind or just any tiddler, such as a minnow, stickleback, or roach fry, is not that important. To a trout, a baitfish (compared to a dry fly) provides much more meat on the hoof – make that meat on the fin. Anglers have long known this, and their attempts to imitate this favoured food source resulted in the *streamer fly,* often referred to as *lures* (but not to be confused with plugs, spinners and the lures we look at in Chapter 12). Such flies are not fished gently like traditional dries or wets, but tweaked or drawn provocatively through the water to get a response. If you fish stocked pools for rainbow trout, this can be an excellent and exciting way to catch.

A sideways feather has the rough outline of a fish and so many traditional streamer patterns started out as a pair of feathers tied lengthwise along the shaft of a hook. And many fish were caught, and continue to be caught, with simple streamers. In later times, and especially with the growth of fishing for aggressive, stocked rainbow trout, more fluid materials such as marabou have taken over, along with synthetic tinsels and fibres that shine, sparkle and wave seductively. Figure 13-5 shows two lures for trout.

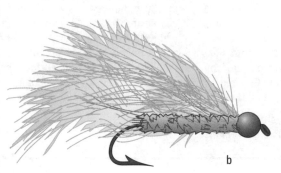

Figure 13-5:
Two modern lures, the Cat's Whisker (a) and a Muddler Minnow streamer fly (b).

Choosing the caddisfly

A *caddis* is a type of insect found in most trout streams and also most lakes. Trout and other fish prey on caddis in addition to the mayfly, which makes a caddisfly another alternative for you. However, using a caddisfly, which can be fished like a dry fly, is like travelling in economy compared to fishing with a mayfly imitation (that's considered first-class trout fishing).

Pick up a rock from the river bottom, turn it over, and chances are you can see some immature mayfly nymphs scurrying for safety. You may also notice a number of little cocoons made of twigs or small pebbles. These little cocoons are *caddis cases*. Inside the cocoons, the caddis larvae grow to their next stage, *the pupa stage,* which is sort of the booster rocket for the mature caddisfly. When the caddis pupa is ready to hatch, it often moves very swiftly to the surface, emerging from the water like a Polaris missile going straight up. Unfortunately, a caddis doesn't usually do as well as a Polaris missile on its first flight attempt. The fly often falls back to the water and tries to take off again. It keeps flapping its wings, bouncing and skittering on the surface. All this activity, both above and below the surface, can excite the trout into feeding. Later, when a swarm of caddis descends on a stream to lay eggs, the trout are on the lookout for these returning adults, which give themselves away by dotting the surface repeatedly as they make their all important deposits.

You can tell a caddis from a mayfly when they are on the water because caddis wings don't stick up like little sailing boats (which is how many anglers traditionally describe the upright wing of mayflies). They lay flat. Caddis are more fluttery too and are often mistaken for small moths.

Fingers on buzzers: Midges for stillwaters

So far we have focused much of our attention on river flies, and mayflies in particular, which provide a good basis to examine how aquatic insects develop and how anglers copy each stage of the cycle. For many anglers, however, the action takes place on stillwaters, from small pools to big reservoirs. The staple diet of fish here is very often *buzzers,* which is simply a generic name for that wide range of smallish insects better known as midges. These hatch year round and are present just about everywhere.

The life cycle of the buzzer demands different fly patterns at each stage, just as that of the mayfly does. The buzzer starts life as an egg, before hatching into a bloodworm. These are wriggling, elongated critters that live on the bottom of the lake or pond, and are often coloured red, hence the name. Anglers sometimes fish bloodworm imitations slow and deep, but the real fun starts when these pupae make their journey towards the surface to hatch. They are small, segmented creatures, often coloured black, brown or olive. Most flies referred to as buzzers replicate this stage and the artificials are deceptively simple, often little more than dark thread on a hook. In fact, the curve of a hook quite nicely mimics the curly, lashing shape of the real thing. Figure 13-6 shows a typical buzzer.

Figure 13-6:
A typical buzzer, ideal food for still-water trout.

You can use just one, but buzzers are often fished as a *team* of up to four flies. We'd recommend you start with just one or two to avoid tangles. A really easy way to set up two flies is simply to tie a really long Surgeon's Loop knot (see Chapter 14 on knots) and then snip the loop within a few inches of the knot so that you have a long section plus a shorter tag (or *dropper)* of six inches to add a second fly. Buzzers are best fished on a long leader – try twelve feet to begin with – and either retrieved very slowly or simply allowed to drift in a breeze. Watch the end of fly line carefully and strike at any little pull. A bite often looks just like someone gave your fly a gentle tug, as a trout intercepts your buzzer.

Just like mayflies, trout also love to grab buzzers as they are emerging at the surface (look out for fish rolling as they take buzzers in or just under the surface). Special emerger buzzers are the answer in this scenario, fished in the surface film so that the fly is not riding high but stuck in the surface film. Much like mayflies, some midges get stuck as they hatch, which is bad news for these little suckers, but good news for the trout.

Extra: Terrestrials

Sometimes on rivers or stillwaters, nothing much is hatching, but the trout can still be seen hitting flies on the surface. Windy lakes are a classic setting for this scenario, as a breeze sweeps flies from the land and deposits them on the water and at the mercy of trout. These flies are called terrestrials because their natural environment is on land, not water. Beetles, moths and daddy-long-legs are all classic terrestrials.

Terrestrials can make up a large part of the trout's diet, especially on blustery days when many insects are blown out of the bushes and trees. Indeed, they can be a godsend during those times when buzzers or mayflies are not hatching and the fish rely on other food sources. Streams with lots of tree growth are often full of beetles, ants and other terrestrial trout food. Another classic setting is in the autumn, when daddy-long-legs (also known as craneflies) are abundant. Unluckily for them they are clumsy when airborne, and with a little wind accidents soon happen. If you thought they made poor fliers, daddies are even more rubbish at swimming. Trout know this and seize them aggressively. Fish a big, leggy dry fly and you could be in for some serious fun.

A Rundown of Flies That Work Everywhere

Zillions of pages have been written about flies. Every fly angler has an opinion, a favourite fly, a neat little trick. Although I have no doubt that every situation has a best fly, you can spend years learning these situations and I would much rather spend my time fishing. If you want to learn a great deal about a great number of flies, don't take this as a warning not to learn. Your continuing study can pay off. Still, as the years go by, I find that I catch more fish with a smaller selection of flies. I really believe that a well-presented fly that gives the *impression* of the real thing is often just as effective as a fly that *duplicates* whatever it is that the fish are eating. And sometimes, the best strategy is to go against the hatch and give the fish something that stands out from the crowd.

So this section contains a list of ten flies that are worth a place in any fly box. In time, you may make up your own slightly different list; but I guarantee that your list will have a good number of the flies I am recommending here because they are tried-and-true fish catchers.

Pheasant Tail Nymph

The pheasant tail nymph (often shortened to 'PTN' by anglers) is one of those fly designs which proves that simple is often best. Don't be fooled though: This modest nymph is a killer. Dating from well before the advent of fancy modern materials, it is little more than a body and tail of pheasant fibres with coils of fine copper wire to give the segmented appearance of a small mayfly or *olive* nymph. It's a pretty good impression, too – sparse, slim and deadly. The PTN is a cracking little fly for just about any shallow trout stream, although they will also catch on still water. Flip over some stones on the river to get an idea of the scale of the natural nymphs you want to copy. Sizes 14 to 16 are especially useful.

Black Buzzer

If there's one trout food item that no stillwater fly fisher should ignore, it's the buzzer. As we've already discussed, they hatch year round and trout thrive on them. The imitations we use are often simple to say the least, just a few turns of thread, a rib and possibly a hint of bright colour on the head. They hardly leap out of the box, but we say let the trout be the judges. The biggest mistake you can make when fishing buzzers is to yank them in fast. In a breeze the best way is often to simply let your buzzers drift, with only the occasional tweak to prevent too much slack line developing.

Klinkhamer

A quite brilliant fly, this emerger-style dry pattern is a superb all-rounder which cleverly copies a juicy, hatching caddis fly or other insect. With a bright wing post above the surface and a curved body hanging below, both angler and trout have no trouble at all spotting this one. It works well for both trout and grayling and is one of those flies that the fish bite even when no insects are hatching. It's also great for fishing New Zealand style on rivers (as described earlier in this chapter), but however you fish it it's best to only apply floatant to the top half. Try a beige or hare's ear coloured Klink on rivers, or even a little black number on lakes.

Hopper

In the summer months, when trout look up for insects dropping into the water, terrestrial dry flies such as the hopper are fun and effective to try. The hopper is usually a decent mouthful tied in sizes 10-12. It's not the neatest affair, but with a bushy hackle and a few knotted trailing legs it looks like a juicy meal whether you cast it on still or flowing water. It doesn't copy any specific insect, but just looks good to eat. Not only does it catch trout on lakes, it's also my favourite fly for river chub, and in warm weather these big mouthed fish clobber the hopper. They come in all colours, but black makes a nice bold outline.

Elk Hair Caddis

Although elk hair gives this fly extra buoyancy, it still has a sleek and delicate profile. The Elk Hair Caddis is a very good prospecting fly when you see a few splashy caddis rises. I usually carry sizes 14, 16, and 18.

Gold Ribbed Hare's Ear

The Gold Ribbed Hare's Ear is a general impressionistic nymph that picks up flash from gold wire coiled around its body. The fur used to tie this fly comes, as its name suggests, from the ear of a hare. It is gold, brown, white and black in colour, and its texture is stubby and filled with many short hairs that stick out at all kinds of angles. To a hairdresser these short hairs would be thought of as unsightly split ends. To a fish, this unkempt look is very buglike. In recent years, some anglers have been fishing the Gold Ribbed Hare's Ear with the addition of a shiny metallic bead head that both helps it sink and gives some more flash. Carry this one in sizes 10, 12, 14 and 16.

Griffith's Gnat

This little all-purpose fly, invented by John Griffith, the founder of Trout Unlimited, is the one I (Peter) go to when there is small stuff on the water. The hook of the Griffith's Gnat is wrapped with a body of peacock herl (fibres of peacock feather) and a palmered small hackle from a grizzly rooster (which has multicoloured feathers of white, black, and gray). To the fish, I think that all those neck fibres sticking out must make Griffith's Gnat look like a buzzing little bug. I've used this fly for gnats, tiny olives, midges and ants. It is one of those flies that fish often take even though it may be bigger than the natural insects on the water. Carry this fly in sizes 16–22.

The Muddler Minnow

Many of the great flies are kind of like folk songs or legends: They're really good, but nobody knows where they came from. Quite often, many people had a hand in the fly's creative process. Not the Muddler Minnow. Don Gapen observed that the sculpin (a bait fish also called the Bullhead by Brits) makes up a large part of the diet of gamefish. To imitate this bait, Gapen took some deer hair and tied it in long strips. He spun it into a ball and then gave it a crew cut to create a bulbous head. Voilà! The Muddler Minnow was born. Fished under the surface, it looks like a sculpins or other struggling bait-fish. Greased up, it's often taken as a large caddis or terrestrial insect. And you can fish it as any of the above simply by adjusting your retrieve. Carry Muddlers in sizes 2–12.

The Daiwl Bach

This little gem of a fly originates in Wales, where Daiwl Bach means 'Little Devil'. An appropriate name, because it is a devilishly effective fly. Dressed with a dark peacock herl body and feather fibres to make a tail and throat, it is one of those flies which doesn't copy any exact trout food, but does a good impression of all manner of small and tasty trout snacks. I (Dominic) am never without a few Bachs, whether faced with a wild lake full of brown trout or a pool stocked with rainbows. Like a buzzer, often the best way to fish it is to just leave it be and let it drift. On one occasion, I remember idly flipping a Daiwl Bach down below my feet as I stopped for a drink on a craggy Dartmoor lake. About five seconds later the line pulled tight as a good sized brownie made off with it.

The Woolly Bugger

When you can only have one fly, many fly rodders will tell you that the Woolly Bugger is probably the one fly to have. With its simple body and a long supple feather tail, this fly catches fish everywhere. Depending on what size of Woolly Bugger you use, it can be taken for a leech, a minnow, or a worm.

I (Peter) will never forget a day on a slough full of enormous rainbow trout in Argentina. Nothing was hatching, and there was no visible sign of fish. I tied on a Woolly Bugger and stripped it in six inches at a time (that is, I retrieved it in short pulls). I caught fish after fish, up to an unbelievable 11 pounds. When one fish struck, I pulled back to set the hook with such violence that the hook pulled out of the trout's mouth, and my momentum carried the fly over my head and into the water about 20 feet behind me where another five- or six-pound rainbow took the Woolly Bugger on my backcast! This was the ultimate case of using the right fly at the right time. Carry this fly in sizes 4, 6, 8 and 10.

Part IV
Now You're Fishing

"All this time at sea, not a sign of fish & now we're grounded!"

In this part . . .

You'll find straightforward advice and clear illustrations on how to tie effective rigs, cast all kinds of rods and reels, and even set the hook and fight a fish. Here, too, is a chapter dedicated to the techniques you'll use to pursue all kinds of fish in all kinds of water. In this part, the world of fish and angler come together.

Chapter 14

Tying Popular Fishing Knots and Rigs

- -

In This Chapter

▶ Practising basic knot-tying techniques

▶ Knowing a handful of super knots

▶ Understanding how to use different float and leger rigs

▶ Using rigs for sea fishing

▶ Adapting all rigs to meet your water's conditions

- -

*R*eading about the fish you can catch in Chapters 4 and 5 will get your blood pumping, and it's exciting to look at Part III of this book and think about the various ways to fool those fish using bait, lures and flies. Chapter 9 covers the all-important terminal tackle like hooks and snaps, and Chapter 8 tells you what you need to know about line. What's left? The crucial link in the middle of this chain – the knots and rigs you use to connect your offering to the line.

Knots are a compromise. Some knots weaken your line, but you need them to attach all your lures, hooks and weights. You couldn't very well go fishing without tying on a hook! Every fisherman loves a particular knot or two, and you'll find your favourites here as well. Some popular fishing knots have been around forever, whereas others were developed in laboratories within the past year. (As new lines are developed, new knots often follow – knots designed to work best with particular lines, like braided or fluorocarbon, for example.) Some are easy to tie; others seemingly require four hands and a magnifying glass.

A knot's goal is to connect your line to something without failing in the heat of battle. A rig's goal is to present your offering to the fish in a way that looks natural and appealing. In this chapter, we give you a handful of reliable, easy-to-tie knots, as well as a few basic rigs. Generally, use the simplest rig you can get away with, requiring the fewest number of knots. The simpler a rig is, the quicker it is to tie, and the less likely it is to fail at some juncture. But, with luck, the knots you tie will hold and allow you to bring a big fish to the boat or bank.

The Knots You Need

The rigs that we cover later in this chapter are formed with a series of knots. Even a simple presentation – such as casting a lure or fly – requires one solid knot. Although every link in the chain connecting you to the fish – including the reel, rod, line, snaps, lure, etc. – could conceivably fail, the knots you tie are the most likely culprit when something breaks. Technicians in labs can measure the point at which knots fail, and the best knots break at close to or over the line strength. (Say, a knot tied with 14-pound line breaks at close to 14 pounds of pressure, or the line breaks before the knot fails.) But a poorly tied knot will unravel long before the line breaks, probably at a fraction of the pressure required to part the line.

The importance of practice is preached throughout this book, and knot-tying is no exception. Learn these knots well, and you'll be able to tie them quickly and efficiently, even in the rain or near darkness. Soon, your fingers will tie them without you even thinking about it.

Every knot you tie is better when you follow these basic steps:

1. **Pull the tag end of your line through the hook eye and leave plenty of room to tie your knot (maybe 12 inches or so).**

   You can always trim off the excess later.

2. **Form the knot, spit on it, and then snug it up with a firm, steady pull.**

   That's right – moisten the knot with your saliva or water to reduce friction. (The heat can harm your line.) This results in a snugger, tighter knot that holds better.

3. **After tying, wetting and snugging the knot, the tag end will stick out. Trim this to about 3-4mm with nail clippers or scissors (cut the end too close and the knot will pull out).**

4. **Inspect and test the knot by pulling on it firmly before casting.**

   Better it fails on the bank than in the water. If the knot looks odd or ragged, or if the line seems nicked or kinked near the knot, cut it off and retie. Cast only what you think are perfect knots.

Rather than attempting to learn 20 knots, we recommend that you master the 6 that we walk you through in the following sections and commit them to memory. If you want to learn how to tie other knots, including the Improved Clinch knot, a simple search online will turn up many good Web sites with step-by-step instructions and even how-to videos.

Picking up on knot-tying lingo

Most knot-tying instructions use a few standard terms. These terms are pretty self-descriptive, but just to make sure that we are all on the same page, here they are:

✔ **Tag end:** The end of your line. This is the part that does the knot-tying. When you are finished tying, the tag end is the sticking-out part that you clip. (Use nail clippers for best results, unless you're using braided line, in which case you'll need to use wire cutters or scissors designed to cut braided line.)

✔ **Standing line:** The rest of your line that runs up toward your reel.

✔ **Turn:** Sometimes called a *wrap.* A turn occurs when you pass the tag end completely around the standing line.

The Arbor knot: It helps if the line is tied to the reel

Actually, you should finish fighting your fish (or the fish should finish with you) a long time before you get to the knot that connects your line to your reel. But even if you never get into this extreme predicament, you need to tie the line to your reel. (For more info on putting new line on a reel, see Chapter 8.) We suggest that you use the Arbor knot, which is shown in Figure 14-1.

Here's how you tie one:

1. **Pass the tag end around the centre post of the reel spool and tie a simple overhand knot, passing the tag end around the standing end.**

2. **Take the tag end and tie another overhand knot with it.**

3. **Pull on the standing line until both overhand knots come tight against each other and against the centre post.**

The Trilene knot: Connecting your line to hook (and about anything else)

This knot was developed by the folks at Berkley, for use with their Trilene monofilament, but it works with all kinds and brands of line. Similar to the Fisherman's knot (often called the *half blood knot*) or Improved Clinch knot, the Trilene knot ties easily and holds up well in harsh conditions. I (Greg) have used this knot for decades and I can't recall when it last let me down. The line will often break before this knot fails, making it a 100-percent strength knot when well tied.

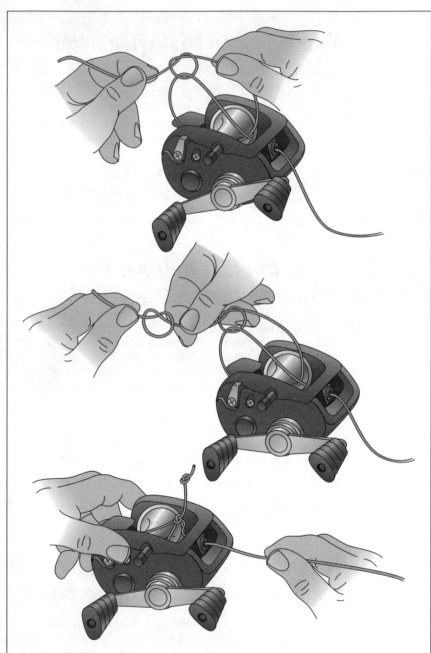

Figure 14-1:
The Arbor knot is one of the best and easiest ways to attach line to a reel.

Use this knot to connect your line to a hook, lure or fly, as well as when using swivels to form various rigs.

To tie the Trilene knot, as shown in Figure 14-2, follow these steps:

1. **Run the tag end of the line through the eye of the hook and pull 8 to 12 inches of line through the hook eye.**

2. **Pass the tag end through the eye a second time, forming a small, double loop you can maintain with your forefinger and thumb of your non-dominant hand. (Figure 14-2a)**

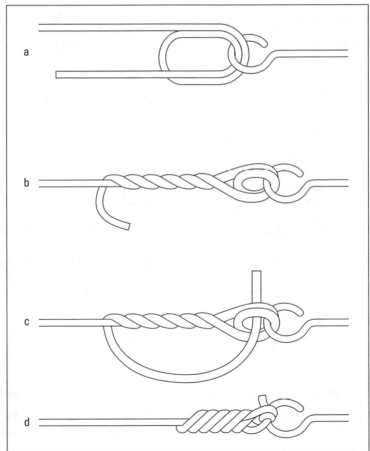

Figure 14-2:
The Trilene
knot.

3. **Wrap the tag end around the standing end for three to five wraps or turns. (Figure 14-2b)**

4. **Now pass the tag end through the double loop next to the hook eye. (Figure 14-2c)**

   You will have formed another loop by making your wraps.

5. **Wet the loops with some saliva to lubricate the knot.**

6. **Hold the bend of the hook and standing line of the line in one hand, then pull with steady pressure on the tag end with your other hand.**

   If you are not sure about safely holding the hook, grip it firmly with needle-nose pliers.

7. **Tighten slowly.**

8. **Clip the tag end so that only 3-4mm are left. (Figure 14-2d)**

The Palomar knot: An easy classic

The Palomar knot is a bit of an oddball because it requires you to double a length of line before you pass it through the eye of your hook or snap. You can use this knot to connect about anything to your line, and it works well with all kinds of line, including braided. I (Greg) use it to tie weights to river rigs, as it's easy to tie and can be quickly whipped together in the dark. Like the Trilene knot, the Palomar retains over 100 per cent of the line strength, and can be tied with all kinds of line. (In fact, in some tests with some lines, the Palomar outperformed the Trilene. But both are excellent knots.)

To tie the Palomar knot, as shown in Figure 14-3, follow these steps:

1. **Double the tag end of the line and run the double line through the eye of the hook and pull 8 to 12 inches of looped line through the hook eye. (Figure 14-3a)**

   If the eye of the lure is too small to easily allow the double line, run the line through once, pull through 12 inches, and then run the line back through the eye before you proceed to Step 2.

2. **Form an overhand loop in the double (looped) line. (Figure 14-3b)**

3. **Pass the hook or snap (whatever it is you're tying on) through the small loop formed beyond the overhand knot. (Figure 14-3c)**

4. **Wet the loops with some saliva to lubricate the knot.**

5. **Hold the bend of the hook in one hand, then pull with steady pressure on both the tag end and standing line with your other hand.**

   If you aren't sure about safely holding the hook, grip it firmly with needle-nose pliers.

6. **Tighten slowly.**

7. **Clip the tag end so that only 3–4mm are left. (Figure 14-3d)**

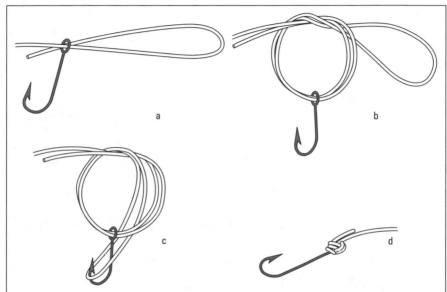

Figure 14-3:
The Palomar
knot.

The Surgeon's knot: Easy for tippet to leader

The well-known fly-fishing author Doug Swisher uses a Surgeon's knot to join the last length of his tippet to the leader, and he convinced Peter to do the same. (See Chapter 15 if you're unfamiliar with the terminology of flyfishing gear.) This knot got its name because it's the same one that surgeons use to close up their handiwork. I (Peter) use it to join two pieces of line that are similar in diameter. More than one fly-fishing buddy has turned his nose up at my scraggly looking Surgeon's knot. Hey, it may not look great, but it works great. And if a surgeon feels that this knot is dependable enough to close up a wound, I am willing to trust it to haul in a trout.

To tie the Surgeon's knot, just follow these steps:

1. **Lay about 10 inches of tag end on top of your standing line, as shown in Figure 14-4a.**

2. **In one hand, hold about four inches of standing line and the tag end and make a loop. Pinch the loop together between thumb and forefinger (see Figure 14-4b).**

3. **Take the other end of the tag end and the end of the standing line and, passing it through the open loop, wrap them twice around the two strands of your loop (see Figure 14-4c).**

4. **Using both hands, pull evenly on all four strands (see Figure 14-4d and e).**

5. **Wet the knot with saliva when you're just about ready to finish pulling the knot tight.**

6. **Clip the tag ends, as shown in Figure 14-4f.**

After a little practice, you'll see that the Surgeon's knot is easy to tie. After you know how to tie this very well, practise tying it in a dark room or step into a closet and tie it. Knowing how to tie a simple knot in the dark can be a handy skill. (I leave it up to you to explain things when someone opens the closet door and finds you standing there with two lengths of fishing line in your hands.)

The Surgeon's Loop knot: to connect hook lengths to main lines, or leaders to fly lines among other things

The Surgeon's Loop Knot is a really easy but dependable loop, a cinch to tie but with good strength. There are many uses for loops in all kinds of .fishing. Quite often, two looped pieces of line are used to make a connection, for example, when you want to attach a slightly finer length of line with the hook on it (called a *hook length*) to your main line (hook lengths are covered in Chapter 8).

Check out Figure 14-5 and follow these steps to tie a Surgeon's Loop:

1. **Create a 4 cm loop and pinch between thumb and forefinger.**

2. **Now double this loop over itself to make another loop, before feeding the first loop through the other twice.**

3. **Wet the knot and pull tight, before trimming off the end.**

Loop to loop connections

There are many times in fishing where you will be required to join two pieces of line together: Joining a finer piece of line to your main line, for example, to add a hook length, or attaching a leader to the end of your fly line. For sheer ease of use, a loop to loop connection is often a good solution. Not only does this make a pretty secure connection, but it can be done in seconds.

With *hook lengths* in particular it is a handy quick fix. Many anglers keep a selection of spare hook lengths ready looped: this way, a fresh one can be attached in seconds should a change be required.

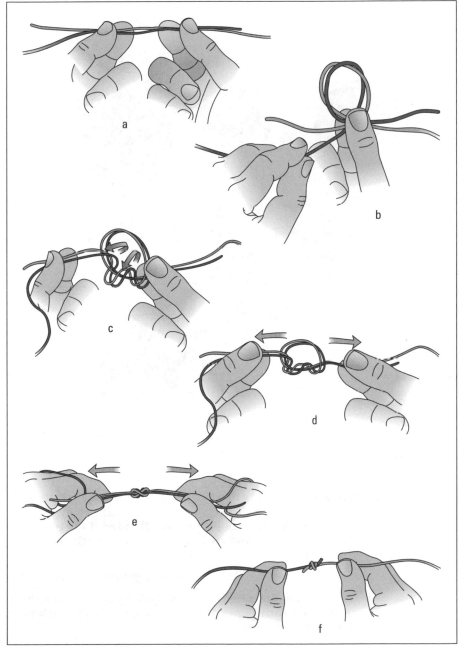

Figure 14-4:
The
Surgeon's
knot.

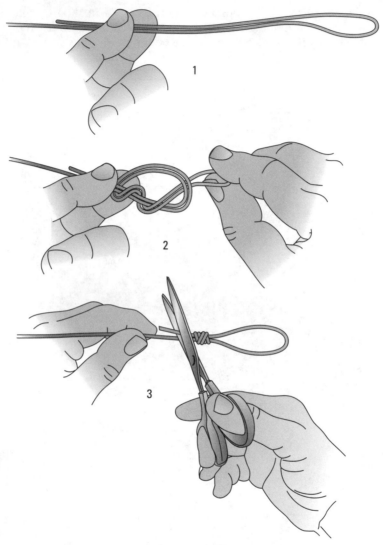

Figure 14-5:
The
Surgeon's
Loop.

Here's how to attach any two loops. Figure 14-6 gives you the detail:

1. **Taking two knotted loops, pass the thinner of the two directly over the thicker loop. The thinner looped line will usually be the connection to your hook.**

2. **Pass the end of the thinner line straight through the thicker loop.**

3. **Now steadily draw tight until everything is joined neatly. You may need to help any tag ends pass through to avoid catching as everything comes together.**

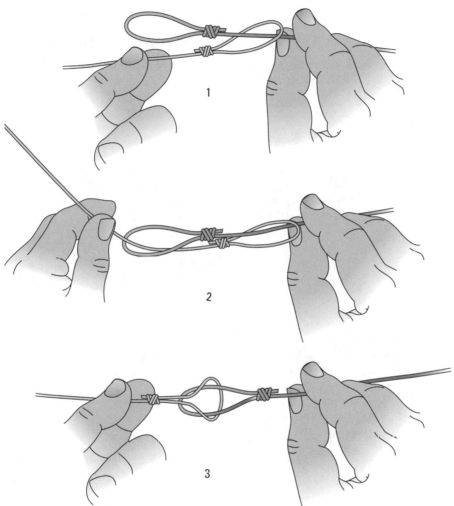

Figure 14-6:
Making a
loop to loop
connection.

The Albright: Joining fat line to skinny line

When joining lines of very different thicknesses, or backing to fly line, I (Peter) use the Albright knot. This knot works well even if the two pieces being joined are very far apart in diameter.

Here's how you tie an Albright:

1. **Make a 3-inch loop in the heavier piece, as shown in Figure 14-7a.**

2. **Pass the tag end of the lighter line through the loop for 7 to 8 inches, as shown in Figure 14-7b.**

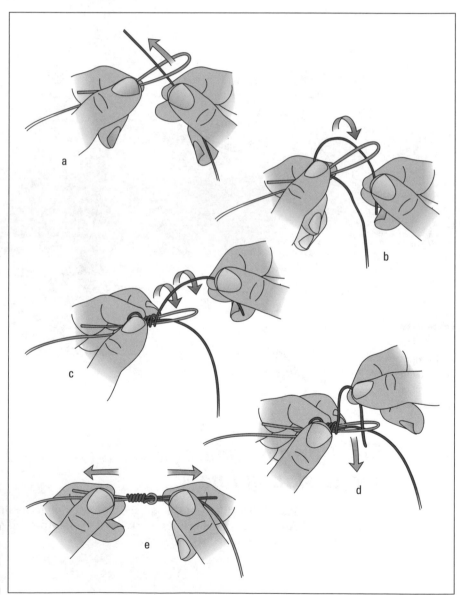

Figure 14-7:
The Albright
knot.

3. **Pinch the loop and the light line together and take the tag end and wrap it six times, trying to include the new wraps in your pinch (see Figure 14-7c).**

4. **Pass the end of the line you have been using for wraps back through the loop on the same side that it entered (see Figure 14-7d).**

5. **Pull gently on both ends of the lighter line so that the wraps slide up against the end of the loop, as shown in Figure 14-7e.**

6. **When everything is lined up and fairly snug, give a good firm pull (not a yank) to finish the knot.**

The Albright knot sounds and looks a little complicated, but as you tie it, you see the logic to it. It really isn't hard to make.

Using the Right Rig to Present Your Offering

After you know how to tie a handful of knots, it's time to master a few basic rigs. At its simplest, fishing only requires one knot on the tag end of your line: the one tying on a hook, lure or fly. Sometimes that's all you need. You might walk to the shore, tie on a spinner, and start casting. Another classic is *freelining*, or the art of simply using a hook and just the weight of the bait to cast, which is ideal, for example, to flick out a piece of bread crust to surface feeding carp.

Often, though, an angling situation will call for a more complex presentation. *Rigs* are methods of presenting a hook to fish, often involving weights, floats or swivels. Different rigs work to reach fish in different environments and present your offering in a natural way. A fish holding on the bottom of the river in strong current or in the bay during a strong tide will be impervious to most float rigs – the current will simply sweep the hook and float away. Equally, if you were faced with a shallow pond and spotted some fish feeding close in, the last thing you'd want to do is cast a heavy lead close to them; a simple, subtle float rig would be much better to avoid scaring them. Knowing when to use the following basic rigs – and how to tie them – should enable you to fish in almost any fishing application.

As a final piece of advice before we look at rigs, fishing legend Richard Walker perhaps summed it up best when he wrote that fishing rigs 'should be your slaves, not your masters.' In the wrong setting, the best tied rig in the world is ineffective. In other words, the type of water and conditions in front of you should be the basis of the rig you decide to use. This isn't always your favourite rig, or the one which worked last week on a different water.

Will snaps save you from knot-tying?

Snaps, covered in Chapter 9, are designed to make it easier to change lures. Instead of tying on every lure, you simply tie on a snap, and then clasp and unclasp the snap to change lures. Easier? You bet. Some snaps incorporate a swivel, as well, which helps eliminate line twist. Snaps can make your life easier, but they come with a price. Not only are they one more thing you need to buy, but their weight can deaden the action of some lures and make your hooks appear more obvious or garish in the water. For that reason, many experts advise you not to use them at all. Depending on where and how you're fishing, though, you might be able to get away with using a snap.

The following sections present a range of basic, effective rigs, along with typical applications. The boundaries are not entirely fixed however. For example, the running leger works just about anywhere, from lakes and rivers to the open sea. The paternoster rig commonly used by sea anglers also works in freshwater. Wagglers and other smaller floats are staples for coarse fish, but can also be used for mullet in a harbor. The more rigs and types of fishing you master, the more adaptable and ultimately successful you'll be at catching fish.

Float Fishing Rigs: Effective and Easy on the Eye

Float fishing is the very heart and soul, the bread and butter of the pleasure angler. There's nothing quite like the sight of a float tip twitching, before dipping under as a fish takes the bait. A float also makes a lovely focal point to watch whilst you wait for a bite, as well as a target to aim your loose feed towards. The author H.T Sheringham perhaps summed up the float best when he wrote: 'Whilst it is pleasing in appearance, it is even more pleasing in its disappearance.'

Float fishing is easy to learn, but also a real art form to master. You can float fish for almost any species and floats vary from dainty little darts for timid biting roach, all the way to big, bold models that you might cast out into a rising tide for sea fish. All work using the same timeless principle, a bright tip being pulled under the surface as a fish bites. It is perhaps the best method of all for a beginner, although even lifelong devotees and the stars of the sport such as Bob James and John Wilson also cite float fishing as their favourite method of all.

Another plus about float fishing is its versatility. For example, you might use a large waggler float to present a bait hard on the bottom, but equally you might rig up a float so that you catch fish closer to the surface or as the bait falls through the water (often described by anglers as catching *on the drop*). The average tackle shop sells many varied floats and it can be confusing to pick the right ones for your own fishing. The next sections break down floats and standard rigs into a handful of clear, user friendly categories to avoid such headaches (Chapter 9 also describes basic float types).

Waggler rigs: Fun and effective

The waggler is probably the most common of all the floats you'll find. No coincidence, because it is easy to use and very versatile. They are excellent for lakes and ponds, but also work on rivers. A waggler is fixed on the line by the bottom end only. They have a little eye at the bottom end which you pass the line through, before using split shot pinched onto the line to 'lock' it in place. Check the float's body to see how much weight you need (most will have a rating such as: '3BB', '4AA' and so on, which correspond to shot sizes). You will still need to test the float out however, and the idea is to add enough shot so that just the coloured tip is showing.

You'll notice from the diagram that with wagglers, most of the weight is used to lock the float in place. This helps the waggler cast well, rather like a dart in flight. Too much weight down the line tends to lead to tangles and it pays to keep things simple with only two or three smaller shot further down the line. By having a little group of shot called a *bulk,* say two feet from the hook, you can make the bait get down quickly towards the bottom. This is useful when tiddlers try to snatch it on the way down. But equally, you might want to catch fish on the drop, well off the bottom, and for this task the shot can be spaced out to provide a slower descent. If the fish are taking high in the water, just a single tiny shot might do the trick.

You'll hear anglers refer to different ways of using shot as *patterns* or *shotting patterns.* A smart angler might alter his shot several times in a session to respond to the fish, for example to make the bait sink more slowly because the fish are coming high in the water to intercept the bait.

Wagglers come in various sizes, from little darts you could fish with right by the bank through to giant, beefy models that can be cast forty yards or more. If you are casting any distance, it pays to use opt for a slightly larger float than is strictly necessary. This way you can overcast slightly and draw the float back, rather than cast onto the heads of the fish, and you're also still in business if the wind picks up.

One advantage all wagglers share is that because they are attached bottom end only, you can sink the line beneath the surface to beat a healthy breeze (usually accomplished by dipping the tip of the rod under the surface and giving a couple of pulls). On the flipside, because the float is attached to the line, or *fixed*, wagglers tend to work best in shallow to moderate depth. If the water is any more than about eight feet they can become quite awkward to cast. Consider switching to a feeder, bomb or sliding float set up. Figure 14-8 shows a typical waggler rig.

Figure 14-8:
A simple waggler rig, the shot can be bulked to get down to the bottom quickly (a) or spaced out evenly for a slower sinking pre-sentation (b).

Telling tales: your little helper, the telltale shot

Sharp eyed readers will notice that most of the float fishing rigs have one final, much smaller split shot closest to the hook. It may be just a baby, but this final weight can make a big difference. When a fish mouths the bait or moves off with it, this little shot also moves, helping to register a bite on the float tip. It's especially useful when targeting shy biters like roach, skimmers and Crucians. The telltale shot is usually positioned from 15-30cm from the hook. How big should it be? On a hard fished canal or calm pond it could be a tiny dust shot (size 9-10). On a big river, the telltale would be quite a lot bigger, say a size 6.

With any float rig, your aim should be to have just the coloured top showing. It's no use having a sensitive float but weighting it so that half of it pokes out of the water. Fish dislike resistance and will often drop the bait if they have to pull lots of float under the water. Many times an angler will *dot down* the float tip to a mere dimple on the surface if possible, so that even the shyest bite results in the tip dipping under. This is especially useful for Crucian carp, roach and other fickle species. Float fishing is a matter of tinkering, however, making subtle alterations as you fish. If the wind picks up, for instance, you might need to remove a little weight to prevent the float from constantly dragging under.

Stick float set-ups: Going with the flow

When it comes to river fishing, the stick float is tailor made for the job of riding the flow and presenting a moving bait, an art form often referred to as *trotting*. Unlike wagglers, stick floats are attached to the line top and bottom by two or three little rubber sleeves called *float rubbers*. Each float has a weight rating, usually printed on the stem of the float, to show you how many shot are required to make it sit properly in the water. They come in various guises, from sensitive wire stemmed models through to lunking great balsa models called *loafers* or *chubbers* which are great for fast water and big baits. River species across the board, from pint-sized dace to large chub, can be tricked with a well presented stick float rig. Figure 14-9 shows you the set-up.

You don't need any shot to fix a stick float in place on the line as you would with a waggler, the rubbers do this job. Instead, place your shot down the line in a pattern to make the bait sink and the float settle correctly, so that just the tip is showing A bulk of tightly bunched shot will get the bait down quickly, for example, whilst shot evenly spaced like the buttons on a shirt (often actually called a *shirt button* pattern) will give a slower, more even descent. The aim is a rig which travels naturally, trundling along with the flow. The angler keeps letting out line (either with a centrepin reel or with the bale arm of a fixed spool open) and gently checking it to keep the bait passing just in front of the rest of the rig.

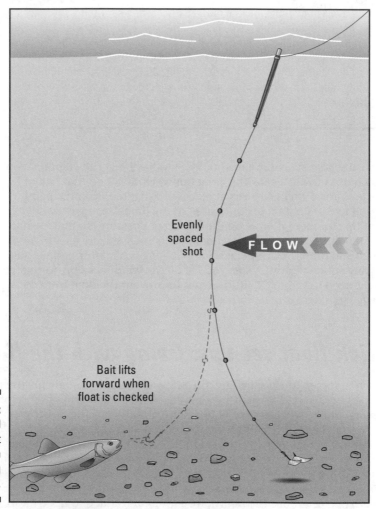

Evenly
spaced
shot

F L O W

Bait lifts
forward when
float is checked

Figure 14-9:
A typical
stick float
rig. Spot on
for running
water.

Pole float rigs: Finesse for success

If you had to pick the best float for pure sensitivity and control, the pole float would win hands down. This makes it a great weapon for small, shy species, but equally such cute presentation could be ideal for bigger fish such as cagey carp that have grown wary of clumsy rigs.

Pole floats come in various guises, but commonly feature a wire stem, bulbous body and a brightly coloured tip (or *bristle*). The really dinky models are ideal for shallow water, whilst large models taking a gram or more of weight would tackle a deep lake or windy ship canal. Models for carp fishing and bigger baits have also evolved, featuring tougher construction and thicker tips. You can check out pole float rigs in Figure 14-10.

Figure 14-10:
Pole float rigs, for fishing on the bottom (a) and higher up or on the drop (b)

How deep is the water?: Plumbing the depth

Before you begin casting a float, one very important job needs taking care of: Plumbing the depth. It's no use casting into a deep swim with your bait several feet above a shoal of fish. Equally, when fishing a shallow area with too much line between float and hook you will either miss bites or only realise what's happening when a fish swallows the bait right down: bad news. Carefully testing the depth will also reveal lots about the swim you're fishing. Is the depth even, or does it drop away? Are there any deeper holes worth investigating? Fish often hug areas such as drop-offs and other sudden changes and time spent investigating depths is never wasted.

To test the depth, you should first attach some extra weight to the hook. A special *depth plumb* with cork to secure the hook is a good idea (available from tackle shops), but you could also gently pinch a shot large enough to sink the float tip, such as an AA, just above the hook. Now cast to where you want to fish with your float rig and watch what happens. Take a look at figure 14-11. If the float buries under the surface of the water (a) you're set too shallow, so try sliding the float away from the hook a few inches. If the float lies flat (b) you're set too deep, with too much line between float and hook. Move the float a few inches down towards the hook and try again. It's a case of trial and error, but you know you've got it spot on when, eureka, Just the tip of the float sits above the water (c).

You should mark this depth carefully before starting to fish. One way is to put the hook in the top of the rod's handle and make a little mark next to the float with correction fluid or a little slip of tape. That way, even if you get tangled later, you still know the exact depth. You could even make two marks, one mark for the water just beyond the rod tip, another for a few metres out in slightly deeper water. Also remember, you don't have to fish bang on the exact depth or *dead depth.* For example, if it's windy and your bait gets dragged about, you could try adding a few inches to the depth to keep the bait on the bottom (anglers call this fishing *overdepth*).

You attach a pole float to the line through a little wire eye on the body, and then via two or three little rubber sleeves (these are sold as *pole float sleeves* or similar). You put the pole float on by threading the line through the eye first, before adding the sleeves, which are then threaded onto thin bottom section (or *stem*) of the float You can easily alter the depth by sliding the float towards or away from the hook. A pole rig can be tied on the bank, but many anglers keep a selection stored on little plastic *winders*. Rigs are roughly the same length of a whip, or the top few sections of your pole. To take an example, if you were fishing a lake around six feet deep you might tie a rig of eight feet in length (that is, the depth, plus a couple of feet between the float and the rod tip). Keeping the rig roughly the same length as your top two or three pole sections allows you to swing in or net fish comfortably. However, it's worth noting that a pole float can also be used with a rod and reel set up when you're fishing close to the bank, under the rod tip.

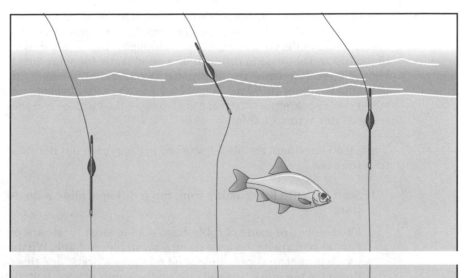

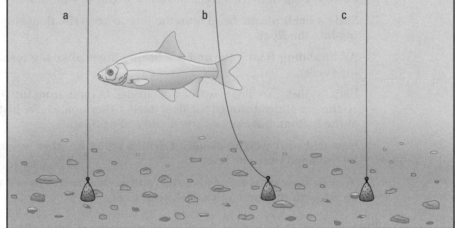

Figure 14-11:
Testing the
depth: (a)-
Too shallow,
(b)-Too
deep, (c)-
Just right

Pike and sea float rigs: slip-sliding away

There is a world of difference between tackling a quiet pool for roach and hunting big pike on a loch, or mackerel in rolling waves. The fish are fiercer and less shy biting for one thing, and they might also patrol much greater depths. You can use various models of sliding float to target pike and sea fish. Even though the quarry is less timid when it comes to dragging a larger float under, it's still a good idea to have only the coloured float top showing by carefully matching your weight and float.

You usually offer sea fish a bait well off the bottom, because species such as mackerel, garfish and pollack are active midwater hunters. For pike, a dead bait is usually offered on the bottom, although a live or dead fish suspended higher up and allowed to drift can be a good tactic for searching the water. Pike will not always pull the float under but may simply take it for a walk, dragging the thing sideways. Whichever way the bite develops, strike early to avoid deep hooking. A wire trace is also essential for pike and these are discussed later in this Chapter.

Typical sliding-floats are also discussed in Chapter 9, but here's a quick guide to setting up:

1. **Start with the line coming from the rod. Then, slide a float-stop on the line.**

   Float-stops are made of rubber and sold in most tackle shops. Or you can tie your own stop knot using a scrap piece of line. Whatever you use, a float-stop should be placed on the line first. Slide this up and down the tag line – this will control the depth of your baited hook.

2. **Slide a small plastic bead onto the line to keep the float-stop from sliding into the float.**

3. **Add a sliding float (pike and sea fishing floats alike are termed as sliding floats).**

   Usually, these are floats with a hole drilled in them from top to bottom, so the line slides through the float itself. Other floats have just one hole at the bottom, but can be turned into sliding floats.

4. **Now add your weight, usually a drilled bullet or other weight that can be threaded onto the line.**

5. **Next tie on a swivel. For pike rigs, add a wire trace. For sea fishing, tie on a length of mono and attach your hook.**

When you cast, the weight will pull line through the sliding float until the float and bead hit against the float stop. When that happens, the hook stays suspended at that depth below the float, or sits on the bottom. See how that works? You can adjust the depth you're fishing by sliding the float stop up or down the line.

If your float lies on its side, that often means the weight is resting on the bottom and not pulling the line taut to the float. Even if you want to be on the bottom, it's best to shallow up a little, so that even if the bait is on the deck the float sits up and you get good bite indication. Figure 14-12 shows a standard sliding float rig.

Figure 14-12:
A sliding
float rig for
sea fish
or pike.

Leger Rigs: Plundering the depths

There are many situations, in whichever branch of fishing you pursue, that require a bait to be presented on the bottom. Fast currents or long distances demand longer casts and more weight. There are also times when conditions rule out the use of a float, strong winds or great depths for example. *Legering* (or ledgering, in traditional spelling) is the craft of fishing on the bottom with a suitable weight.

Another undeniable fact is that large fish often feed on the bottom. They like a bait presented perfectly still, and such an offering may need to sit there undisturbed by wind or currents for a long time before it is picked up. Hence for many specimen anglers in search of monsters, such static presentations are ideal. This is not to say that legering is a simple case of lobbing a baited rig out and waiting. It is an art form all of its own and there are many ways of legering a bait. We deal with all the terminal tackle considerations here, but for information on bite detection for legering methods (such as quiver tips and bite indicators), check out Chapter 16.

The running leger rig: Resistance is futile!

So often in fishing, the simpler your set up the better. The fewer knots and gizmos, the less can go wrong. The running leger rig is a staple for many kinds of fishing, whether that means tackling a river, a lake or the beach. As the name suggests, this leger rig allows the fish to run with the bait, the line passing freely through the eye of your weight. This is ideal for cagey fish that might drop the bait on feeling too much resistance.

The size of the weight and the length of your *trace* or *hooklength* (i.e. the final bit of line between swivel and hook) varies according to the type of fishing. Two feet or so between lead and hook is common, but that might increase or decrease due to different requirements. A shorter hooklength might give you quicker indication if you're missing bites, for example, whilst a longer trace of three or four feet might settle nice and delicately in a weedy swim or give a shy fish more leeway to move with the bait without feeling resistance.

You can use any standard weight with the running leger, provided it has an eye at the top for line to pass through. But it also works a treat with swim-feeders (discussed in Chapter 9) which help to draw fish to your hook by depositing free bait.

For a standard running leger rig, follow these steps and check out Figure 14-13:

1. **Slide the end of your line through the eye in the top of your chosen weight (this could be any suitable bomb, lead or swimfeeder).**
2. **Add a plastic bead to the line.**
3. **Now tie on a swivel. This forms the point at which the lead and bead will stop.**
4. **To the other eye of the swivel, tie on a length of line and a hook. Your hooklength should typically be a little lighter than the main line, not only for a subtler presentation but so that you only lose a hook should you break off.**

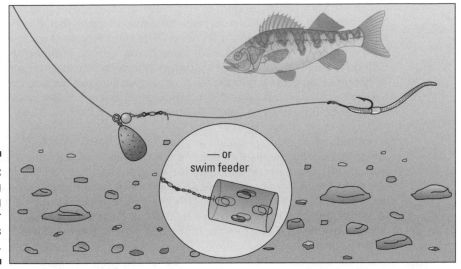

Figure 14-13:
The running
leger rig
works for
many kinds
of fish.

Certain little additions to leger tackle can improve presentation and resistance to tangles. Rubber beads are available, for example, which attach snugly to one end of a swivel, keeping everything tidy. Little rubber sleeves can also help to keep the first few inches of your hook-length straight, preventing tangles on the cast.

Semi-fixed rigs: Bolt rigs and method feeder set ups

Besides letting the fish run with the bait before striking, an alternative strategy is to let the fish hook itself against your chosen weight. Semi-fixed rigs are aimed to achieve just this effect. We refer to these as semi-fixed because no responsible angler uses a 'fixed' system whereby the fish could end up attached to a heavy weight if the line breaks.

Semi-fixed rigs are largely the domain of carp anglers, although they are also popular with anglers seeking barbel and other large species. The *bolt rig* is the staple here. As the name suggests, it works by letting the fish take the bait and then hooking itself as it bolts off, against the weight. Method feeder rigs work on the same principle, only with the hook bait fished close to a sticky mixture of free bait to entice the fish. In either case the recipe for success usually revolves around a fairly hefty weight and only a very short length of line between this and the hook, so that a fish which picks up the bait only has to move a short distance before feeling the pressure and hooking itself.

For the traditionalist the semi-fixed presentation represents lazy fishing; for most others it represents a very effective way to catch fish. It also has the added advantage that the angler needn't be right next to the rod at all times, for example when you might want a few hours snooze while night fishing. So called bolt-rigs are often used in conjunction with bite alarms (see Chapter 10 for more on these). Whether bolt rigging or slinging out a method feeder, hair-raising takes and powerful fish make light line a liability, so in most cases it would be unwise to go below 10 pound line.

So called *in-line* fishing weights are par for the course with such rigs. As you might guess, this means that the line doesn't pass through an eye or swivel, but directly through the middle of the weight. Most have a little rubber sleeve at the bottom end, into which the swivel (which connects a short length of line and the hook) sits. This sleeve keeps everything tight enough to hook fish, yet with enough give to slide off clear should disaster strike and the line break: Vital for the sake of the fish, which don't fare well if tethered to three ounces of lead.

For a standard bolt or method feeder rig, take a look at Figure 14-14, and follow these simple steps:

1. **Take the end of the line from your rod tip and thread through the body of an in-line lead or method feeder.**

2. **Tie on a swivel, and pull this tight so that it sits snugly inside the rubber sleeve in the weight.**

3. **Now add a short hook length (often no more than 8 inches (20 cm) of line, or even less for a method feeder) to the free end of the swivel.**

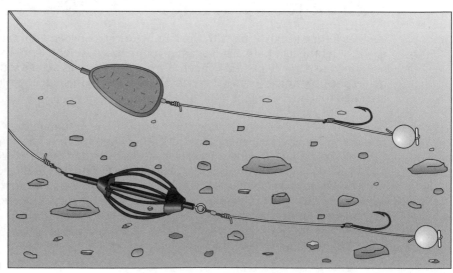

Figure 14-14:
The bolt rig, which works just as well with a method feeder.

Tying the hair rig: Cute presentation

Where bolt rigs dominate, one way of presenting a bait dominates above all others. The hair rig was designed by canny carp anglers to trick hook shy carp. Rather than presenting a bait directly on the hook, they discovered that threading it onto a trailing *hair* (not a hair off your head in this case, but a short trailing length of braid or mono) just off the hook bend was a revelation. A hair-rigged bait not only hangs freely just like the free samples you've dispatched, but provides excellent hooking properties as the hook itself can drive home completely unhindered.

Tying a hair rig is a little more fiddly than standard knotting, admittedly. They can be bought ready tied, but in the long run it's cheaper to tie your own from either special carp braids or high quality mono or fluorocarbon. These can be stored in sealed bags or a purpose made rig container, complete with a swivel to be attached in seconds. Here's how to tie a hassle-free hair rig:

1. **Take a length of your chosen material. Start with at least a foot, because you can always trim it down later. Now tie a small, overhand loop in one end. This is simply a case of making a loop within a loop, and threading the first through the second as shown. A little piece of wire or baiting needle can be a help if you find it fiddly, but the loop must be fairly small. This will be the end of the 'hair' onto which the bait will be threaded.**

2. **Holding the line against the shank, keep the loop you made a little distance below the hook bend. You want enough space for the bait to hang freely below the bend. Now take the other end of the line and put it through the eye, so it passes through to the front.**

3. **Pinching the loop in place, take the other end of the line and make six tight turns around the hook, binding the 'hair' in place against the shank.**

4. **Pass the end back through the hook eye, so that it comes out of the front side as shown. Moisten and pull tight.**

Tying hair rigs takes a little practice. The key is getting the length of the hair right, so that there is a slight gap, but not a chasm, between the hook and the bait, allowing it to move freely. For carp anglers, this is just the start however, and dozens of cunning rigs exist. Having said that, the basic hair rig is all you need to get started and catch some cracking carp. Check out Figure 14-15 to see how to set one up.

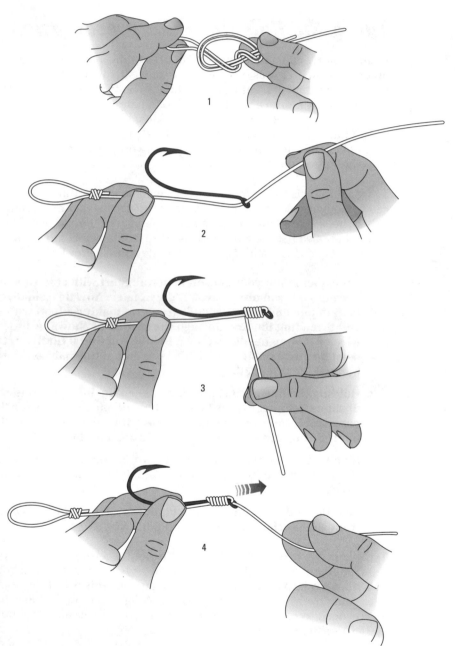

Figure 14-15:
Tying a
hair rig.

Leger rigs for pike and predators

Some fish species require more specialised tackle than others. It's no use
fishing for a large, mean predator with ordinary traces and puny little hooks;

the razor sharp teeth of a pike or zander will simply make mincemeat of them. Equally though, these fish don't respond well to semi-fixed presentations and like to be able to run freely with the bait, in this case a dead fish. Hence the game is altered, and tough rigs incorporating at least 15 pound reel lines attached to tooth proof wire traces are the norm.

Aside from the wire, another common feature of pike rigs is to use a little *leger stem* or other means of keeping line clear of the bottom. Companies such as Greys and Fox produce these, and they form a link to your weight that keeps the line up off the bottom. These work well in the snaggy, weedy swims where pike lurk. The line passes through an enlarged ring, helping to let the fish move off with your bait unhindered. It is vital to spot and strike at bites early however, to avoid deep hooking (for more on bite indication for predators, see Chapter 16). In other ways, you'll notice that the rig illustrated works on similar lines to the running leger. A similar set up will also work for zander, usually with a coarse fish dead bait and slightly smaller treble hooks.

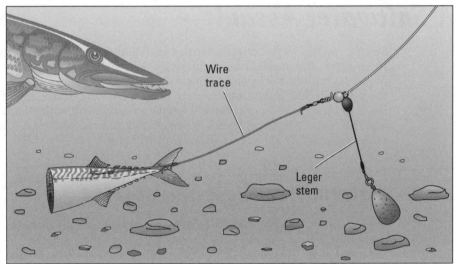

Figure 14-16:
A pike leger rig.

Wire traces: Tooth-proof essentials

Whichever method you use for pike and zander, it is absolutely essential that you use a wire trace. This should always be attached to your main line using a swivel or other link because wire will cut through mono like cotton. You can buy ready-made wire traces and these represent a safe starting point. To tie your own, however, we'd recommend starting off with a flexible, knottable modern wire trace material, available from most tackle shops. Be warned however, even the finest wire isn't as flexible as mono or braid so keep knots simple and secure.

Traces for lure fishing (or indeed fly fishing) are relatively easy. We start with a length of wire of at least 18 inches (pike can twist in the fight so a little extra length is a good idea). To one end, fasten a swivel. This will be where you join the trace to your main line. To the other end, tie a snap link. Having a snap link makes it easy to change lures in seconds without the need to keep re-tying the trace.

Traces for bait fishing are trickier. Most incorporate two treble hooks, usually in sizes 4-8 (or 6-10 for zander). This is a more specialised operation and if you intend to fish for pike regularly and tie your own traces we would strongly recommend you check out the PAC (Pike Anglers Club of Great Britain). Their website (www.pacgb.co.uk) has further information on trace making and lots of sound advice on safe practice for both pike and angler.

Common Sea Fishing Rigs: A Saltwater Assault

Sea fishing rigs have both similarities and differences with those used in freshwater. The most obvious difference is in the strength and size of components. Hazardous rocks and rolling waves present a punishing environment for fishing tackle, hence lines tend to be stronger and hooks, swivels and weights larger and more robust. We have already dealt with sliding float rigs, and the running leger will work at sea as well as anywhere else. A handful of other set ups can quickly be added to the list however.

Paternoster Rigs: Sea staples

In plain terms, the paternoster is a rig with the weight at the bottom and hook traces (sometimes called snoods by sea anglers) attached above in fixed positions. Besides a tidy presentation, this arrangement allows the sea angler to try more than one bait and you'll often find paternosters with two hooks (or even three or four). Effectively this allows us to hedge our bets and try more baits (which could be the same or different types), thereby increasing the scent and attraction. This also means if one bait is trashed or stolen, you still have another one in the water.

In Figure 14-17 you'll see two common paternosters. The very simplest way to make a paternoster rig is with a three way swivel, sold at all tackle shops that sell sea gear. You attach your main line to the swivel, a weight to the opposite end, and a length of line with your hook to the eye coming off the side – and that's it! The line to the weight should be a bit longer than the line to the hook; try around two feet to the weight and one foot to the hook to start with.

A two hook paternoster is trickier, but no sweat once you get the hang of it. These days many rigs are sold ready-made, but in the long run you'll save a lot of cash by making your own, not to mention getting the satisfaction of catching on something you've made yourself.

You could use several knots to make a paternoster, but a much easier and tidier way is to use *crimps*. These are little metal sleeves which slip onto the line. You slide them into place before squeezing them with *crimping pliers* so that they stay fixed to the line, forming a stop. You'll notice that on the two hook paternoster, two pairs of crimps are used, each pair trapping a swivel in between two beads. With the swivel mounted sideways, your hook traces come off at a nice clean angle, which helps avoid tangles. Pay attention to the lengths used however. Keep the hook traces short enough so that they don't overlap and tangle.

The paternoster is also a good set up for the pier or harbour fisher who might be fishing just under the rod tip. In this instance *booms* can be used to keep the hooks clear of the line, which is helpful when your line falls almost vertically down and traces can wrap around the main line.

An open shore mark such as a beach presents a different challenge, however. Where long casts may be necessary, it pays to make the rig as streamlined as possible, without the hindrance of flapping traces or booms. Savvy beach anglers use little bait clips to keep hooks snugly against the line for stream-lined casting.

The rotten bottom rig: For the rough stuff

Rocky, snaggy, rough locations often make for good sea fishing. The fish in such areas are relatively safe from nets and other dangers. Unfortunately, what anglers term *rough ground* can also be a real graveyard for fishing tackle. Quite often it is not the hook which is the problem, but weights, which find holes and crevices and lead to you getting stuck. But rather than bemoan the inevitable risks, smart anglers take action to counter the rough stuff with clever rigs.

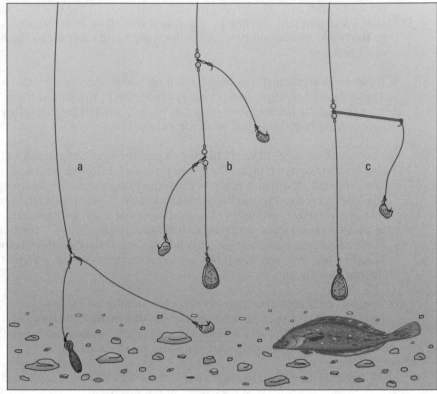

Figure 14-17: Different ways with paternosters: The three way rig (a), and two hook paternoster (b). Booms (c) aid the pier or boat angler.

The rotten bottom rig is a less than beautifully named set up for less than beautiful locations. It is essentially like a running leger, but your lead is attached via a special weak link. This usually consists of a few inches of fishing line weaker than the rest of your set up (so if your hook link and mainline are 20-pound breaking strain, try a 10-pound mono link). Should you hook a fish but become stuck, a solid pull should break off the lead but leave you still attached to your prize. Where losses are really severe you could even try switching costly weights for a cheap substitute (see Chapter 9). For the record, a rotten bottom style rig can be also be used for coarse fish such as barbel or pike in debris strewn areas where leads get stuck. Figure 14-18 shows the set-up.

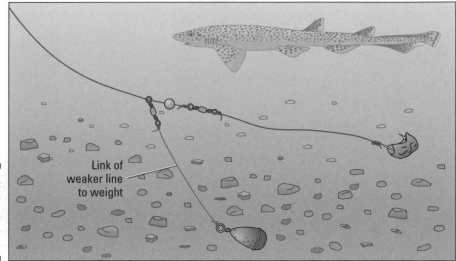

Figure 14-18:
The rotten
bottom rig.
Ugly name,
useful rig.

Link of
weaker line
to weight

Chapter 15

Choreographing Your Cast

. . . .

In This Chapter

▶ Mastering the overhead cast

▶ Figuring out how to cast with fixed spool set-ups

▶ Facing the challenges of casting with multiplier rods and reels

▶ Presenting flies and lightweight lures with fly rods

▶ Dealing with the inevitable snags and snarls

. . . .

*I*f you could walk up to a fish and drop a lure in front of its mouth, you wouldn't need to cast. Unfortunately, fish have an annoying habit of moving around. They cruise, searching for food, or they hover under or near cover that may or may not be close to the bank. The *cast* is the method you use to deliver the fly, lure or bait to a spot where a fish may be enticed, rather than alarmed, by your offering. So in addition to *delivery,* which is concerned with where your offering lands, casting also involves *presentation,* which is how it appears before the fish.

The different kinds of casting gear – fixed-spool, multiplier and fly – all require different casting techniques. (See Chapter 7 for more on the different kinds of rods and reels.) But all casting requires the ability to handle a rod, getting it to flex and release your cast in a controlled way, proper technique with the reel, and sometimes the direct handling of the line. Mastering the basics (say, the overhead cast) will carry over from one kind of gear to another, but we present them in this chapter in order of difficulty so that you can start at the very beginning if you need to.

As with any sport, from football to darts, practice truly does make perfect when it comes to casting. In fact, it's a good idea to begin your fishing trip not on the water, but in flat space on dry land. Tie a small weight or a *lure* (we'd recommend removing hooks first) to your line and cast and retrieve a few dozen times on dry land. (Growing up, Greg and his brothers would 'catch' many local cats by casting and pulling plugs minus hooks through the grass!) As you master the basics, you can hone your skills by placing a ring or similar object some distance away, and then cast towards it until you can reliably strike the target. Practising on the lawn, where there are no fish or snags to distract you, makes casting on the water much, much easier.

In this chapter we use the word *weight* as a general term to refer to all the things you might cast. This could mean a sinker, a float or an artificial lure. How you handle each requires some sussing out: smaller, lighter items such as a little waggler or small lure can be cast with a snappy flick of the wrist. Heavier stuff, such as a three ounce lead, requires a smoother, more progressive casting action. Again, practice makes perfect and getting a 'feel' for the kit you use is the priority. No two people cast quite the same and the most important thing is to find your own style and feel comfortable.

Casting Fixed Spool Gear

Chapter 7 reveals the mechanics of fixed-spool reels, which are used commonly in many types of fishing, whether you're flicking out a waggler float on a pond or launching a grip lead from a windy beach. A fixed spool set up is the easiest for the beginner. to cast with. Indeed fixed-spool reels are versatile, reliable and many anglers find that it is the only reel type they ever need.

Fixed-spool reels feature a *bail arm,* a curved piece of thin metal that lays the line onto the spool (the bit where the line is stored). Casting this gear requires the bail arm to be opened, and on most reels, you do that by hand.

Preparing to cast

Casting with a fixed-spool set up is a bit like riding a bike – after a few wobbly practice sessions it soon becomes second nature. If you've never tried it before though, a little guidance will help. When you prepare to cast, the reel should hang below the rod (as shown in Figure 15-1). To begin the cast, follow these steps:

1. **Hold the rod with your casting hand.**

   Know that most fixed-spool reels allow for the handle to be moved from either the left or right side of the reel, depending on your preference. Most anglers prefer to cast with their right and reel with their left, but left handers will probably feel most comfortable holding the rod in their left hand and reeling with the right. Do whatever works for you.

2. **With your casting hand, grip the line with your forefinger, and hold it against the rod handle under the fleshy part of the first joint (see Figure 15-1a).**

   If you don't hold the line, the weight of whatever you're casting will pull line off the reel when you open the bail. Also, note that your middle finger should be on the same side of the reel stem as your forefinger.

3. **Move the reel's bail over until it clicks into the open position (see Figure 15-1b).**

   Use your free hand to do this. Your forefinger is now the only thing holding the line (and the weight on the end), and you are ready to cast. If you forget to open the bail (we all do it), the lure won't travel very far because all it has to work with are the few inches of line between the lure and the tip ring!

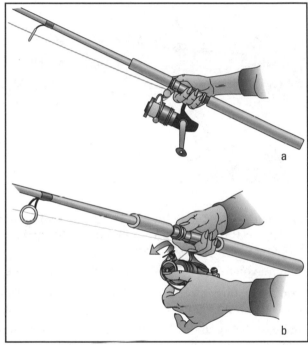

Figure 15-1: Getting ready to cast a spinning reel by gripping the line (a) and opening the bail (b).

A nice, smooth delivery: Perfecting the overhead cast

Ninety out of a hundred times, the overhead cast works well. But even with the more specialised casts, the preparation remains the same. Casting, then, involves following these steps:

1. **Leave the weight hanging around two to three feet below the tip ring.**

   The distance between your casting weight and the tip ring is important. If you have too much of a gap it's hard to generate momentum. If the gap is too small, you might struggle to get a nice, smooth cast. Experiment to see what works for you with the particular tackle you're using – the longer the rod, the bigger the gap you can get away with.

Figure 15-2:
The over-head cast with fixed spool gear.

2. **Grasp the rod with your dominant hand with the reel below the rod, as shown in Figure 15-1a. Square your shoulders toward the target, and check to make sure the area behind you is clear.**

   Checking behind you not only ensures a good cast, but a safe one.

3. **Point the rod at the target, secure the line with your forefinger, and open the bail arm, as in Figure 15-1b.**

4. **To begin the cast, bring the rod back until the tip points between 12 and 2 o'clock (that usually means just slightly behind you). See Figure 15-2, positions 1–3.**

5. **Make the forward stroke by swinging the rod forwards and towards your target. See Figure 15-2, position 4.**

   When casting smaller weights with shorter rods, the backstroke can be snappy, with little or no delay between swinging the rod back and flicking forward to cast. But the rest of the time it's much easier to take your time and simply ease the rod back into position, making the forward cast steadily, in your own time.

6. **Release the line with your forefinger when your rod tip is at about 10 o'clock (or slightly out in front of you), as shown in Figure 15-3.**

7. **Finish the cast by smoothly following through, lowering the rod tip as the cast reaches its target. You may also want to press your forefinger against the line on the spool, which stops more line from paying out.**

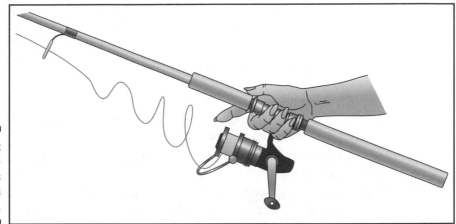

Figure 15-3:
Your forefinger releases the line as you cast.

Most beginners (and quite a few veterans) neglect to use their forefinger as a brake on the spool. But failing to slow the line at all often results in extra slack, all of which must be reeled in before you wait for a bite or begin retrieving the lure. The problem worsens in high wind. As you develop a feel for this technique, you can actually slow down the rate at which line pays out (in much the same way that thumbing will slow down a cast with a multiplier reel). This technique is called *feathering your cast*. Feathers are light, and mastering this method, therefore, requires a light touch. With practice, feathering can also be used to control the distance of the cast. For example, you can dab the reel spool with your finger to gently apply the brakes so that a lure lands neatly in front of an overhanging tree, rather than going straight into it (and making you curse).

Your overhead cast may leave some slack in the line. Once your rig settles you should retrieve this curled line, not so vigorously that you pull your rig out of place, but leaving it tight enough that you can strike effectively when a fish bites. There is a very good reason why anglers say 'tight lines' to wish each other the best. Slack line misbehaves and tangles more easily. And if you leave slack, a fish may bite your bait or lure, smell a rat and spit it out before you have a chance to strike. Get rid of the slack by retrieving the line, but remember to apply some pressure to the line (possibly by pinching it between your thumb and forefinger of the hand holding the rod, or by pressing the line against the rod with your thumb). If you don't keep tension on the line, it will coil loosely onto the reel, and you'll be left with a snarl of line that won't cast smoothly. Your goal is to maintain a relatively tight line between you and your rig or lure.

Trick shots: The side cast

Okay, so it's not really a trick shot, but sometimes you see a great looking place to try or a visible fish, and the only possible way to cast to it is with a sidearm motion (shown in Figure 15-4). Maybe the day is too windy, or an overhang prevents an overhead cast. It's also perfect for flicking out casts on narrow waters such as canals and drains, where an overhead thump would overshoot the mark every time. You'll perfect this maneuver when you truly understand that the rod has to do the work for you. Muscle this cast, and you end up casting way off target. Follow these steps for the sidearm cast:

1. **Leave the weight two to three feet below the tip top.**

2. **Face the target. Righties, put your left foot slightly forward. Lefties, put the right foot forward.**

3. **At waist level, point your rod at the target, secure the line with your forefinger, and open the bail arm.**

4. **If you're right-handed, move the rod with an easy stroke to the right about 45 degrees. If you're left-handed, move the rod left 45 degrees.**

5. **Snap the rod back crisply to the starting position.**

6. **As the rod tip travels forward to where you're aiming at, release the line with your forefinger.**

7. **Point the rod straight at the target and stop the line with your fore-finger as the lure reaches the target.**

Figure 15-4:
The sidearm cast is all a matter of touch and finesse.

Mastering (Sort Of) Multiplier Techniques

Yes, you can handle multiplier gear. As we point out in Chapter 7, many sea anglers and lure fishermen favour multipliers (sometimes called baitcasters by lure fishers) because they love the reliability and smooth cranking power of these reels. With practice, you too will confidently cast your new multiplier reel with no fear of the dreaded backlash. But before you practice casting, make sure you understand how your reel works.

Unlike a fixed spool reel, a multiplier has no bail arm, but instead uses a button or lever to disengage the reel and let the line come off freely when you cast. And unlike the fixed spool, the multiplier has a spool that rotates, and you need to control the rotation of the spool. If you don't, it's likely to rotate too quickly, piling up extra line in the reel housing. Meet the backlash, also known as the overrun, the bird's nest and some terms we can't repeat.

Multiplier reels vary, and unlike fixed spool reels, you can't simply switch the handle, so be sure to buy the reel that's right for you. Many sea anglers learn to reel with their right hands, in other words, casting with their right arm, and then swapping over after the cast so that they reel in and play fish holding the rod in their left hand and cranking with the right. Switching hands like this becomes habit when you learn this way. But be warned, for many others – and especially those who start out with fixed spool reels – a reel described and sold as 'left-hand wind' will feel far more natural. In other words many of us prefer to hold the rod with the right hand, and turn the reel with their left. For left-handers the opposite is true, and they might prefer a 'right-hand wind' model. If in doubt, do visit your tackle shop where you can try out the gear for yourself and get some friendly advice on what might suit you best.

Setting the reel (and using your thumb) to cast better

Most multiplier reels feature a *tension* knob that adjusts the speed of the spool's rotation. You want to set this so that the reel can cast freely, but not so free that you can't control it. More on that later in this section. But your thumb matters here, too – your thumb must learn to control the spool. When you cast with multiplier gear, you need to press the spool with your thumb to stop it from spinning as soon as your weight or lure hits the water. If you don't do this, the reel will keep spinning as the lure splashes down, and that's a sure recipe for a backlash.

The way to learn multiplier casting with minimum heartbreak is to try it a little bit at a time, following these steps and referring to Figure 15-5:

1. **Before you make your first cast, hold the rod at about a 45 degree angle.**

2. **Disengage the reel and hold your thumb on the spool.**

3. **Release some thumb pressure so that the lure descends pretty freely; then, as it does, put more pressure on the spool with your thumb to slow it down so that the spool stops completely by the time the weight or lure hits the ground.**

4. **Adjust the reel's tension. The tension should be light enough that the weight or lure can pull line from the spool, but not so light that the spool spins rapidly.**

   If the tension is too tight, the lure won't be able to pull line from the spool at all. Find the happy medium where the lure can pull line slowly from the spool. Adjust accordingly with the weight of whatever you cast.

This test will give you an idea of how the reel's tension setting and thumb control work together to control real casts. Try short casts at first, using the thumb as a brake (better to use too much braking rather than too little when you start out). Your casts may be short of the mark this way, but you won't tangle.

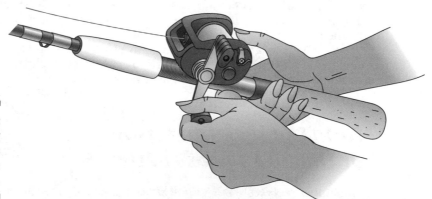

Figure 15-5:
Multiplier gear calls for thumb control.

Casting overhead with a multiplier

To make overhead casts with multiplier gear, you follow the same arm motion you make when casting with fixed spool reels. But multiplier reels are more complicated and it's your thumb that has to do the work. Following these steps will have you casting like a pro in no time:

1. **Grasp the rod with your dominant hand with the multiplier reel above the rod. Your shoulders should be squared towards the target. Check to make sure the area behind you is clear. (This not only ensures a good cast, but a safe one.)**

2. **Put the reel into *free spool* by pushing in the reel's release.**

   You should typically have between two and three feet of line between your casting weight and the *tip ring* (the top line guide on the rod). If you were using a really long rod, say a beachcaster, and a heavy weight this gap could be extended to four or five feet.

3. **Point the rod at your target.**

   If you are a right-handed caster, place your left foot forward. (If you are left-handed, step forward with your right foot.)

4. **Begin the *backstroke* of your cast by bringing the rod directly overhead and behind you, until it reaches the 2 o'clock position.**

   This action will put some flex into the rod as you begin your cast. Keep your thumb on the spool to keep the spool locked all through the backstroke. When casting artificial lures, the backstroke can be snappy, but using heavier weights calls for a softer, gentler backstroke.

5. **Once the casting weight is in position just behind you, begin the *forward stroke* by swinging the rod forward and toward your target, releasing thumb pressure from the spool as you do (so that the lure can pull line off the reel as it travels to the target).**

   Leave your thumb lightly touching, or hovering over, the spool as you release pressure. If the spool begins to overrun on the cast, you can feather (lightly brake) it to slow the turn of the spool. (If it's more comfortable for you, you can also press your thumb to the side of the spool, as opposed to the centre.) The timing of this release – the moment you lift your thumb from the spool – is crucial to a successful cast. Releasing the spool too quickly during the forward stroke will send your weight high above you. Releasing too late will cause the weight to slam down right in front of you.

6. **Finish the cast by following through by pointing the rod again at the target.**

   As soon as the lure hits the water, press your thumb completely on the spool, stopping it and preventing a backlash.

7. **The cast ends and you're ready to fish when you turn the crank and engage the reel.**

   Remember, the reel is disengaged until you do this, so if you cast your lure and a fish bites immediately, you can't set the hook until you engage the reel!

Flycasting: Presenting Flies

Flycasting intimidates anglers, often because their only exposure to it comes from watching fluent casters on film, such as Brad Pitt's artful loops in *A River Runs Through It*. As with some of the more complicated things in angling, we strongly recommend that you have someone who knows how to flycast work with you in the beginning. A well-practised friend can help, but it's well worth contacting a guide or casting instructor otherwise. Some offer half-day or hourly rates to give you an affordable head start. Don't be daunted however, because anyone can learn to cast a fly. Peter can tell you from experience (his) that if you apply yourself, you can master every cast in this chapter in two days. You won't be perfect at these casts, but you will be fly fishing.

Presentation of the fly is the single most important skill in fly fishing. To do it well and to do it with all kinds of wind conditions requires a few more practice casts than conventional multiplier or spinning gear. But if you master the casts, you will be able to catch fish in almost any situation. Those are covered fully in Peter's book *Flyfishing For Dummies* (Wiley). The following sections cover the most basic casts.

Striving for the oneness of rod and line

Apologies for sounding like a wise and ancient kung-fu master, but I (Peter) would like to plant an idea in your head that may help as you approach fly-casting. When flexed, the rod bends into a curve. If you're moving line at the right speed as you cast, your line will shoot off that curve in a straight path. If you hesitate too long at any point and if the arc that your rod moves through is too big, your line will no longer be able to continue the curve, and your cast will lose shape and power. Figure 15-6a shows a rod flexed properly. Note how the line smoothly continues the bend in the rod. Also note how the line curls back. This segment of line, shaped like the crook in an umbrella handle is called a *loop*.

Think of the loop on your rod as the bow of a boat. In the same way that a boat's bow cuts through water, the loop cuts through the air. A nice, slim v-shaped boat will move through the water with little resistance. On the other hand, if you hook up an outboard motor to a bathtub, you will meet a great deal more resistance to your forward motion. The same is true of the cast. A tight loop will slice through the wind. A wide loop (see Figure 15-6b) will just hang there like a – the phrase that comes to mind in describing how it hangs there is *limp noodle*.

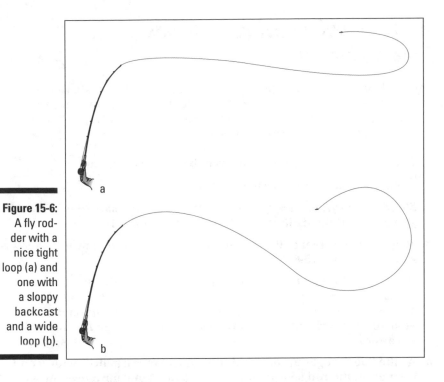

Figure 15-6:
A fly rodder with a nice tight loop (a) and one with a sloppy backcast and a wide loop (b).

There is basically one right way to hold a fly rod, and it involves grasping the rod firmly above and in front of the reel, with the reel under the rod. Keep your thumb extended for more control, as shown in Figure 15-7.

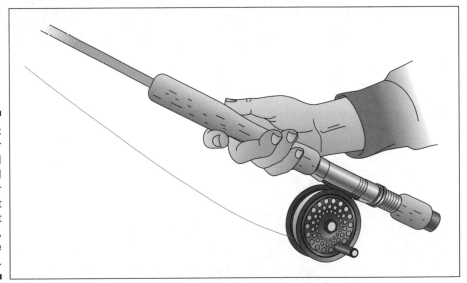

Figure 15-7:
The proper way to hold your fly rod to deliver the most power, most efficiently, is with the thumb up.

The forward (and sometimes sidearm) cast

Peter would estimate that 75 per cent of all your fly-fishing casts will be a version of this basic forward cast. If you're a saltwater fisherman, make that 95 per cent. Figure 15-8 illustrates this fundamental cast. To complete your first practice forward cast, follow these steps:

1. **Pull about 10 feet of line off the reel beyond the tip ring.**

   Pulling line off the reel is called *stripping*.

2. **Stand sideways, or mostly sideways with your left shoulder in front if you are a rightie. (Lefties, point the right shoulder.)**

3. **Strip another 2 feet of line off the reel and hold it in your left hand, as shown in Figure 15-8.**

4. **With the rod held at a 45-degree angle, crisply lift the line in the air, snapping your wrist upward as you do. Your backstroke should stop when your wrist is at 12 o'clock (vertical). Momentum will carry your rod and wrist along the arc you have started and flex the rod backward.**

5. **As the line straightens out behind you, let your arm drift with it and then move the rod sharply forward. Again, stop your power stroke dead on 12 o'clock (it will drift forward); as you do so, continue to drive forward with your wrist as if you were pushing in a drawing pin.**

6. **When your rod reaches the 45-degree angle, drop the rod tip.**

   If you have executed this cast well, you will feel a tug on your left hand, which is holding the extra 2 feet of line that you stripped out in Step 3, before you started the cast. Let go of the line and it will shoot out of your top guide, giving you an extra couple of feet to your cast.

When you're fly casting it's always safest to wear a pair of polarising glasses. A fly travelling at speed could hit you in the eye, and even if you are a well practised caster it only takes a sudden gust of wind for a mistake to happen. Plus, even if you cast like a pro, you'll still spot far more fish with a decent pair of polarising glasses.

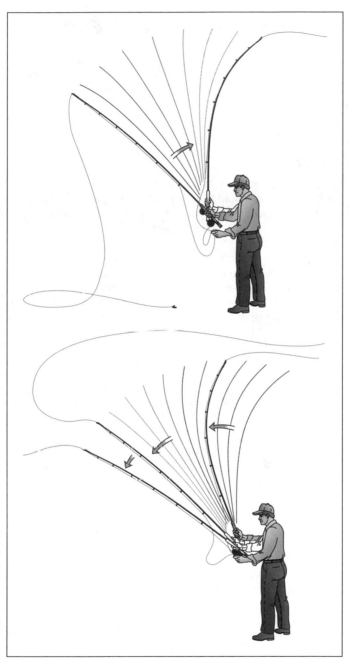

Figure 15-8:
Master the
forward
cast and
you can fly
fish right
away.

Figuring out what you did wrong

With ten feet of line out of the rod rings, you probably performed a reasonable approximation of a cast. Now, do the same thing with 15 feet of line. This will probably begin to show some of the problems in your beginning cast. Try to keep the line in the air as you execute a few false casts. (A *false cast* is the name given to what you do when you flick the line backward and forward before finally delivering the fly.) A false cast serves two purposes:

- ✔ It lines up your cast with your target.

- ✔ It develops *line speed,* which allows you to work more and more line through the rod rings so that you can hold it in the air, get up speed, and shoot a longer cast to your target. With good use of line speed, you can easily add distance to your cast.

But before you worry about distance, concentrate on casting mechanics. You need to get out on the lawn with your 15 feet of line and (standing sideways) watch your line in the air as you cast. This will require you to drop your arm for more of a sidearm delivery, but don't worry about that. Sometimes a fishing situation calls for precisely that manoeuvre, which fulfills a similar role to the side cast for fixed spool users.

As you watch your line, your goal is to keep it moving in the air and parallel to the ground. If the line drops below the horizontal, you are moving through too wide an arc. You're forgetting to stop your forward stroke at 12 o'clock. We can't emphasise this enough. Stop the rod tip high, and the rod will do the work for you.

Another common error is hurrying the cast. Casting a fly isn't like shooting a bullet out of a rifle. It's not just one flick of the finger followed by delivery of the fly. In casting a fly, four things have to happen:

- ✔ You transfer power to your rod.

- ✔ Your rod bends and multiplies that force over distance.

- ✔ Your line is set in motion by the action of the rod.

- ✔ The bullwhip action of the fly line develops even more speed as you finish the casting motion.

All of this action takes time. You back cast. The line straightens out and pulls on the rod. You move through the forward cast, and the line travels forward. You shoot line and drop the rod tip. A beginner's cast often falls apart at a point between the end of the backcast and the beginning of the forward cast. You need to pause just a bit at this part of the cast until you feel a little tug or, if you are not a great tug feeler, pause until you see the line straighten out.

The line tray or 'stripping basket'

During the 1960s, the otherwise forgettable film 'Man's Favourite Sport' showed Doris Day and Paula Prentiss getting Rock Hudson a complete fishing outfit. With inflatable waders and a real geek's hat, nothing could possibly have looked dafter. But that was because line trays weren't around in those days. A *line tray* or *stripping basket* is a basket that an angler ties around his or her waist. When casting long distances from a boat, jetty or shore, a stripping basket, which stores your stripped in line in one safe spot, can keep your line from getting tangled, falling under a rock, or getting swept out by the surge of the waves. So at the risk of looking silly, remember there are worse things in the world than walking around with something that looks like a dish washing basin tied to your waist – like not catching fish! They are especially useful when wading. When bank fishing, a good tip is to place the head of your landing net just in front of your feet to catch the line and keep it clear of snags.

Another common fault is known as 'breaking the wrist'. This means letting the rod handle move around too much in the cast, coming away from your wrist. Remember, you are not trying to use a throwing action and smooth is better than jerky. It's best to keep the rod handle in line with your wrist, so that the rod is essentially just like an extension of your arm. If you can do this, your casts will be smoother.

After the fly is out there, it might interest a fish. For you to catch that fish, which is the point of all this, you need to make the transition from casting the fly to fishing the fly. You wrap the thumb around the rod and extend your index finger so that it holds the fly line against the rod shaft. This trick ensures that anytime a fish hits, you won't have unwanted slack in the line. Your other hand is now free to pull in line as required. This retrieving action is called *stripping* line.

Cast Disaster: Beating Snags and Snarls

Successful fishing is often a game of inches. Come to think of it, which sport isn't? A shot that beats the goalie just inside the post, a return that glances the baseline, a drive over a bunker – these skills require accuracy, too. The same goes with fishing. So if you want to get your cast in there where the fish are, you're going to miss by inches and get stuck from time to time. Everybody does. In fact, a common angling saying proclaims, 'If you aren't snagging occasionally, you aren't fishing where the fish are.' With care, you will snag up less, but you are still going to snag. Sometimes you can also undo it.

With any snag, don't panic. Responding with rage will only drive the hook deeper into the snag, making freeing it impossible, or you'll slingshot the hook back at you. Most casting mistakes can be overcome as long you stay calm and reason your way out of it.

Whether you're fishing from boat or bank, one common casting miscue involves casting too far and wrapping your line around a branch. Sometimes the lure will still fall to the water (where occasionally a fish will strike it!); other times it hangs there in the tree, taunting you. My brothers and I (Greg) call this squirrel fishing, and we never mean it as a compliment. If you cast and your lure sails over a branch or limb, don't panic and jerk back on the rod. Doing that will often only spin the lure around the branch, tangling the line. Instead, follow these simple steps:

1. **Point your rod at the offending branch.**

2. **Very gently, reel up any slack until the lure comes almost up against the bottom of the limb.**

3. **With a gentle upward flip of the rod, the lure will often somersault over the limb, thereby freeing it.**

4. **Retrieve your lure normally.**

Tree branches aren't the only lure, bait, fly and line stealers, of course. You can hang up on underwater rocks (or any other submerged obstacle); in fact, there are as many things to snag on as there are types of cover for fish to hide under and around. And as with catching fish, a number of techniques and strategies (including a couple of important don'ts) apply to getting unsnagged:

✔ If you're snagged on something underwater, don't rear back with your rod and put a lot of pressure on it, and don't savagely jerk it either. You'll break a rod sooner or later (which is a big price to pay, even if the alternative is losing an expensive lure). Instead, try gently tightening up so that the rod is pointing at the snag, before waving the rod up and down, trying to pop the lure loose. It's surprising how often this succeeds. If that fails, try pulling with steady pressure, with the rod pointed right at the snag. When you do this, don't put too much pressure on the (engaged) reel. You could harm the reel's gears. Try holding the spool of a fixed spool reel with your hand before you pull, or hold the line of any type of gear against the rod to take some pressure off the reel.

✔ If firm (but not overpowering) pressure won't free a snagged line, we often put the rod down and strip some more line off. Then we wrap the line around a stick a couple of times and pull straight on the line. (Don't wrap line around your hands or arms! Any fishing line can cut you.) Usually, if the hook has any chance of breaking free, this does the trick.

A gradual, steady pull is best. With strong tackle you might even succeed in bending the hook out. Not ideal but better than breaking off and leaving it in the water.

Whereas this wrap-and-pull technique is good for deep underwater obstacles far away, don't try this method if the hang-up is in a tree (or other above-water obstacle) or barely submerged snag. You can slingshot a lure back toward you with tremendous force, and chances are you'll be looking straight down the line at your lure. Guess what path that hook is going to take as it hurtles out of the brush – right at your face!

✔ If you're snagged in a stream, sometimes walking downstream to change the angle of pressure will free the hook. The same applies on other waters and a change of angle can sometimes quickly free the hook. Walk up and down the bank or move the boat if you have to.

✔ The final decision is to 'call it quits and pull for a break'. After trying to rescue your equipment for a while, you need to consider the following: You wait all week to try and get in a little fishing. When you get right down to it, you don't spend all that much time actually fishing, even when you do get the time. Getting rigged up, in and out of waders, in and out of boats, and the like eats up a great deal of time. How much time do you want to spend trying to save the unsaveable? Sometimes the answer is 'give up and get back to fishing!' You will be amazed at how much better you will feel as soon as you catch a fish.

✔ Don't break your line until you're positive you're not 'snagged' on a fish! Many big fish stories begin with the line, 'Well, at first I thought I was hooked on a log, until the log started to swim off!'

✔ After any snag, check your hook points. Sometimes a nasty snag can dull or roll a hook point. When that happens, sharpen or replace the hook.

Chapter 16

Exploring Different Fishing Techniques

. . . .

In This Chapter

▶ Knowing what makes fish bite

▶ Figuring out static fishing methods with leger and float rigs

▶ Active methods – casting your way toward more fish

▶ Fishing calm water and flowing water

. . . .

*T*he first people to capture fish for food were hunters more than anglers: They used their bare hands, spears or traps to catch fish. Today, you're more likely to pursue fish with a rod and reel, but you still have many options. After you find fishable water (see Chapter 3) and have a sense of the fish living there (see Chapters 4 and 5), you need to figure out how to get those fish to bite. After all, that moment – the bite – is what separates fishing from hunting. Successful angling requires a fish to take your offering, either through choice or instinct. (And if they don't, you go home practising your excuses.)

Fish bite for two primary reasons:

✔ They're hungry, and they see your offering as something to eat.

✔ They're triggered to bite by instinct; they strike out of a sense of aggravation, protection or competition.

So how do you entice fish to bite? First, you need to present something that of the fish likes to eat or thinks it will, whether this means a man-made or natural food source. You need an effective bait, lure or fly, full stop. But that alone won't always catch fish. You must understand how to approach fish with your bait, and that's where your technique comes into play. Little about fishing technique fits neatly into a chapter because with so much of technique, experience matters. Learning how to cast takes practice. Knowing what fishing technique to use, and when, takes experience.

To simplify, whether you fish salt- or freshwater, the water in front of you is either flowing or still. Tides move water; a river's current moves water, too. Fish relate to moving water differently to how they do still water. For that reason, your fishing techniques will vary as you approach the different environments. And here's another simplification: most of your fishing will fit into one of two categories: static or active fishing. This chapter focuses on those categories and provides you with plenty of advice on finding the best technique for you and the fish you're intent on catching.

Static Fishing

Static fishing refers to methods of angling where the bait is presented, either on a float rig or legered on the bottom, and the angler waits for the fish to find it and bite. Don't think of static fishing as lazy fishing, even though you don't cast as many times as you do while working a lure or fly. Although you can cast out a bottom rig and then do nothing but wait for hours, static fishing can be almost as active, or at least as mentally involving, as casting lures or flies. Some fish practically require static fishing. After all, some fish are simply too shy or passive, to go chasing artificial lures. Fish do vary in the intelligence stakes. In one study, carp came out tops when fisheries biologists trained fish to avoid a light source. Rainbow trout placed near the bottom. (Not sure how their GCSE grades turned out.) Some fish can be caught reliably only on bait. Static fishing presents that bait effectively. Besides, no one says fishing has to be work. You can catch about any fish that swims while static fishing.

Floating away

Float rigs, the term given to any rig that utilises a float to present a bait beneath, allow you present your bait either on the bottom or suspended in the water column. This presentation keeps your main line clear of weeds and obstructions on the bottom. (For more on float rigs, see Chapter 14.)

Floats represent good bite indication and also quite an active way to fish in one spot. You might present a bait just touching the bottom and leave it in place (say for tench or carp), but equally you might recast fairly often, letting the bait drop down and settle again, which can excite the interest of the fish. Pike and sea anglers, or those fishing in a river current, will sometimes let a bait drift under a float to search out likely water. At other times, such as casting a waggler on a lake or stillwater, the idea is often to keep to one fairly tight area and throw in free bait (or *loose feed*) to draw fish in.

How static does static fishing need to be? The answer lies with you, but there are often things you can do to increase your chances of success. The most obvious is to keep adding a little free bait by hand or with a catapult and 'little and often' is a good general rule here. You can also alter your presentation in other ways. For example, if little fish are stealing the bait you could try fishing deeper, increasing the size of your bait or casting to the edges of your feeding zone to try and pick off a bigger one. The same applies whether you're float fishing or legering and sometimes a small change can make a big difference.

Legering: Waiting out the fish

Fish in both salt- and freshwater fall for bottom fishing (or *leger*) rigs. Such rigs can present living or natural baits such as worms or fish, but are also perfect for a multitude of other baits from sweetcorn to boilies. Leger rigs let the bait do the work for you, as the bait, either through smell and/or appearance, attracts the fish you hope to catch. Too many anglers, however, mistake this for meaning that you can cast a bottom rig anywhere and expect to catch fish. Bottom rigs work best when placed in the general vicinity of active fish; even a lively worm or a chunk of fresh bait can only do so much when cast into dead water.

We cover standard leger rigs in Chapter 14, but any bottom rig should keep your bait anchored to the bottom while also allowing a fish to take it, notifying you of a bite. Many of these rigs feature a weight that slides on the main line, so fish can take the bait without feeling the drag of the weight. Others, as in the case of many carp rigs, are designed to work as the fish moves away with the bait and is hooked against the weight itself, meaning you don't need to strike.

Legering can often mean sitting it out for a bite. If you were fishing for a big bass or tackling a lake with a few large, wary carp, for example, you wouldn't want to keep casting every five minutes. But on the other hand if you use a swimfeeder for bream, roach or smaller carp, regular recasting will keep a supply of free food going in and help to draw fish to the hook. You also need to consider keeping bait fresh. Sea anglers, for example, don't tend to sit on their hands out for hours on end because the tide soon washes out the bait and a fresh offering works better than one which is tired and tatty. In the case of using a swimfeeder to fish for coarse species, regular, accurate casts to one favoured area will create a steady build-up of free bait. Do it right and the fish should be queuing up for the next helping.

Whether legering or float fishing, it pays to be accurate. It's no use finding the perfect area to fish or carefully loose-feeding a spot unless you can accurately cast to it every time. Practice makes perfect, but other tricks will help. One good way to keep hitting the same spot is to line up with a marker on the horizon – a tall tree for example – to give you something to aim at (don't pick something liable to move, like a boat!).

When casting longer distances you can also trap the line in the line clip on your reel (most modern reels feature a little plastic clip on the spool), so that the cast stops at the same point every time. You can also use a line clip to make your cast stop right by a feature – for example, a tree on the far bank. With leger tackle you could even take a practice cast or two with the sinker on its own to get the perfect distance, before clipping the line and adding your hook to the rig. Be warned though: a large fish could break the line if you trap it, so if you're expecting larger specimens remember to unclip the line once you've cast out.

Top Tips: Using the rod tip to spot bites

With no float to give clues, leger fishing often requires careful observation of the rod tip to detect bites. When coarse fishing with a bomb or swimfeeder rig, this often involves the use of a *quivertip*, which we meet in Chapter 7. Sea anglers from both shore and boat also use the rod tip to detect bites, however.

Whichever branch of bottom fishing you pursue, it is important to get good bite indication. This is achieved by keeping the line tight enough to spot bites, but not so tight that the rod is bent right over. A very slight curve in the rod tip is usually enough to give you an instant sign when a bite comes, but enough flexibility in the tip to let the fish have a good tug and take the bait properly. Having a well-positioned rod rest is vital. On calmer waters such as ponds and lakes, the quivertip angler often sets up the rod low, and almost at a right angle to the bait. However, anglers tackling a heavy flow such as a big river, or a wave strewn beach, prefer to keep the rod tip high. This helps keep the line and rig from getting dragged about in the current. Figure 16-1 shows you how to use a quivertip.

As with a float, there is a definite knack involved at knowing when to strike and when to ignore movements. It can be tricky when wind or waves give false indications, but fish tend to move the rod tip in a twitchier, faster manner than the slower pull of the elements. Whichever species you encounter, a good general rule is to avoid striking at tiny taps and twitches. When the tip makes a decisive pull and holds, or starts bouncing round with a vengeance, strike!

Active Fishing Methods: Casting About

Static fishing has its place and works especially well for certain species of fish. However, many anglers prefer to cast. Casting allows you to cover more water actively, and your lure or fly (casting is most often paired with artificials) can be made to act as enticingly as real prey. Casting also allows you to capitalise on the aggressive nature of some fish. Species such as perch, trout, pike and bass feed by chasing and catching prey, and casting and retrieving lures can trigger that response.

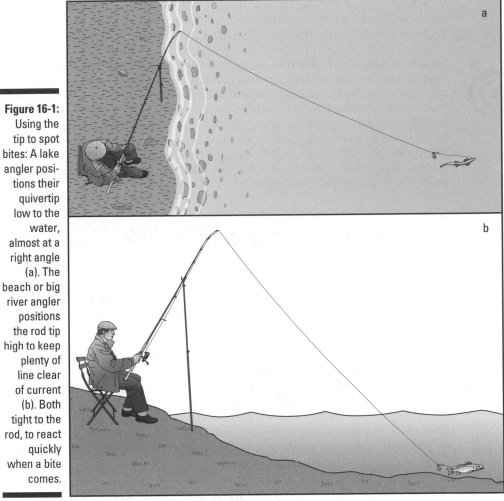

Figure 16-1: Using the tip to spot bites: A lake angler positions their quivertip low to the water, almost at a right angle (a). The beach or big river angler positions the rod tip high to keep plenty of line clear of current (b). Both tight to the rod, to react quickly when a bite comes.

However, we should also note that in some ways even 'static' methods can be pursued with great mobility. Roving the banks with a float, for example, and stopping for no more than half an hour in each spot is hardly an inactive way to fish and allows you to really search the water. With some types of fish, such as perch and chub, the response can arrive quickly and you might catch far more than you would by sitting in one place all day. If the water is clear enough, you can even go and try your luck by presenting bait to visible fish. This is very exciting and often referred to as *stalking* by coarse fishers.

Whichever active method you use though, blind casting is little more than exercise. To catch fish consistently, you need a solid strategy. The following sections provide some tips for active fishing styles.

So how do you decide whether to fish actively or static? The truth is that you needn't stick to one or other approach. Static methods are most suitable when you have identified a good spot where you're confident the fish will be around. If you're fishing an unfamiliar water, however, you would often be better off travelling light and trying several spots; even if you catch little, you are likely to get some clues and hopefully spot a few fish on your travels. Once you've found the fish you can always return armed with static fishing tackle and sit it out in a promising area. Start out active though – it's often the case that the more you explore, the more you catch.

Covering water and taking fish

Watch an expert lure angler at work. Using a practised, polished motion, the angler will cast his lure to a precise spot, say by a sunken log, and work it back in a deliberate manner. As soon as the lure returns, zing, it's placed near the next target. Soon, the whole area has been fished, and the angler has caught several fish. The successful angler has probably seldom stopped moving his lure.

Casting allows you to fish actively, and it's possible to present your lure or fly to a lot of fish. The key? Cast well and cast often. Although it's certainly possible to fish too fast (and miss fish as a result), casting gives you the chance to catch the most active fish in the area – those that are hungry and looking for a good meal. Accurate casts are a must. Practice will help you land your lure or fly precisely where you want it to go. (See Chapter 15 for more on how to cast.)

Matching your retrieve to the conditions

Lures and flies (sometimes called *artificials*) come in different shapes and sizes for a reason. As we explain in Chapters 12 and 13, they vary widely so you can use them in a variety of places and in a range of ways. Your job as an angler is to know two things:

- How a lure or fly is designed to work. Manufacturers build lures with a particular action in mind, and they'll share this information with you. After all, they want you to catch fish on their lures.

- When to use a particular lure or fly. For example, a surface popping plug will catch active predators such as pike and bass looking upwards for dinner, but if they're lying deep it's unlikely to work.

Carry a range of artificials (see Chapters 12 and 13 for advice on which lures and flies to buy), and experiment until you know what conditions call for which lures. With lures, you can quickly see that some demand attention: They're shiny and vibrant and some are loud. Use them to find active fish, or on days when fish feed aggressively. Other lures, like a soft baits and jigs, slip through the water more subtly. Lures like these work better when fish hang near the bottom in a lethargic manner.

Fishing Still (Non-flowing) Water

When fishing calm water you should know that, in the absence of current, fish will relate to features such as structure and cover. (For more on cover and structure, check out Chapter 3.) In flowing water, fish will almost always face upstream because that's where the food, in the form of floating insects or other prey, comes from. In a pond, lake, or a tidal pool at low tide, fish could be facing in any direction. You must choose between static fishing or active methods, bait or lures, but start with this knowledge: The fish are usually close to features. That could mean a weed bed, a deep hole or an island. Find the key areas to fish, and you're half way there. Now you just need to use the right technique to earn bites.

Working the banks: A deliberate approach

When fishing a pond or lake with no current, the first thing to do is visually inspect the water and its surroundings. Think about structure – what clues are there that tell you about the bottom of the body of water? Are there points trailing from the bank into the water? Rocky shorelines? Islands? Coves or narrow stretches? Is there a dam or obvious deeper end of the water? Any of these things can concentrate fish. Cover will be more visible to the naked eye, and equally important. Search the banks features such as fallen trees, weedbeds, docks, bushes or overhanging limbs. Fish use cover for protection and as ambush points, and putting your bait near cover often results in a bite.

From the bank or from a boat, move methodically around the shoreline and fish obvious points of interest. Fish the edges of the cover you can see – cast along a weedbed or along the branches of a submerged tree. Of course you'll snag sometimes, but this means you're really trying to fish in the right spot. Another classic area in so many waters is the *drop off*, where shallow and deep water meet. Whether you're using lures, flies or livebait, keep moving. Fish the structure and cover available to you, and pay attention to bites. Where are most of the fish taking? Are you catching one big fish around every sunken tree? Are fish only close to the rocky shores? Pay attention and look for patterns. Even if you're fishing static, there's nothing that says you have to camp out in one spot all day. Quite often 30 minutes or so is enough time to allow a fish to find your offering. Keep moving and exploring.

Fan casting: Covering the bases

Occasionally, a pond or bay will have no discernible features – it looks like a bowl, uniform in appearance on every side. Reservoirs can be like this, and so are some canals and drains. In this situation, keep busy and cover water. Using a lure like a spinner or a plug, cast parallel to the shore to your left. Retrieve the lure and cast again, this time a little farther out. Think of your casts as an old-fashioned, handheld fan or the spread of a peacock's tail (see Figure 16-2). Cast in a pattern until you're casting parallel to the shore on your right. Doing this will put your bait near the bank, over deeper water, and everything in between. Move down the bank (twice the reach of your previous furthest cast) and repeat. (Go far enough that your casts back toward your original location don't overlap with your initial casts.) Move down the bank and watch for patterns. This method will cover a lot of water and put your lure in front of many fish. It's a good exploratory technique.

Figure 16-2: Fan casting allows you to cover a lot of water from one spot.

Stirring things up: Fishing windy days

A strong, persistent wind acts like a current – it can concentrate fish in one location. Most anglers try to avoid the wind, but the fish often have other ideas. I (Dominic) once learned that lesson clearly on a big windy lake. I had been fishing for bream with no success, when I decided to make a move. The wind was making big waves in a bay further along the bank. The lake looked more like the sea than freshwater. It certainly made for ugly casting, but a swimfeeder cast into the waves quickly rewarded the effort. In the tumult of the lapping water I wondered if I'd spot a bite even if I got one, before the rod tip pulled round and kept going. It happened repeatedly as several real dinner-tray-sized bream came to the net, and it seemed like every fish in the lake was feeding hard in that windswept area.

The moral of the tale is simple: When fishing on a windy day, fish the bank towards which the wind is blowing. It's certainly easier to cast with the wind, but you'll find more success if you cast into the wind. A strong, steady wind pushes waves against the bank, which stirs up sediment, which activates microinvertebrates, which triggers a feeding response in small fish, and so on up the food chain. Insects also get blown onto the water and I've had some of my best trout fishing on those breezy days when casting is difficult.

Fishing Flowing Water

Sea fish follow the tides because the tides concentrate and shift their food supply. In streams and rivers, fish know that the current delivers food in the form of dead or dying prey. For this reason, in everything from saltwater estuaries to mountain streams, fish tend to face into the current, waiting to see what it offers. Luckily for you, in our opinion, these places also tend to be among the most beautiful places to fish. There's something enchanting about moving water.

Casting upstream, retrieving downstream

Fishing streams by wading is certainly the most popular way to pursue trout. Most anglers wade upstream, fishing as they go, then walk back downstream when it's time to head home.

On popular waters, it may be hard to find unfished water during peak times. Just because you haven't disturbed the water yet doesn't mean another angler didn't work the same area an hour earlier. On small streams, there's only so much you can do about crowds, but try to fish on weekdays and be willing to walk/wade further than others.

Predatory fish species will often be near the current, but slightly out of it, hiding behind a rock or other obstacle that blocks the current. Pay particular attention to the following spots:

- **Eddies:** Places where the current swirls back upriver
- **Creases:** Where two currents come together
- **Undercut banks:** Where the current has washed out a hole under the bank

Fish watching the current don't have forever to make up their minds about eating something. If they hesitate too long, the morsel will wash on down-stream. This fact works to your advantage. Fish that reside in flowing water tend to be more aggressive than still water fish and are often stronger, as result of swimming in flowing water their whole lives. Practice bringing your lure or fly downstream in a manner that matches what the fish are used to seeing. In Figure 16-3, notice how the cast brings the artificial right past a log where a fish lies in wait. Notice that not every upstream cast will be directly upstream – many will be at angles, often toward different targets on either side. Work upstream, but cast diagonally or across the current, too.

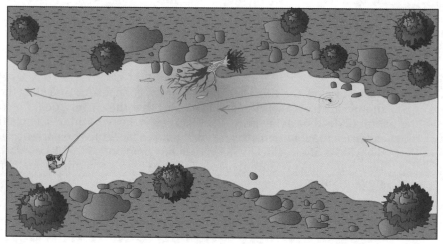

Figure 16-3:
Cast your lures and flies upstream and bring them down-stream past likely haunts.

Trotting with floats: Meals au naturel

Float rigs account for many fish from streams and rivers every season. They work so well because the flowing water carries the float downstream, pre-senting the bait underneath in a natural manner. Because fish that reside in the current get used to the speed of the flow, float rigs allow you to present a bait at exactly the same rate as the current. This looks natural to the fish.

Using a longer rod will benefit you when float fishing. A longer rod allows you to steer your float rig as it manoeuvres downstream. As always, avoid slack line between your rod and the float, and lift and lower the rod tip to direct the float around obstacles. Gently holding back the float a little lets the bait reach the fish first, as opposed to the shot, line and float. So-called *trotting* works for various kinds of fish from dace and roach through to chub and even barbel. The bigger fish often like the bait close to the bottom. You can even drift a deadbait in the flow to target river pike.

Other Fishing Techniques

Most of your fishing will consist of classic static and active fishing methods, and we would recommend getting to grips with simple techniques first before you attempt anything more specialised. Knowing how to set up an extra rod, or trying trolling or night fishing will expand your possibilities for angling success, but we recommend that you try these techniques only after you've mastered the fundamental art of casting and still fishing on your home waters.

Specimen tactics: Waiting for the big one

In some types of fishing, you may wait a long time between bites. This is especially true if the fish are big and cagey, or few in numbers. Most waters contain far more small fish than big ones, and if you want to catch quality rather than quantity you must adapt your style accordingly. You might try using larger, tiddler-proof baits such as large boilies or whole dead fish, for example, along with rigs that will stay put for as long as it takes. In these circumstances you might get a real headache from watching a float for a whole day, so long-stay anglers often use bite alarms to alert them to fish activity.

If you want to target big fish you might also consider using two or even three rods (do remember, though, that you need two licences to fish legally with three rods). In general terms, we would usually recommend fishing with just one rod and giving it your full attention. It's a case of that old adage 'better to do one thing well than two things badly', but if bites are few then a second rod could effectively double your chances by allowing you to cover more water. You might try putting one bait close in, for example, whilst another is cast out at greater distance.

Specimen Carp: Plotting for monsters

An increasing number of anglers are addicted to chasing big carp. We'd strongly suggest you go for the smaller ones with simple float or leger tackle first to grasp the basics. Playing and landing a big one (and many waters now produce them to over 20 pounds) is a real thrill, but only the last stage in a careful and sometimes lengthy process. The first step, before you so much as cast a bait, should be to decide on a likely area. Asking other anglers and fishery owners, as well as using your feet and eyes to locate fish are the first steps.

Besides a measure of patience and knowledge, targeting big carp often calls for special tactics. You might be in for a long wait (which could well include night fishing), so you want your baited rigs to stay in place perfectly without alarming the fish. For this reason carp anglers often use two carefully positioned rigs, often *bolt rigs* (discussed in Chapter 14), which will hook fish even when unattended – in the middle of the night, for example, when you might be dozing off. They also use bite alarms to signal a take, or *run*. Some would call it lazy; and yes, bite alarms and bolt rigs are totally unnecessary on fisheries packed with small to medium-sized carp. But where you might wait many hours for just one big fish, such tactics are perfectly justified.

Wily carp are quickly put on their guard by tight lines cutting through the water, so another common measure is to use a *back lead* to keep the line on the deck. These little weights are clipped onto your line, but only once your bait is in the water. To use one you should first cast out to the desired spot and let everything settle for a few seconds. Next, grab hold of the line just in front of the rod tip, keeping the line under light tension but avoiding pulling your weight out of place. Now clip on the back lead and give it a little push so that it slides out into the water a few yards out. This will keep your line tight to the bottom where the carp won't swim into it, not to mention keeping it clear of swans, boats and other potential nuisances. Figure 16-4 shows the set-up.

Figure 16-4:
In position for carp. A backlead pins the line down tidily whilst the rod is set securely on two rod rests or a rod pod.

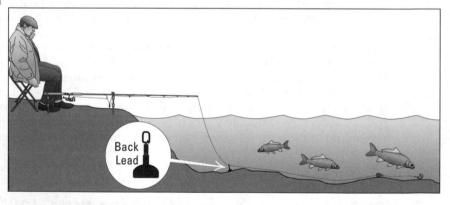

The next step is to set up your bite detection. For the specimen carp angler this is also a case apart. With no float or quivertip, carpers use special bite indicators, which clip onto the line and either lift or fall when a fish moves off with the bait. These are used in conjunction with a bite alarm to add an audible signal. A bite alarm has a little groove through which the line runs and makes a noise when any movement occurs (see Chapter 10 for more on bite alarms) – very useful for night fishing when you may not be able to spot bites with your eyes.

Carp bites are often described as *runs* for the simple reason that fish will often go screaming off with the bait at a rate of knots. For this reason another essential is a special reel featuring a *free spool* or *baitrunner* system. This basically means that the reel has a special switch, which when engaged will let out line freely. Reels should always be switched to free-spool mode when carp fishing, otherwise your rod could simply be pulled into the water when you get a bite. And yes, we've seen it happen! Figure 16-5 shows how you set up the free-spool system.

Figure 16-5:
All set for a run: The line is clipped into a hanging bite indicator just before the bite alarm. The reel is set in free-spool mode to allow a hooked carp to run.

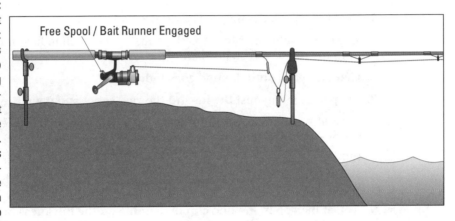

Free Spool / Bait Runner Engaged

Legering for pike and zander: Drop offs and dead baits

Legering is also an excellent method for toothy predators. It's true, you can also float fish (covered in Chapter 14), but where deep water or long distances are involved the leger often works best. A leger rig keeps your bait, usually a dead fish, on the bottom where a scavenging predator can easily pick it up. You might try several spots in a day when predator fishing and your biggest challenge is often simply finding the fish, which won't always come to you. Snaggy areas, sudden depth changes and places where you find shoals of the predator's prey are all likely areas. On rivers, pike like slack water where they can lurk out of the main current.

Again, we'd recommend you begin fishing with just one rod and give it your full attention – although you can add a second when your confidence grows. Predators can wolf down baits however, and deep hooking is bad news for fish and angler alike. This is why you must remain vigilant, strike bites early and use sensitive bite indication.

Bite indication for predator fishing is quite different than for other species when you're legering. The key tool to spot bites is called a *drop off indicator*, so called because it is set more-or-less horizontally under tension and then literally drops downwards when a fish moves off with the bait, giving you a clear, instant signal to strike. If you do eventually decide to use two rods, bite alarms are recommended; you can't watch two things at once and a slow response could lead to a deep hooked fish and fatal consequences. Here's how to set up a drop off indicator (and Figure 16-6 helps, too):

1. **Cast out your bait and put it onto two rod rests.**

   The rod should point towards the bait. The drop off indicator is clipped onto the rear rod rest, just below the level your reel will sit at.

2. **Gently reel in until the line goes tight.**

3. **Keep a finger against the line on the reel spool and open the bail arm.**

4. **Carefully clip the drop-off indicator onto the line, right under the reel spool – virtually touching it is best.**

   Bites are shown when the fish pulls the line out of the clip – or runs straight towards you – and the indicator drops down. Tighten up and strike immediately!

5. **Adjust the gap in the line clip depending on the thickness of your line (most clips feature a twist mechanism to do this).**

   You want it to stay put, but fall off easily when a fish pulls at the bait, and is then able to take line freely (which is why we keep the bail arm open). In windy or tricky conditions you might need to tighten the clip slightly.

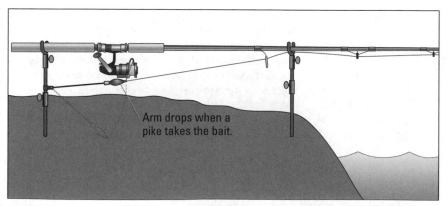

Figure 16-6: A correctly set drop off indicator. Note that the reel's bail arm is open and the drop off is clipped tight to the reel spool.

Arm drops when a pike takes the bait.

Night fishing

Some fish species feed better at night than they do in the day. In the summer heat, for example, carp are often more active during the cooler, quieter hours of the night. Many sea fish, and especially the bigger ones, come closer to the shore at night and there are plenty of spots on the coast where daylight fishing is poor but nights produce well. But there's more to fishing at night than simply staying on the water past sundown. Night fishing is its own technique.

There are other advantages to night fishing, too. Pleasure boaters might crowd a particular lake during the day, making fishing unsafe or at least unpleasant, but they disappear at sundown. Fish facing heavy angling pressure often react by feeding more at night. Many anglers find they catch bigger fish when fishing at night. Quite often large predators of all kinds from catfish, eels and zander through to tope and conger, are more active in the dark.

Almost every challenge that daytime angling presents is amplified by darkness. You're more likely to hook yourself or your partner at night. Tangles and snags become huge obstacles. Even unhooking a fish can be problematic. Any daytime danger – a fall, a dunking, a storm – becomes a bigger deal after the sun sets.

Despite the hazards, night fishing presents so many positives that you might consider it. One big advantage is that you aren't as visible to fish at night as you are in the day. Prepare yourself in this way:

- ✔ **Simplify and organise.** Take only what you need for night fishing, and know exactly where it is.

- ✔ **Carry the right safety equipment.** Always take a headtorch, and at least one other light source.

- ✔ **Don't fish an area you don't know.** Night fish only water you know well from daytime fishing.

- ✔ **Don't night fish at all until you're comfortable as an angler.** Doing even straightforward tasks such as tying knots and baiting up is much trickier in the dark. Get comfortable with the basics before heading out after dark.

Drifting and trolling

One of the biggest advantages of fishing from a boat is that it allows you to do everything a shorebound angler can do, but you can cover even more water while doing it. Anglers in boats often manoeuvre along a shoreline, casting to exposed cover. They're fishing just as bank fishermen do, but they can fish a longer stretch of shoreline, or motor across the bay to cast near the far bank. So they have an advantage, but they're essentially using the same casting tactics of the shore angler.

But bank fishermen can't *drift* or *troll* the way anglers in boats can, and these techniques are two of the most effective ways to put fish in the boat. Trolling means pulling lures, dead bait or livebait rigs behind a boat, using the boat's power (either the engine, electric trolling motor, rowing or paddling). Drifting works the same way, but the boat moves silently with the natural power of wind or current.

Any angler with a boat can drift or troll. Trolling a lure from a canoe or kayak will catch mackerel at sea, for example. In any situation, regardless of what you're fishing for, drifting a livebait behind or underneath a boat covers a lot of water and presents your baits to many fish.

Fly fishermen also benefit greatly from casting from a moving boat. The principle is similar to other methods and you can cover a lot of water. On a big water such as a reservoir, fly fishers often use a device called a *drogue,* which is basically like a parachute, to slow down their vessel to a comfortable speed. Flies are cast and worked back to the boat, often in teams of three or four artificials, and this works well on breezy days when the fish are on the lookout for hatching flies or insects blown onto the water.

As with any technique, drifting and trolling present their own tricks and challenges. But whether you're fishing for trout or pike on a loch, or in a cove for bass, you can learn to use your boat as a tool for presenting your offerings.

Chapter 17

How to Hook, Fight, Land and Release Fish

*L*earning how to cast well can be fun, and you can be proud of fishing a lure properly, with just the right touch of finesse. A beautifully crafted rod and reel is a work of art that you might someday pass on as an heirloom. The act of fishing takes you into some of the most scenic, awe-inspiring places and gives you time with people precious to you. But for all fishing is – the gear, the techniques, the scenery, the companionship – it really comes down to being able to catch fish.

A tackle addict might acquire a garage full of kit, and an expert caster might be able to hit a teacup with a lure at 100 feet, but an angler catches fish. To be a true angler you need to know when to strike at a bite, how to fight (or *play*) the fish and land it. But it's just as important to know how to handle and release it safely, or kill it humanely should that be an option (we explain how to do this in Chapter 19).

Catching a fish is like riding a bike in that the best way to learn how to do it is to actually attempt it. There's only so much you can learn about fighting a fish until you get to do it yourself. Still, preparation helps in all things, and this chapter helps you prepare mentally to improve your chances of success when everything goes right and a fish bites.

Finally! How to Handle a Fish Attack

Different fish have different takes. Whereas a pike may slaughter your lure, a trout may approach your fly in a daintier fashion. A roach may take your bait and spit it out quickly. A big carp might do all but pull your rod in.

The general rule is this: Although there's no one dictate for when to *strike* or in other words drive the hook into the fish's mouth, earlier hooksets usually result in fewer swallowed hooks. (When a fish swallows a hook, it becomes hard to remove the hook without killing the fish.) True, some fish, in some circumstances, will require you to be a bit more patient with your hooksets. For example, when legering for barbel you would be wise to ignore little taps and wait for the tip to bend over decisively. Overall, to be an effective angler, you need to know your fish and its behaviour, and this includes knowing how a particular species of fish bites. Ninety per cent of the time, you can set the hook immediately after a bite.

A savage bite doesn't require a savage response from you. Usually, all this sort of response does is ensure that you jerk your bait, lure or fly away from the fish – or worse still, break the line. You need to come tight to the fish: All the slack must be gone from your line, and you must make direct contact. Again, the more you do this, the better your feel for it will be.

This section helps you pick up the basic skills used to properly set the hook into a fish. Whether you fish with single or treble hooks, bait or lures, you find out all you need to know about moving from 'Hey! I've got a bite!' to 'Here, take my picture with this awesome fish!'

Starting out in the right (positive) frame of mind

A lot can go wrong when you're fishing – you might cast into a tree, snag a sunken log, or fall into the water and be forced to fish all day with a wet backside. All these things and more happen to all of us from time to time. Sometimes it's hard to stay positive. Greg's younger brother, a real hothead, often gets all pouty when he gets outfished (furrowed brow, big scowl, the whole nine yards).

You'll find, though, that fishing works best when your mind is clear and calm. Not to go all Zen on you, but don't take out your anger on the fish. You will miss more bites and lose more fish if you cast, retrieve, and set the hook like a savage. (Not to mention that you'll get fewer bites.) Hooking and fighting a big fish requires rational thought and smooth, collected action. If you get upset while fishing, take a walk until you cool off. Fishing is meant to be relaxing, and you land more fish when you're relaxed, too. If you're stressed you tend to rush your lure or fly in too fast, or recast the bait too often.

While we're on the new-agey subject of never fishing angry, think about the sports psychology of visualising success. A poor penalty taker might be coached to visualise the ball flying into the corner of the goal. Well, for anglers, this means you should picture the fight of the fish going well and ending in your favour. Imagine steering the fish out of danger and bringing it to the net.

This exercise helps you to stay positive, but you also need to prepare for the negative possibilities. We talk about strategies for landing fish successfully later in this chapter, but it helps if you start with a mind that is in the right place. Much can go wrong while fighting a fish, but it seems to happen less often if you think ahead and plan on things going well.

Setting the hook

When a fish bites a baited hook or lure, you've been successful: You've tricked that fish into making a connection with you. But that connection – through the rod and reel, down the line, across any terminal tackle your rig consists of, and culminating in the sharp hook you've selected – is a tenuous one. You need to act quickly and wisely to ensure that the fish stays connected to you. This is called *striking* or *setting the hook*, and it's the process by which the hook passes from merely being in the fish's mouth to being through the fish's mouth. Setting the hook means pointing the rod at the fish (as shown in Figure 17-1), tightening the line, and lifting the rod sharply back toward you, driving the hook into the fish's mouth (shown in Figure 17-2). Setting the hook is like serving a tennis ball – it's a sweeping gesture, but one that should flow smoothly. Brute force is not the answer. This is true whether you're using a single hook with bait or a lure with three treble hooks.

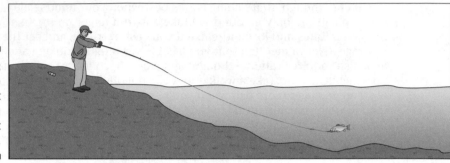

Figure 17-1:
To set the hook, start by pointing your rod at the fish.

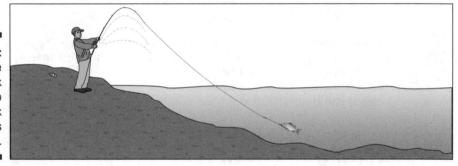

Figure 17-2:
Lift the rod back smartly to set the hook in the fish's mouth.

Different species call for different hooksets, and different baits call for different tactics. For example, a fish picking up a large lobworm in a weedy swim may require an extra second or two to hoover the thing up. Some fish, like dogfish or pike, have hard mouths that require harder hooksets. Others, like perch or bream, will go free if you set the hook too hard. But the following tips should work for you most of the time, with most fish caught on most rigs.

✔ **Keep a relatively tight line between your hook and your reel at all times.** When fishing with a float rig, for example, slack line can form between your rod and the float. When a fish bites and the float sinks, that fish is ready to be hooked, but the slack line can prevent you from driving the hook home. By the time you furiously crank up the loose line, the fish may have spat the bait and moved away. Keep your line tight, and be ready to set the hook at any time. *Note:* If you set the hook and find that you have too much slack in the line, quickly reel in the slack and set the hook again. The fish might still be there!

✔ **Let the rod help you.** As you sweep the rod overhead, the rod should bend. This bend is providing the force that sets the hook. If your rod isn't bending on the hookset, you're not providing enough force.

✔ **Quicker hooksets are usually better.** I'm not one to advise waiting to set the hook. Look at it this way: If you feel a fish tap your bait, or your float goes under, that fish has your hook in its mouth. A fish can't move your bait with its hands! If the bait is in a fish's mouth, then the hook should be able to find purchase. Some folks will tell you to wait, to 'make sure he has it' or something, but most of the time this pause results in a *swallowed hook.* A swallowed hook can lead to an inadvertent fish death, and is usually the result of waiting too long to set the hook. Your goal should be to land every fish that bites, but also to be able to release every fish you land, should you choose to do so.

Playing a Fish the Right Way

After a fish is hooked, the battle begins. If you maintain a tight line to the fish, the hook should remain seated in the flesh of the fish. But you still need to get the fish to you, and that process is called *fighting* or *playing* a fish.

Like playing tennis or any other sport, fighting a fish is a physical sensation. The fish is alive and working against the strange pull in its mouth. You have many tools at your disposal, including a rod and a reel with a drag, but the fish has things like its physical strength, the current, and a full understanding of its underwater domain. It will use all of these things and more to free itself. This section gives you practical advice to help you get the fish you hook into your hand.

Although some consider it more sporty to subdue fish on lighter tackle, you need to use tackle strong enough for the job. Using an outfit that doesn't let you bear down on the fish may still land you a fish after a long fight, but if the fish is totally exhausted when you land it, you didn't use heavy enough gear, or you didn't push your gear to the limit. Match your tackle to the conditions and the kind of fish you're after, so you can catch and release fish in a reasonable time. Otherwise, you may end up exhausting and killing your catch, even inadvertently.

Savouring the most enjoyable part of fishing

Having a big fish on the end of your line is like any other emergency situation: If you haven't been through it before, you may get rattled. But it's only an emergency for the fish. Fighting and landing a fish is one art where you definitely learn from your mistakes, if only because you'll replay them a thousand times in your head. The better the fish, the more times you'll tell yourself, 'Damn, if only I'd just. . . .'

Looking at it philosophically, some fish are always going to get away. That's part of fishing. After all, you don't really want to land every fish that bites – angling is so alluring because of its challenges. In any sport, to form a good rivalry, the other team has to win sometimes, too. And there are variables that lie (mostly) outside your control. Sometimes the fish tangles the line around the sunken limb it was finning under when you cast toward it. Or the line will drag across a rock's rough edge and part. A jumping fish might throw the hook. It happens. It may or may not happen the next time, which is why you try again. These experiences are not all negative because they teach the angler how to avoid the same mistakes in future.

Having a fish hooked is the fun part of fishing. That tug. That pushing and head-shaking and throbbing. That wildness. These are the prime thrills of fishing. It's you against the fish, and the fish is in its element. That you will win is not a foregone conclusion (although the more fish you fight, the better your chances are). Win or lose, the fight is always a thrill. Enjoy it.

As wily as a fish is, and as big as strong as some fish can be, you always have plenty of tricks and tools to subdue even the largest fish. But start with this: When a fish is hooked, it takes precedence over everything else. If you've hooked a big fish, and you're fishing with a partner, he or she should come to your aid. This assistance may involve being ready to net the fish, or simply moving other rods or objects out of your way. (*Note:* He or she doesn't help you catch the fish by actually touching the rod or reel – instead your partner merely assists with the other stuff.)

Focus all your attention on the fish at the end of your line. Not only does this allow you to enjoy the experience, but you're better able to spot obstacles that could break your line and more prepared to counter the movements of the fish. For example, if you see and feel the fish head to the right, you may need to pull your rod back to the left. Experience might tell you to apply the breaks when the fish heads for that hidden snag under the bank.

Letting the rod, reel, and line help you

A good fishing rod can be a great tool if you remember to let the rod do some of the work. It was designed to do just that. Follow the advice of Izaak Walton and keep the fish under the bend of the rod. This means that you should hold the rod at an angle that allows it to bend. (If you were to point that rod directly at the fish, it wouldn't bend at all.) It doesn't have to bend double, but it should flex. This flexing of the rod, more than anything else, will tire (and eventually conquer) a fish. It also acts as a shock absorber, protecting your line from breaking from any sudden pull. No matter how far the fish runs, no matter how much it jumps or shakes, the rod will flex, keeping pressure on the hook. This constant pressure on the hook keeps the fish from coming off. When fighting a fish, the best general rule is to keep the rod tip up and the line taut! However, keeping the rod lower and to one side is another useful ploy and can subdue a big fish quicker. A lower rod is also employed to keep the line out of danger sometimes, when a fish races towards over-hanging branches, for example, you might drop the rod tip right down into the water to avoid disaster.

When fighting a fish, the drag mechanism on your reel serves as another ally. The drag works by allowing some line out while the reel is engaged, provid-ing a little give and thus preventing a fish from breaking the line. When you set the drag properly (as covered in Chapter 15), the drag acts as a brake that further tires the fish. In most cases, the time to set the drag is before you cast. Adjusting the drag while you are fishing becomes just one more thing that you can mess up, and it should only be done if a big fish is on the verge of breaking off. It helps if you know where your reel's drag is located and understand how it works before you reach for it while a big fish is on the line. If the fish is able to pull line from the spool incessantly, you need to tighten the drag a bit. If the fish seems to be forcing your line to its breaking point, and the drag isn't giving any line at all, you should loosen the drag a touch. Adjust it only slightly in either direction!

When a large fish runs off a great deal of line, the resistance of the water against the line creates even more drag, in the form of friction. This works in your favour if you have a sense of how much added pressure your tackle can take. If a fish is about to hit a snag you must try to apply the brakes, but if the fish pulls away into open water, don't panic. Stay calm, and let the fish tow that extra line through the water. Eventually, you'll gain it back on the spool as you work the fish toward you. If the fish takes out so much line that you're in danger of being *spooled* – or losing all of your line – then you need to do something drastic, such as move the boat to follow the fish or wade up or downstream, or you're in big trouble.

Pulling up, then reeling down

When fighting a fish, you want to recover the line so that you can eventually get the fish close enough to grasp or net. With a small fish, you can usually keep the rod tip up and reel the fish in, pausing when it makes a run. But the act of reeling, when you're hooked up with a big fish, can be the longest and most tiring part of the fight, so it pays to know how to do it right.

Most newcomers get a fish on and reel for dear life. This technique does you no good and can even harm you by causing bad line twist or stressing the line to point of breaking. When hooked up with a big fish, apply enough pressure to bend the rod but avoid brute force. You may have to let the fish tire a little before you start to bring it closer to your position. A useful way to bring in a good sized fish is to pull up on the rod to bring the fish toward you; then drop the rod tip and, while you do, reel up line. This 'pump and wind' method is especially favoured by sea anglers, for example, attempting to pull up a big fish from the danger of sunken rocks or a wreck. Repeat as needed. Do not allow the line to go slack while dropping the rod tip!

Remember, too, that every pull up is not going to bring the fish in. Sometimes a fish will take a lot of line before you're able to recover any. Or you may have gained a great deal of line, and then the fish sees the boat and tears away on another run. Keep the pressure on – it's the only way to land the fish.

Getting the fish pointed up

If you can keep the head of the fish up, or pointing toward the surface instead of the bottom, then you can direct the fight. With its head up, the fish is disoriented and can't see where to go (that is, it can't see a rock to slip under or a weedbed to dive for). If the fish can get its head down, you're in the position of reacting while the fish picks where it will take the fight.

Keeping the head up doesn't mean rearing back at all costs. Sometimes a little pressure to one side or the other will do the trick. You're in contact with the fish, and you just have to feel your way through the fight, responding to its twists and turns by pulling back, easing up, or changing direction – whatever it takes. Fighting a fish is mostly about feeling the movements of the fish and reacting to counter those moves.

Using current if it's there

A fish tends to run away from the pressure of hook, line, and rod. If you have hooked your fish in moving water, try to position yourself downstream from the fish. That way, the fish fights not only you and your tackle, but the current, as well. This move may not always be possible, but when it is, do it, even if you have to back out of the water and walk downstream. When boat fishing, it may mean moving toward the stern of the boat. (Assuming the bow is pointed upstream.)

Reacting when the fish jumps

If your tussle with a fish ends suddenly when the fish takes to the air, it can mean only one thing – the fish has jumped free, and your fight is over. It may have broken the line or shaken the hook, but either way, it's off. Trout and pike are especially liable to such leaping episodes. In most such cases, I (Peter) bow when a fish jumps. When I *bow* to a fish, I literally bow. I bend from the waist, drop my rod tip, and extend my arms like a waiter offering a tray full of canapes. As soon as the fish falls back to the water, I come tight again. When a fish is airborne, it may reach a point in its trajectory when all of its weight and momentum snap against the line. Without the buoyancy of the water to act as a shock absorber, this is a very good time for knots to break under the added force of gravity. A hard-mouthed fish, like a pike, may not be very deeply hooked to begin with. The force of a jump may be all that is needed to dislodge a hook.

Handling a snagged fish

Where I (Greg) fish for catfish, the fish live among hundreds of sunken trees. Although the trees make for great cover, it can be a nightmare to fight a big fish near all this timber. What happens with a hooked fish from time to time is that the fight will suddenly lurch to a halt – the fish will wrap my line around a log or limb, and stay put, content to wait it out. This can happen to you, too, any time you're fishing near weeds, docks, rocks or other cover. (In other words, everywhere you should be fishing.) When this happens, you'll feel sick, but you have at least one trick to try. It may not work, but if slow, steady pressure won't free the fish, try giving it slack line. This is the only time you should give a hooked fish slack line, but giving the fish freedom from the pull will sometimes make it swim away from the snag and free itself.

Knowing how long to play a fish

You should always try to get a fish in as soon as possible. The longer a fish fights, the more lactic acid builds up in the fish's muscles, and the harder it is to revive. Releasing a fish that you have fought to the point of total exhaustion makes no sense because the fish may well die anyway. Sometimes the fish can be revived (more on that in a bit), but not always. When it comes to being able to release a fish, a sprinting fight is better than a marathon. If you're consistently taking a long time to get fish in, this may be your cue to use stronger tackle.

The warmer the water is, the more stress the fish will endure during the fight. When fishing warm water during the peak of summer, try to land the fish after a short fight and keep it out of water for an absolute minimum of time.

Netting and Landing Fish

After you have fought a fish to the bank or boatside, your next task is to land or boat it. Most fish can be caught by a lone angler. A word of warning, though: Many, many big fish have gotten away at the last possible moment. More than a few anglers have suffered heartbreak as a specimen fish eluded the net or hand right at boat- or bankside. 'The one that got away' makes a good fishing story, but too many of these escapees are lost right at the net. However, with a little forethought and attention to detail you can minimise such tales of woe.

This section gives you the lay of the land (or the water) for most fish that you can land by yourself. The larger the fish, the more the task calls for at least one helper. When fishing for big fish in salt- or freshwater, think about landing the fish before you hook it – do you have what you need to safely land a large fish? Are there any potential snags the fish must be kept clear of? It's hard to operate both the rod and reel and net by yourself. (To say nothing about posing for and taking the obligatory photograph to come next.)

The right way to use a landing net

For the majority of fishing, a landing net is an essential tool to get a fish on the bank. There are situations, such as when wading and casting for trout or bass, in which you might dispense with the net as you have no need to lift the fish up onto the bank or boat. In any situation however, a lively fish is often not easy to land by hand, and being poorly equipped is a bad deal for both fish and angler. Indeed, many angling clubs insist on the use of reasonably-sized landing nets.

Not all fish are big enough to warrant a net, admittedly. Smaller fish of up to half a pound can often be lifted to hand. On a flat-banked venue such as a beach you can simply beach your catch. Virtually all the other fish you catch need netting.

Your choice of net should reflect the water you fish and also the size of fish you might optimistically encounter. To take one example, a small net with a short handle is as good as useless for landing a large carp or pike on a sloping river bank. A long-handled net with a frame of at least a metre across would be required here. A skimpy little tennis racket of a net could lose the fish of a lifetime, or damage the fish you try to cram into it. Similarly, no decent skipper would take you wreck fishing for big cod or pollack without reasonable means of boating a weighty fish.

Netting a fish is straightforward, in theory at least. It's a job easiest done with a fishing partner at the net, although if you're fishing solo the net can be lowered with your non-rod hand. Netting is a question of simple positioning and timing. As you bring the fish closer to the net and netter, make sure the fish's head is up and the fish is not still totally *green,* or full of fight. (You don't want to fully exhaust a fish, but bringing it in too green will only result in chaos, and the fish will often get away.) As the fish nears your position sink the frame of the net slowly under the water just in front of you. A good general rule is to draw the fish to the net, rather than vice versa. Draw the fish in so that it is comfortably over the net frame and lift the net up in one smooth motion.

Don't try to pull up a large fish by the net handle because you might break it. Instead, grasp the frame or 'head' of the net and lift it by this. Next put the net down somewhere safe, preferably on an unhooking mat (see the later section on these). Otherwise look for soft grass. Conscientious anglers have even been known to use a coat; not great for personal fashion but better than damaging a perfectly conditioned fish.

Never try to net a fish tail-first, and don't chase the fish through the water with the net. Swiping at it is likely to make it bolt or get bumped off the hook. If the fish eludes the net on the first try, keep the net still again beneath your feet and fight the fish back to the bank- or boatside again. When it approaches, make another attempt to net the fish. If you are lure fishing avoid letting the hook or hooks in the fish's mouth get tangled in the edge of the net.

As shown in Figure 17-3, hold the rod tip high and bring the net under the fish, head-first.

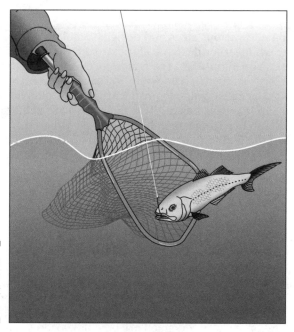

Figure 17-3:
The classic landing net position.

What about a gaff?

Certain things in life are designed so well that you take one look at them and you know what they are for. A *gaff* is one of them. It's really nothing more than a humongous hook on a long shaft. Used almost exclusively in sea fishing from a boat, a gaff allows you to snag a hooked fish and bring it ashore or onboard. Think of it as a net that grabs hold, with fish usually gaffed somewhere in the head, gill, or shoulder region. A gaff should only be used for fish you intend to keep, and many skippers and anglers who practise catch-and-release stick to a landing net. Indeed, to many modern-day anglers gaffs look pretty brutal, although having said this a gaff is a useful tool for subduing a large cod or conger.

Unhooking mats

The unhooking mat is another staple of the modern fishing era, and perhaps no other item could make a more fitting contrast to the gaff. Many fisheries now insist on unhooking mats and certainly no keen carp or pike angler should be without one. Exactly as the name suggests, these mats provide a safe, padded surface on which to lay a good sized fish, preventing your prized catch from being scratched or damaged on the bank.

Unhooking mats come in various sizes and designs. Smaller, fold-up models are highly portable, while larger designs offer extra size and security for the largest of specimens. You should wet the mat before putting a fish on it. Not only are they ideal for holding a fish on while you take the hook out, mats are also great for pictures because you can pose with your catch over the mat so that should you slip it always has a soft landing. Fish are vulnerable on the bank, after all. Scratches from rough banks can get infected and one careless drop could spell the end for a big fish. As a final note, such mats are also useful for the sea angler fishing from rocks, protecting backsides as well as fish from damage!

Keepnets

There are occasions when the angler wants to retain fish for a while. For example, a match angler might want to weigh his catch at the end of the match. Sometimes pleasure anglers also like to see what they've caught at the end of the session. If you are to use a keepnet, though, a few sensible limits apply. Avoid at all costs cheap, small nets. Many of these which have harsh, stringy netting or are way too small are now illegal. So pick a soft-meshed design of at least eight feet long. Modern designs often have fish-friendly 'carp sacking' material and these are ideal.

A keepnet should always be well extended so it gives fish space. Peg one end to the bank with a bank stick, and you can use a landing net handle to push the far end out fully, like stretching out an accordion. You could even use a second bankstick to anchor the far end. You should give keepnets a miss in hot weather and avoid leaving one out all day or cramming too many fish into one. In big matches, anglers often use two. Certain fish, such as barbel and pike, should never be put in a keepnet.

When It's Time to Say Goodbye: Releasing Fish

Fishing in today's world is no blood sport. Most fish are released with minimal harm. In this way it differs greatly from hunting. After you shoot a deer or bird, it's a goner – you can't release it back into the wild. A caught fish is different, in that it can always be returned. Even when you can legally take your catch home you have a choice: Do you kill the fish, or do you let it go?

First, you need to ensure that it is legal to keep the fish. Know your regional laws, and the rules governing the particular body of water you're fishing. Some places have bag (the number of fish in your possession), or size limits (protecting the largest and smallest of a species). Sea fish, for example, must not be taken unless they have reached a certain length. Artificially stocked trout fisheries may dictate that you *must* kill your catch, but the vast majority of coarse fish can't be killed at all. So, before you endanger the fish, it's your responsibility to know the laws. We cover licences more completely in Chapter 2, and you can check regional and national fishing laws through the Environment Agency website (www.environment-agency.gov.uk). Be sure also to check rules for the fishing clubs and fisheries you visit, either on the web or through published information. Always report those who take fish illegally for the table; it's your sport they're damaging.

If the fish is legally yours, so is the decision about the fish's fate. Don't let anybody tell you that you're immoral if you decide to kill fish. If you intend to eat them, killing them is okay with us. However, and this is a big however, if we all killed all the fish we caught, fishing would be pants for all of us.

This is especially true of top predator gamefish like trout, bass and salmon. They're the top predator in their environment, and the way nature has set things up, there are fewer top predators out there relative to animals lower down the food chain. Which means that if you take a load of trout out of a stream, the fishing quality in that stream will definitely decline. The same holds for other species. The world just doesn't have that many top predators left. Humans, the ultimate predator, need to kill other predators responsibly.

Besides the fact that the smaller (but legal) fish of most species taste better than the old warriors, it's also much better for the overall fish population if you take a couple of two-pound sea bass , as opposed to one 8-pounder (which will have taken over a decade to grow that size). Fish such as bass and sea trout are highly localised and you wouldn't want to damage your favourite spot. Leave the biggest adult fish to breed and pass on the big-fish genes. Most bodies of water have many more smaller fish of a species than elders, and taking these younger fish often has less ill effect on the lake's health.

Taking quick action after landing a fish

When you release your catch you must act quickly to allow the fish to survive its encounter with you. A fish can handle getting caught – there's no question that catch-and-release fishing works. I (Dominic) once caught the same large pike twice in two seasons. Because I had been careful the fish was still healthy a year after the first capture. In fact, she was in great condition and had put on weight. Do remember though, that certain species are more fragile than others, and other conditions such as temperature and handling affect mortality rates.

Follow these tips to increase a fish's chances of surviving:

- **Leave the fish in the water as much as possible.**
- **Handle the fish as little as possible.**
- **Wet your hands or use a wet rag (if you have one handy) to hold the fish.** These techniques cause less damage to its scales and protective coating.
- **Use forceps, pliers, hook removers or a disgorger to remove the hook.** You must always have adequate unhooking equipment. You should never fish for small fish without a disgorger, for example, or pike without long nosed pliers or foot long forceps.
- **If the hook is embedded very deep inside the fish's mouth or gullet, too deep for removal, cut the line, leaving the hook in the fish.** The hook may eventually rust out or work itself free, and the fish may be able to feed normally with the hook still in its mouth. By the way, artificials are usually not taken deep, and setting the hook quickly will help prevent swallowed hooks. And for sea anglers, circle hooks often hook the fish's mouth, not its throat or stomach.

Unhooking and handling fish

Like playing and landing, taking the hook out of a fish safely begins with preparation. Always have your unhooking tools to hand. I (Dominic) always carry my forceps and disgorgers in the same pocket in my tackle bag so I know where they are at all times. Many times when the fish is lightly hooked, you can simply pick out the hook with your fingers. If it's further down you'll need a tool.

Before you think about unhooking however, you must be in control. Wet your hands first: fish hate dry, hot hands and will wriggle against them. You could also grasp the fish using the wet mesh of the landing net. A smaller fish can be gripped by the back, just behind the head. A larger fish may jerk and flap, so you must get it under control. You may need to hold the fish down at first, against a wet net at minimum, preferably an unhooking mat.

Smaller fish can be unhooked with fine forceps, but a disgorger is often essential for smaller hooks. Grip the fish firmly but carefully and keep the line tight. A friend can help, or you can even keep the line tight between your lips. A disgorger has a little slot in the head; slip it onto the line via this little slot and run it down the tight line until you stop at the hook. Now give a little push down and the hook should pop out. Once you get the simple knack it's surprisingly easy.

Figure 17-4:
Using a
disgorger.

Big fish and larger hooks require forceps. Once you have landed the fish, keep the line tight and seek out the hook. Unless the fish is lightly hooked you'll probably need to kneel down and look directly into the mouth. Reach in with forceps and aim to get a solid grasp of the hook shank. By applying a little downward pressure and turning the point back on itself the hook should come free. Practice makes perfect, but while you're still learning, barbless hooks are far easier to remove.

Releasing your catch and reviving an exhausted fish

A good angler never throws their catch back. This is not only disrespectful, but puts extra stress on the fish. Instead you should hold the fish facing forwards in a balanced, horizontal position in the water and let it swim off of its own accord. Much of the time, releasing the fish is relatively easy. You simply remove the hook, and once held in the water the fish wiggles vigorously, which lets you know that it is ready to take off for freedom. If you fish from a high bank or somewhere really awkward where you can't reach the water easily, put the fish back in the landing net and lower it into the water rather than dropping it back.

If the fight has been especially long or strenuous, the fish may come in totally exhausted. You'll know this because the fish will float on its side or back, moving very little. If you simply unhook and release an exhausted fish right away, you have a belly-up, soon-to-be-dead fish on your hands. Before you release, you need to let it recover, and the angler can help it do so.

It's never a good idea to go walking about on the bank with a fish in your hands, even the short distance to take it to the water's edge for release. If you drop it, this could cause severe damage to internal organs, especially if it's a heavy specimen. Instead, carry fish back to the water in the landing net or held firmly in the safety of an unhooking mat.

A good rule of thumb to follow in figuring out if a fish needs reviving is this: If the fish lets you hold it and doesn't struggle, revive it. After all, any self-respecting wild animal will take off like greased lightning to escape the clutches of a strange creature. To a fish, a human is a strange creature.

If a fish is merely tired (and not bleeding or otherwise injured), it may spring back to life and be fine if it receives the proper care. Follow these steps to help ensure that a caught-and-released fish survives:

1. **If you're in heavy current, move to gentler current. Hold the fish gently and keep it under the surface of the water, pointing it upstream (that is, nose into the flow).**

   Cradle it from below if you can. If you cannot, hold it gently by its sides. You may grasp some mid-size fish (salmon and pike, for example) by the tail. Always keep the fish sitting upright in a natural swimming position. On lakes or in the sea, however, current usually isn't a factor when reviving a fish.

2. **If the fish is still tired and won't swim off after a few seconds, move it backwards and forwards (mostly forwards, if possible) so that its gills are forced to open and close.**

   When properly done, this technique delivers oxygen to a heavily oxygen-depleted fish. Reviving the fish so that it can swim under its own steam may take a few minutes, and sometimes up to an hour. It lets you know that it is ready to be released when it starts to wiggle.

3. **Release the fish.**

   It should swim slowly away. If it rolls over on its back and lays there, this is not a good sign. Bring the fish back under your control and continue to revive it.

Very occasionally, the fish won't revive. This might well be your cue to use stronger tackle next time, in order to exhaust the fish less. If it was deep hooked, you should try to improve your bite detection and strike earlier next time. If it's very hot, it might be a good idea to give the fish a break altogether. If you can't revive the fish, you might take it home and eat it if this is legal. If not, then leave it in the water where other creatures will make use of it. Know that you did what you could to revive it.

Part V
After the Catch

"How are you getting on with the
cooking of the conger eel I caught?"

In this part . . .

Because catch-and-release fishing is the norm, you'll find a load of advice on taking a good photograph of a trophy fish, and tips for releasing a fish safely back into the water. There's even material here covering the latest in fibreglass replicas, that allow you to release the fish and still have a trophy on the wall. Should you be able to keep and eat your game or sea catch, you'll also find step-by-step instructions for preparing what you've caught and recipes for cooking them.

Chapter 18

Photographing, Weighing and Preserving Fish for Posterity

*T*homas Edison, when asked what went into the glamorous job of being an amazing inventor, replied, '99 per cent perspiration, 1 per cent inspiration.' Sounds like fishing! You spend almost all your time trying to catch fish, and the actual amount of fish-on-the-line time sometimes seems very small by comparison. So how do you make the memories last?

Today's technology makes it possible to keep the memories of your fish alive and kicking – and the fish still alive and swimming! Digital cameras range in price from expensive to very affordable, but even the least expensive cameras take quality photographs. You can easily carry your camera along on fishing trips (we recommend placing it in a bag or waterproof container). If you can stretch the extra few pounds, a waterproof camera is the safest option and not all of these cost an arm and a leg. Video cameras are compact, lightweight and suitable to record fishing memories, too.

In the old days, a specimen sized fish ended up cooked or hanging on the wall. Today's anglers release their biggest fish, but that doesn't mean they can't have wall mounts in their homes or offices. Aside from taking a great picture, fiberglass replicas, produced from photos and measurements of live trophy fish, allow you to have your fish and release it, too.

Catching a big fish is an amazing thing: it's a reward for hard work, a celebration, a gift. This chapter tells you how to make the most of the moment when it happens so that you can enjoy it for years to come.

Hurry Up and Take Your Time: Photographing Fish

Very few people are born with the natural ability to catch big fish consistently, but most of us have a native talent to take lousy pictures. What makes photographing big fish difficult starts with this happy problem: You just caught a big fish, and you're shaking like a leaf! Compounding the issue is the fact that your subject is alive, and if you intend to return it to the water alive, you don't have a lot of time for a photo shoot.

The time to prepare for a great fish photo comes before the fish is hooked. Know where your camera is and how to use it. Check the batteries before each trip and make sure the lens is clear. Then, all you have to do is catch a fish worthy of a picture. I (Greg) take photos of many of the fish I catch. Why not? With digital cameras, the cost is nil. That way, all the photos become a log of sorts of the whole trip.

This section breaks down everything you need to have, do, or think about to photograph your catch in its best light.

Digital cameras: Perfect fishing partners

Your mobile phone may take photographs, but that doesn't mean it's a real camera. A fishing magazine I (Greg) subscribe to recently explained that it can no longer print most reader-submitted fish photos, because most of them were taken with mobiles, and those photos often can't be enlarged enough to print in the magazine. (And we're not talking about a full-page spread.)

You want a quality photo of your big fish, so carry a real camera. Most are small, compact and maybe even water resistant. Keep the batteries fresh or freshly charged, and empty the photos onto your computer or other source from time to time to preserve them, should the camera be lost or damaged.

With digital cameras, not only can you see immediately how well you framed the shot, you can take a ton of photos. Do it. You never know which pictures will turn out. Shoot fast and often, and then release the fish.

One of the most effective tools for good picture taking is a wide-angle lens. Some point-and-shoot cameras have a wide-angle function included. With a wide angle, you can get closer to your subject, which makes the fish that the angler is holding up look a lot bigger in the foreground. You might think this is cheating, but it's not. All it does is ensure that the fish in the photo looks as big, as nice and as exciting as the fish in your memory. Boaters take note – a wide-angle is the only effective way to get the boat *and* the subject in the picture without having to leave the boat to get the shot.

More and more cameras now do more and more of the work, leaving less opportunity to mess up to the photographer. Of course, real photographic artists may want the ability to make their own choice of lenses, exposures and so on. But for most of us, most of the time, all we want is the best picture with the least fuss. If this is your outlook, automatic everything works great. These are called 'point and shoot' cameras.

Of course, as with everything else, there are more and less expensive point and shoot cameras. If you want to spend a few extra quid, look for the following features:

- ✔ Autofocus gets your subject looking sharp without a lot of unnecessary fiddling around while your fish tries to squirm out of your hands. Remember to point the camera at the *most important* thing first because that is what it will focus on. Then lock the focus and finish composing your shot.
- ✔ A simple zoom function will give you more choices, especially close-up capability.
- ✔ In Chapter 6, I recommend polarised lenses for your sunglasses. For the same reason, a polarising filter on a camera works well when taking pictures on the water. Not only does it cut down on glare, but it also enhances the richness of the colours in the scene. Also, a polarising filter will let your camera see into the water to capture the look of a clear lake, or a glimpse of a trout feeding in a pool. This gives you a look into the world of the fish.

Lighting at all times

When you can, follow the basic rule of photography – position the sun over the photographer's shoulder so that it illuminates the subject. The angler holding the fish should look towards the sun (though, of course, not straight at it).

It's easy for me to tell you as a photographer to get the sun over your shoulder, but there are times when the sun doesn't want to go over your shoulder. You could be stuck on a riverbank looking into the sun. Or it might be high noon and the sun hangs directly overhead. In cases like this, a flash will fill in the shadows on your subject.

Because you often fish in low light periods, such as dusk and dawn, poor lighting hurts many fish shots. Get the subject into as much natural light as you can find, and use a flash to brighten the shot, regardless of the time of day. (This is another argument against relying on cellphone cameras, as not all of them have flashes.) The constant use of your camera's flash will brighten anglers' faces hidden under ball caps and any other shady spots.

Working with live subjects . . . or not

You must first decide if you are going to kill the fish. We hope that most of the fish you catch will go back. Our ancestors may have killed many, but they didn't have cameras, or supermarkets to buy food from. But if you are taking a fish home for supper, say a rainbow trout or a bass, take pictures when it's colourful and vibrant. Photos taken hours after a fish's death – sometimes posed in the driveway or garage – don't do much to render the fish's world. In general, a fish looks best when you photograph it fresh out of the water. The wetness makes the colours pop and gives an overall sheen to the fish.

As long as you hold the fish in the water, facing upstream (if there is a current), the fish will survive well for enough time to let you get ready. When you want to snap a picture, lift the fish out of the water, supporting its body as you do so. (Remember, the fish's internal organs are normally supported by the buoyancy of water.) Always handle a fish with wet hands to protect the fish's natural slimecoat.

Another trick is keeping the fish in the landing net, with the net lowered into the water. This forms a temporary holding pen for the fish, and allows you to get ready for a good photograph. Avoid keeping fish out for any longer than you'd want to hold your breath. It's far better to give your catch a quick breather in the water than keeping it on the bank for one long photo session. I (Dominic) prefer to unhook a big fish first and weigh it, before giving it a bath. While it's taking a breather I then pick my background and get the camera set so that I'm ready to roll and the fish spends minimal time out of water while I photograph it.

Hold 'em high: Posing fish for photographs

In your mind's eye, you remember everything about where you caught that big fish. You can see it vividly: the trees in the background, the mountains in the distance, the boat under you, your kid who said 'I don't care about the fish, Daddy. I'm tired and I want to go home.' Don't try to capture all this in a photograph. You'll end up with a picture where everything looks dinky. Instead, remember that anyone looking at your fish photos will respond to two things: the fish and the human. Concentrate on those two elements and have them occupy as much of the photo as you can.

Hardly anyone takes photos the way they used to back in the early days of photography – all those stiff, unsmiling people staring into the lens with all the warmth and happiness of someone who has just swallowed a live toad. A smile never hurts.

The successful angler should always be the one holding the fish, although Greg's wife has been known to refuse to hold some of the 'mean-looking' catfish she has landed. Hold the fish horizontally and across your body. This looks more natural because a fish seldom swims vertically. If you push the fish too far out in front of you, you look like you're trying to fool the camera, making the fish appear bigger than it is. But don't let the fish disappear against your body, either. (And while we're on this subject: a decent shirt makes a better background for a fish than say, a 'Bikini Inspector' t-shirt from Summer, 2006.) Fish sometimes wriggle, so if you're on the bank you should never stand up with a big fish, but kneel over an unhooking mat or, at the very least, soft grass. This way if you drop the fish it'll come to minimal harm.

 A good way to make sure your catch picture is clear is to make sure the eye of the fish is sharply in focus before you hit the shutter. Also try to avoid big gaps in the picture by kneeling down and holding the fish just under your chin.

I (Peter) have a mess of pictures of me with fish. In all honesty, they're just a bunch of mug shots of a grinning goon. Happy, but pretty goofy. I much prefer pictures where the angler is caught in action, such as

- ✔ During the fight with the rod bent. This kind of photo tells a story, and people find it naturally interesting.
- ✔ When landing the fish, when the viewer gets to savour some of the anticipation and excitement of the moment.
- ✔ When releasing the fish. This presents the fish and the angler in the fish's environment. As with the fight, this photo expresses a story.

Taking measurements for bragging rights

They say a photo is worth a thousand words, and this time, they may be right. But anglers always want a figure too, so most carry scales to measure catches (rather than using the old-fashioned method of spreading their arms out in the pub). You can choose from spring or digital scales. Digital scales rely on batteries, but spring scales are ready all the time. Your choice depends on what you fish for. For seekers of specimen carp, catfish or large sea fish a scale that goes up to and perhaps above 50 pounds would be sensible. If you tackle roach, perch and smaller species more detailed scales, running only to 10 pounds, say, are better.

Anglers come with a reputation for stretching the truth, but you're only kidding yourself by not weighing properly. In the bad old days, fish were sometimes weighed straight under the jaw, through the gill cover, a shooting offence in modern times! Today, some anglers use special weigh slings for the task. But the easiest method is to weigh the fish in the net. To do this, first remove the net handle and make sure the fish is sitting flush in the bottom of the mesh and not crumpled or tilted where it may be damaged. Now hook the scales into the net in a suitably secure position. Lift up the lot and let the needle or numbers settle. Once the fish is released you can then deduct the weight of the net. Some anglers zero the scales against the weight of the net first and then transfer the fish. If you use the same net regularly you'll quickly become familiar with its wet weight and can easily subtract this.

As an interesting further point, many Europeans measure fish rather than weighing them. It's certainly quicker and ideal for fish like trout. There are even special formulas out there for converting the length into a weight. Different species require different formulas; a brown trout, for example, weighs almost exactly a pound at 13 inches.

Come On, Everyone's Doing It: Making a Fish Video

I'm (Greg) a photograph guy. But then a few years ago my older brother started bringing his palm-sized video camera along on fishing trips. Suddenly a photograph of a caught fish wasn't enough. Now the whole fight had to be videoed.

At first, like so many things my older brother does, this weirded me out. Wasn't video footage only for those Discovery Channel fishing shows? Apparently not any longer. I must admit, though, he got some pretty exciting battles caught on tape (and that hilarious moment when I threw bait at our younger brother).

More than that, we also documented stretches of river, campsites where we stayed and local wildlife. I still love the understated art of a photograph, but I see the value of a video, and maybe you will, too.

YouTube, here you come

As with digital photographs, when it comes to videoing, the sharing of the images becomes the issue. Popular websites like YouTube have made it possible to post video clips online, where anyone can go and watch it. If you go on a deep-sea charter with five of your mates, you could post an edited clip of the most exciting fish battles online, where everyone from the trip will have access.

Like photo-sharing sites, this allows you to place the clip in one place without having to mess with emailed files. As with photography, there is a skill and an art to taking good video. Editing is the key. Using either your camera's or computer's software, pare the trip down to the good parts. A fishing trip might be slow and contemplative, and that may be the best part of the whole trip. But a fishing video should probably be more action-packed. Adding good music helps.

Downsides to being your own videographer

It takes a second to capture a good photograph. You can pick up the camera, click a shot of your partner fighting a fish, and then get back to the business of readying the net and preparing to land the fish. If you're trying to video-tape the whole struggle, leaping fish and all, you're not being very helpful to your partner. Videotaping works best if you have at least three people along on a trip. One works the camera while the other helps land the fish.

You might also need to think about your goals for fishing. Are you fishing merely to document the act of doing it? Are you hoping to get your clip discovered by Hollywood agents? Probably not. So don't get obsessed.

The other obvious factor with video is that you are in effect showcasing good or bad practice. YouTube is sadly littered with clips of those who mishandle fish – dropping them, not using adequate equipment and all the rest. The presence of the camera should never compromise good practice and safe catch-and-release. Remember, you might be setting an example for others, so make it a good example by being well prepared and respecting your catch.

You Want This Fish Forever: One for the Wall

For some anglers, a photograph or even a videotape is insufficient to memorialise a great fish. You might want a three-dimensional representation of your fish, and if you do, you have two options. You can kill and keep your fish, take it to a taxidermist, and have the fish *mounted,* or turned into a wall mount. This is often illegal today, however, not to mention the crying shame of killing what could be the fish of a lifetime. But if you do go down this route, it is vital to keep the fish as fresh as possible, usually with ice or a freezer, and get hold of a reputable taxidermist, pronto. It's something of a dying art these days, although many a local boozer still displays a locally caught monster on the wall.

The other option is a fibreglass replica. These are done by specialised artists who in many ways offer a much better solution. Not only can you then release the fish, but such replicas are lifelike and age better than old fashioned stuffed fish. On the flipside, you do have to supply some detailed information. Some good quality photos along with length and girth measurements would be a minimum requirement. Like taxidermy, the exercise might not be cheap. You will usually be charged at least £20 per inch, and that's before you've factored in a glass case or mount. But for that fish of a lifetime, it could make a terrific memento, and you also have the pleasure of knowing that the monster fish is still out there, even though it's just a little wiser.

As a final point, if you're lucky enough to catch a record fish you'll definitely want to take careful steps before release. Besides quality pictures, a potential record must also be witnessed by another person and be weighed on two separate sets of scales before the evidence goes to the experts (The Angling Trust: email them at brfc@anglingtrust.net). You never know, that next bite could make history.

Chapter 19

Biting Back: Storing, Cleaning and Cooking Fish

In This Chapter

▶ Dispatching and keeping your catch fresh

▶ Scaling, gutting and filleting

▶ Exploring basic cooking techniques

▶ A handful of favourite fish recipes

Cleaning fish isn't the most fun part of fishing. Gutting a bag of mackerel is a miserable, smelly job. But if you want to eat fish, you have to clean it and keep it fresh. It's a process that demands respect. Our ancestors didn't simply walk to the fish counter at the supermarket, but killed to eat. In today's world, fish stocks are under more pressure than ever and sustainability is the watchword. Fish like mackerel and pollack are still relatively abundant; salmon, eels and others are not. Many species, such as most coarse fish, must be returned by law.

Don't feel guilty about the occasional fish supper though. There is nothing ethically wrong with taking a fish or two home, provided you are allowed to. But if you do take fish to eat, you want them to taste the best they possibly can, so this chapter coveres all you ever wanted to know about readying a fish for cooking by cleaning it, slicing it up and freezing it for maximum freshness.

Acting Fast to Retain Taste and Texture

Before you catch any fish, you should know whether you plan to keep any to eat. If your plan is to fish for food, have a a cool storage space handy, such as a cool bag or bucket of ice. For the sake of good eating, as well as being a nice person, you really should kill the fish right away. With this ugly job done, you then need to store and transport your fish properly so it will taste as fresh as possible on the dinner table.

The best way to dispatch a fish is with a small club called a *fish priest*. If you have no priest, a piece of wood, rock or other weighty object will have to do (at least preferable to using a headbutt or karate chop). It sounds ugly, but it's far kinder than simply leaving it to expire. The quickest way to do this is to hold the fish firmly by the body and deliver a sharp rap to the head, right above the eyes.

Well and Truly Gutted

Since most of the time you won't immediately stop fishing and start cooking when you catch a fish, it makes sense to gut it soon after it's dispatched. If you put off this job, the guts, organs and grisly juices inside the fish will gradually taint the meat. Here's how it's done:

1. **With the blade pointed toward the head, pierce the stomach cavity and make a slit toward the head.** Try not to make too deep a cut, just enough to get through the top layer of skin and flesh.

2. **Now pointing the knife toward the tail, completely open the stomach cavity.**

3. **Reach in and pull out the guts.**

4. **Detach the guts with the knife, or simply pull away. Give the body cavity a quick rinse to wash out any gunk.**

5. **Discard the guts. You could wrap and bin them, but if you're by the water it's far more eco friendly to throw them in where crabs, gulls and other fish will clean up.**

Keeping your catch fresh

If there is anything that smells worse than bad fish, we don't want to know about it. Part of the reason that fish can turn so quickly is because they're so delicate. Handled with proper tender loving care, a well-cooked fish is one of the freshest-tasting things you can eat. When you go fishing, plan ahead if you intend to keep any fish to eat. We suggest the following solutions:

- **Cool bag:** Various lined bags exist for keeping food or bait cool. These are also ideal for smaller quanitites of fish. Ice packs can be included to help keep everything cold. We'd recommend putting the fish itself in a plastic bag to keep things from getting messy.

- **Ice Bucket or cooler box:** A cooler box is less portable, but good for keeping several fish fresh. Fill it with ice packs or ice. It sounds crude, but a bucket works well enough if you're by the sea. A couple of bottles of iced water (kept in the freezer before your trip), along with a dose of fresh sea water should keep your catch perfectly cool whilst you concentrate on fishing.

✔ **Net or bag:** The simplest way of all to keep a fish or two fresh is to keep your catch in a bag or even just the head of a landing net, dunked into the water. If you use a bag, do stake it to the bank with something. *Bass bags* are mesh items sold in tackle shops for exactly this purpose. This simple method isn't such a great idea if the water is warm, but it works well enough for short periods.

A few spare large plastic bags are always handy when keeping fish. This barrier keeps the fish from sliming your storage space, and if you're fishing with pals, it makes it easier to divide up the catch.

Cleaning: A Good Meal Starts with the First Cut

Fish cleaning can be a kitchen-destroying operation: scales flying everywhere and guts sliding around and clogging up the sink. But it doesn't have to be that messy. Our advice to you is that whenever possible, you clean the fish *before* you bring it into the kitchen. The next sections give you everything you need to know about cleaning a fish, from scaling and gutting to filleting and cutting up your very own fish steaks.

You need only one tool to *dress* (another term for cleaning) most fish: a quality, sharp knife. The size of fillet knife you need depends on the size of the fish you're cutting up. For smaller fish, a four-inch fillet knife will work fine. Bigger fish call for longer blades, but a longer knife is harder to handle. For most fish, a six-inch blade is fine. A good cutting board helps, too.

Scaling

You want to *scale* a fish, or remove all its scales, when you intend to cook a fish with the skin on. It can be easier to do this before gutting, and doing this outdoors also avoids scales whizzing around your kitchen. Although most fish have scales, not every fish needs to be scaled. The scales on trout and mackerel, for example, are so small that you don't have to worry about them. In fact, you wouldn't know there were any scales on a trout if someone like me hadn't told you. Here's how to scale a fish:

1. **Take some newspaper and lay out about four spreads.**

2. **Run the knife against the grain of the scale.**

   Your motion should be firm enough to remove the scales, but not so strong that they go flying all over the place. (***Note:*** You can buy a specialised fish scaler, which is a handheld contraption with serrated edges made for rubbing off scales. It's probably worth the small investment because your knife will stay sharper longer if you don't use it for scaling.)

3. **When you have finished scaling, lift the fish and peel back the top sheet of paper. Lay the fish down on the next (clean) sheet of newspaper and throw out the top sheet with the scales.**

4. **Rinse the fish.**

If you're going to fillet a fish and remove its skin, there's no need to scale it.

Filleting

Filleting a fish – that is, removing just the meatiest parts of the fish as efficiently as possible – is the perfect choice for many species of fish, most of the time. The process takes a certain amount of skill and dexterity, but expending a little more effort at the cleaning stage is worth it because it means no bones at the eating stage. When you get the hang of filleting, you can zip through a pile of fish pretty quickly, and it's quite satisfying.

Don't worry too much if you don't get absolutely all the meat off the fish when you first start filleting. The idea at the beginning is to get *some*. If you remove the skin from the fillets, as recommended, you don't have to scale the fish first, because the scales will come off with the skin. You'll be left with two pieces of skinless, scaleless, boneless meat (one from each side of the fish). Obviously, if you like to eat the skin, you can fillet a fish without removing the skin. In that case, you would still scale the fish unless you like to eat scales, too. Figure 19-1 shows the basics of filleting a fish.

1. **Cut down to the backbone just behind the gills (see Figure 19-1a).**

2. **Hold the fish by the head or tail, with the fish's back toward you. With the knife blade pointing away from you and across the body of the fish, begin to cut along the backbone toward the tail or head (see Figure 19-1b). Use the backbone to guide your knife. Use the knife tip to work around the ribcage. If you fillet quickly after catching, you don't need to gut the fish. Don't cut all the way to the tail. Instead, leave about an inch of fillet attached to make removing the skin from the fillet easier.**

3. **Flip the fish over and do the same thing: Free the fillet by following along the backbone. This time, when your knife nears the tail, you can remove the tail (and the two fillets) by cutting through the backbone near the tail.**

You now have a head, guts and backbone ready for the bin. You also have a tail with two fillets, skin and scales still attached.

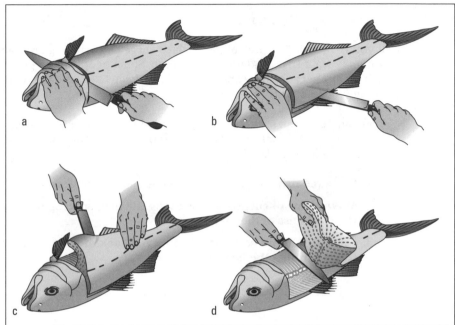

Figure 19-1:
Try this technique for filleting fish.

4. **To take the skin off, begin by holding the fillet by the tail, skin side down. Hold the knife crosswise across the fillet and insert the knife between the skin and the flesh. While holding the skin, cut in the direction of where the head formerly was (see Figure 19-2).**

5. **Repeat Steps 4 through 6 for the other fillet. When done, you'll have the tail still connected to two pieces of skin, which you discard.**

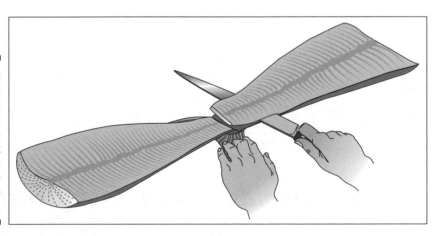

Figure 19-2:
Laying the skin flat on the cutting board, carefully work the knife against it to remove the fillet.

Cutting steaks

If you're cleaning a catch of particularly large fish, say large rainbow trout, you may want to consider steaking them. Some people don't go in for cooking fish steaks because they are too dry. My advice to you: Make thinner steaks, an inch or less, or try baking in foil.

You can make fish steaks by using a wide-bladed chef's knife (like the kind chefs use on TV when they chop vegetables). Just follow these steps (see Figure 19-3 for the visual):

1. **Scale the fish. (**as explained in the earlier 'Scaling' section).

2. **Make a row of cuts crosswise along the fish, spacing them so they're the thickness of the steaks.**

3. **Cut down to the backbone, hitting the back of your knife with a stick to get through the bone, if needed.**

Figure 19-3:
Cutting a
fish into
steaks.

Freezing to Avoid an Oily, Fishy Taste

Frozen fish does not have the consistency of flesh that has never been frozen. The physics behind this are simple. Living cells are filled with water. Water expands when frozen, and this expansion breaks down tissue. However, if you are not going to eat fish right away – within a day or two – then we recommend freezing. I usually freeze fish that I have filleted first. Store them in plastic bags, keeping the fillets flat.

Is It Done Yet?: Cooking Fish

Fish is either cooked, or it isn't. You seldom ask for a medium-rare fish. When cooking fish, one minute the flesh looks milky and semi-transparent, and resists cutting with a fork. Then, just like that, the flesh turns opaque and a fork will flake it easily: the fish is done.

How do you know how long to cook fish? Whether you boil, fry, poach or broil, you should cook fish no longer than *ten minutes for each inch of thickness.* Measure the fish at its thickest part, and multiply it by ten minutes for each inch. Over a barbeque or open fire this becomes harder to guage however, so do keep checking.

Fearless Frying

Crispy, crunchy, salty. Show me someone who doesn't like fried fish and I will show you someone who is possibly an extraterrestrial. The big trick with frying is *hot oil.* If the oil isn't hot enough, you have a greasy recipe for heartburn. If the oil gets too hot, you'll notice excessive smoke. With hot oil, the crust is crisp, light and non-greasy. If in doubt, drop a pinch of bread into the oil. With the oil temperature right, the bread should immediately sizzle and jump.

Your choice of fat for frying is entirely up to you. Sunflower oil works just fine, or try olive or peanut oil. Fish fillets can be fried as they are, but are tastier still when dipped in egg and then flour, breadcrumbs or batter. If you're new to the hob, pre-packaged seasoning and breading products offer an easy solution.

Poaching Allowed

Poaching is a method of cooking fish that is well suited to delicate flesh (and most fish is pretty delicate). It allows the flavour and texture of the fish to come through. It's also a healthy option, with water or broth used rather than oil. This can be achieved easily enough in a large saucepan, with fillets or chunks of fish part submerged into a suitable stock.

Marinate with caution

Everybody likes marinated food. Garlic, salt, wine, soy sauce, lemon juice – all the classic marinating ingredients – sound so good. A duck or a cut of beef can sometimes be marinated for days to the benefit of the completed dish. Marinating gives flavour and/or tenderises tough cuts of meat. Basically, there is no such thing as a tough cut of fish. So by all means, pile on the lemon juice, the white wine, the teriyaki sauce, but half an hour of marinating will give it more than enough flavour without giving your fish the consistency of a wet paper towel.

If the fish is absolutely fresh, you might want to serve it with nothing more than steamed potatoes. Indeed, fresh poached fish needn't be overcomplicated and tastes spot on simply with some dill or tartare sauce and buttered toast.

Grilling and BBQ

Salty, crusty and peppery. Grilling fish is an easy way to make fish into a crispy, tasty meal. It's also very straightforward, whether the grill happens to be in your kitchen or out on the barbeque in your garden.

For basic grilled fish, just brush your fish fillets with some oil, sprinkle both sides with salt and pepper, and slap'em on a hot grill for 10 minutes per inch of thickness. Another way is to marinade in whatever you like; soy sauce, lemon, honey and any number of other ingredients work. The same principles apply to barbeques, although the fish may cook quicker or slower. Foil is also handy if the fish is liable to stick, slide through gaps or come apart.

Simple Fish Favourites

So you have your freshly caught fish. You've filleted it, or at least gutted and fridged it we hope. So what happens next? Okay, so this is *Fishing For Dummies*, not *Cooking Basics For Dummies* (although that might also be worth a read for budding chefs). But cooking fish can be as much fun as hooking fish, and it needn't be difficult.

Everyone has their favourite fish recipes, but we thought the best place to start was with a handful of easy to cook crowd pleasers. Those who regularly target sea fish or rainbow trout, especially, will no doubt benefit from some usful starting points. It might even provide a good excuse (should you need one) to go fishing on a more regular basis.

Beer-Battered Fish and Chips

Fish and chips is not so much a dish as a British institution. You could take your catch down to the local chippy, but it's fun and cost effective to make it yourself. This version uses traditional beer batter. And if it all goes wrong, you can always have a beer.

Prep time: 15 mins **Cook time:** 25 mins **Yield:** 4 servings

Ingredients	*Directions*
8 decent sized potatoes (maris piper are best), cut into chips	*1* In a large mixing bowl, combine the flour and salt together dry. Now whisk in the beer and add cold water gradually until the batter is a smooth, fairly thick consistency. Let this settle for at least 15 minutes whilst you sort out the chips.
2-4 cups of sunflower oil, depending on size of pan	
1 teaspoon salt	*2* Peel the spuds and cut into chips.
1 teaspoon ground black pepper	*3* Add oil to a large frying pan and once hot amd rolling, add half the chips and cook for 3-4 minutes until golden brown. Remove with a slotted spoon and drain chips onto kitchen paper. Do the same with the other half of the chips.
1 cup of cold beer	
½ cup of cold water	
8 fillets of white fish, such as cod or pollack	
2 cups of peas	*4* Now give each batch of chips another minute in the oil, or as long as it takes for them to brown a little more. Drain again and keep them warm in an oven set to very low heat.
Sliced lemon	
Tartare sauce or ketchup	
	5 Time for the fish. Dip a fillet at a time in the batter and place carefully in the oil. Like the chips, the fish is easiest done in batches, say two fillets at a time. Cook each piece of fish for 4–5 minutes or until golden and then drain on kitchen paper. Towards the end, heat the peas.
	6 Serve with sliced lemon, a dollop of sauce and cold beer. Follow up with a deep fried Mars bar and a game of darts (Mars bar and pub sports strictly optional).

Grilled Fish in Mustard Sauce

This is my own favourite way to cook trout (Dominic). It also works well with other fish and especially oily types such as mackerel. I may be no Jamie Oliver, but this is easy and tasty! It works great with fillets, but you could just as happily use fish steaks.

Prep time: 10 mins **Cook time:** 15 mins **Yield:** 4 servings

Ingredients	Directions
Two dozen small new potatoes.	*1* Begin steaming the new potatoes early and then pre-heat the grill to medium-hot level.
One tablespoon of olive oil	
1 teaspoon sea salt	*2* Glaze the fillets with a little olive oil and sprinkle on the salt and pepper. Place under the grill on a sheet of foil. Set the oven timer to ten minutes.
1 teaspoon ground black pepper	
1 tub of crème fraiche	*3* Take a saucepan and add the crème fraiche and mustard. Mix together and add in a good squeeze of lemon juice and a few turns of black pepper.
2 tablespoons of mustard (or more if it's mild stuff)	
4 large fillets of rainbow trout (or 8 fillets of mackerel or smaller fish)	*4* Put your veg on to steam. Heat the sauce mixture on a low to medium heat. Keep stirring for 5 or so minutes or until hot to the touch.
1 lemon	
baby sweetcorn, beans or preferred steamed veg	*5* Remove your fish from the grill, checking to make sure it's properly cooked.
	6 Plate up the trout, potatoes and vegetables, before adding the mustard sauce to the fish.

Spicy Fish Cakes

Everyone who likes fish enjoys fish cakes. And for those who hate fussy preparation or really suck at filleting, they are a dead easy, hands on operation. You can make them pretty much straight up chip shop style, but I (Dominic) like to spice things up with a little heat.

Prep time: 10 mins **Cook time:** 15 mins **Yield:** 4 servings

Ingredients	Directions
500g mashed potatoes.	*1* Cook and mash the potatoes.
1 onion	
500g of any fish meat	*2* Apply a little oil and salt to the fish, before placing in an oven at 200 °C or under a hot grill for 10–15 minutes or until well cooked (if oven-baking the fish, wrap it in foil). Fish should be cleaned, gutted and scaled, but you needn't be too fussy beyond that.
Salt	
1 tablespoon Oil	
1 egg	
1 handful of chopped coriander	*3* While that cooks, finely chop the coriander, garlic and ginger and add to a large bowl. Next chop the onion into fine pieces and add this too.
1 tablespoon paprika	
1 tablespoon chilli powder	
2 cloves of garlic	*4* When the fish is well cooked, flake off the meat into your bowl, taking care to avoid bones.
1 chunk of root ginger	
2-3 tablespoons of oil	*5* Add the mashed potato and start mixing the lot together. Then add the paprika, chilli powder and a couple of good pinches of salt.
Breadcrumbs	
Sweet chilli sauce	
1 lime	*6* Crack the egg into the mixture and continue mixing. The egg helps the mix hold together.
	7 Break off a decent chunk of the mixture at a time, then roll and flatten into a suitable fish cake shape. Gently pat each cake in flour to coat.
	8 Add the oil to a large frying pan and put onto a medium heat. Once the oil is crackling nicely, add the fish cakes and fry for 3-4 minutes on each side until golden brown.
	9 Serve with sweet chilli sauce and a squeeze of lime.

Part VI
The Part of Tens

"The fish certainly are coarse in
'this part of the river."

In this part . . .

In the grand *For Dummies* tradition, this part contains quick reference chapters of our top ten lists. We kick off with ten fishing lessons we learned the hard way – so you don't have to do likewise. Then you can get the scoop on ten important fishing organisations for UK anglers, and for those quiet moments, we finish up with a list of ten great fishing books.

Chapter 20

Ten Fishing Lessons You Don't Have to Learn the Hard Way

. . . .

In This Chapter

▶ Wearing the right clothes and not spooking the fish

▶ Acquiring the right kind of stuff

▶ Investing the time needed for good fishing

▶ Introducing others to the sport we love

. . . .

Throughout this book, we stress the need to pay attention while fishing. We say a lot about experience, and how there really is no substitute for it. All things in fishing – from casting to netting a big fish – get easier the more you do them. Although true, this advice assumes you're learning on your own. Fish with an experienced angler, though, and you can learn a lot about what to do, and even what not to do. This shortens the learning curve.

Avoid Making Bad Vibes

The fish's lateral line enables it to sense vibrations. When a fish picks up vibrations, it pays attention: Is a predator nearby? A scared fish flees; it doesn't bite. Whether you're wading or walking the bank, walk quietly.

In a boat, avoid dropping anything against the hull – that's like hitting a bass drum underwater. Put some old carpet over the floor of your boat to dampen vibrations. People often warn against talking while fishing, but your feet are what really get you into trouble.

Go the Extra Mile

It's amazing just how many anglers always set up by the car, seeing only a small fraction of the waters they fish. But being mobile makes sense on so many levels. It takes you to spots where the fish are not usually bothered by humans. It also helps you find peace and quiet.

Cast No Shadow

Like vibrations, shadows falling on the water's surface often trigger a fleeing instinct in fish. On bright sunny days, and even moonlit nights, avoid letting your shadow hit the water. Keep back while you tackle up. Stay low and keep the sun in front of you and the element of surprise is yours.

Choose Clothing that Blends In

That Aerosmith concert t-shirt may be your lucky shirt, but if it's too garish, it might not be your luckiest fishing shirt. Wear comfortable clothes while fishing, and try to blend into the background. When wading, dark earth tones will blend into the bank better than day-glo orange. While boating, dark clothes stand out against the sky more than light colours. So think like a hunter while fishing – try to disappear against whatever background the fish sees.

Reuse Home Items

I (Greg) am an admitted gear hound. I love acquiring new stuff to make my fishing life easier. But I've learned that a lot of the best items for fishing weren't made for fishing. Kitchen containers and pill bottles make great waterproof units for medicine, sunglasses, mobile phones, you name it. Bar towels work for fish slime. Foam packaging can be used to store ready-made-up rigs. Airtight food containers are ideal for smelly fish baits. Look for fishing gear wherever you go.

Pick a Bait Cooler

If you fish with bait at all, you need a way to carry it and keep it cool. Coolers come in every shape and size. Many tackle companies now produce specially lined bait bags and these are ideal. Buy one that fits the kind of bait you use and label it as your bait cooler. Use it for bait and only bait. Trust me, it makes life easier.

After a day's fishing, rinse out your bait cooler and set it – with the lid open – in the sun to remove most of the odours.

Seek Out Advice

We hope this book helps you learn how to fish. But there's a lot to cover – the fishing world is vast – and your particular kind of fishing will lead you to more questions we didn't think to answer. Don't be the stubborn one who refuses to stop and ask for directions. Most anglers will gladly help a fellow angler. If you see others fishing with success on your home waters, respectfully ask them for advice. Just don't interrupt their fishing!

Keep a Fishing Diary

I (Greg) am in the business of assigning homework, so I know it's no fun. But this isn't homework, even though it involves taking notes. Record data about every fishing trip you take: the weather, water conditions, fish caught and lures used. Over time, this fishing journal becomes an invaluable source of information, as well as a nice way to revisit past successes.

Be Open to Multispecies Angling

Don't be a fish snob. We all have our favourites, but there are so many kinds of fish out there! Branch out and fish for everything. That way, regardless of the season, you'll have something to pursue. And you'll find that the more you understand about different species of fish, the more you understand all fish.

Take Someone Along for the Trip

Some of us like to fish alone, but there can be more advantage to having fishing mates than purely some good banter. Having a few trusted friends is a great way to share information and bounce ideas off each other, and you can also save on petrol costs. Introducing more people to the sport you love benefits us all in the long run. The more anglers there are, the more of us there are who are concerned about the resources and habitat fishing requires. When it comes to tasks like spotting polluters or poachers, the more watchdogs on the water, the better. Plus, why keep such a great thing to yourself?

Chapter 21

Ten Fishing Organisations You Should Know About

. . . .

In This Chapter

▶ Organisations that will help you get more from your fishing.

▶ Specialist groups to help you catch the big one.

▶ Playing your part in the bigger picture of the sport.

. . . .

*I*t's perfectly fine simply to pay for a day ticket, set up your tackle and cast out. But underneath the surface, fishing is a sport where so much can be learned, enjoyed and discovered from others. Equally, so much we take for granted needs a helping hand from ourselves as anglers.

This is where key organisations come in. Special fishing groups are a mine of friendly information. They're also of key importance in protecting the sport and those most precious things of all – the fish themselves and their habitats. Joining with others is a great idea on so many levels. You can make new like-minded friends, learn how to catch more fish and pay your part in making sure that fishing has a bright future in tough times.

One for all: The Angling Trust

Anglers like to categorise themselves into different groups. That can mean distinguishing between fly and bait fishermen, or between coarse, sea or game. But beyond such distinctions, we all share the same love of fishing. Whether it's the open sea or a tiny stream, all those watery environments we treasure most are fragile places which need our protection. This is where the Angling Trust comes in.

Representing sport fishing of all descriptions across the land, the Trust is there to make sure the future is safe, fighting for angling clubs and individuals everywhere on vital issues such as pollution, abstraction, access rights and fish theft, as well as encouraging the next generation of anglers. Every keen angler should give the Trust their support, and for a small annual fee members also get tackle discounts and other benefits. Check out their website: www.anglingtrust.net

Read all about it: Angling Times

For over 50 years, the *Angling Times* has been at the heart of fishing, bringing the biggest stories, news of incredible catches and a wealth of up-to-date information to anglers. Whether you want to learn about the latest methods, find out how your local hotspots are fishing, or simply enjoy reading the best fishing stories, *Angling Times* has it. Find it in newsagents or visit the site: www.gofishing.co.uk/Angling-Times

A Band Apart: The Carp Society

If you're one of the growing band of anglers crazy about catching carp, The Carp Society is the club to join. Providing friendly advise, special events and a wide range of carp fishing info, the organisation has been going strong for 30 years to promote this exciting branch of the sport. It also runs three exclusive big carp waters. Check out www.thecarpsociety.com.

Wild Out West: The Wye and Usk Foundation

Offering outstanding coarse and game fishing in some of the UKs most beautiful locations, this organisation is big on fishing, but equally big on conservation. The Wye was lately voted Britain's favourite river because of its excellent sport, in no small part due to the ongoing work of the Foundation. Book your own slice of great fishing and learn more at: www.wyeusk foundation.org.

For the Future of Our Seas: Fish Fight!

Not a fight using fish as weapons (that's just *too* Monty Python), but a vital campaign on behalf of all those who want to see a brighter future for our seas. Launched by angler and celebrity chef High Fearnley-Whittingstall, Fish Fight is an international project aimed at addressing the chronic overfishing of our seas. See what the campaign is all about at www.fishfight.net.

Wild Trout Fishing for Beer Money

Fly fishing is a sport for posh types with money to burn, right? Wrong! Whether you live north or south, these exciting current projects offer great fishing on some of Britain's wildest streams for as little as a fiver a day. Better still, all the proceeds go back towards protecting and improving fragile eco systems. A win–win deal, we think! Both *Go Wild in Eden* and *The Westcountry Angling Passport* are there to make the difference. Point your mouse at gowild.edenriverstrust.org.uk and www.westcountryangling.com.

Angling with Added Bite: The Pike Anglers Club of Great Britain (PAC)

Catching and handling toothy pike is no job for the faint hearted, requiring care and specialist knowledge. Pike are fragile as well as fierce, hence those unsure would do well to seek out useful info and support. Luckily for pike and angler alike the PAC provide just that, protecting the species and offering special events and access to a whole community of friendly experts to help you bank – and safely return – that monster pike. Their site has great fishing advice, as well as invaluable info on how to handle and return pike safely: Check it out at www.pacgb.co.uk.

Watching Our Waters: The Environment Agency (EA)

Picture the scene: you've just been fishing your favourite spot when you see two dodgy intruders making off with scores of fish – the ones you wanted to catch – dead in an illegal net. Who should you call? The EA are there to help, whether you want to report pollution, get licensed or check up on the fishing rules in your area. Their 24 hour freephone emergency hotline is: 0800 807060. For licences and other info visit `www.environment-agency.gov.uk`.

Bring on the bass!: The Bass Anglers' Sportfishing Society

It's no surprise that sea anglers love bass so much. They're beautifully wild creatures that fight like stink. But they also need our help, with bass populations and the marine environment under threat. Joining B.A.S.S. is not only a positive step for the future, but also puts you in touch with friendly experts nationwide who can help you to success with this elusive species. Visit `www.ukbass.com` for more.

Save our spots: The Wild Trout Trust

Trout streams are vulnerable places: It's a fact. They need our protection if the species is to flourish in an increasingly uncertain future. Another invaluable conservation body, the WTT is responsible for many initiatives looking to improve and protect wild habitat, safeguarding the very future of our native trout. If you're interested in the future of both fishing and the British countryside, take a look at `www.wildtrout.org`.

Chapter 22

Ten Great Fishing Reads

. . . .

In This Chapter

▶ Reading material to inspire and entertain you.

▶ Books to make up for when you can't be on the bank.

. . . .

Sometimes you can't easily go fishing. It blows a gale and the trip is can-celled; something crops up and you miss out; maybe life just catches up with you and your weekly trip only exists in a daydream in the office. It happens to the best of us. All is not lost, however, because even if you can't be there the sport is rich in reading material.

Reading books about fishing might not be quite the same, but a little home-work is no bad thing. You might learn a whole lot more than you bargained for by turning the pages of a classic book. You could learn the secret that turns your next day out into a brilliant one. Or you might just lose yourself in the pages of a great story – fishing has hundreds of them.

Discovering the Joy of Carp Fishing

Confessions of a Carp Fisher (by 'B.B.', otherwise known as Denys Watkins-Pitchford, and published by Merlin Unwin) is perhaps my favourite fishing book of all time. *Confessions* is not a book that will tell you about high-tech rigs or modern baits, but in terms of sheer escapism and capturing the magic, B.B.'s collection of carping adventures is simply delightful. The author takes you into a world of misty, forgotten ponds and dipping floats to cast a spell over anyone who loves fishing – and even if you don't just yet, you will by the end of the book.

A Mixed Catch of Fishing Treats

Fishing anthologies can be hit and miss affairs, but *Fish, Fishing & the Meaning of Life* (edited by Jeremy Paxman and published by Penguin) is one of the best. Revealing a gentler, humorous side, famous broadcaster Jeremy Paxman pulls together a really fascinating mixed catch from the archives here. It's a collection that spans several centuries, with witty commentary from the *Newsnight* presenter himself.

Casting Towards Adventure

Okay, so *Hooked* (by Fen Montaigne; published by Weidenfeld and Nicolson) is not the most original title for a fishing book. But the adventures within are anything but ordinary. Charting one man's travels across the sprawling landscape of Russia with a fishing rod, it's a narrative of danger and possibility, beauty and corruption. From trout and pike to vodka-pickled extras and local intrigue, *Hooked* is a gripping journey into the heart of one of the world's greatest and most mysterious countries, with rod in hand.

When It's More than Just a Hobby . . .

When exactly does fishing cease to be a hobby and start to stick like a bad habit? This and other questions are discussed in a candid and thoroughly entertaining manner by fly fisher John Geirach in his colourful book *Trout Bum* (published by Prentice Hall), which had such resonance that the term 'Trout Bum' is now part of fishing folklore.

A Lesson from the Master of Modern Angling

Not always easy to find, but still inspirational reading some fifty years after its first edition, *Stillwater Angling* (by Richard Walker; published by David & Charles) remains a book that changed fishing forever. Dick Walker's advice on catching big fish of any species remains just as relevant today as ever, and in a modern era obsessed with high-tech rigs and tackle, his seminal work deals with the fundamentals of the sport in a lucid, refreshing manner.

More Fun Than You Can Shake a Rod At

If you thought fly fishing was just for trout and salmon, think again. More and more anglers are learning about the huge range of species that can be caught on the fly. *Flyfishing for Coarse Fish* (Dominic Garnett; published by Merlin Unwin) attempts to give coarse and game anglers alike an entertaining guide to catching all kinds of fish on the fly, from pike and carp right through to oddball species such as zander and barbel. With scores of useful fly patterns and handy tips, the book opens up a whole host of exciting possibilities.

The Magic and the Madness

There are few writers who can evoke the joy of fishing quite like Chris Yates, star of 'A Passion for Angling'. His book *How to Fish* (published by Penguin) will not, as the title might suggest, tell you how to hook maggots or make a perfect cast (you can find that out within these pages, right?). But if ever there was a book to make us ponder the joy of fishing, and the very reasons it fascinates us, then this is it.

Here's One 1 Tied Earlier

There's only one thing better than catching a fish, and that's catching a fish using something you made yourself. *A Beginner's Guide to Fly Tying* (Chris Mann and Terry Griffiths; published by Merlin Unwin) puts the process of creating your own flies into an easy to follow, user-friendly style with aplomb. Not only does it give you a superb guide through a dozen useful patterns, but gives the reader the skills and confidence to embark on a whole new hobby.

The Finer Points of Tackling Freshwater

Written by two legends of the sport, *Freshwater Fishing* (Hugh Falkus and Fred Buller; published by Stanley Paul) covers a multitude of coarse and game fish species and techniques in fine style. The tackle may be dated in places, but the expertise certainly isn't, and for those with an interest in the craft and history of the sport *Freshwater Fishing* is both a fascinating read and a useful in-depth look at Britain's best-loved fish and their habits.

The Greatest Fishing Tale Ever Told?

If you've ever felt that lingering sense of ill fortune after sitting biteless for a few hours on a lake, *The Old Man and the Sea* by Ernest Hemingway (published by Scribner) should put things into perspective. Describing one man's battle against an impossibly big fish, this is not just a classic novel but one of the greatest angling stories ever told.

Index

• G •

• Z •

FOR DUMMIES®

Making Everything Easier!™

UK editions

BUSINESS

Bookkeeping For Dummies
978-0-470-97626-5

Persuasion & Influence For Dummies
978-0-470-74737-7

Starting & Running a Business All-in-One For Dummies
978-1-119-97527-4

REFERENCE

British Politics For Dummies
978-0-470-68637-9

DIY For Dummies
978-0-470-97450-6

Dad's Guide to Pregnancy For Dummies
978-1-119-97660-8

HOBBIES

Growing Your Own Fruit & Veg For Dummies
978-0-470-69960-7

Keeping Chickens For Dummies
978-1-119-99417-6

Beekeeping For Dummies
978-1-119-97250-1

Asperger's Syndrome For Dummies
978-0-470-66087-4

Basic Maths For Dummies
978-1-119-97452-9

Body Language For Dummies, 2nd Edition
978-1-119-95351-7

Boosting Self-Esteem For Dummies
978-0-470-74193-1

British Sign Language For Dummies
978-0-470-69477-0

Cricket For Dummies
978-0-470-03454-5

Diabetes For Dummies, 3rd Edition
978-0-470-97711-8

Electronics For Dummies
978-0-470-68178-7

English Grammar For Dummies
978-0-470-05752-0

Flirting For Dummies
978-0-470-74259-4

IBS For Dummies
978-0-470-51737-6

Improving Your Relationship For Dummies
978-0-470-68472-6

ITIL For Dummies
978-1-119-95013-4

Management For Dummies, 2nd Edition
978-0-470-97769-9

Neuro-linguistic Programming For Dummies, 2nd Edition
978-0-470-66543-5

Nutrition For Dummies, 2nd Edition
978-0-470-97276-2

Organic Gardening For Dummies
978-1-119-97706-3

11-37870

FOR DUMMIES®

Making Everything Easier!™

UK editions

SELF-HELP

978-0-470-66541-1

978-1-119-99264-6

978-0-470-66086-7

STUDENTS

978-0-470-68820-5

978-0-470-974711-7

978-1-119-99134-2

HISTORY

978-0-470-68792-5

978-0-470-74783-4

978-0-470-97819-1

Origami Kit For Dummies
978-0-470-75857-1

Overcoming Depression For Dummies
978-0-470-69430-5

Positive Psychology For Dummies
978-0-470-72136-0

PRINCE2 For Dummies, 2009 Edition
978-0-470-71025-8

Project Management For Dummies
978-0-470-71119-4

Psychometric Tests For Dummies
978-0-470-75366-8

Renting Out Your Property For Dummies, 3rd Edition
978-1-119-97640-0

Ruby Union For Dummies, 3rd Edition
978-1-119-99092-5

Sage One For Dummies
978-1-119-95236-7

Self-Hypnosis For Dummies
978-0-470-66073-7

Storing and Preserving Garden Produce For Dummies
978-1-119-95156-8

Study Skills For Dummies
978-0-470-74047-7

Teaching English as a Foreign Language For Dummies
978-0-470-74576-2

Time Management For Dummies
978-0-470-77765-7

Training Your Brain For Dummies
978-0-470-97449-0

Work-Life Balance For Dummies
978-0-470-71380-8

FOR DUMMIES®

Making Everything Easier!™

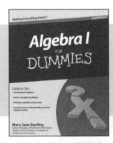

FOR DUMMIES®

Making Everything Easier! ™

COMPUTER BASICS

978-0-470-57829-2

978-0-470-61454-9

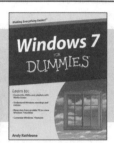

978-0-470-49743-2

DIGITAL PHOTOGRAPHY

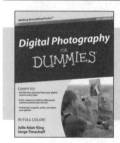

978-0-470-25074-7

978-0-470-76878-5

978-1-118-00472-2

MICROSOFT OFFICE 2010

978-0-470-48998-7

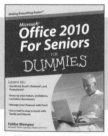

978-0-470-58302-9

978-0-470-48953-6

Access 2010 For Dummies
978-0-470-49747-0

Android Application Development For Dummies
978-0-470-77018-4

AutoCAD 2011 For Dummies
978-0-470-59539-8

C++ For Dummies, 6th Edition
978-0-470-31726-6

Computers For Seniors For Dummies, 2nd Edition
978-0-470-53483-0

Dreamweaver CS5 For Dummies
978-0-470-61076-3

iPad 2 For Dummies, 3rd Edition
978-1-118-17679-5

Macs For Dummies, 11th Edition
978-0-470-87868-2

Mac OS X Snow Leopard For Dummies
978-0-470-43543-4

Photoshop CS5 For Dummies
978-0-470-61078-7

Photoshop Elements 10 For Dummies
978-1-118-10742-3

Search Engine Optimization For Dummies, 4th Edition
978-0-470-88104-0

The Internet For Dummies, 13th Edition
978-1-118-09614-7

Visual Studio 2010 All-In-One For Dummies
978-0-470-53943-9

Web Analytics For Dummies
978-0-470-09824-0

Word 2010 For Dummies
978-0-470-48772-3

WordPress For Dummies, 4th Edition
978-1-118-07342-1